AMERICAN COURTS

AMERICAN COURTS
PROCESS AND POLICY

Third Edition

Lawrence Baum
Ohio State University

HOUGHTON MIFFLIN COMPANY Boston Toronto
Dallas Geneva, Illinois Palo Alto Princeton, New Jersey

To Carol

Senior Sponsoring Editor: *Margaret Seawell*
Senior Development Editor: *Susan Granoff*
Senior Project Editor: *Rosemary Winfield*
Production/Design Coordinator: *Sarah Ambrose*
Senior Manufacturing Coordinator: *Priscilla Bailey*
Marketing Manager: *Karen Natale*

Printed in the U.S.A.

Library of Congress Catalog Card Number: 93-78688

ISBN: 0-395-67539-1

123456789-AM-96 95 94 93

Contents

Preface

No faithful reader of a daily newspaper could doubt the importance of American courts. Headlines often point to the dramatic impact of some court decisions, from a Supreme Court ruling on state regulation of abortion to a jury's acquittal of the defendants in a police brutality case. Equally striking is the steady succession of stories about all the ways that courts affect people's lives.

Looking at all that courts do, some commentators argue that the judiciary is the most powerful branch of government in the United States. Whether or not this view is accurate, one thing is clear: it is impossible to comprehend American government as a whole without a clear understanding of the courts.

Yet public opinion surveys show enormous gaps in public understanding of the courts. And even people with considerable expertise on other aspects of government, such as the presidency or state legislatures, often know a great deal less about courts.

This book has been written to help provide a better understanding of American courts. It examines trial and appellate courts in both the federal and state systems, generalizing about this wide range of courts wherever possible and making distinctions wherever appropriate. The book describes the formal procedures under which courts operate; it also looks at the informal processes that modify these formal procedures and thus help determine how the courts really work.

While the book is concerned with describing the ways courts work, it is equally concerned with explaining what they do. Why, for instance, is plea bargaining so prevalent in criminal cases? What considerations shape the president's choices of people to serve as federal judges? Why do Supreme Court decisions often have less impact than we would expect? In suggesting some answers to these kinds of questions, I will point to a wide array of forces within and outside the courts.

A constant theme in discussion of the courts is reform. People frequently point to what they see as major failings of the courts and propose changes to attack those failings. Such reform proposals often appear attractive on their face, but they cannot be assessed fully without a clear understanding of the courts. One of my goals in writing *American Courts: Process and Policy* is to provide the necessary basis for judging reform proposals.

Features of the Revision

Much has happened since the last edition of this book was published four years ago. This third edition of *American Courts: Process and Policy* reflects these changes, as well as the growth that has occurred in our knowledge of courts.

Every chapter has been thoroughly updated. Among the new coverage in this edition are the following noteworthy additions:

- A section on the sources and nature of law that American courts are called upon to interpret (Chapter 1)
- Examination of effects of recent growth in caseloads on courts (Chapters 2, 7, 8)
- More coverage of the working lives of lawyers, including such matters as salaries for new lawyers and attorneys' satisfactions and dissatisfactions with their careers (Chapter 3)
- Coverage of the growing competitiveness of judicial elections (Chapter 4)
- Analysis of how the new sentencing system for federal crimes works in practice (Chapter 6)
- Discussion of the growing volume of civil cases and the question of whether the United States is truly a society that is fond of litigation (Chapter 7)

In addition, approximately one-third of the tables and charts (now called "Exhibits") are entirely new, and one-third have been updated. The new exhibits include coverage of the Pete Rose case as an illustration of "forum-shopping" between federal and state courts (2.1), a table of starting salaries for various legal positions (3.3), and examples of actions taken by Congress to overturn federal court decisions (9.5).

Finally, new to this edition are two pedagogic features that instructors and students may find useful: a brief annotated bibliography at the end of each chapter and an index of the cases cited in the text, which appears just before the index.

Contents of the Third Edition

The book is divided into nine chapters. *Chapter 1* presents an introduction to the courts and the perspectives that I will take in examining them. *Chapter 2* describes the organization of the federal and state courts, discussing the structure of court systems and how they are administered. This chapter emphasizes how the organization of courts affects the policies they make and shows why seemingly routine issues of court organization sometimes become matters of heated debate. *Chapter 3* looks at lawyers, who do much to determine how the courts actually operate, and provides an overview of careers in law and the legal profession.

Chapters 4 and 5 examine judges. *Chapter 4* deals with the selection of judges. One central concern is the impact of different selection systems on the ways that judges are actually chosen and on the kinds of people who become judges. *Chapter 5* focuses on judges themselves. It begins by looking at judges' backgrounds and the effects those backgrounds can have on judges' behavior. It then examines judges' activities on the bench. Finally, it probes the quality of judges' work and considers proposals for strengthening their performance.

Chapters 6 and 7 look at the work of trial courts. *Chapter 6* deals with criminal cases, focusing on the most important stages in the criminal process: decisions whether to prosecute suspects, plea bargaining, trials, and sentencing decisions. The chapter examines efforts to eliminate plea bargaining and reduce judges' discretion in sentencing. *Chapter 7* takes a similar look at civil cases, focusing on decisions about whether to initiate cases, the processing of cases in court, and patterns of outcomes in cases.

Chapters 8 and 9 deal with appellate courts. *Chapter 8* examines the processes that occur at the appellate level, including choices whether to appeal unfavorable decisions, screening of cases by the courts themselves, and the process of reaching decisions. *Chapter 9* examines appellate courts as policy makers. It discusses the policies made by appellate courts, including a growth in judicial "activism," and explores the ultimate impact of these policies on American society.

Acknowledgments

This third edition continues to reflect the help that a number of people provided during my writing of earlier editions. In addition, I would like to thank those individuals who assisted in this revision of the book. A number of scholars helped me improve the book by suggesting changes in the second edition and in a draft of this edition: David Gray Adler, Idaho State University; Lee Epstein, Washington University in Saint Louis; John B. Gates, University of California, Davis; Kevin T. McGuire, University of Minnesota–Twin Cities Campus; Wayne V. McIntosh, University of Maryland at College Park; William McLauchlan, Purdue University; Laurin A. Wollan, Jr., Florida State University; and Robert A. Wood, North Dakota State University.

Several people aided in my gathering of new information for this edition. These include Ray August, Cassie Dalla Santa, Sheldon Goldman, Marie Hojnacki, Mark Kemper, Mark Miller, David Richert, Kathleen Sampson, Jack Wax, and Karen Winner. I owe special thanks to my parents, Ruth Klein Baum and Irving Baum, for their tireless efforts to locate and pass on material that would be useful for the book. Peter Radcliffe provided very helpful research assistance.

Throughout the life of this book, people at Houghton Mifflin have been enormously helpful to me. For this third edition, I appreciate very much the assistance of Susan Granoff, Margaret Seawell, and Rosemary Winfield.

L.B.

AMERICAN COURTS

1

An Overview of the Courts

Courts play a central role in the United States: they are deeply involved in the collective life of American society and in the lives of many individuals. Courts regularly reach decisions on matters as vital to individuals as termination of marriages, monetary compensation for injuries, and imprisonment. And they shape government policy on an array of consequential issues, ranging from capital punishment to environmental protection and the structure of the telephone industry. The significance of what courts do is suggested by some of their decisions in a single month, described in Exhibit 1.1.

Courts receive the kind of attention that their importance merits. Newspapers and television news programs give a great deal of coverage to major events involving the courts. The trials of former Panamanian leader Manuel Noriega and of the four police officers who had confronted Rodney King in Los Angeles drew extraordinary attention from the mass media; the same was true of the confirmation hearings for Supreme Court justice Clarence Thomas in 1991 and the Court's decision on the Pennsylvania abortion law a year later. In the past few years, there has been a seemingly endless flow of television series and movies about courts and the people who work in them.

Still, American courts are not very well understood. One reason is that the mass media often present incomplete and even inaccurate pictures of lawyers, judges, and cases. But the most fundamental source of this problem is that the range and complexity of the courts and of what they do make them very difficult to fathom. As a result, confusion about courts is widespread—not only in the general public but among political leaders as well.

This book is an effort to help in understanding courts in the United States. It has three related goals: to lay out a clear description of courts and their activities; to suggest explanations of these activities and of the behavior of people who work in the courts; and to offer ways of evaluating the work of courts.

In this introductory chapter, I provide an overview of the courts, outlining some ways of thinking about courts that may help in understanding them. Starting with the relationship between courts and law, the discussion then moves on to an examination of courts as institutions and of their roles in

1

A state court of appeals overturned an administrative decision and ordered an insurance rate increase for about 1 million New Jersey drivers.

A federal district judge in Seattle ruled that the U.S. Forest Service plan to protect the northern spotted owl was inadequate under federal environmental laws.

State trial judges in Ohio and California held that state laws regulating abortion were unconstitutional.

The U.S. Supreme Court held that the Constitution severely limits state taxation of mail-order sales from out of state unless Congress acts to authorize such taxes.

A Virginia trial judge issued a temporary restraining order to prevent a Republican effort to take over a county school board.

Source: Newspaper reports.

EXHIBIT 1.1 A Sampling of Court Decisions in May 1992

government and society. The chapter also discusses the perspectives from which court processes and outcomes can be explained and the task of evaluating courts. Many of the topics discussed in this chapter will be examined more closely in the chapters that follow; the brief discussions in this chapter are intended to provide some background with which to begin.

COURTS AND LAW

Courts deal with law, and it is useful to consider the sources and types of law. Although the concept of law itself is complex, it can be defined simply— adapting Herbert Jacob's formulation—as authoritative rules made by government.[1] The rules are authoritative in the sense that they are intended to be binding on government itself, on people and institutions outside government, or on both. The job of courts is to interpret law; in doing so, courts also make law.

Sources of Law

Law comes from a variety of places in government. The most fundamental sources of law are *constitutions*. The federal and state constitutions establish basic rules about the powers of government and the procedures by which government is to operate. State constitutions also contain a great many rules about the substance of government policy that one might not expect to find in a constitution. The Kentucky Constitution, for instance, includes a provision dealing with intersections of tracks belonging to different railroad companies.[2]

Whatever their subject matter, the legal rules in a constitution are the highest law for that level of government. State constitutions are superior to any other state laws, and the federal constitution is superior both to other federal laws and to state laws—including state constitutions. This superiority of constitutions provides the justification for courts to declare other forms of law unconstitutional on the ground that they are inconsistent with constitutional rules.

Second highest in the hierarchy of laws are *statutes,* laws passed by legislatures. (Laws passed by local legislative bodies are usually called *ordinances.*) Legislatures are free to pass statutes of any type, so long as their action is consistent with the relevant constitutional rules. While constitutions focus primarily on government, statutes are more often directed at society as a whole. Some familiar subjects of statutes are prohibitions of certain kinds of conduct, such as damage to the environment, and the provision of benefits, such as Social Security.

Chief executives make law in the form of *executive orders.* Such orders may be based on statutes or on the inherent power of a president or governor derived from the federal or state constitution. Far more common is law adopted by administrative agencies in the form of *rules* or *regulations.* Statutes outline the law; the agency responsible for carrying out a statute fills in the outline by adopting more detailed legal rules. Thus, for instance, the federal Equal Employment Opportunity Commission has established regulations for the civil rights statutes that it implements. Statutes take precedence over regulations, and a regulation can be challenged on the ground that it is inconsistent with the relevant statutory provisions.

Courts are called upon to interpret all these forms of law. In doing so, as noted earlier, they make law themselves. This function is particularly clear when courts write and publish opinions laying out the legal rules—often, new rules—on which their interpretations are based. In some fields of law, such as contract and tort (which concerns primarily personal injuries), English and American courts first developed rules of law in the absence of statutes. Such independent judge-made law is sometimes referred to as the *common law,* though the term has other meanings as well. Legislatures increasingly have moved into these fields, and their statutes override any contrary judge-made rules.

Categories of Law

The law established by government policy makers ranges widely in its subject matter. Of the various distinctions that can be made among categories of law, a few are particularly important for an understanding of courts.

One distinction is between *public* and *private* law. Public law has been defined in different ways, but basically it involves the government acting as government—as opposed to other roles, such as property owner. Public law includes such matters as taxation, regulation of business practices, public welfare programs, and foreign policy, along with criminal cases. Law that does not involve government as government is private. Common kinds of private law cases are those concerning disputes over personal injuries or provisions of contracts.

Another distinction is between *criminal* and *civil* law. Criminal law involves the prohibition of certain conduct and the threat of punishment for the prohibited conduct. Criminal cases are those in which individuals (or sometimes corporations) are prosecuted by government for alleged violations of criminal laws. Everything else is civil (though civil law sometimes has a narrower meaning). Much of the civil law also places prohibitions on conduct, but here the consequences of a violation ordinarily do not involve punishment as such; most often, violators are required to compensate those who suffered losses as a result of the prohibited conduct. The same situation may bring both criminal and civil law into play; an alleged assault, for instance, may lead to both a criminal prosecution and a civil lawsuit for damages by the injured party.

Within these broad categories, law is often subdivided further. Criminal statutes deal with *felonies,* the more serious offenses, and with *misdemeanors.* Civil law covers a variety of fields such as *contracts, property*, and *domestic relations*. As Chapter 3 shows, categories of law in practice are defined largely by the ways that lawyers specialize in their work.

UNDERSTANDING COURTS AS INSTITUTIONS

The judicial branch of government is composed of trial and appellate courts in both the federal system and the fifty state systems—altogether, thousands of courts. As institutions, these courts share some important traits. Most fundamentally, all courts interpret and apply the law in individual cases. And judges and lawyers play the central roles in nearly every court. Because of these shared traits and because courts are all situated in the judicial branch, people tend to think of courts as a distinct set of institutions.

Yet this view of courts obscures two important realities: courts differ from each other in fundamental ways, and they are not unique in their characteristics. Each of these realities requires some elaboration.

The differences among courts can be illustrated by comparing the U.S. Supreme Court and a municipal court, which many states have established as a trial court for cases with relatively small monetary or other stakes. Such a comparison might seem unreasonable, because these two courts represent extreme cases. But it highlights some important differences among courts.

1. The municipal court is a *trial court,* whereas the Supreme Court is an *appellate court*. Cases are heard first in trial courts. When cases go to trial, the emphasis is usually on ascertaining facts, chiefly through the testimony of witnesses. Appellate courts review lower court decisions. They hear arguments that deal primarily with the application of the law to the facts that have already been ascertained at trial. In trial courts, a single judge presides, and either this judge or a jury renders a decision.

In appellate courts, cases are heard and decided by a group of judges, usually ranging from three to nine in number. (Members of the Supreme Court and of state supreme courts are usually called justices rather than judges.)

2. Public proceedings in the two courts look quite different. Municipal court sessions typically involve action on large numbers of cases, which are often handled informally, as well as speedily. Someone who walks into a courtroom probably will find it difficult to follow the action, and the overall impression is likely to be one of chaos. In contrast, the public proceedings of the Supreme Court are conducted with considerable formality in a rather majestic setting. To the observer, the difference between the Supreme Court and a municipal court may seem like the difference between a well-staged show and a three-ring circus.

3. To continue the metaphor, the casts of characters in the two courts are also different. Somewhat different kinds of lawyers generally handle cases in the Supreme Court and in municipal courts. Perhaps most important, lawyers who appear in the Supreme Court are more likely to come from the most prestigious segments of the legal profession. And the judges usually differ even more. In both courts, they usually have law school training, experience in legal practice, and a background in political activity. But Supreme Court justices come primarily from the legal and political elites, whereas judges reach municipal courts from lower levels of the legal and political systems.

4. Different kinds of cases appear in the two courts. Municipal courts handle criminal and civil cases with relatively small stakes under state laws and local ordinances. Common types of municipal court cases include small claims and misdemeanor criminal offenses (among them, traffic and parking violations, which are generally classified as misdemeanors in most states). The Supreme Court hears cases raising broad legal issues under the Constitution and federal statutes (laws enacted by Congress); the largest numbers of these cases concern civil liberties and government regulation of the economy. Nearly all cases heard by the Supreme Court were originally decided by some trial court, and occasionally a case that began in a municipal court is eventually decided by the Supreme Court. Even in such a case, however, the central issues generally change so much—from narrow factual questions to broad questions of federal law—that the Supreme Court in effect decides a different case from the one that was heard in municipal court.

Taken together, these characteristics show basic distinctions between municipal courts and the Supreme Court. The more general lesson should be clear: courts do not constitute a homogeneous set of institutions; rather, they vary along several dimensions.

A second and related point is that courts share attributes with other institutions. Indeed, scholars such as Martin Shapiro have noted that a great many nonjudicial institutions are similar to courts in their functions, their operation, or both.[3] Some of these institutions are easy to identify because they look like courts and are labeled as such. The executive branch of government, for example, contains some administrative courts, which hear appeals of decisions of agencies such as the Social Security Administration. In their procedures, these bodies resemble courts in the judiciary. Indeed, the federal Court of International Trade, which originated as an administrative tribunal, changed relatively little when it moved from the executive branch to the judicial branch.

The private sector also contains institutions that resemble courts. Many of these institutions were set up as alternatives to courts in the judicial branch. An example is arbitration, commonly used in disputes between businesses, in which two parties present their cases to an arbitrator for a decision. Some religious and ethnic groups set up their own courts to resolve disagreements within their communities.

Other institutions that do not look like courts on the surface share some important attributes with them. Indeed, both the Supreme Court and municipal courts have common functions and operations with some seemingly quite different institutions in other branches of government. The Supreme Court is similar to Congress in many respects. Both set their agendas by selecting issues for consideration from a much larger body of requests. Both reach decisions through a series of group processes. Both establish general policies on national issues, policies that must be put into effect by other people and institutions.

For their part, municipal courts have much in common with bureaucratic agencies that apply the law by processing large numbers of similar cases. Political scientist Michael Lipsky has made a more specific analogy, comparing trial courts with other "street-level bureaucracies," such as police and welfare departments, that deal directly with the public.[4] Like police officers and welfare workers, trial judges hold a great deal of power over the people with whom they interact, and they must exercise considerable discretion in using this power. For instance, trial judges usually have a wide range of options and few clear standards in setting bail for criminal defendants. According to Lipsky, the behavior of each street-level bureaucracy is shaped by its limited resources and by official goals that are often difficult to achieve. And each bureaucracy develops routines for the rapid processing of cases.

These analogies underline the differences among courts, as well as their similarities to nonjudicial institutions. Both are noted throughout the book.

THE ROLES OF COURTS: FUNCTIONS AND IMPACT

A central goal of this book is to discern the roles that courts play in American government and society. In the process, two related questions are explored: what do courts do, and what impact do they have? In the chapters that follow, these questions are addressed in specific contexts; here, however, I discuss them in more general terms.

The Functions of Courts

Courts engage in a wide variety of activities. These activities can best be understood in terms of their functions within government and society. The work of courts in the United States could be linked to a great many functions, but a few of these stand out as particularly important.

The first is *dispute resolution*. Civil cases explicitly involve disputes between at least one plaintiff (the party that brings the case) and one defendant (the party against whom the case is brought). A great many criminal cases also arise from disputes between a complainant and the defendant. (A complainant is someone who calls a possible criminal case to the attention of the police or the prosecutor.) Thus courts provide a forum for the ventilation and resolution of disputes. In the great majority of civil cases that are filed in court, the parties themselves agree on a settlement prior to trial. Similarly, in most criminal cases the defendant pleads guilty, settling at least one important aspect of the dispute. In a minority of cases, of course, courts themselves determine how disputes are resolved by reaching decisions.

By establishing courts as a forum for dispute resolution, the government provides an important service for its citizenry. In this sense, courts are similar to other public institutions, such as health and fire departments. At the same time, the government is also serving its own collective goals. From the government's perspective, it is generally desirable to control and channel conflicts in a society and to help set the terms on which conflicts are resolved.[5]

This last point suggests a second function, *behavior modification*. Courts reward certain kinds of behavior and penalize others, with the goal of encouraging what is rewarded and discouraging what is penalized. This function is clearest on the criminal side of the law. In criminal cases, courts are part of a system for the enforcement of the criminal laws, a system designed to reduce activity that is labeled criminal by threatening serious penalties for that activity.

Similar purposes underlie the civil side of the law; here the government allows lawsuits for damages against people who engage in certain types of behavior, hoping thereby to discourage such behavior. A negligent driver may face a suit brought by someone who has suffered an injury through the driver's actions. Or a business that violates the terms of a contract may be sued by the other party to the contract. In this sense, private individuals or groups who bring civil cases are unintentionally acting as agents of the government.

The government sometimes goes to considerable lengths to link its behavior modification goals with the self-interest of potential litigants. To help deter false monetary claims against the federal government, Congress has given people an incentive to expose such claims: individuals can bring lawsuits in the name of government against people who allegedly have made false claims and to recover a portion of the proceeds of the case.[6] To take a different kind of example, Congress encourages enforcement of drug laws by allowing law enforcement agencies to seize and retain assets such as homes and cars that are connected with drug offenses.[7]

A third function of courts, one tied to the first two, is the *allocation of gains and losses*. In criminal cases, courts impose penalties on defendants in the form of monetary fines, imprisonment, and even death sentences. In civil cases, courts often order transfers of money from one party to another. They also determine such matters as the custody of children and the control of corporations. In this process, civil courts often take something from one party and give it to another.

This allocation function is quite significant in its direct effects on litigants, for each year millions of people gain or lose through their involvement in court cases. Beyond the individual level, courts can be thought of as allocating gains and losses between entire groups in American society, such as creditors and debtors in contract cases or insurance companies and injured people in accident cases. In doing so, courts may benefit some groups systematically at the expense of others.

A fourth function of courts, *policy making,* is implicit in the first three. Policy making can have many different definitions; what I mean here is the creation and application of authoritative rules. This function, of course, is one in which the other branches of government are also heavily engaged.

The distinction between creating new legal rules and applying existing rules seems clear in itself, and it helps to distinguish different kinds of policy making in the courts. A state supreme court may create a new rule for liability in accidents caused by defective products; a trial jury then may apply that rule in determining whether an individual can recover damages for an injury from the manufacturer of a product.

In practice, however, the distinction between creating and applying legal rules is not always a sharp one.[8] In announcing a seemingly new rule, a court sometimes says that it is simply refining or clarifying the rules that already exist, and Supreme Court justices sometimes have heated disagreements in their opinions about whether the Court has changed the law. For their part, trial judges or jurors who seem to be applying legal rules to individual cases in a routine way may implicitly be creating new rules with their decisions. A judge who regularly imposes the maximum allowable sentence on individuals who are convicted of burglary is thereby helping to determine the law of burglary in practice.

Of the four functions just described, the first three are dominated by trial courts. This is because the great majority of court cases are terminated at the trial level—through a settlement, through a choice by the initiating party not to pursue the case, or through the acceptance of the court decision by all the parties. Thus most of what courts do in resolving disputes, modifying behavior, and allocating gains and losses is done by trial courts. Appellate courts, which hear a small proportion of all cases, play a more limited role in performing these functions directly. Because of their roles in policy making, however, appellate courts are institutions of considerable significance.

The Impact of Courts

Just how important *are* the courts in terms of their impact on American society? Observers have expressed a wide range of views on this question. For instance, some scholars and commentators write about government policy making without paying much attention to courts, as if their activities were insignificant. In contrast, others have depicted the courts as a dominant force; one commentator referred to "the judicial takeover of America."[9] The difference between these two views suggests how difficult it is to pinpoint the courts' importance. It *is* possible, however, to explore their impact.

At the outset, it is useful to distinguish between trial courts and appellate courts because the two kinds of courts are important in somewhat different ways. Trial courts gain their impact chiefly through the large numbers of decisions that they make in individual cases. Each year millions of individuals are subject to court action involving such matters as criminal offenses, divorces, auto accidents, and traffic and parking violations. In some instances, such as decisions over child custody or imprisonment, court decisions have an enormous impact on people's lives. And what courts do in these cases affects still more people—those who resolve matters out of court—because predictions of what a court would decide can help determine the bargaining positions of people who negotiate about a dispute.

Appellate courts exert influence primarily through the broad impact of the legal rules that they proclaim. This impact follows from the doctrine that a court's interpretation of the law is binding on courts below it in the judicial hierarchy. Thus a state supreme court ruling on the obligations of landlords to tenants can affect decisions on landlord-tenant relationships in every court in the state. A ruling by the U.S. Supreme Court on the definition of obscenity affects every state or federal judge who hears an obscenity case. And because appellate courts influence what courts below them do, they also affect what happens outside of court. A Supreme Court decision on obscenity can help determine the language that legislatures put into obscenity laws, the ways that police departments enforce them, and even the content of published material.

Important as these effects are, they should not be exaggerated. For one thing, courts are only one part of the larger set of institutions that make government policy in an area. In deciding a criminal case, for instance, a trial court is applying rules that the legislature established. The case came to court because of decisions by police officers and prosecutors. How much time a person spends in prison may be determined not only by the court's sentencing decision but also by decisions of parole boards whether to release the convict.

The impact of appellate court decisions depends heavily on the actions of other policy makers. A Supreme Court decision on censorship of school newspapers or on the questioning of suspects by the police must be interpreted and applied by lower courts. Ultimately, administrative officials—school principals, police officers—determine the effect of such a decision in practice. And Congress or a state legislature might limit the impact of a decision or even overturn it altogether.

Furthermore, even though their concerns are broad, courts do not play a major role in all the areas of government activity. Most notably, in part because of judges' reluctance to intervene in this field, foreign policy features little judicial activity. Courts have been a minor participant in the shaping of American trade policy, and they have had almost no effect on most international conflicts that have involved the United States.

A second limitation on the impact of courts applies to government in general. Government is only one of many forces that shape society, and it is not necessarily the most powerful. Important nongovernmental forces—including the family, the mass media, and the economy—all help determine the impact of court decisions on conditions such as race relations and criminal activity. For this reason, the sweeping claims that are sometimes made about the impact of the courts on society seem extravagant. In 1981, for instance, one scholar argued that court decisions expanding the rights of public school students on issues such as suspensions and free speech had helped bring about high levels of "youth suicides, homicides, and out-of-wedlock births."[10] It seems unlikely, however, that the impact of courts on these kinds of trends could rival that of more fundamental social forces, such as the family.

I emphasize these limitations because they are sometimes given insufficient attention. But, as I have suggested, these limitations are not unique to courts; other government institutions face similar constraints on the effects of their policies. And we should not lose sight of the impact that courts do have. Judicial activities directly affect a high proportion of people in the United States and affect many of them quite significantly. Court decisions also have important effects on the nation as a whole. Therefore, courts certainly merit the attention that we give them, and one cannot understand American government and society without understanding the judiciary.

EXPLAINING COURT PROCESSES AND OUTCOMES

One of the aims of this book is to explain both the processes by which courts operate and the outcomes of cases that are brought to court. Thus I will discuss explanations for such matters as the prevalence of plea bargaining in criminal cases, the outcomes of automobile accident cases, and the disagreements among judges in appellate court decisions. These matters seldom have simple explanations, and our ability to explain them is often handicapped by a lack of needed information. Still, it is important to explore ways of understanding what goes on in courts.

It is difficult to explain what courts do in general terms because different aspects of their work are best explained in different ways. Nevertheless, we can begin by thinking about general perspectives from which the processes and outcomes that take place in court might be understood. Most of these explanations fit within three broad categories, which might be called the legal, the environmental, and the personal. Each of these perspectives has both value and limitations.

The Legal Perspective

Courts work within a legal framework. Decisions by judges and juries involve the application of legal rules to the facts of specific cases. These rules are found in the federal and state constitutions, in the statutes adopted by legislatures, and in past court decisions. Court procedures are also governed by legal rules.

Judges, lawyers, and observers of courts disagree sharply about the importance of this legal framework in shaping what the courts do. Some people, particularly judges, argue that courts do little more than follow the law. At the other extreme, some critics argue that the law is primarily a rationalization for judges and other people in the court system who act on other bases, such as judges' attitudes about the policy issues involved in the cases they decide. The reality, I think, is somewhere between these two views.

The law is important in courts chiefly because judges and lawyers believe that they are in the business of applying the law. To a degree, this belief is embedded in American culture, with its strong emphasis on the rule of law. And lawyers undergo intensive law school training in legal reasoning—training that is reinforced by their later experience in the legal system.

For these reasons, courts generally are pervaded by an atmosphere in which people speak and think in terms of legal principles. As a result, the law channels and constrains activity in courts. Lawyers seek to win cases by showing that their clients' positions are consistent with the best interpretation of the law. In turn, judges seldom reach decisions that cannot be justified as interpretations of the applicable body of law, and their reasoning reflects their training in the law. To take one example, legal education emphasizes reasoning by analogy, so it was not surprising when an Alaska judge resolved a dispute between a divorcing couple over where their dog would live by applying principles developed for custody of children.[11] And in 1992 a federal court of appeals felt obliged to interpret an old statute literally, despite an apparent typographical error, and upset a long-established practice by holding that national banks in small towns no longer could sell insurance.[12]

The impact of the law is most apparent when it seems to overcome other considerations that move judges toward a different decision. In 1992, for instance, an Alaska court reluctantly ruled that a ship captain could not be prosecuted for actions resulting in a massive oil spill in 1989.

> The unparalleled environmental devastation wrought by the grounding of the Exxon Valdez is hardly lost upon this court. But while we may feel sorely tempted, as individuals, to recast the law in a mold better suited to our personal sense of justice, we are bound, as judges, to resist this temptation.[13]

Yet the law is an incomplete explanation of what courts do, for two fundamental reasons. First, the law frequently leaves considerable discretion to judges and juries. In some instances, legislatures create this discretion deliberately. State legislatures, for example, often give judges a wide range of alternative sentences to impose for a particular criminal offense in the belief that sentences need to be fitted to the characteristics of individual cases and offenders. Thus in Nebraska a judge can mete out a prison sentence that ranges anywhere from one to fifty years for first-degree arson or assault on a police officer.[14]

More often, discretion results from ambiguities in the law and its application. Jurors are asked to apply the law to the facts of a particular case, but if there are two or more plausible readings of the facts, conscientious jurors may reach different conclusions. Similarly, many provisions of constitutions and statutes contain vague language, such as "due process of law," which requires judges to choose among credible alternative interpretations. And even seemingly clear language is often difficult to apply to a specific situation, as the case in Exhibit 1.2 shows.

The other reason that the law fails to explain court activities fully is that the motivations of people in the courts go beyond simply trying to follow the law. Undoubtedly, most judges strongly believe that they *should* follow the law in deciding cases and supervising court proceedings. But judges also hold preferences about public policy issues and feel external pressures to

EXHIBIT 1.2 The Virginia Supreme Court Disagrees over Application of a Statute

A police officer in Falls Church, Virginia, found a man in a parking lot, sleeping behind the steering wheel of his car, with the engine off but the key in the ignition. The officer concluded that the man was intoxicated, and the man was convicted of drunk driving under a statutory provision that makes it "unlawful for any person to drive or operate any motor vehicle . . . while such person is under the influence of any . . . self-administered intoxicant." Another statute defines a vehicle "operator" or "driver" as anyone who "drives or is in actual physical control of a motor vehicle upon a highway."

The defendant argued that, under the circumstances, he was not actually "driving" or "operating" the car and thus could not be convicted under the statute; ultimately, the state supreme court ruled on the issue. A four-member majority concluded that "because the presence of the key in the ignition switch in the off position did not engage the mechanical or electrical equipment of" the defendant's car, he did not "drive or operate" the car under the meaning of those terms in the statutes. But three judges dissented vehemently, arguing that "when a drunk is sitting in the driver's seat of a parked, operable motor vehicle, and he is alone and has inserted the key in the ignition switch, he is in 'actual physical control' of the vehicle" and thus falls under the statute. Thus, by a 4–3 vote, the conviction was overturned.

Source: Stevenson v. City of Falls Church, 416 S.E.2d 435 (Va. 1992).

handle cases in certain ways. These factors affect the behavior of judges, even of judges who wish only to apply legal rules faithfully. Federal judge Patricia M. Wald points out some of these nonlegal factors:

> Despite much protestation to the contrary, a judge's origins and politics will surely influence his or her judicial opinions. Judges' minds are not compartmentalized: their law-declaring functions cannot be performed by some insulated, apolitical internal mechanism. However subtly or unconsciously, the judge's political orientation *will* affect decisionmaking.[15]

The limitations of the law as an explanation of court behavior are highlighted by disagreements among judges and among jurors. On the Supreme Court, whose nine members apply the same body of law to the same case, only a minority of decisions are unanimous—38 percent in the 1991-1992 term.[16] And there are so many conflicting interpretations of the law by federal courts that the Supreme Court has time to resolve only a portion of them. In one conflict that the Court did resolve in 1992, about forty federal district courts had addressed the issue of whether the Red Cross could require that any case brought against it in state court be moved to federal court, with only a small majority on one side of the issue, the Supreme Court itself decided the issue by a 5–4 vote.[17] Such disagreements reflect both the ambiguity of the law and the influence of other motivations on those who decide cases.

It is worth reiterating that legal rules offer a good guide to much of what courts do. Without a legal perspective, it is impossible to understand what happens in courts, and the law is often the best starting point for an explanation of court behavior. But it is only a starting point, and other perspectives must be considered in order to gain a more comprehensive understanding of courts.

The Personal Perspective

In its strongest form, the legal perspective assumes that people who make decisions in courts are motivated only by a commitment to the law. In contrast, what might be called the personal perspective allows for a broader range of motivations that can influence behavior. Judges, for instance, may act on the basis of their own values, self-interest, or personality characteristics, such as a strong need for approval. Thus the processes that occur in courts and the outcomes of cases can be seen in terms of the motivations of the people who are involved in them.

A focus on individuals has proved very useful in the study of Supreme Court decision-making. Many scholars view the Court's decisions primarily as reflections of one motivational factor, the justices' policy preferences. According to this view, divisions on the Court can be explained by differences in values, and the Court's collective position results from the sum of the nine justices' views on policy.

On the Supreme Court, as well as on other courts, judges' personal policy preferences and court policies are often described as either *liberal* or *conservative*. These labels require some discussion. On most issues that courts decide, the competing positions generally are given one label or the other; Exhibit 1.3 summarizes what are usually considered to be the liberal and conservative positions on some major judicial issues. One common thread binding together positions on different issues is that the liberal position on most issues is the one more favorable to equality rather than to competing values, such as the autonomy of businesses. In part because of this common thread, people tend to be consistent in their ideological positions; in other words, a judge with liberal views on one issue is likely to have liberal views on most other issues. For this reason, the terms *liberal* and *conservative* are useful in summarizing both a judge's general views and the direction of a court's policies.

EXHIBIT 1.3 Liberal and Conservative Positions on Some Common Judicial Issues

Issue Area	Liberal Position	Conservative Position
Criminal cases	Relatively sympathetic toward defendants and their procedural rights	Gives greater emphasis to effectiveness of criminal justice system in fighting crime
Personal liberties	More supportive of liberties such as freedom of speech and right to privacy	More supportive of values that may conflict with these liberties, such as public order and national security
Disadvantaged groups	More strongly supports expanded rights and improved status for groups such as African-Americans, women, and the poor	Gives relatively great weight to the costs of these expansions and improvements, such as the monetary costs of public welfare
Regulation of business	More favorable to government regulation on behalf of such goals as protection of the environment	More protective of the autonomy of businesses
Businesses vs. individuals	In economic conflicts, such as disputes between insurance companies and injured drivers, more likely to support the individual	Less likely to support the individual; more favorable to business

Note: Positions of liberals and conservatives should be read in relation to each other; for instance, liberals are more likely to support individuals in disputes with businesses than are conservatives.

A different motivation, self-interest, is highlighted by the *plea bargaining* that takes place in criminal courts. In plea bargaining, lawyers, defendants, and judges resolve cases through negotiation rather than through trials. Plea bargaining is prevalent chiefly because it offers important advantages to each group. Among other benefits, prosecutors avoid the risk of an acquittal at trial, defendants and their attorneys limit the severity of the sentence, and judges save the time that trials would require. Efforts to eliminate plea bargaining tend to fail because of this mutual self-interest in maintaining it.

An implication of the personal perspective is that courts should be understood as institutions with their own dynamics. We can think of the set of people who participate in a particular court as an organization or a work group.[18] All the participants bring to the work group their own motivations, and court processes and case outcomes emerge from the interaction of these motivations. One result is that legal mandates can be distorted. Legislatures, for example, may establish a mandatory minimum sentence for an offense, only to discover that judges and prosecutors who disagree with such a requirement have found ways to avoid imposing it.

Another implication is that it often makes a considerable difference who participates in the courts generally and in particular cases. As a Pennsylvania judge pointed out more than a half century ago,

> we must, if realists, recognize that courts controlled by a "conservative" personnel and those dominated by a "liberal" membership are more than likely to decide constitutional questions from different angles and with different results.[19]

The general recognition of this reality is reflected in the attention focused on appointments to the Supreme Court. People interested in the Court understand that even a single new justice can shift the Court's ideological balance and thus its policies. This is the primary reason that presidential nominees to the Court, such as Clarence Thomas, have received so much scrutiny in the Senate.

It is not just ideology that makes individuals important in the courts. For instance, some judges are more aggressive than others in their handling of cases. For more than a decade, Judge Harold Greene of the federal district court in Washington, D.C., has played an active role in supervising the nation's telephone system under the settlement of an antitrust suit. Another judge might have carved out a more limited role, seeking to extricate the court from conflicts over the form of the system.

The internal focus that leads to such insights also constitutes a limitation on the personal perspective; a narrow concentration on people within the courts may cause an observer to lose sight of the broad forces that shape their behavior. A focus on individuals helps a great deal in understanding why a Supreme Court justice has selected the more liberal position of the two that are debated in a particular case. It is less useful in identifying a position that no justice has considered because it cannot be reconciled with federal law or because it lacks sufficient support outside the Court. Today, for instance, the Supreme Court could hardly rule that the Constitution prohibits federal minimum wage laws; that position and its broader implications are unacceptable to too many people in and out of government. Nor does the focus on individuals point to the social forces and political currents that help produce a liberal or a conservative Court in any given period. Thus the personal perspective must be supplemented with a broader perspective on court behavior.

The Environmental Perspective

The environmental perspective views courts in relation to the government and society of which they are a part, looking to the ways in which courts are affected by external forces.

Certainly, courts are affected by their environments in a number of ways. The values and perceptions of lawyers and judges are shaped by their experiences in American society. Other branches of government influence courts by writing laws, by providing resources for the judiciary, and by selecting judges and other court participants. Interest groups sponsor significant cases and influence judges' perceptions of the issues in those cases. Similarly, the state of the economy and social trends help determine what kinds of cases reach court and how judges and jurors think about them.

From this perspective, it can be argued that courts tend to mirror their society. But what exactly is it that they mirror? To some degree, they reflect the pattern of social values and attitudes in the United States. One reason is that dominant attitudes are likely to exert at least subtle pressures on courts; another is that judges and other court participants are likely to share these attitudes. For both reasons, to take one example, widespread concern about illegal drugs in the past few years has had a considerable effect on the courts. Many judges impose longer prison terms in drug cases. The Supreme Court gives more weight to government success in attacking illegal drugs than to the individual liberties that might be weakened by those efforts.

Courts also tend to reflect the distribution of economic and political power. Those segments of society that have the most power are generally in the best positions to influence what courts do. Most lawyers and judges come from higher-status backgrounds. Those with the greatest economic resources are the most capable of bringing cases to court and presenting them effectively, and they also hold disproportionate influence in the legislatures that write statutes for courts to apply. For these reasons, one might expect, for example, that courts would serve the interests of business corporations more diligently than the interests of low-income individuals.[20]

Courts also respond to more direct pressures from their environments. Elected judges want to retain public support, and this goal may move them to take popular positions in their decisions. And even judges who hold their positions for life might alter judicial policies that have incited outrage in the other branches of government. Today, in an era when the work of the courts receives close attention, such pressures are especially likely to arise.

Although environmental influences are powerful, their impact is limited by the relative autonomy of courts. Through such mechanisms as the life terms of federal judges and the norms that restrict direct lobbying of judges and juries, courts are partially insulated from external pressures. And people who become judges have undergone intensive training, in which they are taught that they should withstand pressures in order to follow the legal rules that apply to cases. This insulation is reflected in some actions by judges. Many federal judges have ordered school busing for racial integration despite the great unpopularity of this policy; their tenure in office enables them to take this position, which is much more dangerous for elected members of Congress. To use a somewhat different example, a trial judge who receives strong advice from the mass media to impose a heavy sentence on a notorious criminal may well bend to that pressure, but the judge is quite unlikely to impose a sentence more severe than the law authorizes.

Thus courts reflect society imperfectly. Strong currents of thought and power in American society inevitably affect courts, but other influences and motives also help determine what happens in the courts.

General Implications

The discussion so far has pointed out several different perspectives—each with its strengths and weaknesses—from which one can explain the behavior of courts. It has also indicated that court processes and the results of court cases are shaped by a good many forces, so that few significant court phenomena can be explained in simple terms.

The examination of courts in this book reflects these lessons. Although I will give primary emphasis to the personal perspective, and especially to the motives that underlie choices made by people in the courts, the book employs other perspectives as well. The effects of outside influences on court processes and on the outcomes of cases receive considerable attention. And the legal framework within which courts work, a framework that in itself reflects social thought and power in complex ways, is also taken into account.

EVALUATING COURTS

American courts are constantly being evaluated. Indeed, it is almost impossible to write about Supreme Court decisions or criminal court processes without assessing the performance of those courts. This book contains a good deal of evaluation, addressing such issues as the quality of judges and the effectiveness of trials in discovering the truth. But more often than not, my evaluations are tentative rather than firm. This reflects my feeling that, as with other government institutions, a conclusive appraisal of courts is virtually impossible to achieve.

One difficulty is that it is frequently unclear what criteria should be used for evaluation. Almost any significant aspect of court outputs or processes can be assessed on two or more different bases. And the mere choice of a particular criterion may predetermine whether an evaluation is positive or negative.

Perhaps the classic example of this difficulty involves the work of trial courts in criminal cases, work that has received considerable scrutiny and criticism during this century. Using a distinction made by Herbert Packer, we might evaluate criminal courts on the basis of either a *due process* model or a *crime control* model.[21] In the due process model, which some political liberals support, courts are judged primarily by their procedural fairness to defendants and their care in reaching appropriate decisions in cases. In the crime control model, more popular in society as a whole, courts are judged primarily by their efficiency and effectiveness in convicting and punishing criminals. Clearly, a court that looks good according to one model might look quite bad according to the other; this is one reason for the great disagreement about how well the criminal courts actually work.

It is important, then, to be clear about one's criteria for evaluating courts and to recognize that alternative criteria might lead to quite different conclusions. People who disagree in their evaluations often are talking past each other because they have based their arguments on different premises.

But agreement on criteria does not end the difficulties of evaluation, for the application of these criteria to a particular situation also tends to be problematic. This is especially true when the criteria are broad or vague, as is often the case. We might agree, for instance, that the task of trial courts in adjudicating civil cases is to do justice. But the concept of "justice" is complex, and its meaning and application to specific circumstances are matters of almost continuous debate. Businesses that come to court to collect debts from individuals are generally quite successful. Is that a just result? Beginning with one conception of justice in the context of American society, we may view the success of businesses as just, on the ground that courts are properly requiring people to pay their debts. Starting with a different conception, we may view this result as unjust, on the ground that it allows an advantaged segment of society to exploit those who are often economically vulnerable.

It is not much easier to evaluate a court according to how well it interprets the law. What is a good interpretation of the Constitution when the relevant constitutional language is vague and several conflicting methods of interpretation are available? Legal scholars generally write commentaries on Supreme Court decisions in the style of movie reviews, presenting one point of view and ignoring the possibility that other legitimate viewpoints exist. But commentaries on a decision, like reviews of a movie, often differ sharply in their conclusions. Such differences are inevitable, given the ambiguity of legal interpretation.

Sometimes a lack of information increases the difficulty of evaluation. For example, people in the legal profession probably could reach at least moderate agreement as to what constitutes competence in a trial lawyer. But there are so many trial lawyers across the country that no single observer could make a definitive judgment as to how competent trial lawyers actually are. Thus there has been a long-standing debate on this issue, one that is unlikely to be resolved.

Even more problematic is evaluation of court decisions on the basis of their intended impact. Many people feel that the primary goal of criminal sentencing should be to limit the future incidence of crime, and one long-standing purpose of court decisions in personal injury law is to minimize the frequency of accidents. But at this point we know too little to determine what kinds of sentences or personal injury doctrines will best achieve these goals. For this reason, some of the strong judgments that people make about the work of courts in such areas are open to question.

Despite all these difficulties, we should not be deterred from making tentative evaluations of courts; their work is too important not to be evaluated. In most areas, however, these evaluations must proceed with considerable caution and modesty. To offer a definitive assessment of court activities when both the appropriate criteria and their application are uncertain has little value.

This is also true of efforts to describe and explain court processes and the outcomes of court cases, for there is a great deal that we do not know about courts—including some things that many people think we know.[22] Caution is always appropriate in examining the courts. Yet our knowledge is considerable, and it is growing rapidly. The remaining chapters of this book lay out what we do know about these institutions that play so central a part in American life.

NOTES

1. Herbert Jacob, *Law and Politics in the United States* (Boston: Little, Brown, 1986), pp. 6–7.
2. *Kentucky Constitution*, sec. 216 (Ky. Revised Statutes, 1988 ed.).
3. See Martin Shapiro, *Courts: A Comparative and Political Analysis* (Chicago: University of Chicago Press, 1981), ch. 1.
4. Michael Lipsky, *Street-Level Bureaucracy: Dilemmas of the Individual in Public Services* (New York: Russell Sage Foundation, 1980).
5. Austin Sarat and Joel B. Grossman, "Courts and Conflict Resolution: Problems in the Mobilization of Adjudication," *American Political Science Review,* 69 (December 1975), 1213–17.
6. *United States Code*, tit. 31, sec. 3730 (1988 ed.).
7. *United States Code*, tit. 21, sec. 881(e) (1988 ed.).
8. Lynn Mather, "Policy Making in State Trial Courts," in *The American Courts: A Critical Assessment,* ed. John B. Gates and Charles A. Johnson (Washington, D.C.: CQ Press, 1991), pp. 123–129.
9. James McClellan, "The Judicialization of the American Republic," in *The Judges War: The Senate, Legal Culture, Political Ideology and Judicial Confirmation,* ed. Patrick B. McGuigan and Jeffrey P. O'Connell (Washington, D.C.: Free Congress Research and Education Foundation, 1987), p. 61.
10. Edward A. Wynne, "What Are the Courts Doing to Our Children?" *The Public Interest,* 64 (Summer 1981), 3.
11. The decision is reported in "Strange Things Done in the Midnight Sun," *Alaska Bar Rag,* 16 (January–February 1992), 1, 14–15.
12. *Independent Insurance Agents of America v. Clarke,* 955 F.2d 731 (D.C. Cir. 1992).

13. Andrew Blum, "Alaska Appeals Valdez Reversal," *National Law Journal*, December 14, 1992, p. 9.
14. *Revised Statutes of Nebraska*, ch. 28, secs. 105, 502, 929 (1989 ed.).
15. Patricia M. Wald, "Some Thoughts on Judging as Gleaned from One Hundred Years of the *Harvard Law Review* and Other Great Books," *Harvard Law Review*, 100 (February 1987), 895.
16. "Unanimous Decisions," *National Law Journal*, August 31, 1992, p. S2.
17. *American National Red Cross v. S.G.*, 120 L. Ed. 2d 201 (1992), and *Petition for Writ of Certiorari* in the case, at pp. 10–11. In citations of court decisions, the first number is the volume of the court reports in which the decision and accompanying opinions are found. The abbreviated designation of the court reports follows that number. (In this instance, "L. Ed. 2d" stands for the second series of the Supreme Court Reports, Lawyers' Edition, one of the unofficial reporters of Supreme Court decisions; the official reporter is the U.S. Reports, designated "U.S.") The second number is the page on which the decision and opinions begin.
18. The concept of work groups is presented in James Eisenstein and Herbert Jacob, *Felony Justice: An Organizational Analysis of Criminal Courts* (Boston: Little, Brown, 1977), ch. 2.
19. Horace Stern, "Book Review," *Harvard Law Review*, 51 (November 1937), 179.
20. See Marc Galanter, "Why the 'Haves' Come Out Ahead: Speculations on the Limits of Social Change," *Law and Society Review*, 9 (Fall 1974), 95–160.
21. Herbert L. Packer, *The Limits of the Criminal Sanction* (Stanford, Calif.: Stanford University Press, 1968), ch. 8.
22. See Marc Galanter, "Reading the Landscape of Disputes: What We Know and Don't Know (and Think We Know) About Our Allegedly Contentious and Litigious Society," *UCLA Law Review*, 31 (October 1983), 4–71; and Michael J. Saks, "Do We Really Know Anything About the Behavior of the Tort Litigation System—And Why Not?" *University of Pennsylvania Law Review*, 140 (April 1992), 1147–1292.

2

Court Organization

The federal judicial system is divided into twelve circuits, each with a court of appeals. By any measure, the Ninth Circuit is the largest of the circuits. The Ninth Circuit contains nine states and two territories; it stretches from Alaska to Arizona, from Montana to Hawaii, and then to Guam. The Ninth Circuit Court of Appeals has twenty-eight full-time judges, as well as a number of retired judges who serve part-time, to consider and decide more than five thousand cases a year.

In 1990 the Senate considered a bill to split the Ninth Circuit into two parts. The states of California, Arizona, and Nevada would constitute one circuit; the other states and territories another.[1]

During the hearings on the bill, those who favored a division of the circuit focused on administrative issues: whether the circuit was too large to handle its business efficiently and whether the large membership of the court of appeals created too many conflicts among three-judge panels over interpretations of the law. But if administrative issues were the only concern, it was difficult to explain the lineup of supporters and opponents of the bill. Why was the bill sponsored and favored by senators from northwestern states, while the California senators vehemently opposed it? And why would the Sierra Club and other environmental groups argue fiercely against a proposal relating to judicial administration?

The primary answer is that the proposal to split the Ninth Circuit was more than simply a technical matter of administration. The bill's sponsor, Senator Slade Gorton of Washington, suggested what was involved when he complained that "Northwestern states are simply dominated by California judges and by California attitudes."[2] California's Senator Pete Wilson made the matter more explicit when he described the proposal as "environmental gerrymandering."[3] The Ninth Circuit Court of Appeals, with a majority of judges from California, had given broad interpretations to environmental protection laws. Many people in the Northwest, including conservative senators, saw these decisions as quite damaging to timber and other industries in that area. Splitting the circuit would prevent California judges from ruling on environmental cases in the Northwest, and judges who came from the

Northwest themselves might be more sympathetic toward industries that were important to the region's economy.

The proposal failed. But the battle over dividing the Ninth Circuit underlines the importance of court organization. The ways in which individual courts and court systems are structured and administered help shape judicial policies and thus make a difference to those who use the courts and those who are affected by court decisions. Hence even seemingly routine matters of court organization are often a focus of political contention.

This chapter examines the organization of courts in the United States. I give primary attention to the mechanics of court organization. But I also consider the politics of court organization: the debates that arise over organizational arrangements, and the impact of those arrangements. The first section of the chapter discusses the general principles of court organization, the second section focuses on the organization of the federal court system, and the third examines patterns and variations in state court systems.

GENERAL PRINCIPLES OF COURT ORGANIZATION

Before looking at the specifics of court organization, we need to consider two broad matters: the relationship between the federal and state court systems and general patterns in the organization of each court system.

Federal and State Court Systems

Perhaps the most important feature of court organization in the United States is the existence of multiple court systems. Each of the fifty states, as well as the District of Columbia and the territories, has a court system. The federal government has its own court system.

Separation of Court Systems   The state systems are, of course, clearly divided from each other by geography. In contrast, the federal and state systems overlap geographically, with federal and state courts sometimes located near each other in a particular city. Each type of court, however, is part of a different organization.

Cases ordinarily stay within a single system. A case brought to a federal court almost always remains in the federal courts. Under certain circumstances, a case may begin in a state court system and then move to the federal courts; for instance, some cases go from a state supreme court to the U.S. Supreme Court. But such a move is very much the exception to the rule.

Each system is organized and managed by its own government. The form of the Colorado court system, for instance, is determined by the constitution and statutes of Colorado. As a result, the Colorado system need not take the same form as that of other states or of the federal court system. Indeed, court systems vary considerably in such characteristics as the structure of trial courts and the methods used to select judges. Of course, the laws that courts carry out also differ from one system to another. In part for these reasons, each court system develops its own distinctive ways of operating.

Federal and State Court Jurisdiction   The concept of *jurisdiction* refers basically to the power of a court to hear cases; that concept is central to the organization of court systems. Rules of jurisdiction, set primarily by state and federal constitutions and statutes, determine what kinds of cases each court can hear. At the same time, they indicate which court or courts are appropriate forums for any specific case. Jurisdiction may be based on several characteristics of a case, including its subject matter (criminal versus civil, for instance), the parties (for example, whether the federal government is a party), and its geography (where the parties reside and the location of the events from which a case stems). Jurisdiction can be considered a characteristic both of court systems as a whole and of individual courts. The jurisdiction of the state court system in Missouri, for instance, is the sum of the jurisdiction of all the individual state courts in Missouri.

The dividing line between the federal and state courts can be understood in terms of the jurisdiction of the federal court system. Federal courts may try only those classes of cases that are designated to be within their jurisdiction by federal law; some of these cases can be heard in either federal or state court. By default, everything else is within the jurisdiction of the state systems. The Constitution outlines the scope of federal court jurisdiction, which is developed in more detail in federal statutes. Although the rules of federal jurisdiction are complex, the cases they admit to the system fall primarily into three categories.

1. *Federal question jurisdiction* is based on the subject matter of cases. Under this jurisdiction, federal courts are entitled to hear all cases that are based on the U.S. Constitution, on treaties with other nations, and on federal statutes. This category includes both civil cases and criminal cases that are based on federal law.
2. *Federal party jurisdiction* gives federal courts the general power to hear cases in which the federal government is a party. Consequently, nearly all cases brought by or against the federal government, a federal agency, or a federal officer can be heard in federal court.
3. *Diversity jurisdiction* is based on geography, granting federal courts the right to hear cases in which there is a diversity of citizenship between the parties (if they are citizens of different states or if one is a citizen of a foreign nation) so long as the suit is for fifty thousand dollars or more.

Jurisdiction over a particular class of cases may be exclusive to a particular court, or it may be concurrent (shared by two or more courts). This distinction can also be applied to court systems as a whole. With some exceptions, such as criminal cases based on federal statutes, the jurisdiction of federal courts is concurrent with that of state courts. Thus, for example, most kinds of civil cases brought by the federal government can be heard in either state or federal courts.

Cases based on diversity of citizenship illustrate the workings of concurrent jurisdiction. When citizens of different states become involved in a controversy involving at least fifty thousand dollars, the plaintiff has the option of filing a case in either federal or state court. But if the plaintiff chooses state court, the defendant can have the case removed to federal court. Thus either party can take an appropriate case to federal court.

Diversity cases also illustrate the politics of jurisdiction. Congress first established this jurisdiction in 1789 as a protection against state bias; it was feared that state courts would favor their own citizens against those of other states. The diversity jurisdiction has survived for two centuries, even though some people think that the bias that concerned Congress in 1789 is no longer a problem. In recent years federal judges have sought to limit or eliminate the diversity jurisdiction because it adds a large and burdensome set of cases to their workload.

But Congress has responded to this campaign only by raising the minimum monetary amount in 1988 from ten thousand to fifty thousand dollars. The main reason is that lawyers want to retain the option of bringing diversity cases to federal court. They like the choice between federal and state courts because it allows them to engage in "forum-shopping" by choosing the court whose judges seem more likely to favor their clients. The 1989 battle in baseball between manager Pete Rose and commissioner A. Bartlett Giamatti, described in Exhibit 2.1, illustrates this kind of forum-shopping. And some prefer federal courts because of perceived advantages, such as a less hurried pace of proceedings.

Criminal justice issues also illustrate the politics of jurisdiction. To take one example, some criminal offenses could be prosecuted under either federal or state laws. The Bush administration sought to bring federal prosecutions in many of these cases—particularly when the cases involved drugs or crimes committed with guns—because federal sentences for those offenses tend to be heavier. The result was to add further to the heavy caseloads of federal courts. In Washington, D.C., where the United States Attorney prosecutes both federal cases and the equivalent of state cases, a recent U.S. Attorney battled with some federal judges over what they regarded as his policy of bringing minor cases to federal court to gain a sentencing advantage. In one gun possession case, a judge in the District of Columbia complained that "this court shouldn't be the place for the local police to try their petty crimes."[4]

Most cases that fall under federal jurisdiction do end up in federal court. Yet only a small proportion of all court cases are tried in federal court because the great majority of cases fit under no category of federal jurisdiction and thus go to the state courts by default. Every year the largest group of cases throughout the country results from traffic and parking violations, and almost all of these fall under state law. In addition, criminal law is primarily a state matter, and people charged with common crimes, such as burglary and assault, ordinarily are tried under state law. Similarly, most common types of civil cases, such as those that arise from personal injuries or contract disputes, are based on state law and involve citizens of the same state.

In March 1989 the office of the commissioner of major league baseball announced an investigation of Cincinnati Reds manager and former star player Pete Rose, based on allegations of gambling by Rose. After an investigator submitted a report to Commissioner A. Bartlett Giamatti, the commissioner scheduled a hearing for June 26 to allow Rose to respond to the report.

On June 19 Rose filed suit to prevent the hearing from taking place, arguing that Giamatti had shown bias against him. Rose could have brought the case in federal court under diversity jurisdiction because he was a citizen of Ohio, whereas Giamatti and his office were located in New York. Instead, Rose brought the case in Ohio state court. By doing so, he could have it heard by an elected judge in Cincinnati, where Rose was very popular. Indeed, Rose's attorneys brought the case at a time when emergency motions were to be heard by a judge facing election in 1990 rather than a later year.

That judge, Norbert A. Nadel, scheduled his announcement of a decision for June 25 and allowed the announcement to be televised. When Nadel "started the hearing with a microphone check," wrote an editorial writer, "you knew Pete Rose had the home-court advantage." And Nadel did rule in favor of Rose, issuing a temporary restraining order to delay Giamatti's hearing and discipline of Rose for two weeks while Nadel considered a preliminary injunction.

On July 3 Giamatti's lawyers asked to have the case removed to federal district court, using the right of a defendant to such removal on the basis of diversity jurisdiction. The case was then transferred from Cincinnati to Columbus, also in the Southern District of Ohio, where it would be heard by a nonelected judge who did not live in Cincinnati. Judge John D. Holschuh, assigned the case, scheduled a hearing to decide whether the federal court had jurisdiction. On July 31 he ruled that there was federal jurisdiction, and on August 17 the federal court of appeals for the Sixth Circuit refused to consider the jurisdictional issue.

On August 24, while a hearing on Rose's request for a preliminary injunction was pending, Rose reached an agreement with Giamatti under which he would drop his case and accept a permanent prohibition on participation in baseball that could be rescinded at some point.

On November 6, 1990, Judge Nadel was elected to a new term on the court of common pleas, winning the largest majority of any Hamilton County judicial candidate who faced opposition.

Sources: The chronology is based primarily on "Rose's Woes," *Cincinnati Enquirer,* August 25, 1989, p. A9. Additional information comes from *Rose v. Giamatti,* 721 F. Supp. 906 (S.D. Ohio 1989). The quotation is from "Paint the Robe Red," *Cleveland Plain Dealer,* June 27, 1989, p. 14B.

EXHIBIT 2.1 Diversity Jurisdiction and Pete Rose

On the other hand, a disproportionate number of cases that raise major policy questions come to federal court, for many of these cases arise under the Constitution or federal statutes, and only federal cases have the potential to produce legal rules that apply to the country as a whole. As a result, the federal courts are a good deal more important than the numbers of their cases alone would indicate.

General Patterns of Court Organization

Despite the diversity of American court systems, some general patterns exist in the structure of the courts within these systems and in the ways in which the courts are administered.

Court Structure   The jurisdiction of a court system must be divided among courts within that system. Thus, both at the federal level and within each state, constitutional provisions and statutes create a set of courts and establish the jurisdiction of each. Such jurisdiction is always divided along two lines, vertical and horizontal.

Vertically, some courts are designated primarily as trial courts and others as appellate courts; put another way, a court's jurisdiction may be mostly trial or mostly appellate. In addition, most systems in the United States make a further distinction: between first-level appellate courts, which hear appeals from trial court decisions, and second-level appellate courts, which hear primarily cases brought from first-level appellate courts. A strong hierarchical element exists in every system. Higher courts review the decisions of the courts below them. Their judgeships are also more prestigious (and, in most systems, better paying) than those on lower courts.

Horizontally, jurisdiction may be divided among different sets of courts at the same level. Such a division occurs primarily at the trial level. In most states one set of courts is designated to try cases with larger stakes, while other courts try cases with smaller stakes. In addition, certain courts may be given relatively narrow responsibilities, such as tax cases or domestic relations cases. Sometimes two or more sets of courts in a system hold concurrent jurisdiction over a particular type of case.

Related to horizontal jurisdiction is *venue*, which concerns the place and court in which a case may be brought. Particularly at the trial level, several different courts of the same type often sit in different places. For instance, there are ninety-four federal district courts spread across the United States. Venue rules are complex, but generally the place in which a case may be brought depends on the location of the parties' residences and of the actions from which the case derives. Although venue seems like a technical matter, courts take it quite seriously. In 1989, for instance, a federal court of appeals overturned the convictions—after a three-month trial—of two officials of the Beech-Nut Corporation for distributing phony apple juice. The court made this decision on the ground that the officials had been tried in the wrong federal district.[5]

Sometimes a case can be brought in only a single place; sometimes in two or more places. In the latter situation, as in cases that could go to either a state or a federal court, the litigant can engage in forum-shopping. Judges in Manhattan, for instance, tend to interpret legal rules in ways that favor both bankruptcy lawyers and companies seeking to reorganize under the bankruptcy law; as a result, it is common for companies whose business activities are centered elsewhere to file their bankruptcy cases in New York on the basis of some corporate activity there. Eastern Airlines did not file for reorganization in Miami, the site of its headquarters, or in Houston, where its corporate parent was located. Instead, it filed in New York, where its airport club operation for customers ("The Ionosphere Club") was based.[6]

A special case of forum-shopping involves motions by criminal defendants for a "change of venue" to avoid potential prejudice in the place where the alleged offense took place. Such requests seldom are granted. In the first prosecution, under state law, of four police officers for the videotaped beating of Rodney King, a successful request for change of venue moved the case from Los Angeles to a neighboring county, whose potential jurors were likely to have considerably greater sympathy for the defendants. In the view of one reporter, "the outcome of the case may well have been decided" when the case went to that county.[7]

Court Administration   The actual running of individual courts and court systems is called court administration. Power and responsibility for court administration are divided between the courts and the other branches of government. Constitutional provisions and legislation determine such basic matters as the kinds of courts that a system includes and the places where court is held. Within the limits established by constitutions and statutes, courts administer themselves. Individual courts have their own administrative structures to handle their business, and court systems have administrative bodies to help run these systems as a whole.

Many judges are traditionalists. They resist centralized control over their work and are reluctant to change well-established ways of doing things. According to one Colorado judge, "Courts would still be using quill pens if there were enough people raising geese."[8] One commentator suggested that "judges don't want to govern themselves, but they don't want anyone else to do it either."[9]

Traditional patterns of administration have been challenged in recent years by growth in court workloads and the failure of court budgets to keep pace with these workloads. Indeed, resource problems increasingly dominate the concerns of judges and court administrators. A variety of programs have been adopted to dispose of cases more quickly, primarily by providing more incentives and opportunities for pretrial settlement. Courts resort to ad hoc measures to overcome limited space: an Oklahoma judge held a session on the courthouse lawn when courtrooms were busy, and an Arizona court took up residence near a karate school and a Burger King in a shopping mall.[10] Judges increasingly lobby the other branches for larger budgets or legal changes that would reduce the flow of cases into court. In 1991 the chief judge of New York's highest court sued Governor Mario Cuomo and the state legislature for allegedly failing to meet a constitutional requirement to fund the courts adequately. (Cuomo tried unsuccessfully to move the case into federal court, arguing that he could not get a fair hearing in a state court system headed by his adversary; later, the case was settled out of court.)[11] It should be emphasized that both resource problems and efforts to cope with them can influence the handling of cases and their results. One recurring theme of this book is the impact of heavy caseloads on court processes and outcomes.

THE FEDERAL COURTS

It is appropriate to begin with the federal court system because its basic structure is relatively simple. The organization chart in Figure 2.1 shows a bewildering array of courts, but the bulk of the system's work is done by the three sets of courts in the center of the figure. The district courts serve as the primary trial courts of the system, and the courts of appeals as the primary first-level appellate courts. The Supreme Court is the only second-level appellate court.

Paralleling the district courts and courts of appeals are several other courts that are specialized by subject matter. These courts, taken together, also constitute a significant part of the system.

Federal District Courts

For the great majority of cases, the district courts are the point of entry into the federal judicial system. Most cases go no further. Thus these courts are the primary center of activity in the federal system.

Geographic Division: Districts   There are ninety-four federal district courts, one in each judicial district. These districts cover the fifty states, the District of Columbia, and some of the U.S. territories. Every state has at least one district of its own, and twenty-six of the states consist of a single district. The rest of the states are divided into two or more districts, with three states (New York, Texas, and California) having four districts each.

Many districts are divided into divisions, in each of which the court holds proceedings. Even as routine a matter as the divisional structure of a district is sometimes controversial, as indicated by the proposal to create two divisions within the Maryland district. Prior to the creation of divisions, judges in the district sat only in Baltimore. While lawyers in the Maryland suburbs of Washington, D.C., wanted a federal court in their area, Baltimore lawyers sought to keep all the judges in their city, and the district judges themselves preferred to stay where they were. Because of that opposition, Congress approved the division only after two decades of debate.[12]

Personnel   In federal district courts, as in other trial courts, cases are generally tried before a single judge, with or without a jury. Each district is

1991 Cases		
Type of Case	Number	Percentage
By source of jurisdiction:		
Federal party cases	52,654	20.8
Federal question cases	149,231	58.9
Diversity cases	50,944	20.1
Other	648	0.8
By subject matter:		
Criminal prosecutions	45,735	18.0
Prisoner petitions	42,262	16.7
Civil rights	19,340	7.6
Labor laws	14,686	5.8
Social Security laws	7,692	3.0
Torts	37,309	14.7
Contracts	42,418	16.7
Other	44,035	17.4

Total Cases Filed		
Year	Number	% Change
1991	253,477	−14%
1986	296,318	+40%
1981	211,863	+23%
1976	171,617	+26%
1971	136,553	—

Notes: The actual periods covered are fiscal years. Cases handled by bankruptcy judges and petty criminal offenses handled by magistrates have been excluded. Criminal cases are included in the federal question category. Figures given under "% Change" indicate change in the total number of cases over the preceding five years.
Sources: Annual Report of the Administrative Office of the United States Courts, 1991 (Washington, D.C.: Government Printing Office, 1992), pp. 190–191, 230); *Annual Reports* for earlier years.

EXHIBIT 2.2 Composition of Cases Filed in Federal District Courts in 1991 and Total Cases Filed in Selected Years

there were positions for 345 full-time and 130 part-time magistrate judges in the various federal districts. Federal law allows a considerable range of possible duties for magistrate judges. They may conduct many types of pretrial proceedings, rule on matters such as petitions challenging prison conditions, and (with the consent of the parties) try and decide civil cases and criminal misdemeanor cases. Depending on the type of case and other circumstances, a magistrate judge's decision can be appealed either to a district judge or to the court of appeals. With a few exceptions, the judges in a particular district determine which of these duties are actually given to a magistrate.

The activities of magistrate judges and the importance of their role in decision-making vary considerably from district to district. In general, however, they have come to perform a significant part of the district courts' judicial work. Along with their extensive involvement in preliminary proceedings, they take final action in large numbers of cases. In 1991, for instance, magistrates disposed of ninety-five thousand misdemeanor cases through trial, dismissal, or the acceptance of a guilty plea.[15]

The status and role of magistrate judges have been enhanced over time with relatively little controversy. In contrast, the position of bankruptcy judges has been the subject of great disagreement.[16] This controversy concerns their appropriate status. As bankruptcy business grew, district judges increasingly delegated the actual processing of bankruptcy cases to referees (designated as judges in 1973). District judges were happy to do so, because these cases were time-consuming and seemed unrewarding. As their responsibilities increased, bankruptcy judges sought higher status, including greater job security and recognition as judges. But district judges did not want their own status diminished by the designation of large numbers of bankruptcy judges as their equals or near-equals.

The result has been a series of conflicts between bankruptcy judges and district judges. In response to these conflicts, in 1978 and 1984 Congress adopted legislation that enhanced the status of bankruptcy judges while maintaining a clear distinction between them and district judges. In the current system, bankruptcy judges are adjuncts of the district courts, but they are appointed (for fourteen-year terms) by the courts of appeals rather than by district judges. Their decisions can be appealed to the district court or to a panel of bankruptcy judges, as determined by the district court and court of appeals.

The number of bankruptcy cases has risen tremendously over the past decade, from 370,000 in 1982 to 970,000 in 1992.[17] As a result, the number of bankruptcy judges has been increased (there were 326 judgeships in 1992), and so has their impact. More and more, for instance, they help determine the fates of major corporations that go into bankruptcy proceedings. A bankruptcy judge in Washington, D.C., attracted attention in 1987 when he ruled that the Justice Department had forced a company out of business by taking its computer software illegally, a ruling later upheld by a district judge. A year later the judge was denied reappointment for a new term, and some people concluded that the Justice Department had exerted pressure to remove him from the bench. Whether or not this was the case, it suggests the significance of life tenure—or its absence.[18]

The increasing importance of both magistrate judges and bankruptcy judges is one aspect of what some observers call the bureaucratization of the federal courts—a diffusion of effective decision-making power from judges on the major federal courts to other people. Of course, a similar process has also occurred in the other branches of government, as illustrated by the growing role played by congressional staff personnel. Nevertheless, bureaucratization in the judiciary remains particularly troublesome to many people, largely because of the traditional view that judges should make their own decisions. Indeed, one federal judge has referred to bureaucracy as "the carcinoma of the federal judiciary."[19]

Three-Judge District Courts   The three-judge district court illustrates the use of judicial structure to serve policy goals.[20] This type of court, which is ordinarily composed of two district judges and one court of appeals judge, is set up to hear a single case. Its decision may then be appealed directly to the Supreme Court.

Under a series of statutes beginning in 1903, Congress required that certain kinds of cases be heard by three-judge courts. The primary purpose of these courts was to take decisions of great importance out of the hands of single district judges. For example, when state officials expressed unhappiness at the power of single district judges to hold state laws unenforceable on constitutional grounds, Congress acted in 1910 to require three-judge courts in such cases. As these statutes accumulated, three-judge courts became increasingly common. In 1973 they heard 320 cases.

But with such frequent use, three-judge courts also became a burden on the federal court system. Not only did each case require that three judges from two levels of courts find the time to meet, but the provision for a direct appeal of their decision to the Supreme Court also added to that court's workload. These burdens seemed to outweigh the original purposes of three-judge courts, and in 1976 Congress eliminated most of the grounds for convening them. They are now largely restricted to suits that challenge the drawing of legislative districts and to certain civil rights cases. In 1991 only fourteen cases were heard by three-judge district courts.[21]

Federal Courts of Appeals

If the district courts are the primary location of activity in the federal court system, the courts of appeals rank second. Most appeals from federal trial courts go to the courts of appeals. Because the Supreme Court accepts so few cases, these courts also represent the end of the line for nearly all litigation that continues beyond the trial level. For these reasons, the courts of appeals are policy makers of considerable importance.

Geographic Division: Circuits   The basic geographic unit at this level is the circuit, which has a court that hears appeals within its area. The twelve circuits are shown in Figure 2.2. The District of Columbia is a circuit in itself, and the states and territories are divided into eleven numbered circuits, each of which contains three or more states. The number of court of appeals judges in the circuits ranges from 6 in the First Circuit (New England and Puerto Rico) to 28 in the Ninth Circuit (the Pacific), with a total of 167 in the twelve circuits.

The controversy over possible division of the Ninth Circuit has been discussed at the beginning of the chapter. A similar controversy raged over division of the Fifth Circuit in the Deep South during the 1960s and 1970s.[22] The court of appeals had a majority that was sympathetic to claims of racial discrimination, and anti–civil rights senators favored a split because the new southeastern circuit was likely to be dominated by judges who were more conservative on civil rights issues. Pro–civil rights judges in the Fifth Circuit and their allies fought successfully against the division proposal for more than a decade; the court finally was divided in 1980, after concerns about civil rights had lessened.

Ordinarily, court of appeals cases are decided by panels of three judges, which are not permanent but rather are rotated for each set of cases. Along with active judges from the circuit, these panels often include visiting judges (primarily district judges from the same circuit) and retired judges.

By majority vote, a court of appeals can hear or rehear a case en banc, a term that in most circuits means participation by the court's full membership of judges. However, this procedure is not often used; it is employed primarily in cases of special importance and cases involving issues that have divided the court.

Geographic arrangements vary by circuit, with some courts sitting in a single city and others dividing their time among several cities. In most circuits, the judges themselves reside in different cities, which complicates the task of scheduling hearings and conferences. In 1992, for example, the judges on the Ninth Circuit Court of Appeals resided in nine cities, including Phoenix, San Francisco, Boise, and Fairbanks.

Like the district courts, the courts of appeals employ a great many people other than judges. Each judge has three law clerks. Each court of appeals also has a central legal staff whose members have become subordinate judges in fact if not in name. The staff screens appeals and helps decide those that it designates as routine, thereby saving the time of the judges. This important development is examined more closely in Chapter 8.

Jurisdiction and Business   The courts of appeals have jurisdiction primarily over the decisions of district courts. A dissatisfied litigant may appeal to the court of appeals after nearly any final district court decision and after some preliminary decisions during the course of a case. Appeals from the decisions of three-judge district courts go directly to the Supreme Court, and appeals in patent cases go to a specialized court, the Court of Appeals for the Federal Circuit (discussed later in this section). The general rule is that

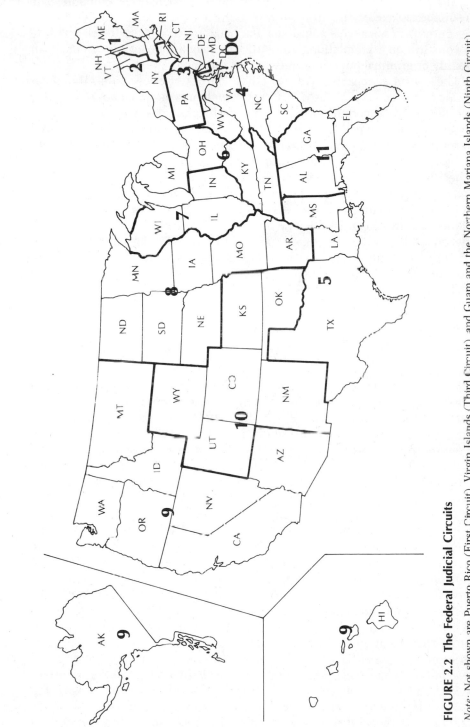

FIGURE 2.2 The Federal Judicial Circuits

Note: Not shown are Puerto Rico (First Circuit), Virgin Islands (Third Circuit), and Guam and the Northern Mariana Islands (Ninth Circuit).

litigants have the right to appeal district court decisions to some court. The only important exception is the proviso that the federal government as criminal prosecutor may not appeal acquittals. Such an appeal is regarded as violating the constitutional prohibition against double jeopardy (putting a person in jeopardy of criminal punishment twice for the same offense).

The courts of appeals have two other sources of cases. First, they hear appeals from decisions of the Tax Court, which acts as a trial court for some tax cases. More important, orders of certain federal administrative agencies may be appealed directly to the courts of appeals without going first to the district courts. In 1991 such administrative appeals made up about 7 percent of all the cases brought to the courts of appeals, and 37 percent of the cases in the District of Columbia circuit.[23]

The caseloads of the courts of appeals have grown even faster than those of the district courts. Like the district courts, the courts of appeals have obtained congressional help in the form of additional personnel. Legislation between 1978 and 1990 increased the total number of judges from 97 to 167. And, as noted earlier, the courts of appeals have also responded by giving their central legal staffs substantial responsibilities for decisions in some cases.

The Supreme Court

The Supreme Court is a single national court that decides cases with its full membership. The Court's size is determined by Congress, and the number of justices was changed several times in the nineteenth century; some of these changes were motivated by the desire to affect the Court's policies. But there have been nine justices since 1869, and that number is unlikely to change. In contrast, the Court's staff has grown considerably and now includes more than three hundred people. The most important of these staff members are the justices' law clerks. Most justices now have four clerks, who perform such tasks as drafting opinions and screening requests to hear cases.

The Supreme Court's jurisdiction is almost entirely appellate. As Figure 2.1 indicates, cases come to the Court from several sets of lower courts. The two primary sources of cases are the federal courts of appeals and the state supreme courts, but a case can be brought from a state system to the Supreme Court only if it contains an issue of federal law. A case that is initiated in a state court on the basis of state law sometimes develops a federal-law issue, such as interpretation of a criminal defendant's constitutional rights. When this happens, such cases are eligible for Supreme Court consideration, although they must go through the full set of appeals in state courts before the Supreme Court has jurisdiction to hear them.

With one minor exception—cases decided by three-judge district courts—the Supreme Court's appellate jurisdiction is discretionary. This means that the Court has the freedom to choose which cases it will hear. Because of this freedom, cases generally come to the Court not as appeals but as petitions for writs of certiorari. If the Court grants such a writ, this means that it calls up the case from the lower court for its consideration. But if the Court denies the writ, as it does in the overwhelming majority of cases, the lower court decision is left standing.

The Constitution also gives the Supreme Court original (trial) jurisdiction over some cases involving states as parties and cases involving foreign diplomatic personnel; these cases are relatively rare. When the Court does hear such a case, it delegates the task of gathering evidence and reaching a proposed decision to a special master, often a retired judge, who has been selected for that purpose.

Because of the Supreme Court's screening power and the fact that its cases come from many sources, its agenda looks somewhat different from those of the lower federal courts. A large share of its decisions involve issues arising under the Constitution, and in the past quarter century it has concentrated heavily on civil liberties.

Like other federal courts, the Supreme Court has faced a growing caseload. The number of cases brought to the Court did not reach two thousand until 1961; by 1990 filings had exceeded the five thousand mark. Even though the Court can limit the number of cases that it hears, the mere increase in the amount of certiorari petitions has added considerably to its burdens. Several justices have expressed concern about the Court's workload.

After several years of urging by the justices, Congress acted in 1988 to eliminate nearly all of the Court's mandatory jurisdiction. As a result, the Court gained almost complete freedom to reject cases that the justices do not wish to decide. The Court itself has acted to reduce its workload by accepting fewer cases for full decisions. In recent years, even as the number of petitions for hearing kept growing, the Court reduced considerably the number of cases that it accepted.[24]

A more sweeping set of proposals in the 1970s and 1980s involved the creation of a new court, located in the organizational structure between the courts of appeals and the Supreme Court. In one version, this court would screen petitions for certiorari on behalf of the Supreme Court. In another, it would actually decide some cases in place of the Court—cases involving issues that seem to require resolution but are not sufficiently important to demand Supreme Court consideration. Despite support by several justices and respected legal scholars, bills to create a new court did not go far in Congress. Most policy makers are hesitant about adopting such a fundamental change in the judicial system, especially when its full impact is difficult to predict. And some scholars thought that the new court would violate the constitutional requirement of "one supreme Court."[25]

Specialized Courts

The three sets of courts discussed so far may be called generalists, in that they deal with a broad range of cases. The federal system also includes specialized courts, which have narrower jurisdiction. The characteristics and responsibilities of these courts are summarized in Exhibit 2.3. As the table shows, there are two distinctions among them. First, some courts have their

Court	Type of Judge	Level	Status Under the Constitution	Areas of Activity
Tax Court	Permanent	Trial	Article I	Federal taxes
Claims Court	Permanent	Trial	Article I	Claims against the federal government
Court of Veterans Appeals	Permanent	Trial	Article I	Veterans' benefits
Court of International Trade	Permanent	Trial	Article III	International trade issues
Court of Appeals for the Federal Circuit	Permanent	Appellate	Article III	Patents, trademarks, international trade, claims against the federal government
Rail Reorganization Court	Borrowed	Trial	—	Railroad reorganization
Foreign Intelligence Surveillance Court	Borrowed	Trial	—	Foreign intelligence surveillance warrants
Foreign Intelligence Surveillance Court of Review	Borrowed	Appellate	—	Foreign intelligence surveillance warrants

Note: Military courts are not included.

EXHIBIT 2.3 Selected Characteristics of Specialized Federal Courts

own permanent judges, and others borrow judges from the generalist courts. In the latter instance, judges are assigned to the specialized court for a limited period and serve on that court in addition to their regular duties on a district court or a court of appeals. The second distinction among the specialized courts is that some of those that have their own judges are, like the generalist courts, established under Article III of the Constitution; consequently, their judges have lifetime appointments and their salaries may not be reduced. Others with their own judges are called legislative courts because they are established under Article I, which deals with Congress; their judges lack these protections.

The specialized courts are hybrid institutions. In most respects they resemble other courts. But their focus on a relatively narrow set of issues also gives them characteristics that are more typical of administrative agencies. Such agencies frequently develop a strong point of view on the policy issues that they address. One reason is that agency officials with specialized responsibilities often develop narrow and parochial perspectives. Another reason is the special opportunity for influence that an interest group gains when an agency deals continuously with that group's area of concern. Specialization can have similar effects on courts. Indeed, according to one scholar, courts that are not generalists thereby "lose the one quality that clearly distinguishes them from administrative lawmakers."[26]

Partly for this reason, many members of Congress are suspicious of specialized courts, and Congress has rejected a good many proposals to create them. But some proposals have been accepted, largely because they seemed to offer important advantages: the expertise of judges who specialize in a technical field such as tax law, the opportunity for a single court in a field to avoid the legal conflicts that develop among district courts or courts of appeals, and reducing the caseloads of generalist courts. And officials in the federal government or groups in the private sector sometimes have anticipated that a specialized court would rule more favorably toward them than would the district courts or courts of appeals. The cumulative result has been to make specialized courts a major part of the federal judicial system, handling issues as important as patent rights and international trade.[27]

One of these courts, the Court of Appeals for the Federal Circuit, illustrates both how such courts are created and what their potential effects can be. Congress established this court in 1982 by combining two existing courts, the Court of Claims and the Court of Customs and Patent Appeals (CCPA). The most important feature of the combined court is that it has jurisdiction over appeals from district courts in patent cases, which were formerly heard by the courts of appeals. This transfer was attractive to many people in Congress because it would eliminate conflicts among courts of appeals over the standards for determining whether a patent was legally valid. Congress approved the transfer largely for this reason.

But some people had favored creating the new court because they wanted changes in patent law. Many courts of appeals had established high standards for patent validity, which meant that a large proportion of patents coming to court were found to be invalid. In contrast, in deciding a special set of patent cases, the CCPA had supported more lenient standards. Those who preferred lenient standards expected a new court with five CCPA judges among its twelve members to adopt such standards. Indeed, this has occurred.[28] Thus the transfer of jurisdiction from generalist courts to a specialized court has produced a fundamental change in judicial policy.

Federal Court Administration

The federal court system has a tradition of independence for individual courts and even individual judges. But the federal system also has a substantial and growing set of administrative structures.

Administration of Individual Courts   Individual federal courts have chief judges (called the chief justice in the Supreme Court). When a chief justice leaves the Supreme Court, the president makes an appointment to fill the vacancy, either elevating a sitting justice to that position (as was the case with William Rehnquist) or selecting a chief justice from outside the Court (as with Warren Burger). In lower courts, with some exceptions, the chief judge is simply the judge who has served on the court the longest.[29]

A chief judge has general administrative responsibility for a court. This responsibility covers such matters as assigning judges and panels to cases, supervising nonjudicial personnel, and budgeting. Chief judges of the courts of appeals also have some administrative duties related to the district courts in their circuits, and the chief justice has such duties for the federal court system as a whole.

Chief judges generally seem to get along well with their colleagues. Occasionally, however, the administrative leadership of chief judges creates conflicts. One example is the long-running dispute in the Northern Ohio district court between Chief Judge Frank Battisti and most of his colleagues.[30] In 1985, after dissatisfaction with Battisti's leadership had developed, nine of the other ten judges on the court voted to take away some of the chief judge's powers; Battisti then contested their right to do so. The Sixth Circuit judicial council intervened several times, finally ruling that administrative decisions should be made by the judges as a group. The battle between Battisti and his colleagues continued; while the judicial council was working on another effort to resolve the battle, Battisti resigned as chief judge in 1989.

As in the state courts, growth in the number of judges and in caseloads has demanded that greater attention be paid to administration. One consequence has been a substantial increase in personnel other than judges, from about one thousand in 1925 to twenty-five thousand in 1991.[32] Courts also have instituted mechanisms to process cases more efficiently and with less time required of judges. In 1990 Congress adopted the Civil Justice Reform Act, which required district courts to initiate plans to reduce expense and delay in civil cases. This legislation underlined the degree of concern about problems resulting from growing caseloads; it also underscored the ultimate power of Congress to impose administrative structures and procedures on the federal courts.

Administration of the System as a Whole   The administrative structure of the federal court system is largely a product of a statute called the Administrative Office Act of 1939.[32] This act created both the Administrative Office of the United States Courts and the Judicial Councils that serve each federal circuit (usually called circuit councils); it also expanded the responsibilities of a body called the Judicial Conference. The Administrative Office is responsible for the administration of the federal court system as a whole.

The Judicial Conference is made up of the chief judges of the courts of appeals and one district judge from each circuit. The chief justice of the Supreme Court presides. The conference develops rules of practice and procedure for federal courts, subject to Supreme Court approval. It also takes positions on legislative proposals, and judges and judicial administrators lobby Congress on behalf of conference positions. In addition, the Judicial Conference puts together the proposed budget for the federal courts. The prestige of the Judicial Conference is suggested by an incident in 1989: when Chief Justice William Rehnquist proposed legislation to limit death penalty appeals despite opposition from most conference members, their stance seriously weakened his position.

The circuit councils, established in 1939, were restructured and strengthened by congressional legislation in 1980.[33] Each of these councils is composed of judges from the court of appeals and district courts in the circuit; the chief judge of the court of appeals presides. By statute, each council has sweeping authority to "make all necessary and appropriate orders for the effective and expeditious administration of justice within its circuit," with the added proviso that "all judicial officers and employees of the circuit shall promptly carry into effect all orders of the judicial council."[34] (Court personnel have the same obligation to the Judicial Conference.)

The councils also have several more specific powers. Their most important and most controversial power, a product of the 1980 law, involves the disciplining of judges within the circuit. According to the statute, a council may investigate a complaint of misconduct against a judge, and if that complaint is found to be justified, it can take any appropriate action short of removing a judge from office. Such action can include a temporary order that no further cases be assigned to a particular judge or a recommendation that Congress consider impeachment. In 1986 the council for the Eleventh Circuit recommended impeachment of district judge Alcee Hastings after he was acquitted of conspiracy to receive bribes, and Congress removed Hastings through impeachment proceedings in 1989. In 1992 the council for the Fifth Circuit reprimanded district judge James Nowlin for consulting with a Texas state legislator, a fellow Republican and former legislative colleague, in drawing up Texas legislative districts; the council, however, found him innocent of "a corrupt or evil motive."[35]

To what extent do these administrative structures create centralized control of federal judges? The picture is mixed and ambiguous. Certainly, the autonomy of individual judges has been reduced in a variety of ways. It is clear, for instance, that the centrally established rules of procedure have produced what one expert calls "nationalizing tendencies" in the district courts.[36] And the disciplinary powers of circuit councils are a potentially enormous source of control. Thus it is understandable that some judges complain of constraints from administrative bodies.

On the other hand, some important factors work in favor of continued autonomy for judges. The Administrative Office and the Judicial Conference possess only limited powers, and judges on administrative bodies are reluctant to engage in coercion over their colleagues. Even with the enhanced powers of circuit councils, one district judge said that "the council just doesn't seem to influence my life."[37] As this observation suggests, federal judges retain primary control over their work.

THE STATE COURT SYSTEMS

The state court systems are quite diverse. With the independent power that results from federalism, each state has created its own structure through constitutional provisions and statutes. Inevitably, the results have varied greatly. Indeed, hardly any generalization about these systems applies to all the states.

Fragmentation and Unification

As they often do in policy making, however, the states have borrowed freely from each other in court organization; they have also been subject to common influences. Consequently, there are many similarities among the state court systems. Until fairly recent times, one important similarity was a quality that can be called fragmentation.

The traditional fragmentation of state court systems has both structural and administrative aspects. Structurally, the most important feature has been a multiplicity of trial courts. New courts were set up by both state and local governments on an ad hoc basis to serve specific needs. As a result, most states eventually found themselves with many sets of trial courts. Many of these courts had very narrow jurisdiction, and the jurisdiction of different courts often overlapped in confusing ways.

The administration of the state court systems was also fragmented, with each court quite independent of the others. Management and financing of these courts were divided between state and local governments, and local governments were primarily responsible for trial courts.

Since early in this century, efforts have been made to reduce the fragmentation of state court systems and in this way to reform and modernize them. This movement for court unification, to use its most common label, was sparked by legal scholar Roscoe Pound in a 1906 speech to the American Bar Association (ABA).[38] Pound gradually won support from the ABA, from state and local bar groups, and from individual lawyers. In 1913 lawyers established the American Judicature Society, which has been an important arm of the unification movement since that time. "Good government" groups, such as the League of Women Voters, have also joined in the effort.

The court unification movement has put forward a variety of policy proposals, but two general prescriptions stand out. The first is consolidation of trial courts into one or two sets of courts. The second is centralization of court administration so that all courts are financed by state governments and administered by professionals under the supervision of the state supreme court.[39]

Several premises underlie these prescriptions. One is a perception that the traditional fragmented system is highly inefficient and thus serves the public badly. Another is a belief that control by the other branches of government, particularly local governments, weakens the judiciary. These premises are not universally accepted. While fragmentation sounds like an undesirable quality, it has been argued that a fragmented system is more responsive to the needs of local areas and may even be more efficient than a unified system.

In practice, participants in the debates over consolidation have taken sides largely on the basis of their own situations and self-interest. Supreme court justices, for instance, have reason to favor consolidation because it strengthens their own court's power over the judicial system. In contrast, judges on courts that might be consolidated or even eliminated through unification have a strong incentive to support the traditional system. In addition, officials and residents of rural areas tend to oppose unification because they prefer to maintain local courts with which they are comfortable and over which they have some control.

Across the states, intermittent battles over court unification have raged for several decades. In this conflict, the opponents of consolidation hold the advantage of defending the status quo, and the backing of rural judges and officials provides them with considerable strength. But the unification movement has two offsetting advantages: the association of its prescriptions with widely accepted values, such as efficiency, and the prestige of many lawyers and judges who have been among the movement's leaders. The outcome of these battles has varied from state to state. However, proponents of court unification have secured enough victories to change the state court systems a good deal. In examining the structure and administration of state courts, we will see evidence of victories for both sides.

State Court Structure: An Overview

The wide variety of state courts fit into four general categories, two at the trial level and two at the appellate level.[40] The trial courts may be divided into *major* and *minor* courts, and the appellate courts may be divided into supreme courts and intermediate appellate courts.

Major Trial Courts   A few states, such as Idaho and Massachusetts, have fully consolidated their trial courts; thus they have a single set of trial courts with jurisdiction to hear cases of all types. But most states retain multiple sets of trial courts, ranging in number from two to ten. Where multiple courts exist, they are usually divided into two categories. Sometimes these categories are labeled *general jurisdiction* and *limited jurisdiction*, but those terms are misleading since most courts in both groups are limited in the kinds of cases they can hear. The terms *major* and *minor* courts are preferable, if imperfect, because the chief distinction between the two types of courts is in the seriousness of the cases brought before them.

Most states have a single set of major trial courts, commonly known as district courts, superior courts, or circuit courts. Typically, such a court conducts trials involving criminal offenses for which the most severe penalties are possible (felonies rather than misdemeanors) and in civil cases involving relatively large sums of money. In many states, some special categories of cases are also heard in major trial courts: juvenile criminal offenses; domestic relations cases (primarily divorces); and probate cases (primarily the handling of wills).

In most states, major trial courts also have appellate functions, hearing appeals in at least some types of cases originally tried in minor trial courts. In many states, these appeals are de novo, meaning that the case is actually retried in the major court. As a result, a party who is unhappy with what may be a relatively informal trial in the minor court can obtain a trial with a fuller set of procedural rights, such as a trial by jury, in the major court.

Despite the campaign for consolidation, a few states retain multiple sets of major trial courts, with the jurisdiction of each based on geography and subject matter. Even when there is a single court, it is often split into divisions according to the subject matter of the cases, with judges serving permanently or temporarily in a specialized division. This system is especially common in courts serving populous areas, which have enough judicial business and enough judges to allow such specialization.

Like federal district courts, major state trial courts are geographically dispersed. In some states, each county has its own court, while in other states the counties are grouped into circuits. In that system, each circuit has a set of judges who serve the whole area, traveling from county to county to hear cases.

Major trial courts have a great deal of business: in 1990 about 27 million cases were filed in these courts across the country.[41] This number is enormously large in comparison with the number of cases filed in federal district courts.

The cases that come to major trial courts, shown in Exhibit 2.4 for 1990, range widely. Nearly half involve traffic violations. Among the other cases, most are civil rather than criminal. Within the civil category, domestic relations cases stand out in frequency. The numerical importance of juvenile cases, most of them criminal in content, is also noteworthy.

Minor Trial Courts   Below their major trial courts, most states still have minor courts, which handle less serious civil and criminal cases. These courts may also have jurisdiction over special categories of cases, such as juvenile criminal offenses. In several states, such as Michigan and Rhode Island, the minor courts handle the preliminary stages of felony cases as well. As a result, cases routinely move from one court to another before trial.

Subject	Major Courts		Minor Courts	
Civil	34%		12%	
Family		11%		
Contract	·	5%		
Tort		3%		
Other		15%		
Criminal	14%		13%	
Felony		4%		
Misdemeanor		8%		11%
Drunk driving				1%
Other		2%		1%
Traffic	48%		74%	
Juvenile	4%		1%	

Note: Percentages for subcategories of cases are based on data from fewer than fifty states. In criminal subcategories, "Other" includes drunk driving cases for major courts and felony cases for minor courts, along with some miscellaneous cases.
Source: Court Statistics Project, *State Court Caseload Statistics: Annual Report 1990* (Williamsburg, Va.: National Center for State Courts, 1992), pp. 10, 18, 33.

EXHIBIT 2.4 Subject Matter of Cases Heard by Major and Minor State Courts in 1990

State systems became most fragmented at this level. The fragmentation of minor trial courts has been reduced a good deal over time, but only a few states, such as Kansas and Virginia, have a single set of minor courts. Other states retain multiple courts—sometimes a great many.

There are two common lines of division among sets of minor courts. The first is geographic, with urban areas often served by municipal courts and rural areas by county courts or justices of the peace. The second line of division is functional, as separate courts are frequently established to carry out specific duties. Jurisdictional lines are often confusing. Seemingly parallel courts, such as municipal and county courts, may have somewhat different jurisdiction, and in some states the jurisdiction of different courts overlaps.

In most states, minor trial courts are highly decentralized. It is common for every city of moderate population to have its own municipal court. And in states that have retained justices of the peace, there are sometimes several hundred separate justice courts. As a result, in 1987 there were more than thirteen thousand separate minor trial courts—along with more than two thousand major trial courts.[42]

The division of jurisdiction between major and minor trial courts varies among the states, but minor courts generally have more business. In 1990 minor trial courts received 73 million cases, more than twice the number in major courts, even though several states lack minor courts.[43] As Exhibit 2.4 shows, however, the work of minor courts is dominated by cases with relatively small stakes, particularly traffic offenses. The volume and composition of the business in minor trial courts make their operation distinctive. Because most cases involve small stakes and few are really contested, cases are typically handled in routine fashion. Often cases are processed and disposed of by administrative personnel rather than by judges. Even when judges handle cases, they may do so quite rapidly and informally.

Intermediate Appellate Courts   At the beginning of this century, state systems generally included only a single appellate court, the supreme court. But growth in the volume of appeals gradually caused state policy makers to create one or more intermediate appellate courts below the supreme court level. Today about three-quarters of the states have intermediate courts as first-level appellate courts, most of them known as courts of appeals or something similar.

The structures of intermediate appellate courts vary in several respects. While some states have only a single court, others follow the federal model and provide separate courts for different regions. In a few states, one court hears criminal appeals and another hears civil appeals. In most states, intermediate courts sit in panels, either with judges permanently assigned to a particular panel or with rotating panel membership.

The jurisdiction of intermediate courts also varies. All share the function of hearing appeals from the decisions of major trial courts, although certain kinds of cases may go directly to the state supreme court. In some states, some or all appeals from minor trial courts go to the intermediate appellate court rather than to the major trial courts. And in many states, appeals from at least some administrative agencies are heard by intermediate courts. In general, the jurisdiction of intermediate appellate courts is mandatory because of the doctrine that the parties to a case are entitled to one appeal. But the Virginia Court of Appeals has discretionary jurisdiction over criminal cases, and many other courts have discretion over narrower categories of cases.

Despite the mandatory jurisdiction of most intermediate courts, only a small fraction of the cases handled by trial courts reach them. In 1990, for instance, state trial courts in Indiana received about 1.3 million cases, while the state's intermediate court received about 2,000.[44] Of course, the cases that do come to appellate courts generally have much larger stakes than average. Courts that can hear both civil and criminal cases receive substantial numbers of both, with the balance between civil and criminal business varying by state.

Supreme Courts   Whether or not it has created an intermediate court of appeals, every state has a court that serves as its supreme court. With a few exceptions, this court is actually called the supreme court or some variant of that name. In effect, Oklahoma and Texas each have two supreme courts;

their supreme courts hear only civil cases, while their courts of criminal appeals serve as the final courts for criminal cases.

Supreme courts have between five and nine justices. (The Oklahoma Court of Criminal Appeals has three justices.) Even the larger courts generally sit en banc rather than in divisions or panels. Some courts hear cases not only in the state capital but in other cities as well.

The Louisiana and California supreme courts sit primarily outside the capital, residing in New Orleans rather than Baton Rouge and San Francisco rather than Sacramento. According to a former chief justice, the Louisiana court originally located in New Orleans because "there wasn't a road you could count on" until well into this century, and after that the court stayed in New Orleans "mostly from habit."[45] The California court seems simply to have a preference for San Francisco; in 1992, after the court had upheld a voter-mandated reduction in the legislative budget, some legislators threatened to punish it by moving its headquarters to Sacramento.[46]

The state supreme court, like its federal counterpart, is the final appellate court within its system. The functions of this court depend in large part on the presence or absence of an intermediate state appellate court. Where that court exists, the supreme court is a second-level appellate court; as such, it receives most cases from the intermediate court and has discretionary jurisdiction over most of those cases. Typically, some classes of cases come from the intermediate court on a mandatory basis. Others bypass the intermediate court altogether, going directly from trial courts to the supreme court.

Because of their discretionary jurisdiction, these courts have considerable control over their agendas. Indeed, in some states the supreme court is highly selective in choosing cases to hear. In 1990, for instance, several supreme courts granted hearings in less than 10 percent of the discretionary cases they considered, and the Michigan supreme court in only 3 percent.[47] Even so, because the range of state cases is so broad, a supreme court is likely to deal with a diverse set of legal issues in any given year.

In states without an intermediate appellate court, the functions and business of the supreme court resemble those of an intermediate court. Most cases come to such a supreme court from trial courts on a mandatory rather than a discretionary basis. But the supreme court of West Virginia has primarily discretionary jurisdiction, and in 1979 the New Hampshire supreme court adopted a rule under which it could refuse to hear cases. Thus these two states deviate the furthest from the general principle that litigants are entitled to one appeal.

Two Examples of State Court Structure

Two examples provide a clearer sense of state court structure. The states chosen, Illinois and New York, are both populous ones, with a great deal of judicial business. But they also represent two extremes, for their organizational structures are fundamentally different. Illinois has adopted one of the simplest systems; New York has one of the most complex.

Illinois   The simplicity of the Illinois court system, resulting from a full consolidation of trial courts in 1962, is obvious from the diagram in Figure 2.3.[48] The highest court is the supreme court, which sits in Springfield, the state capital, and in Chicago. Cases come to the supreme court primarily from the intermediate appellate court, and its jurisdiction is mainly discretionary. The supreme court also hears appeals directly from trial courts in some types of cases, such as those with death sentences.

The intermediate appellate court, known in Illinois as the Appellate Court, hears all other appeals from trial courts. It also hears appeals from several administrative bodies, such as the Pollution Control Board and three boards dealing with labor relations. This court is split into five divisions on a geographic basis.

The most noteworthy aspect of the Illinois system is the single set of trial courts, the circuit courts, which handle the functions of both major and minor trial courts. The trial court structure is not quite as simple as it seems, however, because the circuit courts may be subdivided. In Cook County (Chicago), which has nearly four hundred judges, the subdivision is quite detailed: the circuit court includes a county department with seven specialized divisions for functions such as probate and domestic relations, as well as a municipal department with six districts. Within these subdivisions, judges are assigned to hear particular categories of cases in a given time period, and some courtrooms are devoted to very specific types of cases, such as gun offenses.

New York   As Figure 2.4 shows, the New York court system is exceedingly complex.[49] In 1961 it underwent a partial consolidation, but a large number of separate courts and multitudinous routes for appeals were left

FIGURE 2.3 Organization Chart of the Illinois Court System

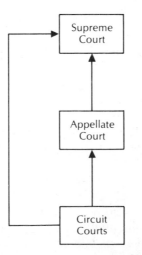

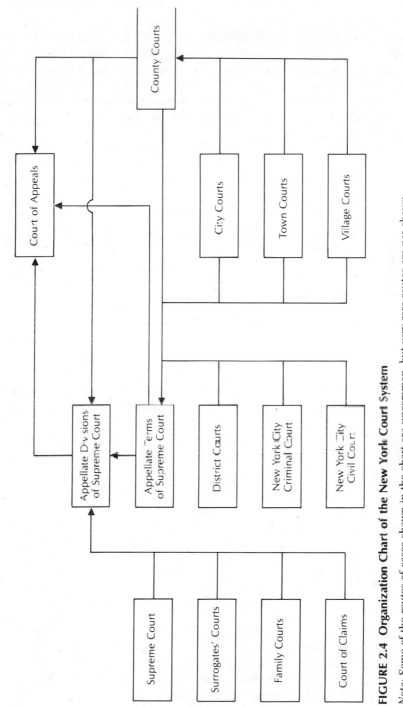

FIGURE 2.4 Organization Chart of the New York Court System

Note: Some of the routes of cases shown in the chart are uncommon, but very rare routes are not shown.

Source: State of New York, *Report of the Chief Administrator of the Courts for the Calendar Year January 1, 1989–December 31, 1989* (New York: New York Office of Court Administration, 1990), p. 11; League of Women Voters of New York State, *The Judicial Maze: The Court System in New York State* (New York: League of Women Voters, 1988), p. 7.

standing. Efforts at further consolidation have been made from time to time but so far have not succeeded.

While the organization of Illinois courts can be described rather easily, any attempt to trace the position and functions of each New York court produces great confusion. Only at the top of the system, where the state's court of appeals is equivalent to the supreme court in most other states, is there much clarity. This court of appeals primarily hears cases brought from the intermediate appellate courts, but it also hears appeals from trial courts in cases involving only the constitutionality of a statute. Its jurisdiction is partly mandatory and partly discretionary.

At the intermediate appellate level, the structure begins to become complicated. Here jurisdiction is divided among the county courts and the appellate divisions and appellate terms of the supreme court. The county courts and the supreme court are also trial courts. (It is symbolic of the confusing structure of New York courts that the state has a lower court called the Supreme Court, and a supreme court called the Court of Appeals.) Where an appeal goes depends on the trial court from which it came, its subject matter, and the section of the state in which it was tried.

The New York supreme court is one major trial court, divided into eleven districts. It has unlimited trial jurisdiction, but it generally hears cases outside the jurisdiction of other courts. The county court, which is the other major state trial court, exists in each county outside the city of New York.

Minor trial courts are the most numerous, with hundreds of city, town, and village courts scattered throughout the state. Two Long Island counties also have district courts, and the city of New York has its own civil court and criminal court. Special courts exist for matters related to children (Family Court), for probate (Surrogates' Court), and for claims against the state (Court of Claims).

The contrast between this complex structure of minor trial courts and the simpler system in Illinois, where such courts are absent altogether, underlines the extent of the differences among the court systems of the various states.

Administration of State Courts

Like court structures, the administration of state courts varies considerably from state to state. In general, however, the efforts of the court unification movement and the pressures created by growing caseloads have strengthened central administration of individual courts and court systems.

Individual Courts   The chief judges of state courts are selected in a variety of ways. Like their federal counterparts, they hold administrative authority over their courts. But in trial courts their control often is weakened by the independent power of court clerks and other personnel who are elected or appointed by officials other than judges. The potential for conflict is illustrated by a recent battle in Fairfax County, Virginia. Traditionally, judges on the circuit court (the major trial court) had relied on the court clerk's staff; when the court's chief judge obtained county funding for judges to hire their own staffs, the clerk attacked the move as unconstitutional and fought it in the state legislature. As often is the case in these situations, the underlying conflict was about effective control over operation of the court.[50]

Chief judges do possess real power over the operation of their courts and the work situations of their fellow judges. For instance, the presiding judge of the Los Angeles superior court (the major trial court) has taken such actions as eliminating night court and transferring judges to different courts against their wishes. One judge who complained about an action by the presiding judge was told by colleagues to "Cool it, or you're going to be sitting in Lancaster"—an outlying city with a small court.[51] Conflicts between chief judges and other judges are not rare.

State Court Systems   Historically, individual state courts were largely independent of each other. Typically, each made its own procedural rules and operated in its own way. One observer, comparing various Connecticut trial courts in 1957, concluded that any similarity in the handling of judicial business is largely coincidental.[52] In addition, the funding of court systems and the control connected with that funding were divided between state and local governments.

Supporters of court unification have sought to centralize administrative control and responsibility for court systems, primarily in the state supreme court. Some local governments, which fear losing control over their trial courts, have opposed this centralization. Lower-court judges have also tended to oppose it because they like the freedom to operate their courts as they see fit.

The unification movement has secured a great many formal changes in court administration, but it has suffered defeats as well. Where states have changed their formal administrative system, outcomes in practice have varied. The result is a mixed pattern of administration, with some states highly centralized and others retaining most of their traditional decentralization.

This variation is illustrated by the roles of court administrators. Nearly all states now have professional administrators under supreme court control, but their power over the management of lower courts differs considerably. One study found that the Connecticut Office of Chief Court Administrator exercised considerable control over trial courts, while the Administrative Office of the Courts in Georgia had such limited responsibilities that the state's trial courts remained effectively independent.[53]

Of particular importance is the right to make rules of practice and procedure for the courts. Many states have followed the prescription of the unification movement and lodged this power entirely in the supreme court. Formal powers aside, supreme courts differ a good deal in the extent to which they have used rules to direct the lower courts.

Perhaps the most common use of formal rules by supreme courts has been as a means to speed the processing of cases in trial courts. Rising caseloads, funding shortages, and inefficiencies often combine to create long backlogs of cases to resolve. Mechanisms such as recommended time standards for the processing of cases are now common, and state chief justices sometimes engage in informal campaigns to encourage administrative innovations and other means of attacking case backlogs.

As supreme courts gain power over lower courts, conflicts are inevitable. One example was a 1991 battle between the Pennsylvania Supreme Court and the Philadelphia Traffic Court, a minor trial court. Acting on behalf of his court, supreme court justice Nicholas Papadakos sought a reduction in the traffic court staff. George Twardy, presiding judge of the traffic court, refused to go along. "Twardy said 'Go to hell' in effect," Papadakos reported after one meeting. Papadakos finally set up a panel under a supreme court order to make the staff cuts directly—thus partially taking over traffic court administration.[54] The outcomes of such conflicts vary, depending on the distribution of both legal and political power between supreme courts and lower courts.

Changes in court funding have been relatively limited. Nearly every state provides some funds for trial courts, but in most states the preponderance of money still comes from local governments. Undoubtedly, one reason for the absence of more substantial change is the importance to local governments of maintaining fiscal control over local courts, including control over fines and fees paid to those courts. Perhaps even more important in a time of tight budgets is the reluctance of state governors and legislators to take on a new and substantial financial burden. In 1991 California passed legislation that would increase state funding of trial courts in return for procedural changes to improve court efficiency, but the state government's serious budget problems raised questions as to whether it could keep its part of the bargain.[55]

Court Unification and Its Impact

The success of the court unification movement has differed from state to state, but the movement has secured considerable change in the structure and administration of court systems. Proponents of unification, of course, believe that these changes improve the functioning of state courts. We know little about whether the improvements that are sought actually occur, in part because such qualities as efficiency are often very difficult to measure. Nor do we know much about other possible effects of changes in the state court systems. But a few points can be made concerning the impact of court unification.[56]

First, it is not certain that unification actually produces all the benefits that have been ascribed to it. Consolidating courts and centralizing authority do not necessarily improve the system's capacity to process and dispose of cases. Nor does unification appear to diminish the influence of other political institutions on the courts.

One reason for these results is that unified and fragmented systems may differ less in reality than they do on paper. A consolidated set of trial courts, such as the Illinois circuit courts, may include divisions that are largely independent and judges who specialize in specific types of cases. And even in a system with a strong central authority, individual courts and judges retain a great deal of autonomy.

Perhaps more fundamentally, advocates of unification underestimate the strength of factors other than court structure. One example is the capacity of courts to process cases efficiently. Consolidation can improve efficiency by eliminating a situation in which some judges have too much to do and others too little. However, efficiency is also affected by the work habits and styles of individual judges and by the ways in which attorneys handle cases. If these factors work against efficiency, consolidation may accomplish relatively little.

Nor can structural changes shield courts from the intrusion of political considerations. For example, a shift from local to state funding may reduce court involvement in local politics but increase its involvement in state politics. As one commentator said, "No matter what the funding source, budgeting is politics."[57] And it is not clear that courts are in a stronger political position at the state level.

More generally, court unification, like other reforms, can have unexpected and sometimes undesirable consequences. The efforts of supreme courts in states such as Ohio and Kansas have improved efficiency in case disposition but also may have reduced the care with which cases are handled. The consolidation of a city and a county court (both of them minor trial courts) in Georgia increased costs for city residents and made court policies less consistent with their preferences.[58] Such unforeseen results are inevitable when major system changes occur.

What then can we conclude about the desirability of court unification? Definitive judgments are impossible for the same reasons that evaluation of the courts in general is difficult. Part of the problem is that people disagree about the values that are associated with unification. Not everyone believes, for example, that the courts should be insulated from external politics. And though everyone presumably does agree that efficiency is desirable, the weight given to this goal in relation to others varies a good deal. Furthermore, we know so little about the actual consequences of unification that it would be folly to try to reach firm conclusions about its good and bad effects.

For these reasons, there has been something of an irony in the history of the court unification movement. Although the movement developed a strong collective view about what a court system should look like and has engaged in a strong and sustained effort to move state court systems closer to that ideal, the people laboring in the movement have little reason to be confident about the effects of the changes that they advocate. In this respect, the campaign for court unification is similar to other campaigns for reform in the courts, including some that will be discussed in later chapters.

CONCLUSIONS

The last two sections of this chapter have sketched the general patterns of organization in the federal and state court systems. In the process, they have illustrated two important themes: court organization is based on "political" as well as technical considerations, and organizational arrangements have a decided impact on the courts.

Although systematic evidence on the effect of court organization is limited, it should be clear that organizational features can make a difference. Specialized courts may resolve policy issues differently from generalist courts. And a supreme court's possession of rule-making power may allow it to alter the ways in which trial judges process cases. Indeed, policy makers usually change the organization of courts in order to change their operations or outputs. Yet such changes do not always have the intended effects. In fact, they sometimes have consequences that were neither intended nor desired.

Because court organization is thought to make a difference, it is the subject of political conflict. Battles over state court unification have raged for several decades, and issues such as the diversity jurisdiction of the federal courts and the creation of a new court to do some of the Supreme Court's work have roused considerable contention.

Of course, court organization is not static. As political realities and ideas about desirable arrangements change, so will those arrangements themselves. Both the federal and the state court systems look different today from the way they looked half a century ago, and continued change is inevitable. This is particularly true when courts face strong pressures from their workloads and there is widespread dissatisfaction with the functioning of American courts.

FOR FURTHER READING

Barrow, Deborah J., and Thomas G. Walker. A *Court Divided: The Fifth Circuit Court of Appeals and the Politics of Judicial Reform*. New Haven, Conn.: Yale University Press, 1988.

Dubois, Philip L., ed. *The Politics of Judicial Reform*. Lexington, Mass.: Lexington Books, 1982.

Fish, Peter Graham. *The Politics of Federal Judicial Administration*. Princeton: Princeton University Press, 1973.

Hellman, Arthur D., ed. *Restructuring Justice: The Innovations of the Ninth Circuit and the Future of the Federal Courts*. Ithaca, N.Y.: Cornell University Press, 1990.

Heydebrand, Wolf, and Carroll Seron. *Rationalizing Justice: The Political Economy of Federal District Courts*. Albany: State University of New York Press, 1990.

Smith, Christopher E., *United States Magistrates in the Federal Courts: Subordinate Judges*. New York: Praeger, 1990.

NOTES

1. This discussion is based primarily on *Ninth Circuit Court of Appeals Reorganization Act of 1989: Hearing Before a Subcommittee of the Senate Committee on*

the Judiciary, 101st Congress, 2d sess., on S. 948, March 6, 1990 (Washington, D.C.: U.S. Government Printing Office, 1990); and Thomas E. Baker, "A Background Paper on the Circuit Boundaries of the United States Courts of Appeals," in *Federal Courts Study Committee: Working Papers and Subcommittee Reports* (1990 Mimeographed), 16–27.

2. Harriet Chiang, "Environmentalists Fight Bill to Break Up 9th Circuit Court," *San Francisco Chronicle*, March 9, 1990, p. A14.

3. *Ninth Circuit Reorganization Act*, p. 284.

4. Tracy Thompson, "Stephens Assailed by Judge," *Washington Post*, May 25, 1991, p. B1.

5. John M. Doyle, "Court Reverses Convictions in Beech-Nut Juice Case," *Washington Post*, March 31, 1989, p. A5.

6. Lynn M. LoPucki and William C. Whitford, "Venue Choice and Forum Shopping in the Bankruptcy Reorganization of Large, Publicly Held Companies," *Wisconsin Law Review* (1991), 11–63; Brett D. Fromson, "Putting in Their Orders for a Court," *Washington Post*, April 22, 1992, pp. F1, F6.

7. David Margolick, "Switching Case to White Enclave May Have Decided Outcome," *New York Times*, May 1, 1992, p. A10.

8. Rita Henley Jensen, "Computer Age Eludes the Courts," *National Law Journal*, May 30, 1988, p. 1.

9. Doris Marie Provine, "Governing the Ungovernable: The Theory and Practice of Governance in the Ninth Circuit," in *Restructuring Justice: The Innovations of the Ninth Circuit and the Future of the Federal Courts*, ed. Arthur D. Hellman (Ithaca, N.Y.: Cornell University Press, 1990), p. 271.

10. "Law on the Lawn," *National Law Journal*, October 28, 1991, p. 39; Gail Diane Cox, "The Malls of Justice," *National Law Journal*, April 20, 1992, p. 59.

11. Joseph F. Zimmerman, "New York Updates," *Comparative State Politics*, 12 (December 1991), 32–34; Kevin Sack, "Cuomo and Chief Judge Settle Court Budget Fight," *New York Times*, January 17, 1992, p. B4.

12. Eric Pianin, "Md. Bar Governors Endorse Splitting U.S. District Court," *Washington Post*, November 27, 1987, pp. B1, B5; Paul Duggan, "Senate Enacts Bill to Place U.S. Court in Md. Suburbs," *Washington Post*, October 1, 1988, pp. B1, B2.

13. Susan F. Rasky, "Congressional Poker Chips: Judges, Water, Oil and Beer," *New York Times*, October 29, 1990, p. A13.

14. Sources of information for the discussion of magistrates include United States Judicial Conference, *The Federal Magistrates System* (Washington D.C.: Government Printing Office, 1981); Carroll Seron, "Magistrates and the Work of Federal Courts: A New Division of Labor," *Judicature*, 69 (April–May 1986), 353–359; and Christopher E. Smith, *United States Magistrates in the Federal Courts: Subordinate Judges* (New York: Praeger, 1990). The term *subordinate judges* is taken from Smith.

15. *Annual Report of the Director of the Administrative Office of the United States Courts, 1991* (Washington, D.C.: Government Printing Office, 1992), p. 108.

16. Sources of information for the discussion of bankruptcy judges include Carroll Seron, *Judicial Reorganization: The Politics of Reform in the Federal Bankruptcy Court* (Lexington, Mass.: Lexington Books, 1978); and Lawrence P. King, "The Unmaking of a Bankruptcy Court: Aftermath of *Northern Pipeline v. Marathon*," *Washington and Lee Law Review*, 40 (Winter 1983), 99–120.

17. *Annual Report of the Administrative Office 1991*, p. 104; "President Signs Bankruptcy Judgeship Bill," *The Third Branch*, 24 (September 1992), 1.

18. Elizabeth Tucker, "Judge Says Justice May Have Ousted Him," *Washington Post*, January 18, 1988 (Washington Business section), pp. 1, 38, 39; Elliot L. Richardson, "A High-Tech Watergate," *New York Times*, October 21, 1991, p. A15.

19. Patrick E. Higginbotham, "Bureaucracy: The Carcinoma of the Federal Judiciary," *Alabama Law Review,* 31 (Winter 1980), 261–272.
20. Charles Alan Wright, *The Law of Federal Courts,* 4th ed. (Saint Paul, Minn.: West Publishing, 1983), pp. 295–297.
21. *Annual Report of the Administrative Office 1991,* p. 147.
22. Deborah J. Barrow and Thomas G. Walker, *A Court Divided: The Fifth Circuit Court of Appeals and the Politics of Judicial Reform* (New Haven, Conn.: Yale University Press, 1988).
23. *Annual Report of the Administrative Office 1991,* p. 170.
24. See Joan Biskupic, "Supreme Court Shows Willingness to Cut Caseload," *Washington Post,* January 12, 1993, p. A4.
25. *U.S. Constitution,* art. III, sec. 1.
26. Martin Shapiro, *The Supreme Court and Administrative Agencies* (New York: Free Press, 1968), p. 53.
27. Lawrence Baum, "Specializing the Federal Courts: Neutral Reforms or Efforts to Shape Judicial Policy?" *Judicature,* 74 (December–January 1991), 217–224.
28. Gerald Sobel, "The Court of Appeals for the Fifth Circuit: A Fifth Anniversary Look at Its Impact on Patent Law and Litigation," *American University Law Review,* 37 (Summer 1988), 1087–1139.
29. Sources of information for the discussion of court administration include Philip L. Dubois, "Court Executives for the Federal Trial Courts: Learning from the Circuit Executive Experience," *Justice System Journal,* 7 (Summer 1982), 180–212; John T. McDermott and Steven Flanders, *The Impact of the Circuit Executive Act* (Washington, D.C.: Federal Judicial Center, 1979); John W. Macy, Jr., *The First Decade of the Circuit Court Executive: An Evaluation* (Washington, D.C.: Federal Judicial Center, 1985); and Steven Flanders, "Court Executives and Decentralization of the Federal Judiciary," *Judicature,* 70 (February–March 1987), 273–279.
30. Jim Parker and John Griffith, "Judges Usurp Power; Battisti a Figurehead," *Cleveland Plain Dealer,* June 9, 1985, pp. 1A, 30A, 31A; Katherine L. Siemon, "Panel Aims to Resolve U.S. Court Feud Here," *Cleveland Plain Dealer,* July 1, 1989, pp. 1A, 12A; Katherine L. Siemon, "Battisti Plans to Resign as Chief Judge," *Cleveland Plain Dealer,* July 8, 1989, pp. 1A, 10A.
31. *Annual Report of the Administrative Office 1991,* p. 127.
32. The development and functioning of this structure are discussed in Peter Graham Fish, *The Politics of Federal Judicial Administration* (Princeton, N.J.: Princeton University Press, 1973).
33. Michael J. Remington, "Circuit Council Reform: A Boat Hook for Judges and Court Administrators," *Brigham Young University Law Review* (Summer 1981), 695–736.
34. *United States Code,* title 28, sec. 332 (d) (1988 ed.).
35. Roberto Suro, "Texas, in Redistricting Conflict, Seeks Delay in State Senate Vote," *New York Times,* February 14, 1992, p. A19; "Order and Report in In re: The Complaint of Lewis H. Earl against United States District Judge James R. Nowlin under the Judicial Conduct and Disability Act of 1980" (5th Cir. 1992).
36. Fish, *Politics of Administration,* p. 431.
37. Provine, "Governing the Ungovernable," p. 277.
38. Roscoe Pound, "The Causes of Popular Dissatisfaction with the Administration of Justice," *Journal of the American Judicature Society,* 20 (February 1937), 178–187. The court unification movement and the politics associated with it are discussed in Henry R. Glick, "The Politics of State-Court Reform," in *The Politics of Judicial Reform,* ed. Philip L. Dubois (Lexington, Mass.: Lexington Books, 1982), pp. 17–33; and Larry Berkson and Susan Carbon, *Court Unification: History, Politics and Implementation* (Washington, D.C.: National Institute of Law Enforcement and Criminal Justice, 1978).
39. Berkson and Carbon, *Court Unification,* p. 2.

40. This discussion of state court organization is based largely on Conference of State Court Administrators, *State Court Organization 1987* (Williamsburg, Va.: National Center for State Courts, 1988).
41. Court Statistics Project, *State Court Caseload Statistics: Annual Report 1990* (Williamsburg, Va.: National Center for State Courts, 1992), p. 10.
42. Conference of State Court Administrators, *State Court Organization 1987*, p. 8.
43. Court Statistics Project, *State Court Caseload Statistics 1990*, p. 10.
44. Ibid., pp. 72, 110. The figure for trial courts does not include appeals from minor to major courts.
45. A. J. Liebling, *The Earl of Louisiana* (New York: Simon and Schuster, 1961), p. 12.
46. Vlae Kershner, "Willie Brown Backs Moving High Court from S.F. to Capital," *San Francisco Chronicle*, March 18, 1992, p. A13.
47. Court Statistics Project, *State Court Caseload Statistics 1990*, p. 59.
48. This discussion of the Illinois court system is based primarily on Administrative Office of the Illinois Courts, *1990 Annual Report to the Supreme Court of Illinois* (Springfield: Administrative Office of the Illinois Courts, 1992).
49. The discussion of the New York court system is based on State of New York, *Report of the Chief Administrator of the Courts for the Calendar Year January 1, 1989–December 31, 1989* (New York: New York Office of Court Administration, 1990); and League of Women Voters of New York State, *The Judicial Maze: The Court System in New York State* (New York: League of Women Voters, 1988).
50. DeNeen L. Brown and Thomas Heath, "Fairfax Courts Dispute Heats Up," *Washington Post*, January 16, 1991, p. B2.
51. B. J. Palermo, "The Judge With an Attitude," *California Lawyer*, 12 (June 1992), 17.
52. David Mars, "Court Reorganization in Connecticut," *Journal of the American Judicature Society*, 41 (June 1957), 8.
53. Thomas A. Henderson et al., *The Significance of Judicial Structure: The Effect of Unification on Trial Court Operations* (Washington, D.C.: National Institute of Justice, 1984), ch. 8. On state court administrators, see James Duke Cameron, Isaiah M. Zimmerman, and Mary Susan Dowling, "The Chief Justice and the Court Administrator: The Evolving Relationship," 113 *Federal Rules Decisions* 439 (1987).
54. Linda Loyd and Susan Caba, "New Panel to Cut Traffic Court Staff," *Philadelphia Inquirer*, May 30, 1991, p. 5B.
55. Reynolds Holding, "Critics Give Trial Reform Little Chance of Success," *San Francisco Chronicle*, July 29, 1991, p. A13.
56. Glick, "Politics of State-Court Reform"; Henderson et al., *Significance of Judicial Structure;* Carl Baar, "The Scope and Limits of Court Reform," *Justice System Journal*, 5 (1980), 274–290.
57. "Funding State and Local Courts: Increasing Demands and Decreasing Resources," *Judicature*, 76 (August–September 1992), 89.
58. Josef M. Broder, John F. Porter, and Webb M. Smathers, "The Hidden Consequences of Court Unification," *Judicature*, 65 (June–July 1981), 10–17.

3

Lawyers

I n the United States, the legal profession is widely regarded as a powerful
one. That perception is correct. Through their representation of clients,
lawyers make a great deal of difference in people's lives. Their impact
often extends well beyond the people they represent and oppose. When representing businesses and governments, for instance, attorneys take part in
decisions that can affect society as a whole, such as whether two large companies will merge or to what extent abortions can be restricted under the law.

Perhaps what is most striking about lawyers in the United States, however, is how much their activities extend beyond the practice of law. Attorneys
frequently serve in other significant roles such as labor union leaders, university presidents, and social critics and commentators. Lawyers also play a
prominent part in government and politics. They serve as campaign managers
and as official and unofficial advisers to presidents and governors. And lawyers
are elected to high offices in large numbers. As a lawyer in the White House,
Bill Clinton is hardly unusual; a majority of the presidents have been attorneys.
Lawyers far outnumber members of any other occupation in both houses of
Congress. In addition, as one critic of lawyers noted ominously, "a mind-
boggling percentage of the U.S. judiciary are attorneys."[1]

Of course, critics of the legal profession are not difficult to find; perhaps
no other occupation in the United States is the subject of so many attacks.
Whether or not such attacks are justified, they reflect the power and significance of lawyers in American society.

This chapter focuses on lawyers as participants in the courts, but that
role should be seen in the context of other roles that lawyers play. By examining what lawyers do as representatives of legal clients, we can gain some
understanding of their importance—and of the criticisms that they receive—
in American society.

One theme throughout the chapter is the variation among lawyers, particularly the distinction between those who represent primarily institutions and
those who represent primarily individuals. Among its other effects, that distinction has considerable impact on the quantity and quality of legal services
that people receive.

The chapter has three parts. The first deals broadly with the structure of the legal profession and the work that lawyers do. The second examines access to the services of lawyers. The final section explores relationships between lawyers and their clients.

THE LEGAL PROFESSION

To understand law as a profession, we need to look at several aspects of the profession. This section discusses the educational and licensing processes that determine who may practice law, the work of lawyers and the settings in which they work, specialization among lawyers, and the organization and regulation of lawyers.

Entry into the Legal Profession

Like many other professions, the practice of law is regulated by the states. Most important, the states control entry into the profession. People cannot act as attorneys simply by labeling themselves as such. In order to represent clients or perform other work identified as that of lawyers, a person must be licensed to do so. The most significant exception is that nonlawyers can represent themselves in legal proceedings. Licensing, like the regulation of other aspects of legal practice, is supervised by state supreme courts and generally administered by boards of lawyers.

The legal profession as a whole has worked hard to limit what nonlawyers can do, seeking a broad definition of the practice of law and limiting that practice to licensed attorneys. The "unauthorized practice of law" by nonlawyers is a criminal offense in most states. Lawyers argue that limitations on nonlawyers are needed to protect people from unskilled practitioners, though critics respond that lawyers are primarily interested in protecting themselves against competition from such groups as accountants (on tax matters) and real estate agents (in sales of property). In recent years there has been growing support, even within the legal profession, for allowing nonlawyers to undertake some of the activities that have been restricted to lawyers. But thus far the restrictions have been relaxed only a little.

Occasionally, it is discovered that a person who is practicing law, sometimes with considerable success, actually lacks a license. For instance, a man was arrested in 1988 for impersonating a lawyer when he acted as a criminal defense attorney in New York City. A judge before whom he appeared reportedly said, "I should have suspected he wasn't a lawyer. He was always so punctual and polite."[2]

Law School Training   In the nineteenth century most American lawyers received their training through apprenticeship with practicing attorneys. Gradually, however, the system of legal education evolved to the one with which we are familiar today: a structured law school curriculum that requires three years of full-time study or its equivalent.

This evolutionary process was both reflected in and strengthened by changes in the licensing requirements for attorneys. Today only four states—California, Vermont, Virginia, and Washington—permit prospective attorneys to bypass law school altogether and gain their training by apprenticeship. Three others—Maine, New York, and Wyoming—allow a combination of law school and law office training.[3] But even where these options exist, relatively few people use them; in 1987 fewer than thirty new lawyers obtained their training through study with an attorney.[4]

Most states require not only that applicants be law school graduates but also that the school be accredited by the American Bar Association (ABA). The ABA's requirements for accreditation are highly detailed. They include, for example, a list of materials that the school library must contain. (Among these required materials is a large set of ABA publications.) In a few states, however, students from unaccredited law schools are eligible to practice under certain circumstances. One such state is California, which has thirty-five unaccredited law schools (some of which have state accreditation). But fewer than 1 percent of the new lawyers in the United States in 1987 were graduates of such unaccredited schools.[5]

Admission to accredited law schools is competitive, and the effective standards for admission have risen dramatically with the number of applications. In general, admission is based primarily on undergraduate grades and scores on the Law School Admission Test, with other considerations such as letters of recommendation also playing a role.

Most law schools resemble each other in the general type of legal training they provide. The heart of their curricula is a series of classes on various areas of the law, such as contracts, property, criminal procedure, and constitutional law. In such courses, the primary texts are the opinions of the appellate courts, the study of which is intended to provide students with both an understanding of the substance of the law and a capacity to undertake legal analysis. The conventional form of teaching is the Socratic method, in which professors question students closely about the reasoning in opinions in order to illuminate particular cases and sharpen the students' thinking. One law professor has explained how this method achieved its dominance in law schools:

> Christopher Columbus Langdell of Harvard was one of the first advocates of the Socratic method of law teaching. His teaching style was so unpopular that Harvard's law school enrollment plummeted, and rumors circulated that Langdell might be fired. When law professors across America learned how much students despised the method, however, they immediately rushed to adopt it, and Langdell's job was spared.[6]

Both the content and the form of law school education have been criticized. The main complaint about content is that a focus on appellate court opinions does not give students much of the practical knowledge they need. Students learn little from such opinions about how to run a law office or try a case in court. Many new lawyers find that their education is just beginning when they leave school.

In response to this complaint, law schools have sought to diversify their curricula. Most now have clinical programs, in which students work with actual legal matters in order to gain such practical skills as interviewing clients and conducting negotiations over cases. As part of some programs, students may even make supervised appearances in court. But clinical programs still constitute only a small portion of the law school curriculum, and both faculty and students tend to view them as peripheral to the mainstream of a legal education.

There has been some movement away from the Socratic method, partly because of the anxieties that it produces in students. But such anxieties are only one source of the pressures that most law students feel—pressures stemming largely from heavy workloads and competition to perform well. One study reportedly found that 6 percent of a group of law students suffered from clinical depression before beginning law school; by the third year, 40 percent had depression.[7]

A kind of hierarchy exists among law schools that is based on their prestige. The most widely respected, such as Michigan, Yale, Stanford, and Harvard, can be the most selective in choosing their students. In turn, because of their reputations and the abilities of their students, these schools provide the widest opportunities for graduates. Large law firms recruit disproportionately from the most prominent schools, and Supreme Court justices usually draw from them in choosing law clerks. Ultimately, graduates of these schools are the most likely to achieve eminence. For instance, President Clinton and his two leading rivals for the Democratic nomination in 1992 all went to Yale Law School. So did Supreme Court Justice Clarence Thomas, law professor Anita Hill—who accused Thomas of sexual harassment when he was nominated to the Court in 1991—and Thomas's Senate supporters John Danforth and Arlen Specter.[8] But law schools with quite different levels of prestige have far more similarities than differences in what they teach and how they teach it.

Law school as a prerequisite to the practice of law has several effects on the legal profession. Some of these effects are financial. Since they usually must earn an undergraduate degree before entering law school, most prospective attorneys go through at least seven years of higher education. The costs of this education prevent some people with limited financial resources from obtaining it.

Those who do go through law school often incur substantial debts. In 1990 the average debt for a graduate from the Harvard Law School was $46,000. A Georgetown University law student who would be paying $700 per month on her law school debt said that "it's like having a whole mortgage without having a house to show for it."[9] These debts reinforce the desire of most law students to find high-paying jobs after education—to the extent that such jobs are available to them.

The second effect of a law school education is that its intensive training influences students' attitudes and ways of thinking. Law students are instilled with the belief that the courts should operate on the basis of the law; indeed, it is largely for this reason that much of what lawyers and judges do can be understood from the legal perspective discussed in Chapter 1. There is some evidence that law school affects students' attitudes in other ways, particularly by increasing their interest in the more remunerative types of law practice, but studies disagree about these effects.[10]

Licensing Requirements   The states vary a good deal in the conditions that a person must meet to become an attorney, but a predominant pattern does exist.[11] Nearly all states require that an applicant be of good moral character. This requirement creates difficulties primarily for people who have been convicted of serious crimes, and several states prohibit the admission of people who were convicted of felonies.

The most important requirements, however, are gaining a law school education—discussed already—and passing the bar examination. With some exceptions in Wisconsin, every prospective attorney must submit to a two- or three-day bar examination.[12] This test consists of essay questions on the laws of the state and, in all but four states, a multiple choice Multistate Bar Examination, administered by a national testing service. Most states also include a short section on professional ethics, called the Multistate Professional Responsibility Examination. In nearly all states, the examination is offered in February and July.

Typically, about two-thirds of the applicants across the nation pass the bar examination each year; 70 percent passed it in 1991. But success rates vary among the states—in 1991 the variation ranged from 91.8 percent in North Dakota to 53.4 percent in California.[13] The examination in California is notoriously difficult; among the people who failed it at least once are Governor Pete Wilson; Jerry Brown, a former governor and presidential candidate; and a former member of the Reagan cabinet, William Clark, who was once a justice on the California Supreme Court.[14] Every state allows those who fail the bar examination to retake it at least once, and most allow unlimited retries. In 1991 an applicant passed the California bar examination on his forty-eighth try.[15]

The possibility of failure makes the bar examination a fearsome prospect for applicants. After completing law school, most take special "bar review" courses to prepare themselves for the test. The traumatic character of the examination is suggested by the test day in New York City in 1989. Ten minutes before the exam began, one prospective lawyer let out a "bloodcurdling scream." She was ushered out; as she returned twenty minutes later, another test taker stood up, cursed, and left the examination permanently.[16]

Not surprisingly, the grading of questions and the scores required to pass the test occasionally lead to disputes. In 1990 complaints about grading of the most recent Ohio bar examination led the state supreme court to change procedures for grading the test, and a year later a grand jury found that bar exam grades for nine Ohio applicants in 1986 had been altered upward.[17]

Attorneys who are licensed to practice in one state do not automatically gain the right to practice in other states. Indeed, in nearly half of the states, outsiders must pass all or part of the bar examination before doing business in the new state. In the others, a lawyer can be admitted to the bar on the basis of some period of experience in another state, most often five years.

However, courts usually grant permission to appear in a single case to an attorney who is a resident of another state.

Federal courts also establish their own requirements for the right to practice before them. In most instances, a lawyer need only be licensed in the state in which the federal court sits, but some courts have set up more stringent requirements. In ten federal districts, attorneys must pass a written examination or have a certain amount of trial experience before they can try federal cases.

The Size and Composition of the Legal Profession   Over the past four decades, the number of lawyers in the United States has grown tremendously, as Figure 3.1 shows. According to one survey, in 1951 there were 222,000 lawyers in the United States. By 1970 that number had reached 355,000. The number of lawyers in 1992 was calculated to be 799,760, representing a growth rate of about 125 percent since 1970 and 260 percent since 1951.

FIGURE 3.1 Growth in the Number of Lawyers in the United States.

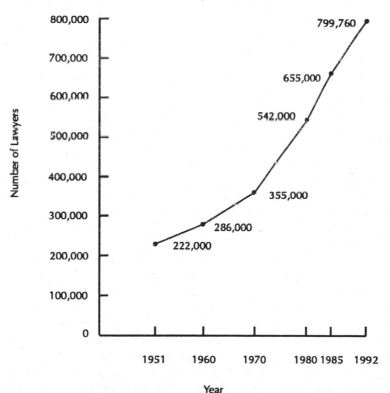

Sources: Barbara A. Curran, "American Lawyers in the 1980s: A Profession in Transition," *Law & Society Review*, 20 (1986), 20: Barbara A. Curran, *Supplement to the Lawyer Statistical Report: The U.S. Legal Profession in 1985* (Chicago: American Bar Foundation, 1986), 3; information provided by the American Bar Association.

This growth, of course, results from massive increases in the number of new lawyers. In 1963, 11,000 people were admitted to the bar; since 1978, in contrast, the average number of admissions per year has been over 40,000. This increase reflects a substantial rise in both law school enrollments and the proportion of law students who actually graduate.[18]

But why are more people going to law school? One careful analysis suggests that a number of forces are involved.[19] For one thing, there is more legal work to be done. (If we control for population, the increase in the number of lawyers since 1951 has been about 120 percent rather than 260 percent. If we control for economic activity, as measured by the real gross national product—GNP controlled for inflation—there has been essentially no increase at all.) Other contributing factors include the baby boom, which increased the pool of potential law school entrants; a growing perception of the impact that lawyers can have on society; and possibly a sense—perhaps exaggerated—of the economic rewards available to attorneys.

Inevitably, this growth in the legal profession affects lawyers. It intensifies economic competition, and this helps explain the more aggressive marketing of legal services in recent years. Combined with the national recession of the early 1990s, the growth in their numbers has tightened the job market for new lawyers somewhat; more graduates have been failing to find the kinds of jobs they seek or even any satisfactory positions in the law.[20]

Not surprisingly, in light of these developments, most attorneys—64 percent in a 1992 survey—think that there are too many lawyers.[21] The same view is widely held by nonlawyers, particularly those who think that lawyers encourage lawsuits and thus affect the economy negatively.[22] Such critics argue that the United States stands out among other countries in regard to the number of lawyers per capita; former Vice President Dan Quayle said that the United States has 70 percent of all the lawyers in the world. Other commentators have calculated much lower proportions, and one scholar concluded that the United States in 1987 ranked thirty-fifth among one hundred countries in the number of "law providers" per capita. As that term suggests, disagreement about the standing of the United States in this respect is based largely on differences in how one defines the equivalent of American lawyers in other nations.[23]

Until quite recently almost all lawyers were white and male; in 1963 fewer than 3 percent of practicing attorneys were female, and in 1970 about 1 percent were black.[24] This pattern stemmed in part from restrictive practices by law schools and law firms. For example, few southern and border state law schools admitted black students until the 1950s, and many law schools throughout the country were equally restrictive for women. Until 1950 Harvard did not accept women as law students. Columbia had the same policy in 1922, when its dean, future Supreme Court Chief Justice Harlan Stone, justified the refusal to admit women by saying, "We don't because we don't."[25] And most law firms were unwilling to hire women or members of racial minority groups.

As barriers have been broken and aspirations have risen, more women and nonwhites have entered law school; the growth has been more substantial for women. Of the first-year students in the 1990–1991 academic year, 42 percent were women and 16 percent were minority group members.[26] Exhibit 3.1 shows the change that has occurred in the demographics of law school enrollments in recent years.

This trend guarantees that the proportion of lawyers who are not white men will grow substantially. It also means that women and members of racial minority groups increasingly will occupy important positions as lawyers; President Clinton's selection of Janet Reno as the first female U.S. attorney general symbolizes this trend. But both women and minority group members continue to face discrimination within the legal profession—discrimination that ranges from hiring by law firms to treatment by judges and other lawyers in court.

Lawyers come primarily from families with above-average economic status.[27] Aside from other factors, the cost of a college and law school education makes it easier for people to become lawyers if their parents are well off.

The Work of Lawyers

The major activities of lawyers fit into several overlapping categories.[28] The first is litigation, which involves handling cases in court and preparing for court appearances. This is the part of lawyers' work that we know best because television and movie portrayals of lawyers emphasize litigation. In reality,

EXHIBIT 3.1 Enrollments of Women and Members of Racial Minority Groups in Law Schools

Year	Women		Minority Groups	
	Number	%	Number	%
1965–66	2,374	4.2	—	—
1970–71	6,682	8.6	5,568	6.1
1975–76	26,020	23.4	8,703	7.8
1980–81	40,834	34.2	10,575	8.8
1985–86	47,486	40.0	12,346	10.4
1990–91	54,097	42.5	17,330	13.6

Notes: Enrollments are in programs leading to the J.D. degree in law schools approved by the American Bar Association. Percentages are enrollments of students in that group as a percentage of all students. Data on minority group enrollment are not available for 1965–1966; figures for minority group enrollment in 1970–1971 are actually for 1971–1972.

Sources: American Bar Association, *A Review of Legal Education in the United States Fall 1990*, pp. 66–68 (Chicago: American Bar Association, 1991); American Bar Association, *A Review of Legal Education in the United States—Fall 1977*, pp. 50–51 (Chicago: American Bar Association, 1978).

however, litigation is only a small part of most attorneys' work, and many lawyers seldom or never go to court.

Similar to litigation is representation of clients—nearly always businesses—in the other branches of government. For example, lawyers present their clients' cases in formal administrative proceedings before such agencies as the federal Interstate Commerce Commission and the state public utilities commissions, and they also deal informally with these and other agencies. In addition, lawyers lobby on behalf of clients in legislatures, seeking results such as an advantageous provision in federal tax law or a favorable city council ruling on a variance from zoning rules.

A third major activity is negotiation—efforts to work out an agreement between a client and another party. Some negotiation occurs in the context of litigation, as lawyers seek to resolve cases prior to trial. In fact, a high proportion of serious criminal cases are ultimately resolved by the prosecution and the defense attorney through a plea bargain, and an even higher proportion of serious civil cases are settled by an agreement between the parties. Lawyers frequently negotiate to avoid litigation altogether, helping clients settle disputes at an early point or preventing disputes from developing in the first place.

Lawyers also engage in securing—a term that means providing security through the writing of documents. The most important such documents are contracts, which are central to the functioning of the economy. Another common example is the will, which allows individuals to designate how their assets will be allocated after death. Wills illustrate the importance of securing because a properly written will can ensure that an estate is settled quickly and in the way that the writer had wished.

The final activity of lawyers, counseling, involves helping clients find the most favorable course of action to handle a particular problem. Every area of the law entails a good deal of counseling. The primary task of many antitrust lawyers, for example, is to advise companies as to whether certain decisions might lead to federal antitrust investigations or lawsuits by other companies. Similarly, tax lawyers provide advice on the tax consequences of different activities. One important aspect of counseling consists of helping clients to decide whether to file lawsuits and whether to accept negotiated settlements of cases. Counseling is, of course, linked to everything else that lawyers do. And, almost inevitably, much of it goes beyond the realm of strictly legal knowledge.

Attorneys are often accused of encouraging lawsuits in order to create business for themselves, but this list of activities suggests a somewhat different conclusion. Although lawyers sometimes do stir up litigation, most of them spend the bulk of their professional time in other activities. In fact, much of what they do is intended to keep clients out of court by settling disputes, by preventing confusion that might lead to court battles, and by avoiding conduct that might expose someone to a legal challenge. As one scholar found in a study of consumer grievances, lawyers may even try to discourage action by potential clients who seem to lack a reasonable claim. "Rather than pour gasoline on the fire of indignation," the researcher concluded, "almost all of the lawyers interviewed in this study seem far more likely to use some type of fire extinguisher."[29]

Where Lawyers Work

Lawyers perform their activities in several different settings. Most are in private practice, but a significant and growing minority work in the business sector or for the government.

Private Practice   In 1985 about 70 percent of all attorneys were engaged in private practice.[30] This proportion represents a significant decline; in 1948 it was nearly 90 percent.[31] Nevertheless, private practice remains the dominant form of work for lawyers.

Lawyers in private practice are members of a profession who are also engaged in a business. At least ideally, they do their work in accordance with the standards of the legal profession. Yet they must also obtain enough work from clients and make a sufficient profit from that work to maintain a successful practice.

The private practice of law follows no single model. Some lawyers specialize narrowly, while others deal with a broad range of legal matters. Strategies to attract clients differ considerably. One important difference, linked to most others, is the size of the firms in which lawyers work.

Historically, most lawyers were solo practitioners. Over time, however, a growing number of lawyers have formed cooperative arrangements with colleagues. By 1985 a little more than half of the lawyers in private practice were involved in such cooperation, which can range from a simple sharing of office facilities by two attorneys to a highly structured firm employing several hundred lawyers.

This trend has resulted primarily from considerations of efficiency, since groups of lawyers can pool both the costs of a law practice and their personal expertise. It is also much easier for an inexperienced attorney to join an established group of lawyers than to start out alone, bearing all the costs of a legal practice and searching out sources of business. The advantages of practicing with other lawyers are reflected in incomes: lawyers practicing in large firms do far better than solo practitioners, with lawyers in small firms falling in between.[32]

All this being true, even today the majority of lawyers in private practice are solo practitioners or have only loose cooperative arrangements with other attorneys. Understandably, this kind of practice predominates in rural areas, and it is relatively common in medium-sized cities. Even in big cities, lawyers who serve individual clients in fields such as divorce are likely to work alone or in small groups.[33]

At the same time, a growing minority of lawyers practice in firms of substantial size. If we define large firms as those with fifty or more attorneys, there has been massive growth in both the number and size of large firms. Part of that trend, illustrated by Exhibit 3.2, is the spread of large firms from New York City to other large and medium-sized cities. Even in the current

EXHIBIT 3.2 Largest Law Firms in Selected Cities, 1992

City	Firm	Number of Lawyers
New York	Skadden, Arps, Slate, Meagher & Flom	976
Los Angeles	Gibson, Dunn & Crutcher	724
Chicago	Sidley & Austin	697
Houston	Fulbright & Jaworski	659
San Francisco	Morrison & Foerster	651
Cleveland	Baker & Hostetler	497
Milwaukee	Foley & Lardner	467
Seattle	Perkins Coie	339
Tampa	Holland & Knight	266
Rochester, N.Y.	Nixon, Hargrave, Devans & Doyle	245
Hartford	Day, Berry & Howard	222
Omaha	Kutak, Rock	206

Notes: Cities are those in which firms have their principal offices; firms with no principal office are omitted. The numbers are for lawyers in all offices of the firm.
Source: "The NLJ 250," *National Law Journal,* September 28, 1992, pp. S1–S27. Reprinted with the permission of *The National Law Journal.* Copyright © 1992. The New York Law Publishing Comapany.

era, large firms hardly dominate the practice of law; of all the lawyers in private practice in 1985, 11 percent were in large firms.[34] But this segment of the profession has a significance far beyond its share of lawyers. Moreover, most characteristics of large firms are more extreme versions of those found in medium-sized firms. For both reasons, a closer look at large firms is useful.

Large Law Firms   The significance of large firms derives chiefly from their clienteles; they represent primarily business corporations, with an emphasis on major corporations. In 1991 one large firm did work for Ford, Pepsi, and Boeing, along with at least 35 other industrial corporations among the 250 largest in the country.[35] Through their legal advice and action, large law firms affect the fortunes of the businesses they represent. They frequently provide advice and shape decisions on nonlegal matters as well, such as the economic consequences of a proposed merger between companies. Many law firms even have attorneys on the boards of major clients.

The services that large firms perform for their corporate clients frequently have a political tinge. Because their clients' interests are affected by legislation and administrative policy, particularly at the federal level, lawyers do considerable work to influence decisions in the legislative and executive branches. To provide this kind of representation, all of the twenty largest law firms in

1992 had offices in Washington.[36] Such representation occurs in the states as well: the nation's largest firm, working on behalf of a corporation that was fighting a hostile takeover, successfully lobbied the Kansas legislature to change corporation law in a way that helped protect against the takeover.[37]

Among the lawyers in large law firms, as in their smaller counterparts, the primary status distinction is between partners and associates. (The distinction was so sharp at one New York firm that its "chief of protocol" refused to allow an associate to bring in his own furniture because it "had partner's legs, not being perfectly straight and squared off, and couldn't be used by an associate."[38]) Attorneys generally enter firms as associates. If they remain with a firm for some period of time, typically five to ten years, they are considered for promotion to partnership status, which traditionally gives lawyers a permanent position in the firm and a share in its profits. Associates who are denied partnerships usually must leave the firm.

Large firms seek to recruit the top-ranked graduates of the most prestigious schools. To attract these lawyers, large firms can offer high salaries, extensive support services, general freedom from the difficult task of finding business, and, perhaps most important, the prospect of partnership. Competition among firms for the most impressive graduates is reflected in the upward spiral of salaries at the biggest firms.[39] Exhibit 3.3 shows 1992 starting salaries for lawyers in a variety of organizations; as it illustrates, new lawyers in large firms do far better than their counterparts in other kinds of organizations, though there is wide variation in salaries among firms.

In exchange for the benefits of a large firm, associates typically work long hours under considerable pressure. The length of their workdays is a matter of legend, as illustrated by one story about a large-firm associate interviewing law students for jobs.

> One student asked if the associates ever do anything fun together. "Sure," the interviewer replied. "About two o'clock, we knock off for an hour and go

EXHIBIT 3.3 A Sampling of Starting Salaries for Lawyers, 1992

Position	Salary
Davis Polk & Wardwell (large firm), New York City	$87,000
Morrison & Hecker (large firm), Kansas City	52,000
Hawaii Attorney General's office	36,000
Internal Revenue Service	32,423
NOW Legal Defense and Education Fund, New York	30,000

Note: Salaries for lawyers in small firms are not available; these salaries generally are considerably lower than those in large firms.
Source: "What Lawyers Earn," *National Law Journal,* April 27, 1992, pp. S1–S8. Reprinted with the permission of *The National Law Journal.* Copyright © 1992. The New York Law Publishing Comapany.

play a game of racquetball." The student observed, "What a great way to break up the afternoon." The interviewer responded, "Afternoon?"[40]

The work that associates do is likely to seem uncreative and uninteresting, and few have much contact with clients. As one observer put it, "The work of young associates . . . is often so boring or trivial that many lawyers would refuse to do it if the money weren't so good."[41]

Attractive though it is, partnership is difficult to achieve. In most large firms only a small proportion of associates become partners, the others leaving early or receiving a negative decision from the firm. In the early 1990s the proportion went even lower—to one in ten in New York City's thirty largest firms.[42]

Because of highly selective recruitment and promotion, lawyers who become partners generally have considerable ability and ambition. But such strengths are not universal. In a prestigious Philadelphia firm, one associate was promoted even though a partner warned that his "intellectual laziness will some day embarrass us," while another successful associate had been described by a partner as "a bit of a con man."[43]

In large firms, all partners are not equal. Relatively new partners enjoy neither the financial returns nor the power of senior partners, and at first their work may differ only marginally from what they did as associates. Over the course of their careers, however, partners come to do less strictly legal work. In the terms used by one lawyer, young partners and associates are "the grinders who do the work," while older partners are "finders," who attract clients, and "minders," who help manage the firm and take care of existing clients.[44] To earn their high incomes, senior partners charge clients the highest rates for their time—in many firms, more than $300 per hour.[45] In one matter, former U.S. Attorney General Griffin Bell, a partner in an Atlanta firm, charged E. F. Hutton $1,711 an hour for his services.[46]

The personnel of large firms includes a great many nonlawyers, from administrators to clerical workers. Of increasing importance are paralegals—nonlawyers with some legal training who perform routine work. Many firms now have more than one hundred paralegals, thereby enhancing considerably the volume of legal work they can perform.

The world of large law firms has changed a great deal in recent years.[47] There are more big firms, and the successful firms are growing faster. Conditions for big firms have become more competitive. While their growing size requires that they find more business, their corporate clients are using their own salaried lawyers to do more work, and corporations "shop around" more among outside law firms rather than maintaining stable long-term relationships with firms.

One result is more aggressive marketing by firms. Another is the growing frequency of mergers between firms and hirings of partners from other firms, largely in an effort to add lawyers who can bring and attract valuable business. Firms are now geographically more dispersed; one-third of all lawyers in the 250 largest firms now work at branches of those firms.[48] In this less stable situation, some firms fall behind and others fail altogether. The most spectacular failure was at Finley, Kumble, the fourth largest firm in the country; the firm became bankrupt in 1988, after a period of enormous growth financed heavily by borrowing. Even the firms that survive and prosper are more vulnerable to the loss of business, and in the recession of the early 1990s some firms laid off associates or asked newly hired lawyers to join them later than originally planned. The growing fluidity of the world of large firms is symbolized by a lawyer who changed firms four times between 1987 and 1990—twice because firms failed and twice because of his own preferences.[49]

Inevitably, these changes have affected the internal structure of large firms. Some firms hire associates for a nonpartnership track, and firms increasingly retain some lawyers as permanent associates rather than partners. There are more distinctions among partners, based on their work and their ability to attract business, and occasionally partners are asked to leave firms; partnership is less secure than it once was.

Business   About 10 percent of all lawyers work directly for businesses.[50] The employment of attorneys as "house counsel" has increased substantially over the past few decades, as more businesses have established their own law departments and the size of existing departments has grown. In 1991–1992 thirty-five companies had legal staffs with a hundred or more lawyers.[51]

This growth is largely a response to the greater legal needs of businesses. However, it also reflects a growing preference for house counsel over outside lawyers. Corporations now spend more money on their own legal departments than on fees to outside law firms.[52] This trend toward in-house work has at least two sources. One is an interest in saving costs, an interest that has grown with the fees charged by big law firms. Estimates suggest that legal work done within the company costs one-third to one-half less than the same work done by outside law firms.[53] Another is the greater control that companies can exert over the legal work done by their own employees.

Traditionally, house counsel concentrated on a company's routine and recurring legal work, and companies turned to outside law firms for less routine work, such as litigation. Today, as businesses try to use outside law firms less, house counsel do more of their own litigation work—about one third of that work, according to a 1990 survey of major legal departments.[54] General counsel—the heads of legal departments—manage and oversee the legal work done by outside firms. Even more than outside counsel, in-house lawyers are likely to be involved in nonlegal decision-making. Some general counsel in Chicago reported that they frequently advised on such matters as corporate acquisitions, labor negotiations, and even advertising campaigns.[55]

The dominant image of in-house legal departments contrasts strongly with that of large law firms: legal departments hire young lawyers with less impressive credentials and pay them less but give them greater security and shorter work hours. This image fits reality to a considerable degree, but the difference between in-house departments and large firms is not as sharp as it once was. A 1991 survey of larger legal departments suggested that the gap in both pay and working hours has narrowed considerably.[56] The continuing differences make in-house departments attractive to many lawyers, and it is common for attorneys to come to these departments from large firms.

Not all attorneys in the business world actually work as lawyers. Many can be found in fields such as banking and real estate, where their legal knowledge provides an advantage even if they are not practicing law as such.

Government   In 1985 about 12 percent of all attorneys worked for the government in some capacity. Of these, about one-third were in the federal government, while the other two-thirds were scattered among the state and local governments. A small proportion worked in legislatures, and more than a quarter in the judiciary. In this discussion, however, I focus on those who serve in the executive branch.

The executive branch engages in a good deal of litigation, both as a criminal prosecutor and as a plaintiff or a defendant in civil cases. A considerable volume of "internal litigation" also occurs within government agencies, such as the Internal Revenue Service and the Social Security Administration, and lawyers represent the agency's position or serve as judges in these cases. In addition, government agencies, like private parties, require expert advice on issues that involve legal questions.

The federal government, which employs about twenty-two thousand attorneys, provides an example of the ways in which government legal work is structured.[57] Nearly a quarter of the federal government's lawyers work in the Department of Justice. The largest concentration of Justice Department lawyers is in the U.S. Attorneys' offices in the ninety-four federal judicial districts. U.S. Attorneys and their assistants represent the government in criminal prosecutions and civil litigation in the district courts. The Justice Department also has several divisions—Civil, Land, Antitrust, and Civil Rights, for example—that help set general departmental policy and advise the U.S. Attorneys. These divisions handle some civil litigation at the trial level and take over cases from U.S. Attorneys at the appellate level. Of particular importance within Justice is the Office of the Solicitor General, which must approve most federal government appeals to the courts of appeals and nearly all government appeals or petitions to the Supreme Court; the office itself handles litigation in the Supreme Court, thereby shaping the federal government's position on major legal issues.

Every other executive-branch agency of significant size has a legal staff, and some are substantial. (The Department of Defense, with a legal staff of several thousand, has even more lawyers than the Justice Department.) These legal staffs advise agency officials and handle internal litigation within agencies. In a few instances, they also conduct litigation in court, as attorneys for the Internal Revenue Service do when they represent the government in the Tax Court.

At the state and local levels, government legal services are organized in a variety of ways, although in most states they are highly decentralized. The state attorney general and other state agencies may have substantial legal staffs, but most lawyers work for local governments in prosecutors' offices and other structures. Some attorneys serve as prosecutors or city solicitors on a part-time basis, primarily in rural areas where government legal business is limited.

The impact of government attorneys merits emphasis. Prosecutors play a critical role through their decisions about which cases to bring and how to handle them, a role that is examined further in Chapter 6. Each state's attorney general influences government practices through advisory opinions on the law, and the legal advisers to federal agencies shape policy on both legal and nonlegal matters. Lawyers within the White House often play a critical role in developing presidential policy positions. Less visible lawyers in lower-level positions also can influence policy a good deal through their work in litigation.

Lawyers who work for the government are chosen in several ways. Some, such as the federal attorney general, are appointed by the chief executive. But in most states the attorney general and county prosecutors are elected. Lawyers who hold lower-level positions are usually selected by their superiors.

The great disadvantage of government service is relatively low salaries.[58] But there are compensating advantages: opportunities to try cases and take on other major responsibilities much earlier than associates can do in law firms, the chance to participate in making public policy, and often high job security. Partly because of the tightening job market, these advantages have attracted an increasing number of lawyers to government in recent years. In 1991, for instance, a new federal public defender in Florida was overwhelmed with applications from what he called "top-quality people."[59]

Many young lawyers come to government for a short time before moving to the private sector. Prosecutors often move into private practice as criminal defense attorneys, and lawyers with government regulatory agencies join firms that represent regulated businesses. Thus a lawyer in the federal Securities and Exchange Commission who had made a mark in prosecutions for "insider trading" in the 1980s moved to a private law firm in 1989 and took on representation for clients who were the targets of federal investigations concerning securities matters.[60] As a result, a high proportion of government attorneys are enthusiastic but inexperienced. Other lawyers stay in government for much or all of their careers. Some high-level lawyers, such as the federal attorney general, come to government from the private sector and return there after a few years.

Specialization in the Practice of Law

Some people have an image of lawyers as generalists, that is, as professionals who handle any kind of legal task for any client who comes to them. This image is largely and increasingly inaccurate: most lawyers specialize to a considerable extent. This specialization occurs along three lines.

The first is by type of activity. A small proportion of attorneys engage primarily in litigation. In contrast, many other lawyers seldom, if ever, go to court. Within large law firms, even trial lawyers may be " 'paper litigators,' logging legal lifetimes taking depositions and exchanging motions." One lawyer became head of his firm's litigation group, with earnings of about $750,000 a year, without ever having helped pick a trial jury.[61]

The second form of specialization is by type of legal issue. In a complex legal system, no attorney can be an expert on everything. Largely for this reason, most lawyers devote themselves to a few fields or even to a single one. In a sample of Chicago lawyers, 22 percent practiced exclusively in one field, while another 39 percent gave more than half their time to one field.[62] Common specialties include tax law, criminal law, personal injuries, and real estate.

Finally, lawyers can specialize by type of client. Some lawyers, for instance, serve the various legal needs of corporations. Others combine client specialization with legal specialization, as in the case of lawyers who represent primarily personal injury plaintiffs or criminal defendants. This combination helps produce some relatively narrow specialties, such as defense of white-collar criminal defendants or class-action suits by stockholders against corporations.

Patterns of specialization are influenced by social and legal developments, as reflected in the needs of current and potential clients. For example, the growth in corporate bankruptcies in recent years has attracted more lawyers to that field. Some lawyers choose their specialties quite consciously; others develop specialties largely by chance, based on such circumstances as the tasks they are given as associates in law firms.

The degree of specialization varies according to the setting in which lawyers practice. Lawyers in big cities are far more specialized than their rural counterparts; surveys found that 70 percent of Chicago lawyers considered themselves specialists, compared with 56 percent in Springfield, Missouri, and 22 percent in rural Missouri.[63] And lawyers who practice alone are less specialized than those in large firms, partly because those firms can combine specialists in different fields to offer a broad range of services.

Because lawyers specialize, their perspectives and their self-interest differ. These differences often come to the surface on public issues. Today, for instance, lawyers who represent manufacturers strongly support proposals to limit legal liability for injuries caused by defective products, while lawyers who represent personal injury plaintiffs fight hard against these proposals. Because of differing needs and interests, most lawyers orient themselves primarily toward their own group of specialists rather than toward the legal profession as a whole.

The Two Hemispheres

> Washington has two distinct groups of lawyers. There's the "uptown" bar, feasting off the specialized and usually dry legal work generated by the Federal Government. And there's the "downtown" bar, a grittier group whose members are here because Washington, like any other city, has its share of mayhem and conflict thrusting people into the legal system.[64]

The reporter who made that distinction correctly perceived an important pattern in the practice of law. The various differences among lawyers that I have described are not random; rather, to a considerable extent, lawyers cluster into what John P. Heinz and Edward O. Laumann have called "the two hemispheres of the profession."[65]

These hemispheres are separated most sharply by the kinds of clients that lawyers represent. Some lawyers serve primarily large organizations, while others represent mainly individuals and small businesses. Relatively few do substantial work for both types of clients. As Exhibit 3.4 shows, this distinction between the "corporate" and the "personal" sectors is related to other important distinctions. Lawyers in the two sectors tend to specialize in different kinds of legal issues. Lawyers in the corporate sector are also considerably more likely to work for large firms (or, of course, for businesses themselves). Furthermore, lawyers in the corporate sector tend to serve a small number of clients over long periods of time, while those in the personal sector tend to serve a succession of clients on single matters. As I discuss later, one result is that attorneys in the corporate sector are generally subject to greater control by their clients.

Corporate lawyers are somewhat more likely to come from higher-status backgrounds and elite law schools, a difference reflecting the higher income and prestige of practice in the corporate sector. And the gap in income has widened considerably since the late 1960s; lawyers in solo practice have actually suffered a substantial decline in real income.[66]

EXHIBIT 3.4 A Comparison of Legal Practice on Behalf of Corporations and Individuals

	Primary Clients	
	Corporations	Individuals
Socioeconomic background of lawyers	Higher status	Relatively lower status
Law school attended	Relatively high percentage from elite schools	Primarily nonelite schools
Type of practice	Large firm or business legal department	Small firm or solo practice
Typical number of clients each year	Fewer	More
Control by clients	Higher	Lower
Prestige within profession	Higher	Lower
Income	Higher	Lower

Source: John P. Heinz and Edward O. Laumann, *Chicago Lawyers: The Social Structure of the Bar* (New York: Russell Sage Foundation, 1982).

The distinctions between the two hemispheres should not be exaggerated, however. Indeed, in some respects, according to one scholar, "there's a continuum rather than a bifurcation."[67] But real distinctions do exist, and they have important consequences. Inevitably, most lawyers and prospective lawyers aspire to enter the corporate sector. As a result, this hemisphere probably contains a disproportionate share of the most skilled lawyers. Furthermore, the good support services and other attributes of practice in the corporate sector are more conducive to effective legal work. For both reasons, the legal services provided in the corporate sector are probably superior, on the whole, to those provided in the personal sector. Hence, in the words of John Heinz, these two hemispheres make up "two systems of justice, 'separate and unequal.' "[68]

Organization and Regulation of Lawyers

As noted earlier, regulation of the legal profession is almost entirely a function of the state governments.[69] For the most part, state legislatures have turned over to their supreme courts the power to regulate the legal profession, including admission of lawyers to the bar and disciplinary action. Most of the actual regulation is performed by lawyers themselves, under the supreme court's direction. About two-thirds of the states have an integrated bar, which means that all lawyers must belong to the state bar association; these associations are then given the primary role in professional regulation. In states such as Nevada and California, the power of these mandatory associations has stirred controversy in recent years. In the other states, the supreme courts establish commissions to undertake regulation in cooperation with voluntary bar associations.

Besides these regulatory functions, the legal profession has a great deal of other organized activity. Its most important single group is the American Bar Association (ABA), to which about half of the nation's lawyers belong. The ABA is divided into a number of sections, some based on specialized areas of practice. Both the ABA and its sections engage in a variety of activities; these include meetings and publications intended to improve the skills of members, as well as work in government on behalf of ABA positions on legal issues. The ABA also seeks to influence the selection of federal judges by giving ratings to potential or actual nominees.

The state bar associations, whether compulsory or voluntary in membership, usually resemble the ABA in organization and activities. There are also many city and county bar associations. In addition, each legal specialization has its own separate associations, some of which play significant roles within the profession and in politics. For example, the Association of Trial Lawyers of America, an organization of sixty-five thousand lawyers who represent plaintiffs in personal injury cases, exerts considerable impact on law and policy in its area of specialization.[70] Perhaps most important, in recent years the association has fought against tort law "reform," a movement to change major legal rules about personal injuries in ways that favor defendants. For many lawyers, these specialized groups are more important than those that are open to all lawyers because they more fully represent their members' interests and serve their professional needs.

Satisfaction with Law as a Profession

Much of what is written about lawyers suggests that they are happy people who make a great deal of money and exercise considerable power. Like any other generalization about lawyers, this one applies far better to some than to others. The incomes of lawyers differ enormously, and those differences have grown considerably in the last two decades. Some lawyers exercise a large measure of political or social power, while most have relatively limited impact. There is also a good deal of variation in lawyers' contentment, ranging from the 31 percent who indicated in one survey that they were very satisfied with their careers to the 5 percent who said that they were very dissatisfied.[71]

That survey suggested that most lawyers are basically happy with their jobs. Yet in recent years there have been signs of substantial and growing dissatisfaction.[72] It appears that lawyers are leaving the profession at a higher rate than in the past;[73] some leave out of economic necessity, but others leave because they dislike their work too much to stay. Among people who remain in the profession, a high proportion complain of long hours—not surprisingly, since half of the lawyers in private practice reported that they worked at least twenty-four hundred hours a year.[74] In the same survey, 75 percent of the lawyers in private practice said that they felt substantial pressure and tension in their jobs.[75] A medical study found that lawyers had the third-highest rate of major depression among 105 occupations; only data-entry keyers and computer equipment operators exceeded that rate.[76]

These signs of dissatisfaction undoubtedly reflect some inherent difficulties in the jobs of most lawyers. They also reflect changes in the profession that have increased economic and other pressures on attorneys. Although the degree of unhappiness among lawyers should not be exaggerated, it underlines the evolution that is occurring in the practice of law.

ACCESS TO LEGAL SERVICES

An attorney's services can be helpful in a variety of situations. We might expect people to seek out a lawyer whenever those situations arise—when, for instance, they feel that their legal rights have been violated or when they need to make an agreement with someone. Yet many people who find themselves in these situations do not consult lawyers.

Why does this nonuse of lawyers occur? "Use of lawyers is an acquired habit," according to one legal scholar; "most people never surmount the barriers of fear, ignorance, and unfamiliarity."[77] The primary fear is that going to a lawyer will worsen a situation rather than improve it. Besides, people may not know in what situations a lawyer could help them or how to find an appropriate lawyer. Thus, even if legal services were free, by no means would everyone with a law-related problem go to an attorney.

But the monetary costs of legal services can add another important deterrent to their use. Most people who consider going to a lawyer lack a clear sense of how much a lawyer's help will cost them, but they often perceive that the cost will be more than they can afford or feel comfortable in paying. Indeed, standard rates for lawyers' services can make those services quite expensive.

Yet various mechanisms have been developed to overcome this monetary barrier. Such mechanisms have grown considerably in number and scope over the last quarter century. Important because they have made legal services more available, these mechanisms have also become a significant part of the legal system in themselves.

Overcoming the Cost Barriers to Legal Services

The types of mechanisms that allow litigants to avoid the usual costs of legal services fall into two general categories. One consists of programs, primarily governmental, to meet the legal needs of the poor. The other includes an array of developments in the private sector that reduce cost barriers for the population as a whole.

Criminal Defense Services for the Poor   There is a long history of efforts to provide free legal services to indigent criminal defendants, but until the 1960s these efforts were limited and unsystematic. Although low-income defendants in federal cases and in most states gained a legal right to free services, this right was not implemented very effectively.

The primary impetus for strengthening this right was *Gideon v. Wainwright* (1963), a case in which the Supreme Court held that indigent criminal defendants in serious state cases must be provided with free counsel.[78] Although the Court's decision did not change the law in most states, it underlined the obligation to back the legal requirement to provide counsel with a meaningful financial commitment. Spending for this purpose increased dramatically at all levels of government, and in 1990 governments spent about $1.7 billion for legal defense of the poor.[79] At least in felony cases, government-funded systems now represent most defendants.[80]

Across the country, two systems for defense of the poor predominate. The first is the public defender system, in which public employees (sometimes part-time) represent defendants. The second is the assigned counsel system. In this system, judges appoint private attorneys, usually from a list of volunteers, on a case-by-case basis to represent defendants. About one-quarter of the states have statewide public defender systems. Most other states employ both systems: public defenders' offices are used chiefly in urban counties, which have enough cases to make them practical, while most rural counties use assigned counsel.

Despite the great increase in financial support for defense of the poor, both systems suffer from serious monetary problems; these problems have been aggravated in recent years by growth in criminal cases and by the worsening fiscal problems of state and local governments. In the assigned counsel system, the problem lies in low hourly fees and limits on the maximum amounts allowed per case, both quite widespread. These low fees discourage attorneys from seeking case assignments, although the depressed legal market of the early 1990s has made such assignments more attractive in some places.[81] More subtly, low fees discourage lawyers who do take assignments from giving sufficient time and effort to cases. In the public defender system, the problem lies in the total funding provided to offices—funding that tends to be inadequate to meet an office's responsibilities. Consequently, public defenders are burdened with large caseloads, and they too may be unable to give sufficient attention to each case.

There is considerable evidence that these financial problems have produced significant weaknesses in defense of the poor. In recent years, for instance, studies have found highly inadequate public defender systems in Tennessee and in Atlanta.[82] Low fees have contributed to severe weaknesses in the quality of counsel in southern death penalty cases—probably the most serious deficiency in providing assistance to indigent defendants.[83] And in 1992 the federal budget to pay defense lawyers was used up three months early, causing some lawyers to withdraw from cases or seek postponements; five weeks later money was found from other sources to resume payments.[84]

Yet the average level of performance by assigned counsel and public defenders may equal that of privately hired defense attorneys.[85] Working-class and middle-class defendants, the primary users of private hired attorneys, are limited in the quantity and quality of services they can purchase. And indigent defendants often receive very good legal services. This is particularly true of public defender systems, in which lawyers typically gain considerable expertise quickly through their specialization in criminal cases. One recent study, more positive than most, states its conclusion in its title: attorneys representing the indigent "Get the Job Done and Done Well."[86]

Civil Representation for the Poor   The first legal aid societies were set up in American cities in the late nineteenth century to provide legal assistance to low-income people in civil matters. The number and size of these societies grew in the twentieth century. The early legal aid societies accomplished a good deal, but they had only limited funding and often depended on volunteer staffing. As a result, they met only a small portion of the legal needs of the poor.[87]

In 1965, as part of President Johnson's War on Poverty, the federal government established its own program of legal assistance to the poor in civil matters. In 1974, after some evolution and political controversy, Congress created the Legal Services Corporation to fund federal legal services to the poor on the civil side of the law.

The Legal Services Corporation operates as an administrator of grants to more than three hundred local agencies that provide assistance directly to the indigent. Most of these agencies set up law offices to which clients can come for help. These offices handle more than a million legal matters each year, encompassing a wide variety of problems that reflect the situations of the poor. In one fairly typical agency, 29 percent of the problems handled in

1991 involved family matters, 24 percent housing, 16 percent health and income maintenance, and 12 percent consumer and personal finance issues.[88]

Most of the business of local agencies funded by the Legal Services Corporation is fairly routine and is resolved without litigation. But attorneys in this program and its predecessor have used lawsuits and other activity for the broader purpose of shaping the law, sometimes through challenges to the legality of government practices. To support this work, Legal Services has special centers in fields such as youth law and consumer law. The emphasis given to "law reform" litigation varies from program to program. This kind of litigation has brought protests from government officials and private groups such as the American Farm Bureau Federation. It has also angered congressional conservatives, and Congress has placed a variety of restrictions on the kinds of cases that Legal Services can handle.

Legal Services fared poorly during the Reagan administration, under a president who had developed an antipathy toward the program when he was governor of California. To a lesser extent, this was true of the Bush administration as well. Both presidents appointed to the corporation's board of directors people who were hostile to the program. Reagan sought to eliminate all federal funding for Legal Services; Congress balked, but funding declined under Reagan and Bush. In 1988 the Legal Services board took the step, perhaps unprecedented, of hiring lobbyists to help convince Congress to cut its budget. In contrast, during his 1992 campaign, Bill Clinton stated his strong support for Legal Services, and he pledged to "appoint to the board people who are absolutely committed to the mission" of the program.[89]

The Legal Services Corporation has radically increased the availability of lawyers to low-income people. But it appears to handle only a small portion of the legal needs of the poor—less than 15 percent in New York state, according to a bar association study.[90] And the funding cutbacks of recent years have limited the program's capacity to handle problems and cases.

Legal Services is not the only source of help for the poor in civil matters. Many lawyers donate a portion of their time pro bono publico (literally, for the public good) to meet what they see as a professional obligation. A portion of this work is on behalf of the indigent. A few local bar associations have established pro bono requirements for their members, and in 1992 the Florida Supreme Court ruled that every lawyer in the state must do at least twenty hours of pro bono work in each year or pay $350. Public officials and bar associations in other states have encouraged attorneys to increase their pro bono efforts. Such encouragement is not fully effective; a 1990 survey in Washington, D.C. found that 41 percent of the lawyers in large firms did twenty hours or less of pro bono work for the poor per year despite a minimum of forty hours recommended by the local bar's code of ethics.[91]

Advertising   Though the poor have the most obvious financial difficulties in using lawyers, people with moderate incomes also may face substantial financial barriers to lawyers' services. Government has done little directly to tear down these barriers, but several developments in the private sector have increased the availability of lawyers to people who are neither indigent nor wealthy. To some extent, these developments simply overcome people's fears about the cost of lawyers; to some extent, they actually reduce these costs.

Advertising by lawyers is significant in itself and a foundation for other developments. Until 1977 state rules prohibited most forms of advertising by lawyers; that year, however, the Supreme Court struck down state prohibitions of advertising by lawyers as a violation of free speech rights.[92] Since then, state supreme courts and bar associations have adopted a great many rules limiting the forms of attorney advertising. The Supreme Court has indicated that the states have only limited power to restrict advertising, but an equivocal decision in 1990 has encouraged many states to adopt new restrictions in the belief that the Court might uphold them.[93]

Lawyers were slow to begin advertising, but by 1987 about one-third of all attorneys advertised.[94] Most lawyers who do so only buy space in the yellow pages of telephone directories. But some lawyers go further, using such media as newspapers, television, and direct mail. About 3 percent of all lawyers now advertise on television, spending more than $100 million a year.[95]

The content of advertising varies a good deal; most is fairly restrained, but some lawyers take a more flamboyant approach. In one classic television ad, a Wisconsin lawyer named Kenneth Hur "played a convict whose final words to the chaplain from the electric chair were that he wished he'd called Mr. Hur's legal clinic."[96] Exhibit 3.5 describes the range of material and approaches in a sampling of advertisements in the yellow pages, to provide a sense of what advertising lawyers see as the most useful appeals to potential clients.

The lawyers who advertise to the general public are those who seek business from individuals. Thus one study found that solo practitioners and those in small firms were the most likely to advertise in the yellow pages, while lawyers in large firms were the least likely.[97] The same is true of newspaper and television advertising. But large firms increasingly advertise in ways more appropriate to their needs. Perhaps the most common method, one used by most firms, is distribution of brochures about the firm and its services.[98] Some firms use more active approaches. One New York firm even sent a letter to potential clients who wanted to influence tax law, arguing that the lawyers in the firm who had served in the Treasury Department and Internal Revenue Service gave it "direct access" to senior officials in those agencies and to members of the congressional tax committees.[99]

Many lawyers are unhappy about the growth of advertising, feeling that it demeans the profession and serves consumers badly. Others claim that advertising has lowered fees and made lawyers more accessible to individuals. At present, we lack sufficient information to resolve these issues. But advertising clearly has become an important means for people to locate attorneys; one study found that 20 percent of the people who consulted lawyers after they had been injured in accidents found those lawyers through advertising.[100]

Legal Clinics   In the 1970s bar associations began to abolish minimum fee schedules, rules that prohibited lawyers from charging less than a certain amount per hour. In 1975 the Supreme Court eliminated these schedules

Those lawyers who place display ads in the yellow pages aim overwhelmingly at middle-class and working-class individuals. This aim is reflected in the services most often advertised: personal injury cases stand out; divorce and criminal problems such as drunk driving are also common. The ads present several kinds of themes.

Overcoming Fears About Lawyers

Ads frequently indicate that lawyers provide free consultations and that there will be no fee in personal injury cases if no money is recovered. Also common is an emphasis on convenience: lawyers available at all hours, locations that are easy to reach, willingness to visit clients "in the hospital or your home" (New York City).

Competence

Many ads point to lawyers' experience and credentials. Some go beyond the routine. Across a Philadelphia lawyer's picture are the words "Rated one of the 'Best Lawyers in America'." A Miami lawyer quotes the *Miami Herald:* "Master of Traffic Technicalities." A Dallas lawyer states that he is "Licensed By The Supreme Court of Texas," a credential shared with all the other attorneys who are entitled to practice in the state.

Results

Some lawyers suggest that the chances of favorable results for their clients are good. A New York City firm is "known for our frequent multi-million dollar awards for our clients." A Los Angeles firm that handles bankruptcy cases tells potential clients, "KEEP EVERYTHING! . . . PAY BACK NOTHING!!" (Asterisks direct readers to the phrase "in most cases.") A Philadelphia lawyer's ad, sprinkled with dollar signs, reassures that there will be no fee "until you receive settlement $$$"; the word "until" suggests that the client can be assured of receiving money in a settlement.

Fear

A few ads address people's fears about legal problems, particularly in criminal cases. One full-page Minneapolis ad has the message "Call our number before they hang one on you." Below it is a picture of a well-dressed defendant in a lineup with a booking number across his chest; the face is indistinct. Another Minneapolis lawyer provides a picture of a man sitting in a jail cell and announces that the lawyer handles "trials and appeals from DWI to death row."

Source: Selected telephone books distributed in 1991 and 1992.

EXHIBIT 3.5 Themes of Lawyers' Advertisements in Telephone Book Yellow Pages

altogether by ruling that they violated the antitrust laws.[101] This development, combined with the legalization of advertising, made possible the creation of legal clinics. As one author has defined them, these clinics are "firms that use advertising to attract a high volume of middle-income clients, and use technological tools and paraprofessionals to offer prices that are generally lower than those of traditional firms."[102] Clinics work primarily on legal matters that are relatively common for middle-income people, such as divorce and personal injuries, and advertising provides the means to attract people who need help with these matters.

Two firms that operate as clinics stand out for their size, both ranking among the one hundred largest law firms in the country. Hyatt Legal Services, founded in Cleveland in 1977, had 302 lawyers in 112 offices in 1991. Jacoby & Meyers, established in Los Angeles in 1972, had 305 lawyers in 87 offices.[103] By contrast, a study by the American Bar Association found that other legal clinics averaged fewer than three lawyers.[104]

When clinics first developed, some people saw them as a means to expand the availability of lawyers' services to people with moderate incomes. Overall, they have not made a fundamental difference in this respect. Some limitations lie in the ways that clinics operate in practice; for instance, they may not be able to offer fees that are substantially lower than those of other firms. But the primary limitation is that there simply are not very many clinics. The ABA study estimated that fewer than two thousand lawyers in the United States worked in legal clinics.[105] However, other firms have adopted some of the practices of legal clinics, thus providing competition for clinics but also making lawyers more available to individuals. According to the study, "it is in the traditional law firm setting, if anywhere," that the mechanisms pioneered by legal clinics "are going to increase access to justice for moderate-income people."[106]

Prepaid Legal Services   The term *prepaid legal services* refers to a variety of mechanisms under which a payment allows people access to a lawyer's services at some future time—in other words, insurance for those services.[107] Prepaid legal services were made possible by a series of court and legislative actions to remove traditional restrictions on legal insurance, beginning with a 1963 Supreme Court decision. As a result, prepaid legal services plans have become a significant part of the legal marketplace. It has been estimated that more than 17 million people are covered by some form of legal insurance.[108]

People obtain prepaid legal services primarily in two ways. The great majority are enrolled in group plans through their employers, either as part of their benefit package or by paying a monthly fee to participate. Others enroll in individual plans, some of which operate through credit unions or are sold to charge card customers. Companies such as Amway and Montgomery Ward market legal insurance plans.

The various legal insurance plans differ in what they provide. Some entitle their participants to a certain amount of a lawyer's time per year. One national program provides unlimited telephone advice and consultation, along with some other services. Some plans have open panels, which allow those enrolled to consult any attorney; more common are closed panels, under which people must choose from a specified group of lawyers.

Like legal clinics, the plans are used most often for the kinds of matters that are most common among working- and middle-class people: marriage and divorce, real estate, landlord-tenant relations, and wills. Because they reach far more people, they have a greater potential for expanding the availability of lawyers' services to individuals.

The Contingent Fee   Somewhat different from all these other developments is a long-standing system under which a lawyer's fee in a case is contingent upon its outcome.[109] Under the contingent, or contingency, fee system, a lawyer will represent a client who has a legal claim for money without requiring an advance payment (except, in some instances, for the lawyer's expenses). If the client recovers money, either through a court decision or through a settlement with the other party, the attorney's fee will be a proportion of that sum. But if the client wins nothing, the attorney also receives nothing.

The contingent fee is used almost entirely in the representation of individuals rather than institutions. It is employed most often in personal injury cases, where it is the predominant form of payment; one study found that contingent fees were used 97 percent of the time in this area.[110] The proportion the lawyer receives can vary, although a fee of one-third of the recovery is common. Lawyers often charge a higher proportion for a case that goes to trial.

The existence of the contingent fee increases the availability of attorneys to people who have legal claims. If a sizable advance payment were required, many people could not hire a lawyer, and if a significant fee had to be paid regardless of the outcome, this would strike many people as an unacceptable risk. However, as long as a substantial monetary recovery is likely, a person with a legal claim will generally be able to find a lawyer to take the case on a contingent basis. Thus, for one important type of legal problem, the contingent fee overcomes much of the financial barrier to the use of legal services. One effect of legal advertising is to inform individuals of the contingency fee and thus to allay their fears about the financial risks of litigation.

Nonetheless, the system has been criticized a good deal. Those who think that there is too much personal injury litigation often blame the contingent fee for fostering lawsuits.[111] Not surprisingly, in recent years groups representing defendants in this area have sought to reduce the level of contingency fees that lawyers can charge. They have been most successful in medical malpractice, where many states have adopted some form of statutory limit or mechanism for regulating contingency fees.

The Overall Picture

The cost of legal services would seem to make it difficult for most people to take advantage of them; it would also seem to create a strong relationship between wealth and the ability to hire a lawyer. On the other hand, several mechanisms have been developed to overcome the usual financial barriers. In light of all this, what is the impact of costs on the use of lawyers?

We can first consider the situation of individuals who are not wealthy. Such individuals still face great constraints when they need to use lawyers. Some people under some circumstances can avail themselves of very good legal services: the indigent criminal defendant in a city with an excellent public defender's office or the injured person who has a strong case involving a large potential recovery. But by and large nonwealthy individuals are limited in the quantity and quality of services they can obtain. They must refrain from using lawyers at times when legal help would be useful, and when they do employ an attorney they may have to settle for less than the full level of the services they need. Furthermore, they cannot afford to use the most expensive attorneys.

These constraints have their clearest impact when people would like to take a case to trial but have no special help in paying the extensive lawyers' fees that usually result. As federal judge Shirley Hufstedler noted, a regular civil trial "is beyond the economic reach of all except the rich, the nearly rich or the person seriously injured by a well-insured defendant."[112]

If we leave aside the wealthy, the relationship between individuals' income and their ability to use a lawyer is not a simple one. Most people are in about the same position, in the sense that they cannot afford the most expensive lawyers, nor can they hire less expensive lawyers for the most time-consuming problems. They can, however, use a lawyer on a contingency basis or for relatively inexpensive matters, such as the writing of wills. The near-poor may now be in a weaker position than the poor, and the relative positions of low-income and middle-income people vary with such factors as the strength of a local Legal Services program and the availability of legal insurance. As a result, surveys of the public have not found a strong relationship between income and a person's use of lawyers to deal with legal problems.[113]

Of course, wealthy individuals are in a far better position than most other people to use lawyers' services. That difference becomes apparent when such individuals become criminal defendants. When William Kennedy Smith was prosecuted for rape, his defense was estimated to cost $1 million; along with several lawyers receiving $250 to $500 per hour, Smith employed a pollster and at least five private detectives.[114] According to Brendan Sullivan, who represents some wealthy defendants, "The bad thing is that by the time somebody comes to me, they are pretty far up the creek. The good thing is they will pay almost anything."[115]

Similarly, there is a sharp contrast between individuals and large institutions, such as corporations and the state and national governments; large institutions are far better able to afford legal services. Large corporations are in a particularly strong position, both because of their wealth and because legal fees are tax deductible as a business expense—in effect, a very large government subsidy. Thus major corporations can afford to pay a great deal for legal services—frequently, millions of dollars a year.

Until fairly recently, large corporations seemed to feel no cost constraints at all. The head of IBM in the 1970s liked to say of Nicholas Katzenbach, the former U.S. attorney general who was chief legal counsel for the corporation, "Nick Katzenbach is the only guy at IBM with an unlimited budget for his department, and he always exceeds it."[116] Companies were often lax in scrutinizing bills from outside law firms, and this laxity led to extravagant and questionable charges in some instances.

In the past few years some corporations have increased their vigilance over legal costs. Perhaps the most important result, noted earlier, is an increasing reliance on in-house lawyers. Another sign of change is the development of companies to monitor legal bills for businesses. One of these companies has found such abuses as a lawyer billing a client for fifty-hour workdays and another who charged for the clothes that he bought during a long out-of-town trial.[117] Although governments rely on outside lawyers far less than does business, the cost of such services to governments has also caused concern. The savings and loan bailout made the Federal Deposit Insurance Corporation the single largest user of outside lawyers' services, paying more than $500 million a year in the early 1990s. Internal studies suggested that these costs were highly inflated, and members of Congress pressed for better controls over costs.[118]

We should not infer too much from the high levels of corporate spending for lawyers. Large institutions pay as much as they do for legal services primarily because they are engaged in so many activities that require lawyers. But the ready availability of attorneys does provide a great advantage in utilizing the legal system. This advantage becomes most evident in a dispute between parties that differ in their access to attorneys. For example, in a tax controversy, the Internal Revenue Service is likely to have the edge over a middle-income individual or a small business because it has a staff of tax specialists who can go to court with relatively little worry about expenses. But in an antitrust dispute, even the federal government may be at a disadvantage against a large corporation, which can hire the most expert antitrust attorneys and assemble a much larger legal staff than the one available to the Justice Department. And a small town is likely to be at a similar disadvantage in dealing with businesses such as land developers.

This kind of advantage is also reflected in corporate influence on government policy. By employing attorneys as advocates in all three branches of government, large corporations can shape the development of the law. Where legal issues involve conflicts between corporations and sectors of society with less access to attorneys (as in consumer law), corporate interests generally have a greater capacity to achieve favorable rules of law.

However, there are exceptions. Legal Services lawyers have sometimes done quite well in securing judicial doctrines favorable to low-income citizens. And some interest groups and public interest law firms enjoy considerable success in their efforts to obtain rulings favorable to relatively powerless segments of society, such as minority groups and consumers. But large institutions retain the greatest ability to use lawyers to shape the law.

THE LAWYER-CLIENT RELATIONSHIP

Clients come to lawyers with problems or opportunities related to the legal system. Their lawyers then serve them in their efforts to achieve their goals. This service may place lawyers in a variety of roles—those of "the gatekeeper who teaches clients about the costs of using the legal system, the knowledge-able friend or therapist, the broker of information or coach, the go-between or informal mediator, the legal technician, and the adversary bargainer-litiga-tor."[119] How lawyers perform these roles—how they serve their clients—is a matter of considerable importance for those clients and for the legal system.

In allowing their lawyers to play these roles, clients put themselves in a dependent position. A client who hires an attorney turns over to that attorney some control over the course of events. As a result, an attorney's ability and willingness to serve a client effectively go a long way to determine the client's success in dealing with the legal system. An incompetent lawyer or one who does not serve a client's interests faithfully may do considerable damage to those interests.

Competence

Differences among lawyers in their skills have an obvious but important impact: the more competent an attorney is, the better off are the lawyer's clients. This is especially evident in the courtroom, where the litigant with the better attorney may gain a visible advantage over the other party. This reality is disturbing. But differences in lawyers' skills are inevitable, and so we may have to tolerate their impact on the legal system.

Less tolerable is work by lawyers that falls below what we would regard as a minimal level of competence. When people give responsibilities to their lawyers, they typically assume that those lawyers have at least a moderate degree of ability. If that assumption is incorrect, the client may suffer griev-ously. A poorly drafted contract, inaccurate tax advice, and ineffective court-room advocacy can all have very serious consequences.

Because lawyers are licensed only after intensive training and a lengthy examination, we might assume that few of them are incompetent. But, argues legal scholar Richard Abel, "it is absurd to pretend that any test of competence administered to someone at the age of twenty-five, no matter how well con-structed, can ensure quality throughout a fifty-year career."[120] A number of critics have pointed to what they see as widespread inadequacies in the work of lawyers, with emphasis on their performance in trials. One of these critics was federal judge David Bazelon; referring to the constitutional provision that guarantees the right to counsel, Bazelon remarked that many criminal defense lawyers are "walking violations of the Sixth Amendment."[121]

A 1987 survey of judges suggested a mixed picture. A majority of judges rated the lawyers who came before them, on the whole, as "very competent," and almost none viewed them as "incompetent." But about one-third chose the "marginally competent" category.[122]

In recent years considerable effort has been devoted to improving lawyer competence through legal education. As noted earlier, many law schools have established clinical programs to give students more practical training, though these programs play only a limited part in the education of most law students. Some lawyers and educators have proposed more radical changes in law school education, but such changes will not come easily.

One major development is an increase in formal education after law school. Continuing legal education programs have become common as a means for lawyers to refresh and expand their knowledge. These programs use a variety of techniques, from formal courses to publications aimed at practical needs. In 1992 thirty-nine states required a certain amount of continuing education classwork for lawyers to renew their licenses; four other states were considering such a rule.[123] A common requirement is fifteen hours of work per year. It is uncertain how much effect such requirements have on lawyers' competence, though they undoubtedly enhance the skills of some attorneys.

Another avenue taken by several states, such as Alabama and Minnesota, is to give official status to some legal specialties so that clients can identify lawyers who have expertise in particular fields; states certify specialists on the basis of experience or an examination. One of these states, California, certifies specialists in such fields as criminal law, workers' compensation, and taxation. A 1990 Supreme Court decision allows attorneys to advertise as specialists on the basis of certification by private organizations,[124] and several specialized lawyers' groups have established such certification programs.

There have also been proposals for mandatory certification, under which lawyers could practice in certain fields only if they met certain requirements. But lawyers prize their freedom to practice in whatever fields they wish, and no state has adopted such a plan.

Faithful Representation

The ethical rules that bind lawyers impose on them a strong duty to represent their clients faithfully. The American Bar Association's Model Code of Professional Responsibility, widely used by the states as a benchmark for ethical conduct, holds that "a lawyer should represent a client zealously within the bounds of the law." Furthermore, a lawyer's professional judgment "should be exercised, within the bounds of the law, solely for the benefit of his client and free of compromising influences and loyalties."[125]

Because it is not absolute, the first of these requirements is ambiguous in some situations. How far must a lawyer go to serve a client's interests? There has been disagreement, for instance, about the proper course of action when a lawyer believes that a client will commit perjury.[126] Of course, situations sometimes arise when lawyers clearly go further than allowed. According to a 1990 indictment, for instance, three New York City lawyers committed such offenses as having a private investigator widen a pothole with a pickax to make it appear more dangerous and using the same person twice as an "eyewitness"—once for an accident that occurred when he was in prison.[127]

But the second requirement is more problematical on a day-to-day basis. In practice, the self-interest of lawyers frequently fails to coincide with that of the people they represent. Those situations create a conflict of interest for lawyers and a potential problem for their clients.

One example concerns lawyers' fees. A lawyer who is paid on an hourly basis may have a financial incentive to devote more time to a case than a client needs. In contrast, a lawyer who is paid a flat fee has an incentive to resolve a matter by spending the minimum time necessary. Even the contingent fee system, which seems to meld the interests of lawyer and client, often creates a conflict of interest. The additional expenditure of time necessary to gain the maximum settlement for a plaintiff may not provide the lawyer with an adequate return to be financially worthwhile.

In situations that involve a conflict of interest, clients are at a disadvantage. Even though lawyers have a duty to elevate clients' interests over their own, in practice they have a strong temptation to follow the course of action most favorable to their own interests, especially because clients often have difficulty in evaluating a lawyer's decisions. As a result, clients do not always receive the most faithful representation from their attorneys.

Some lawyers depart from their client's interests in a much more extreme way: they behave dishonestly. Among the more serious forms of dishonesty, two seem to be the most common.

One is the misuse of clients' funds. Attorneys entrusted with the proceeds of an estate or money to be placed in a trust may sometimes "borrow" these funds for their own use, intending to pay back what they have taken. A few simply steal money—in some instances, a great deal of money. In recent years, for instance, lawyers in New York and Maryland have been accused of taking millions of dollars from clients and other victims.[128]

The second form of dishonesty involves fees. In a legal scholar's survey, "nearly all of the lawyers interviewed reported some amount of deception in practices relating to billing clients," deception that ranged from charging for nonessential work to billing for more time than the attorney worked.[129] Even more serious, lawyers sometimes accept money for services they never perform. As a result, the unsuspecting client may forfeit legal rights. For example, an attorney's inaction can cause a client to miss the deadline for filing a lawsuit.

One means to improve the ethical behavior of lawyers is education. Law schools now require their students to take some coursework dealing with a lawyer's professional responsibilities. Most states include a section on ethics on their bar examinations, and many require some study of ethics as part of mandatory continuing legal education. A knowledge of ethical rules is unlikely to deter lawyers who have larceny in their hearts, but it may prevent some lawyers from engaging in less obvious forms of unethical behavior through ignorance.

Variation in the Lawyer-Client Relationship

The character of the relationship between lawyer and client varies from situation to situation. Most important, some clients are in better positions than others to ensure that lawyers serve their interests. As Heinz and Laumann argue, corporations generally can exert considerably more control over their lawyers than can individuals.[130]

In the sector of the bar that serves individuals, lawyers generally represent clients on a one-time basis, and they have a great many clients. In Chicago, Heinz and Laumann found that, on the average, lawyers who represent individuals in nonbusiness matters, such as divorce and personal injury, have a hundred clients a year.[131] Thus no single client is particularly important to a lawyer's professional position or income, and the lawyer need not worry a great deal about incurring a client's disfavor.

For their part, few individual clients have an opportunity to scrutinize the performance of a lawyer over time or to develop independent expertise in the law. As a result, the lawyer is in a good position to shape the client's perception of the situation,[132] and the client may have great difficulty in getting good representation for appropriate fees. For instance, a study by the New York City Department of Consumer Affairs found that lawyers in contested divorce cases frequently engage in questionable practices concerning fees, so that clients pay more than they expected without receiving satisfactory service. The problems found in the study were epitomized by one lawyer's explanation for not providing monthly bills to clients: he "told Consumer Affairs that he and his secretary make mistakes in the bill and that if clients scrutinized the bills and asked questions, he'd have to charge them for the phone calls."[133]

All this does not mean that lawyers for individuals typically fail to represent their interests effectively. Lawyers for criminal defendants and personal injury plaintiffs often display quite clearly the zealous representation that the ABA's code demands. It does mean, however, that individuals who are one-time clients of attorneys have relatively limited ability to assess and control the performance of their attorneys.

The situation in the sector of the bar that serves institutions is rather different. Here some lawyers are employed by a single client, a business corporation. This arrangement gives the corporation a high degree of control because corporate executives can evaluate a lawyer's work over time and because the lawyer depends on the corporation for employment. Indeed, a number of court cases have arisen when lawyers were fired by their companies after they sought to place ethical responsibilities, such as refraining from illegal conduct, above the interests of their employers.[134] (Full-time government lawyers are in a similar situation in some respects, though their "clients" often are in other agencies and thus may have little direct control over them.)

Because of their independent status and their multiple clients, large law firms would seem to be in a much stronger position than lawyers who work for a single client. But large firms often provide continuing services to a set of corporate clients. These long-term relationships give clients a good chance to scrutinize and evaluate their lawyers' work, and they also require lawyers to satisfy their clients in order to maintain their business. Moreover, corporations are powerful institutions that can do much to affect the standing of a lawyer or firm.

This dependence of lawyers in the corporate sector on their clients is reflected in the ways that law firms structure their practices to serve major clients—even opening new branches to serve their needs better. Some critics argue that lawyers who represent corporations are too dependent on their clients, causing them to be too uncritical in representing their interests. These critics point to the role that lawyers play in protecting companies from environmental and safety regulations and to the seeming complicity of some lawyers in corporate actions of questionable legality. Many law firms have been attacked for their role in the savings and loan scandals of recent years. In 1992 a New York firm paid $41 million to the federal government to settle a lawsuit charging it with helping to hide the wrongdoing that later produced the collapse of Charles Keating's Lincoln Savings and Loan Association, which was expected to cost the government $2 billion.[135]

Although these criticisms and charges have been debated, it is clear that significant clients exert considerable influence over what big law firms do. Heinz and Laumann point to an extreme example of client influence, one that occurred after a major Chicago firm allowed some of its lawyers to spend time on pro bono work:

> All went well until a young lawyer reported to the firm that he had been assigned to defend a man accused of bank robbery. It happened that one of the principal clients of the firm was a major bank. The bank that was the firm's client had no connection with the bank that had been robbed . . . but the firm nonetheless ordered the young lawyer to withdraw from the representation of the defendant. . . . The reason for the firm order to withdraw, apparently, was that bank robbers are the enemies of banks, and for the firm to permit one of its lawyers to represent a bank robber might therefore be seen as disloyalty to a major client.[136]

Differences between individual and institutional clients should not be exaggerated. Lawyers who represent individuals in personal injury and criminal cases are also criticized for zealous representation of their clients. Moreover, lawyers who represent institutions often achieve considerable autonomy from their clients. In his study of medium-sized litigation, Herbert Kritzer concluded that "there is little evidence of significant control of the lawyer by the client, regardless of whether the client is an individual or an organization (even if that organization is a large insurance company on which the lawyer is highly dependent)."[137] It should be recalled that corporations, as well as individuals, are victims of outrageous and even dishonest billing practices.

On the whole, however, institutions do achieve greater control over their attorneys. Thus they gain one more advantage in their use of legal services. Not only do they get more and often better services, they also get services that are more likely to be consistent with their interests.

Remedies

As I have discussed, education programs and certification of specialists have been used to improve the representation that lawyers provide to their clients. For people who feel that they have been badly served by their lawyers, there are more specific remedies: malpractice suits and complaints to disciplinary bodies. These mechanisms can provide redress to a disgruntled client, and their existence may deter lawyers from engaging in undesirable practices.

Malpractice Suits   Like other professionals, lawyers can be sued for malpractice for failure to serve their clients adequately. Suits can also be brought by other people who claim that they have suffered losses because of a lawyer's representation of a client. In law, as in other professional fields, there is considerable disagreement about what kinds of actions constitute malpractice.

Although lawyers are frequently blamed for the growth in malpractice actions against physicians and others, they too have faced a burgeoning of such actions. It appears that only about one-third of all malpractice claims result in some kind of payment to the claimant.[138] But some jury verdicts and out-of-court settlements produce substantial payments, suggesting that attorneys made serious lapses in these cases. Both the increase in suits and the large verdicts and settlements have contributed to rising rates for malpractice insurance and some difficulties in obtaining insurance.

About half of all malpractice claims stem from litigation; the others result from aspects of office practice. Claims of alleged incompetence are more common than claims of dishonesty. More than two-thirds of the claims relate to deficiencies in legal knowledge or poor office administration; only about one in eight are related to intentional error. (Probably the most common allegation is that an attorney missed a deadline for legal action.)

It seems doubtful that the quality of lawyers' work has declined significantly in recent years; more likely, the increase in lawsuits reflects a heightened skepticism about that work and a greater willingness on the part of clients to seek redress when they feel that they have been badly served. In any case, the growth in claims is making lawyers more careful about their handling of cases and dealings with clients, and it may have at least a marginal effect in improving the quality of legal work.

Discipline   Clients or others who feel that a lawyer has acted unethically can complain to the agencies in each state that are responsible for disciplinary action against attorneys. Discipline is ultimately the responsibility of state supreme courts, but typically most of the disciplinary process is delegated to bar association committees or to lawyers' disciplinary groups established by the supreme court. In this process, a lawyer's conduct is assessed against standards adopted by the state supreme court; these standards are usually similar to those in the American Bar Association's Code of Professional Responsibility.

Most disciplinary proceedings begin with a complaint to the appropriate agency. The agency may set a complaint aside without further action or investigate it. After an investigation, it may file formal charges against the attorney and hold a hearing. Based on what it finds, the agency can then recommend disciplinary action, which may range from a private reprimand to permanent disbarment from legal practice in that state. The state's supreme court must make the final decision to impose disciplinary action.

The pattern of action by disciplinary agencies can be illustrated with data from Colorado in 1991. Colorado had about 15,100 active attorneys, 10,600 of them in private practice; a total of 1,219 "grievances" were filed against lawyers. The Office of Disciplinary Counsel determined that only 40 percent of the grievances that it considered merited full investigation. Ultimately, the supreme court suspended 35 lawyers from practice for some period and permanently disbarred 15 others.[139]

It is impossible to evaluate the disciplinary process on the basis of figures such as these. But that process has received a good deal of criticism, primarily on the grounds that too few complaints are given serious consideration and that the discipline applied to miscreant lawyers is too lenient. There is considerable support for this criticism: complaints often seem to be dismissed too readily, and sanctions for serious misconduct are not always heavy. As the example of Colorado indicates, however, many lawyers do receive severe sanctions. In 1989, according to one compilation, the states suspended 948 lawyers from practice for some period, and 572 were disbarred or resigned from the bar as a result of disciplinary proceedings. Frequently, these sanctions are for criminal activity unrelated to legal practice; the most common reason for state disciplinary action, however, is neglect of clients and client interests.[140]

In response to criticism, some states have made significant changes in their disciplinary systems. Among them is California; a monitor of the state's system who had reported in 1987 that it did not approach "a minimum level of acceptability" praised its "remarkable" improvement in 1991.[141] But not everyone is satisfied. In 1992, one lawyer surveyed some recent disciplinary cases and asked, "What does it take to get disbarred in California?"[142] The sampling of cases in Exhibit 3.6 provides a partial answer to his question.

CONCLUSIONS

This chapter offers only a first look at lawyers. Later discussions of their roles in specific areas of the court system, such as the criminal courts, provide a fuller picture of what lawyers do and how they fit into the judicial process.

Even this first look should make clear the importance of lawyers both in the legal system and in American society. Lawyers provide the means by which individuals and organizations use the law to their benefit; in practice, legal rights are meaningful only to the extent that people can call on lawyers to assert those rights. And through their individual work and their organizations, lawyers play key roles in shaping the law.

This chapter also shows differences among segments of society in the use of legal services. The most fundamental difference is between the great majority of individuals and large organizations. For the most part, these two

> In one matter, an attorney was hired to incorporate a business. Because of his handling of the matter, the incorporation was canceled, but he told his clients that the incorporation was still valid. In another matter, he misappropriated $19,000 of a client's money. Sanction: disbarment.
>
> In two matters, an attorney did not communicate with his clients, stopped representing them without acting to protect their interests, and did not perform competently. In one of these matters, he also failed to refund an advance fee. He had been disciplined in the past for similar misconduct. Sanction: suspension for nine months and until the attorney makes restitution, probation for the remainder of a two-year period.
>
> In three matters, an attorney failed to keep clients adequately informed, failed to perform competently, and withdrew without acting to safeguard the clients' interests. Sanction: public reproval, one year's probation, and remedial education.
>
> In one matter, an attorney failed to take actions needed to protect his client's legal claim and evaded the client's efforts to communicate with him. Sanction: private reproval, remedial education, and submission to binding arbitration in a malpractice action resulting from his misconduct.
>
> ---
>
> *Source:* Descriptions are paraphrased and summarized from descriptions in *California Lawyer*, 12 (July 1992), 79–80, and 13 (August 1992), 147, 158, 160.

EXHIBIT 3.6 Selected Disciplinary Cases Resulting in Sanctions Against California Attorneys, 1992

groups are represented by two different sectors of the bar, and the corporate sector that represents large organizations tends to serve its clients more fully than the personal sector.

The past few years have seen major changes in the legal profession. One key source of these changes is the growing number of lawyers; that number will continue to increase for many years, and it will help spur further alterations in the work and situation of lawyers. Yet, with all the changes that have come, much about the practice of law has remained remarkably stable; this stability reflects the deep roots of the ways that lawyers do their jobs. For this reason, most of the patterns described in this chapter are likely to endure well into the future.

FOR FURTHER READING

Abel, Richard L. *American Lawyers*. New York: Oxford University Press, 1989.

Galanter, Marc, and Thomas Palay. *Tournament of Lawyers: The Transformation of the Big Law Firm*. Chicago: University of Chicago Press, 1991.

Heinz, John P., and Edward O. Laumann. *Chicago Lawyers: The Social Structure of the Bar.* New York: Russell Sage Foundation, 1982.

Kritzer, Herbert M. *The Justice Broker: Lawyers and Ordinary Litigation.* New York: Oxford University Press, 1990.

Landon, Donald D. *Country Lawyers: The Impact of Context on Professional Practice.* New York: Praeger, 1990.

Nelson, Robert L. *Partners With Power: The Social Transformation of the Large Law Firm.* Berkeley: University of California Press, 1988.

Spangler, Eve. *Lawyers for Hire: Salaried Professionals at Work.* New Haven, Conn.: Yale University Press, 1986.

NOTES

1. Stephen P. Magee, "How Lawyers Sap the U.S. Economy," *Los Angeles Daily Journal,* February 29, 1991, p. 6.
2. "The Phony Lawyer Who Fooled 4 Judges," *San Francisco Chronicle,* May 27, 1988, p. A6.
3. American Bar Association, *A Review of Legal Education in the United States, Fall 1990* (Chicago: American Bar Association, 1991), pp. 75–82.
4. "1987 Bar Examination Statistics," *The Bar Examiner,* 57 (May 1988), 25–27.
5. "1987 Bar Examination Statistics," pp. 25–27.
6. James D. Gordon III, "How Not to Succeed in Law School," *Yale Law Journal,* 100 (April 1991), 1685 n. 3.
7. G. Andrew H. Benjamin, Alfred Kaszniak, Bruce Sales, and Stephen B. Shanfield, "The Role of Legal Education in Producing Psychological Distress Among Law Students and Lawyers," *American Bar Foundation Research Journal,* (Spring 1986), 225–252.
8. David Margolick, "Another Public Drama Puts Yale Alumni Out Front," *New York Times,* March 20, 1992, p. B9.
9. Michel Marriott, "Aid for Law Graduates Who Want to Aid the Poor," *New York Times,* December 13, 1991, p. B10.
10. Howard S. Erlanger and Douglas A. Klegon, "Socialization Effects of Professional School: The Law School Experience and Student Orientations to Public Interest Concerns," *Law and Society Review,* 13 (Fall 1978), 11–35; Robert V. Stover and Howard S. Erlanger, *Making It and Breaking It: The Fate of Public Interest Commitment During Law School* (Urbana: University of Illinois Press, 1989).
11. Sources of information for the discussion of licensing requirements include American Bar Association, *A Review of Legal Education in the United States, Fall 1990* (Chicago: American Bar Association, 1991); and American Bar Association, *Comprehensive Guide to Bar Admission Requirements 1991–1992* (Chicago: American Bar Association, 1991).
12. Information on the bar examination is taken primarily from "1991 Statistics," *The Bar Examiner,* 61 (May 1992), 21–36.
13. "1991 Statistics," pp. 23–24.
14. Jay Mathews, "California's Bar Exam Breaks More Lawyers Than It Makes," *Washington Post,* August 2, 1983, p. A2.
15. David Margolick, "At the Bar," *New York Times,* September 13, 1991, p. B9.
16. Joan M. Cheever, "A Scream and a Curse Open the Bar Exam," *National Law Journal,* August 7, 1989, p. 8.
17. "Ohio Supreme Court OKs Bar Exam Changes to End Variations in Grading," *Columbus Dispatch,* December 13, 1990, p. 7D; Catherine Candisky and Robert Ruth, "Grades on 9 Bar Exams Altered," *Columbus Dispatch,* May 8, 1991, pp. 1A, 2A.

18. American Bar Association, *Review of Legal Education 1990,* p. 66; Richard H. Sander and E. Douglass Williams, "Why Are There So Many Lawyers? Perspectives on a Turbulent Market," *Law and Social Inquiry,* 14 (Summer 1989), 463.
19. Sander and Williams, "Why Are There So Many Lawyers?"
20. Ken Myers, "Surprise! The Employment News Isn't as Bad as Had Been Feared," *National Law Journal,* September 14, 1992, p. 4.
21. Fred Strasser and Bryan Greenwald, "Lawyers Reject Bush for Clinton," *National Law Journal,* August 10, 1992, p. S4.
22. Magee, "How Lawyers Sap the U.S. Economy," p. 6.
23. Mark Hansen, "Quayle Raps Lawyers," *American Bar Association Journal,* 77 (October 1991), p. 36; Ray August, "The Mythical Kingdom of Lawyers," *American Bar Association Journal,* 78 (September 1992), pp. 72–74. For other views on this issue, see Marc Galanter, "Pick a Number, Any Number," *Legal Times,* February 17, 1992, pp. 26–28; Christopher Ocasal, "How to Count Japan's Lawyers," *Legal Times,* April 6, 1992, pp. 22, 25; and "The Legal Profession," *The Economist,* July 18, 1992, pp. 3–18.
24. Cynthia Fuchs Epstein, *Women in Law* (New York: Basic Books, 1981), p. 4; Robert Benenson, *Editorial Research Reports: Lawyers in America* (Washington, D.C.: Congressional Quarterly, 1984), p. 535.
25. Epstein, *Women in Law,* p. 51.
26. American Bar Association, *Review of Legal Education 1990,* pp. 66, 68.
27. Richard L. Abel, *American Lawyers* (New York: Oxford University Press, 1989), pp. 87–90.
28. See Martin Mayer, *The Lawyers* (New York: Harper & Row, 1967), p. 29.
29. Stewart Macauley, "Lawyers and Consumer Protection Laws," *Law and Society Review,* 14 (Fall 1979), 155.
30. Except where noted, all figures on the distribution of lawyers are taken from Barbara A. Curran, *Supplement to the Lawyer Statistical Report: The U.S. Legal Profession in 1985* (Chicago: American Bar Association, 1986).
31. Bette H. Sikes, Clara N. Carson, and Patricia Gorai, eds., *The 1971 Lawyer Statistical Report* (Chicago: American Bar Foundation, 1972), p. 10.
32. Sander and Williams, "Why Are There So Many Lawyers?", pp. 447–451, 474–475.
33. Donald D. Landon, *Country Lawyers: The Impact of Context on Professional Practice* (New York: Praeger, 1990), p. 24; John P. Heinz and Edward O. Laumann, *Chicago Lawyers: The Social Structure of the Bar* (New York: Russell Sage Foundation, 1982), p. 65.
34. Curran, *Supplement to Lawyer Statistical Report,* p. 4; Barbara A. Curran, "American Lawyers in the 1980s: A Profession in Transition," *Law and Society Review,* 20 (1986), 28. See also Marc Galanter and Thomas Palay, *Tournament of Lawyers: The Transformation of the Big Law Firm* (Chicago: University of Chicago Press, 1991), p. 123.
35. "Who Represents Corporate America," *National Law Journal,* June 1, 1992, pp. S2, S4, S6.
36. "The NLJ 250," *National Law Journal,* September 28, 1992, pp. S5–S7.
37. Jeff Lyon, "Chicago Law," *Chicago Tribune Magazine,* June 9, 1991, p. 16.
38. Lawrence Lederman, *Tombstones: A Lawyer's Tales from the Takeover Decades* (New York: Farrar, Straus and Giroux, 1992), p. 36.
39. See Michael H. Trotter, "How Firms Trapped Themselves," *National Law Journal,* November 16, 1992, pp. 13–14.
40. Gordon, "How Not to Succeed in Law School," p. 1702.
41. Ruth Marcus, "Gloom at the Top: Why Young Lawyers Bail Out," *Washington Post,* May 31, 1987, p. C1.
42. Edward A. Adams, "Becoming Partner: The Impossible Dream," *National Law Journal,* June 22, 1992, p. 2. The figure was obtained from a survey by the *New York Law Journal.*

43. Marcia Chambers, "Partnership: Court Gives Inside Look," *National Law Journal*, January 28, 1991, pp. 13–14.
44. Robert L. Nelson, *Partners with Power: The Social Transformation of the Large Law Firm* (Berkeley: University of California Press, 1988), pp. 69–70.
45. "Billing," *National Law Journal*, November 23, 1992, pp. S6–S8.
46. Morton Mintz, "Griffin Bell Set Hourly Fee at $1,711," *Washington Post*, January 30, 1987, pp. F1, F2.
47. This discussion is based in part on Galanter and Palay, *Tournament of Lawyers*, and Nelson, *Partners with Power*.
48. Rita Henley Jensen, "Branching Fever Still Runs High," *National Law Journal*, October 21, 1991, p. 34.
49. David Margolick, "At the Bar," *New York Times*, June 29, 1990, p. B9.
50. This discussion is based in part on Eve Spangler, *Lawyers for Hire: Salaried Professionals at Work* (New Haven, Conn.: Yale University Press, 1986), ch. 3.
51. "The 50 Largest Corporate Legal Shops," *Of Counsel*, June 15, 1992, pp. 8–9.
52. James S. Wilber, "Support Staffing Ratios Remain High In-House in Spite of Automation," *National Law Journal*, May 20, 1991, p. S6.
53. Spangler, *Lawyers for Hire*, p. 71.
54. From table in *National Law Journal*, November 5, 1990, p. S8.
55. Jeffrey S. Slovak, "Working for Corporate Actors: Social Change and Elite Attorneys in Chicago," *American Bar Foundation Research Journal*, Summer 1979, p. 483.
56. Jonathan P. Bellis and Rees W. Morrison, "Inside, Looking Out," *National Law Journal*, December 2, 1991, pp. S1, S2, S4. This article reports a 1991 Law Department Spending Survey by Price Waterhouse.
57. Figures on federal government lawyers are taken from Marianne Lavelle, "The U.S. Lawyer Corps," *National Law Journal*, October 31, 1988, p. 40.
58. This discussion is based in part on Spangler, *Lawyers for Hire*, ch. 4.
59. Rosalind Resnick, "Associates Jump Ship, Go Public," *National Law Journal*, August 5, 1991, p. 1.
60. Stephen Labaton, " 'Mr Enforcement' for the Defense . . . ," *New York Times*, March 8, 1992, sec. 3, p. 11.
61. David Margolick, "At the Bar," *New York Times*, September 9, 1988, p. B5.
62. Heinz and Laumann, *Chicago Lawyers*, p. 53.
63. Heinz and Laumann, *Chicago Lawyers*, p. 54; Landon, *Country Lawyers*, p. 129.
64. Neil A. Lewis, "Washington's 2 Law Worlds Clash in Barry Case," *New York Times*, January 26, 1990, p. B11.
65. Heinz and Laumann, *Chicago Lawyers*, p. 319. This discussion of the "two hemispheres" is based primarily on Heinz and Laumann.
66. Sander and Williams, "Why Are There So Many Lawyers?", 474–475.
67. Murray Schwartz, quoted in Francis J. Flaherty, "The Myth—and Reality—of the Law," *National Law Journal*, August 6, 1984, p. 43.
68. Ibid., p. 45. In this passage, John Heinz was quoting a 1968 federal commission report on race relations in the United States.
69. This discussion is based in part on Hedvah L. Schuchman et al., *Self Regulation in the Professions: Law* (Glastonbury, Conn.: The Futures Group, 1981).
70. The membership figure is taken from Deborah M. Burek, ed., *Encyclopedia of Associations*, 27th ed. (Detroit: Gale Research, 1993), I, 633.
71. Margaret Cronin Fisk, "Lawyers Give Thumbs Up," *National Law Journal*, May 28, 1990, p. S2.
72. See ibid.; and American Bar Association, *The Report of "At the Breaking Point"* (Chicago: American Bar Association, 1991).
73. Sander and Williams, "Why Are There So Many Lawyers?", 467–468.
74. American Bar Association, *"At the Breaking Point,"* p. 3.

75. Ibid., p. 4.
76. "Depressing News," *California Lawyer,* February 1992, p. 93.
77. Abel, *American Lawyers,* p. 129.
78. *Gideon v. Wainwright,* 372 U.S. 335 (1963).
79. Bureau of Justice Statistics, *Justice Expenditure and Employment, 1990* (Washington, D.C.: U.S. Department of Justice, 1992), p. 3. Information on defense systems was drawn from Norman Lefstein, *Criminal Defense Services for the Poor* (Chicago: American Bar Association, 1982); and Bureau of Justice Statistics, *Criminal Defense for the Poor, 1986* (Washington, D.C.: U.S. Department of Justice, 1988).
80. Roger A. Hanson, Brian J. Ostrom, William E. Hewitt, and Christopher Lomvardias, *Indigent Defenders Get the Job Done and Done Well* (Williamsburg, Va.: National Center for State Courts, 1992), p. 14.
81. Caryle Murphy and Patricia Davis, "Low Fees Cut Legal Services for the Poor," *Washington Post,* March 30, 1987, p. A1; Resnick, "Associates Jump Ship," p. 10.
82. David Margolick, "Volunteers or Not, Tennessee Lawyers Help Poor," *New York Times,* January 17, 1992, p. B10; Peter Applebome, "Study Faults Atlanta's System of Defending Poor," *New York Times,* November 30, 1990, p. B12.
83. Marcia Coyle, Fred Strasser, and Marianne Lavelle, "Fatal Defense: Trial and Error in the Nation's Death Belt," *National Law Journal,* June 1, 1990, pp. 30–44.
84. Claudia MacLachlan, "Funds Stop, Criminal Lawyers Quit," *National Law Journal,* July 20, 1992, p. 7; Randall Edwards, "Court-Appointed Attorneys to Get Paid for Back Work," *Columbus Dispatch,* July 23, 1992, p. 2C.
85. See Roy B. Flemming, "If you Pay the Piper, Do You Call the Tune? Public Defenders in America's Criminal Courts," *Law and Social Inquiry,* 14 (Spring 1989), 393–414; and Hanson et al., *Indigent Defenders.*
86. Hanson et al., *Indigent Defenders.*
87. See Emery A. Brownell, *Legal Aid in the United States—Supplement* (Rochester, N.Y.: Lawyers Co-Operative Publishing, 1961).
88. Legal Aid Society of Columbus, *1991 Annual Report* (Columbus, Ohio: duplicated, 1992), p. 4.
89. Bill Clinton, "Judiciary Suffers Racial, Sexual Lack of Balance," *National Law Journal,* November 2, 1992, p. 16.
90. Kevin Sack, "Judge Pushes Lawyers to Give Services to Poor," *New York Times,* May 2, 1990, p. A13.
91. Saundra Torry, "D.C. Lawyers Lag in Work for Poor," *Washington Post,* October 1, 1990, pp. D1, D5.
92. *Bates v. State Bar,* 433 U.S. 350 (1977).
93. Rosalind Resnick, "State Tries to Rein in Legal Ads," *National Law Journal,* January 21, 1991, pp. 1, 22. The decision was *Peel v. Attorney Registration and Disciplinary Commission,* 496 U.S. 91 (1990).
94. Paul Reidinger, "Lawpoll: More Lawyers Now Advertise Their Practice," *American Bar Association Journal,* 73 (November 1, 1987), 25.
95. Gail Diane Cox, "Battle on Legal Ads Comes Down to Class," *National Law Journal,* August 10, 1992, p. 1; Saundra Torry, "Selling Legal Services Amid the Soap and Dog Food Commercials," *Washington Post,* July 27, 1992 (Washington Business section), p. 5.
96. Cox, "Battle on Legal Ads," p. 44.
97. William E. Hornsby, Jr., and Charles Dainoff, "Let the Yellow Pages Do Your Talking," *The Compleat Lawyer,* Spring 1992, p. 29.
98. Fred Setterberg, "Creating an Image," *California Bar Journal,* August 1989, pp. 44–45, 49–51.

99. Anne Swardson, "Lawyers' Unsubtle Solicitation," *Washington Post,* May 27, 1988, pp. A1, A14.

100. Deborah R. Hensler et al., *Compensation for Accidental Injuries in the United States* (Santa Monica, Calif.: Rand Corporation, 1991), p. 134.

101. *Goldfarb v. State Bar,* 421 U.S. 773 (1975).

102. Lori Andrews, *Birth of a Salesman: Lawyer Advertising and Solicitation* (Chicago, ABA Press, 1980), p. 13.

103. "The NLJ 250: Annual Survey of the Nation's Largest Law Firms," *National Law Journal,* September 30, 1991, pp. S16–S17.

104. This figure and those that follow are from Special Committee on Delivery of Legal Services, *Report on the Survey of Legal Clinics and Advertising Law Firms* (Chicago: American Bar Association, 1990), p. 64.

105. *Ibid.,* p. 134.

106. *Ibid.,* p. v.

107. This discussion of legal insurance is based in part on William A. Bolger, Sandra De Ment, and Joanne F. Pozzo, eds., *Group Legal Service Plans: Organization, Operation and Management* (New York: Harcourt Brace Jovanovich, 1981); and Roger Billings, "Legal Services," in *Encyclopedia of the American Judicial System,* ed. Robert J. Janosik (New York: Charles Scribner's Sons, 1987), pp. 645–652.

108. Saundra Torry, "Joining the Ranks of the Prepaid Services Attorneys," *Washington Post,* January 27, 1992 (Washington Business section), p. 5.

109. One source for the discussion of the contingent fee is Patricia Munch Danzon, *Contingent Fees for Personal Injury Litigation* (Santa Monica, Calif.: Rand Corporation, 1980).

110. Herbert M. Kritzer, *The Justice Broker: Lawyers and Ordinary Litigation* (New York: Oxford University Press, 1990), p. 151.

111. Walter K. Olson, *The Litigation Explosion: What Happened When America Unleashed the Lawsuit* (New York: Truman Talley, 1991), pp. 32–50.

112. Warren Weaver, "The Legal Profession Takes a Look at Itself," *New York Times,* February 10, 1974, sec. 4, p. 9.

113. Barbara C. Curran, *The Legal Needs of the Public: The Final Report of a National Survey* (Chicago: American Bar Foundation, 1977), pp. 152–157; "Project: An Assessment of Alternative Strategies for Increasing Access to Legal Services," *Yale Law Journal,* 90 (1980), 140–141; Bruce Campbell and Susette Talarico, "Access to Legal Services: Examining Common Assumptions," *Judicature,* 66 (February 1983), 313–318.

114. Mary Jordan, "Smith Trial Mobilizes Armies of Legal Support," *Washington Post,* October 22, 1991, p. A5.

115. "Lawyer's True Colors—Green," *Chicago Tribune,* March 4, 1991, sec. 1, p. 12. The quotation was originally in the *Washingtonian* magazine.

116. Aric Press, "The Highest Legal Fees," *Newsweek,* August 24, 1981, p. 71.

117. David Margolick, "At the Bar," *New York Times,* March 20, 1992, p. B9.

118. Jeff Gerth, "U.S. Said to Squander Millions for Legal Work on the Bailout," *New York Times,* November 16, 1991, pp. 1, 30; Sherry R. Sontag, "Congress Challenges the FDIC," *National Law Journal,* December 9, 1991, pp. 3, 35.

119. Macauley, "Lawyers and Consumer Protection Laws," 152.

120. Abel, *American Lawyers,* pp. 151–152.

121. Laurence Meyer, "Conference to Weigh Lawyer Competency," *Washington Post,* May 21, 1979, p. C1.

122. "The View from the Bench," *National Law Journal,* August 10, 1987, p. S6.

123. "State-by-State Update: 39 Now Require CLE, 4 States Propose Rules," *National Law Journal,* June 8, 1992, pp. 31–32.

124. *Peel v. Attorney Registration and Disciplinary Commission.*

125. American Bar Association, *Model Code of Professional Responsibility and Code of Judicial Conduct* (Chicago: American Bar Association, 1982), pp. 32, 24.
126. See *Nix v. Whiteside*, 475 U.S. 157 (1986).
127. Dennis Hevesi, "8 at Law Firm Accused of Bribing Witnesses and Faking Evidence," *New York Times*, January 12, 1990, p. 28.
128. Edward A. Adams, "Lawyer's Flight Investigated," *National Law Journal*, February 4, 1991, p. 10; Ed Bruske, "Hard-Driving Md. Lawyer Drives Himself Into Disgrace," *Washington Post*, January 24, 1990, pp. B1, B5.
129. Lisa G. Lerman, "Lying to Clients," *University of Pennsylvania Law Review*, 138 (January 1990), 705–720. The quotation is from p. 705.
130. Heinz and Laumann, *Chicago Lawyers*, pp. 353–373.
131. Ibid., p. 70.
132. See Austin Sarat and William L. F. Felstiner, "Law and Strategy in the Divorce Lawyer's Office," *Law and Society Review*, 20 (1986), 93–134.
133. New York City Department of Consumer Affairs, *Women in Divorce: Lawyers, Ethics, Fees and Fairness* (New York: Department of Consumer Affairs, 1992), p. 23.
134. Lawrence Dubin and Donald Jolliffe, "Recent Discharge Cases Focus New Attention on Counsel as Employee," *National Law Journal*, May 20, 1991, pp. S2, S4, S19.
135. Stephen Labaton, "Lawyers Agree to Pay Big Fine in S. & L. Case," *New York Times*, March 9, 1992, pp. A1, C5.
136. Heinz and Laumann, *Chicago Lawyers*, pp. 372–373.
137. Kritzer, *The Justice Broker*, p. 167.
138. Data on malpractice claims in this and the following paragraph are taken from William Gates, "Charting the Shoals of Malpractice," *American Bar Association Journal*, 73 (July 1, 1987), 62–65; and Ronald E. Mallen, "Malpractice at a Glance," *California Lawyer*, 5 (July 1985), 34–35.
139. "1991 Annual Report of the Colorado Supreme Court Grievance Committee," *Colorado Lawyer*, 21 (May 1992), 891–896. The cases in which action was taken at various stages in 1991, of course, were not exactly the same as those filed in that year. Some lawyers may have agreed to suspensions or disbarments that did not have to be imposed by the supreme court.
140. American Bar Association, *Statistical Report: Sanctions Imposed in Public Discipline of Lawyers 1985–1989* (Chicago: American Bar Association, 1990); and *Statistical Report . . . 1986–1990* (Chicago: American Bar Association, 1992).
141. David O. Weber, " 'Still in Good Standing': The Crisis in Attorney Discipline," *American Bar Association Journal*, 73 (November 1, 1987), 59; " 'Remarkable' Improvement Cited in Bar's Disciplinary System," *California Lawyer*, 11 (November 1991), 78.
142. Matthew J. Nasuti, "What Does It Take?" (letter), *California Lawyer*, 12 (February 1992), 10.

4

The Selection of Judges

J udges are at the center of the judicial process. In the cases that come to court, judges preside over proceedings and make decisions. Indirectly, their decisions also influence the outcomes of disputes and situations that never get to court. This chapter deals with the processes by which these important figures are selected, and the next chapter examines their characteristics and their behavior as judges.

The judicial selection process merits close consideration for several reasons. How judges are chosen helps determine what kinds of people become judges and what they do as judges. In addition, analysis of judicial selection reveals some important realities about the courts, the larger political system, and the relationship between the two.

The selection of judges has been a matter of debate throughout our history as a nation. That debate has focused chiefly on formal rules for judicial selection because of a widespread belief that formal rules have great impact on the results of the selection process. In reality, as I show, differences among the various formal systems used in the United States have more limited effects than many people think. Perhaps their most important similarity is that each formal system provides considerable room for the influence of other political institutions, including political parties and the other branches of government. Indeed, the selection of judges is the point at which courts are shaped most directly by their political environments.

GENERAL ISSUES IN JUDICIAL SELECTION

Debates about methods for selecting judges are largely debates over goals for the courts and how to achieve them. In these debates, two questions have been dominant.[1] The first is whether to give priority to judicial independence or to political accountability. Many people argue that judges should be selected in a way that maximizes their freedom from control so that they can apply the law as they see it. But others contend that judges are important policy makers and thus must be accountable to the people they serve, either directly or through the other branches of government.

The second question is how to obtain the most competent judges. Lawyers and judges differ about which selection system produces the best judges; these differences stem in part from disagreement over the kind of competence that is desirable. Some people seek only legal competence, a mastery of the law and legal procedures; others, however, see a broader understanding of politics and government policy making as important for judges.

The United States stands out from most other democratic nations in its emphasis on accountability in the selection process and its relatively limited emphasis on legal competence. In continental Europe, for instance, judges typically enter a professional corps that resembles a civil service system after receiving special training as judges. In this country, in contrast, the general public and elected officials play the central roles in putting judges on the bench and determining whether they stay there. And American judges attain office through a highly unstructured process, one in which no specialized training or experience in lower courts is required.

Within this general pattern, there is considerable variation in the formal rules of selection. The federal and state governments use several distinct selection systems, which differ not only in the goals they emphasize but also in the ways they are designed to achieve these goals.

There is a strong historical element to the mix of judicial selection systems in the United States. Different systems have enjoyed popularity in different periods, reflecting changes in people's views about goals and the best means to achieve them.[2] Until the 1840s the federal government and most states gave power over judicial selection to the other branches of government— either the chief executive or the legislature, or both. This approach reflected a desire to minimize direct popular control over the judiciary. And the federal government and most states gave judges lifetime terms in order to maximize their independence.

In the nineteenth century a growing movement for popular control over government led to the use of partisan elections of judges who would serve for terms of limited length.[3] In the 1840s and for several decades after, most new states and many existing states adopted this system.

By the late nineteenth century, however, the political parties had come into some disfavor. Because party leaders exercised so much power, many people came to see parties as barriers to popular control of government rather than as means to achieve it. Accordingly, nonpartisan elections gained support as a means of selecting public officials. The movement for nonpartisan elections had perhaps its greatest success in the judiciary; in the half century that began in the 1880s most new states and several existing ones chose this system.

Early in this century prominent lawyers, such as former president William Howard Taft, expressed dissatisfaction with all the existing methods of judicial selection, arguing that they provided for too little judicial independence and gave insufficient weight to legal competence. This feeling was reflected in the reform agenda of the American Judicature Society (AJS), founded in 1913; its leaders sought a new method of judicial selection, along with unification of state court systems. The AJS helped devise a complex system in which a state governor would choose a new judge from a list of nominees provided by an independent commission, with the voters later having the chance to approve or disapprove the governor's choice.

Supporters of this new system had their first success when Missouri adopted it for some of its courts in 1940. Other states followed, at first slowly and then more rapidly. Since 1950 nearly every state changing its system for selecting judges has adopted some variant of this system. Because of its history, it is often called the *Missouri Plan,* although its supporters prefer the term *merit selection.*

Today the Missouri Plan remains the primary focus of debates over formal methods of judicial selection. Supporters seek its adoption by individual states and, in a modified form, by the federal government. Although they continue to enjoy considerable success, they suffer defeats as well. In the late 1980s Connecticut and New Mexico voters approved modified versions of the Missouri Plan, but Rhode Island and Ohio voters rejected it—in Ohio, by a 2–1 margin.

Debates over alternative selection systems reflect not only disagreement about the intrinsic merits of those systems but calculations about political advantage as well. In the early 1970s, the Tennessee legislature abolished a modified Missouri Plan for its appellate courts because its Democratic majority wanted to take selection power from the Republican governor. The Democrats' primary concern was not with the courts themselves but with the patronage dispensed by the state building commission; in Tennessee the supreme court selects the attorney general, who sits on the building commission, and Democratic legislators wanted to have a Democratic attorney general to maintain their majority on the commission.[4]

Debates over formal systems of judicial selection have also reached the federal level, and in 1977 President Jimmy Carter incorporated part of the Missouri Plan into his procedure for selecting lower-court judges. But there has never been a sufficient consensus to change the constitutional procedures for selecting federal judges, and these procedures continue to reflect the views about judicial selection that predominated two centuries ago.

THE SELECTION OF FEDERAL JUDGES

The formal rules for selection of federal judges are fairly simple. All judges are nominated by the president and confirmed by the Senate, with a simple majority of senators present required for confirmation. When the Senate is out of session, the president can sometimes make a *recess appointment,* under which a nominee takes the bench immediately, to be confirmed after the Senate returns. With the exception of the specialized courts established under Article I of the Constitution, such as the Tax Court and the Claims Court, judges hold their positions for life. This means that vacancies on federal courts occur at irregular intervals: when a sitting judge resigns, retires, or dies—or, occasionally, when new judgeships are created.

The actual selection process is considerably more complicated than the formal rules suggest. It also differs a good deal among the three major sets of federal courts.

The Supreme Court

Most people see the Supreme Court as unique among courts in its importance. This perception makes the selection of Supreme Court justices unique as well, both in the way that justices are chosen and in the mix of criteria used to choose them.

The Nomination Process   Every president must select hundreds of federal officials, but presidents make the great majority of these appointments in name only. A few appointments are deemed too important to delegate to subordinates, and foremost among these are positions on the Supreme Court. Thus, when a vacancy occurs on the Court, the president usually plays a very active role in filling it. One reflection of this role is the common practice of having a president meet personally with one or more potential nominees before making a final choice.

Presidents do not act alone. They usually get considerable assistance from Justice Department officials and from members of their own staffs to help in identifying and investigating candidates and in choosing among them. In choosing Clarence Thomas in 1991, for instance, President Bush worked with the attorney general, the chief of the White House staff, and his White House counsel.

The extent to which the president relies on others in selecting justices varies with the president's general style and interest in the Court. Ronald Reagan gave his subordinates a larger role in the selection process than did Bush; Bill Clinton, a lawyer with a strong interest in the courts, probably will delegate even less responsibility to his staff and to the Justice Department.

A variety of individuals and groups outside the executive branch seek to influence the president's choice. One important group is the American Bar Association, which has created a committee to rate candidates for federal judgeships. Recent presidents have given the ABA committee no advance word on potential nominees, so it cannot affect the nomination process directly. Still, the prospect of ABA scrutiny sometimes affects the selection of nominees.

Among other interest groups, those that are close to the administration may participate privately in the nomination process; if not, their positions will be taken into account as nominees are considered. In the Clinton administration, for instance, civil rights groups undoubtedly will have an impact on any nominations to the Supreme Court. Groups that lack ties to the administration sometimes seek to exert pressure through the mass media—by indicating, for instance, that they will fight against Senate confirmation of a particular candidate if that candidate is nominated. Presidents would prefer to minimize such pressure; for this reason, Bush chose both David Souter and Clarence

Thomas within four days after their predecessors announced they were retiring.

Other participants in the nominating process can include sitting members of the Court and people who would like to be nominated themselves. Sitting justices sometimes play an important role by identifying and endorsing candidates for the Court. To take one example, President Nixon might not have nominated Harry Blackmun in 1970 if Chief Justice Warren Burger had not suggested that the president consider Blackmun.

Aspiring justices occasionally take direct action to secure Supreme Court nominations; Burger's successful campaign for a Nixon nomination as chief justice reportedly included a promise to retire in time for Nixon to name a successor.[5] More often people campaign indirectly, through decisions and public statements that they hope will appeal to presidents. And in 1981 Robert Bork accepted a judgeship on a federal court of appeals because Reagan administration officials told him that doing so would make him a strong candidate for the Supreme Court.[6]

Criteria for Nominations   Presidential nominations to the Supreme Court can be based on many different criteria. The most important of them fall into four categories.

The first includes what might be called the qualifications of prospective nominees: their *competence* and *ethical standards*. A nominee who falls short on either criterion may fail to gain Senate confirmation, and an unqualified candidate who does get confirmed but serves poorly on the Court may embarrass the appointing president. As a result, relatively few nominees are susceptible to attack on either ground. Indeed, most rate very high for their legal competence, and some (for example, Oliver Wendell Holmes and Benjamin Cardozo) have brought truly distinguished records to the Court. It is unusual, though not unknown, for presidents to name nominees whose competence or ethical standards are known to be questionable.

The second category concerns the attitudes of the nominee toward issues with which the Court deals—that is, the nominee's *policy preferences*. Because Supreme Court decisions are so important, presidents seek appointees who share presidential views about policy. A liberal president, for example, will want to select justices who take liberal positions on most issues. As a result, administration officials usually scrutinize the views of potential nominees with considerable care. All the Reagan and Bush nominees were lower-court judges, primarily because their votes and written opinions as judges helped in predicting their behavior on the Court.

A president is not guaranteed that a justice will actually behave as expected. The liberalism of Earl Warren and William Brennan was a source of great disappointment to President Eisenhower, who had selected them. But such unexpected developments are the exception rather than the rule. More typical is the record of the five Reagan and Bush justices, chosen in the hope that they would take conservative positions on the Court. To varying degrees, all five of these justices *have* taken primarily conservative positions, though their votes and opinions have not always pleased the presidents who nominated them.

The third category of criteria might be labeled *reward*. Nominations often go to personal and political associates of the president; in fact, more than half of those nominated to the Court have known the president personally.[7] Frequently, a nominee is a personal acquaintance who has also been a political ally. Former Justice Byron White, a long-time friend of President Kennedy, had worked in the 1960 Kennedy campaign for president and then served in the Justice Department. More broadly, 90 percent of all nominees have come from the president's party;[8] one reason is the belief that such important prizes should be awarded to people within the party.

The final category is *pursuit of political support*. Some nominations are used to appeal to important interest or demographic groups. Most often a president tries to appeal to voters in a large demographic group by selecting a member of that group. Thus President Reagan chose Sandra Day O'Connor in 1981 partly in order to strengthen his support among women. President Bush's selection of Clarence Thomas in 1991 was intended to appeal to black voters, particularly because Thomas would replace the Court's only black justice, Thurgood Marshall. When presidents cross party lines to choose nominees, they often do so to gain a political benefit; in 1971, for instance, President Nixon chose Democrat Lewis Powell of Virginia largely because Nixon wanted to strengthen his support in the South, and Powell was likely to win easy confirmation.

Presidents differ in the weight they give to particular criteria, but in recent administrations policy preferences have had the highest priority. This was true of Reagan and Bush, who emphasized finding strong conservatives. Although their selections often served other goals very well, those goals were clearly secondary. President Clinton is likely to give equal emphasis to the goal of choosing liberals for the Court.

The preeminence of this goal reflects the growing recognition that the Supreme Court plays a significant role in national policy making. More directly, it also reflects the current salience of Supreme Court policies to people whose support is important to presidents. George Bush's effort to appoint strong conservatives to the Court was in part a response to conservative groups in the Republican party, for which some issues before the Court, especially abortion, were critical. Likewise, the nomination of strongly liberal justices will be one way for Bill Clinton to keep the support of the Democratic groups that care greatly about issues such as abortion and civil rights.

Senate Confirmation   The Senate confirms the great majority of the nominees that it considers—twenty-two out of twenty-six since 1949—and usually with just a few negative votes or none at all. Yet confirmation is never automatic, and in recent years the Senate has consistently given nominations a close collective scrutiny. The most public form of this scrutiny is the public hearings held by the Judiciary Committee, in which nominees are questioned at length and other witnesses are heard.

The combination of a high rate of success and close scrutiny of nominees reflects some basic realities about the confirmation process. Senators generally begin with a presumption in favor of confirmation. Although that presumption usually holds up, it can be overcome under the right circumstances—or, from a nominee's perspective, the wrong ones.

Several circumstances can weaken a nominee's position.[9] One is strong and widespread opposition to the views of the nominee on legal issues, particularly if interest groups sharing that opposition mobilize against a nominee. Liberal senators and interest groups sought to defeat some Reagan and Bush nominees who seemed to have strongly conservative views on civil liberties issues—particularly Robert Bork in 1987 and Clarence Thomas in 1991. Conservative groups can be expected to respond in the same way if Clinton nominates people with records of highly liberal positions.

Another unfavorable circumstance is a credible challenge to the competence or ethical behavior of a nominee. Nixon nominee G. Harrold Carswell was defeated in 1970 after opponents mustered evidence of his limited legal skills. Reagan choice Douglas Ginsburg withdrew in 1987 before his formal nomination because disclosures about his use of marijuana made confirmation unlikely. Evidence of ethical weaknesses is important in swaying moderate senators who would not oppose a nominee on ideological grounds alone.

Several situational factors also play a part in confirmation decisions. Inevitably, these decisions are affected by the partisan makeup of the Senate; nominees of a president whose party controls the Senate are in a relatively good position. Nominations may be more vulnerable near the end of a president's term or if the seat in question is seen as especially important. Presidents generally become weaker politically as their terms progress, and senators from the other party may want to keep a seat open in case their own party wins the next election. When the Supreme Court is closely divided between liberal and conservative justices, as it was in the late 1980s, contention over nominees tends to increase.

In the current era, nominees generally win confirmation by wide margins unless both widespread opposition to their views and questions about their competence or ethics are present. To take one example, liberal Democrats in the Senate were quite unhappy with what they perceived as Clarence Thomas's extreme conservatism, but Thomas still would have been confirmed easily had doubts not arisen about his competence and character. The exception to this rule was Robert Bork, defeated for confirmation despite his very high level of legal skills and the absence of serious concerns about his personal behavior. Exhibit 4.1 describes these two confirmation decisions, along with the others since 1987.

The Lower Courts

The district courts and the courts of appeals differ from the Supreme Court in their geographical decentralization, and individual judgeships on these lower courts are less important. For both reasons, the process and criteria for selection have differed from those for the Supreme Court.

Robert Bork, 1987. President Reagan nominated Bork to succeed retiring Justice Lewis Powell. Bork's record as a major legal scholar and federal judge indicated that he was a strong conservative, and liberal senators and interest groups feared that he would shift a closely divided Court to the right. A strong campaign against Bork in the Senate and the country at large gained strength from Bork's testimony before the Senate Judiciary Committee, which increased concerns about his policy views. Bork was defeated by a 42–58 vote, with all but eight senators voting along party lines; Democratic control of the Senate and Reagan's weakened position were key to his defeat.

Anthony Kennedy, 1988. After Bork's defeat, the nomination of Douglas Ginsburg was withdrawn because of questions about his personal conduct. Kennedy, a court of appeals judge, was then nominated. He was known as a conservative but did not have the extensive record of strongly conservative views that had caused difficulty for Bork. The contrast helped Kennedy, who was confirmed by a 97–0 vote.

David Souter, 1990. President Bush chose Souter, recently selected as a federal judge, to succeed retiring liberal Justice William Brennan. Liberals reacted to Souter's nomination with some concern because of its potential impact on the Court's policies. But Souter had very little record of positions on public issues, making him difficult to attack. His Senate testimony disclosed little further information about his views and gave some observers an impression of moderation. Souter was confirmed by a 90–9 vote.

Clarence Thomas, 1991. After the retirement of Thurgood Marshall, the Court's one remaining strong liberal, President Bush nominated Thomas, a federal judge with a highly conservative record. Opposition to Thomas built slowly; some liberals thought that even his defeat would not prevent a conservative majority on the Court, while others thought that continued African American representation on the Court was desirable (Thomas is African American, as was Marshall). But Thomas's Senate testimony, in which he disavowed some past statements of views, raised doubts about his legal skills and personal credibility. Allegations that he had engaged in sexual harassment of a former assistant produced a new set of hearings, which ultimately changed few senators' positions; Thomas was confirmed by a 52–48 vote.

Sources: Various press reports and books.

EXHIBIT 4.1 Senate Action on Supreme Court Nominations, 1987–1991

The Nomination Process   The large number of vacancies on the lower courts makes it impractical for a president to participate regularly in the selection of their judges. The president usually sets down general guidelines for subordinates to follow and intervenes only in a few specific cases.

Most administrations have given the task of selecting judges chiefly to officials in the Justice Department. The Reagan and Bush administrations involved the White House more directly in the process, reflecting the importance of judicial appointments to those presidents.

In making their choices, the officials who act on behalf of the president are subject to a variety of pressures and constraints. The most important is the practice of senatorial courtesy. Under this practice, when a presidential nomination to a federal position within a state requires Senate confirmation, the Senate as a whole gives some deference to the wishes of the senators from that state—very strong deference to a home-state senator of the president's party, who is accorded something of a veto power.

The existence of senatorial courtesy provides home-state senators of the president's party with leverage that they can use to intervene in the original nomination process, since they hold so much power over the subsequent confirmation. Indeed, such senators often seek to dictate a nomination by submitting a name to the administration. But such names may be rejected if administration officials have strong reasons to disapprove of a senator's choice. If senatorial courtesy grants certain senators veto power over nominations, the president's ultimate power to choose a nominee gives administration officials a veto power as well.

A home-state senator who is not of the president's party usually has limited influence. If a state's two senators are from different parties, the senator from the president's party can monopolize influence over nominations. In some instances, that senator agrees to share some power; during the Bush administration, for instance, New York Republican Alfonse D'Amato allowed Democrat Daniel Patrick Moynihan to choose one of every four judges.[10]

If neither senator is a party colleague of the president, one or both senators may have some impact on nominations. But the administration will shift much of its attention to important public officials and leaders of its own party from that state. During George Bush's presidency, when both senators from Ohio were Democrats, the Republican state party organization and Republican House members both participated in suggesting nominees; not surprisingly, this shared role led to some frictions between them.[11]

The extent of a senator's power over nominations partly depends on the senator's power in the Senate. When the president's party controls the Senate, for instance, the majority leader and chair of the Judiciary Committee wield considerable influence. Thus it is not surprising that Bush gave a district court nomination to someone who had served on the staff of Senator Strom Thurmond of South Carolina, ranking Republican on the Judiciary Committee. Nor is it surprising that this nominee was confirmed with unusual speed, despite some questions about his qualifications.[12]

A final element in the relationship between the president and the Senate— an element that shapes the whole process of selection—is the importance of lower-court judgeships to the administration. Some presidents, such as John Kennedy, gave a low priority to judgeships. But since Kennedy's time, presidents have given increasing weight to judgeships, and as a result they are less willing to cede power to senators.

The Reagan and Bush administrations, for instance, saw the appointment of lower-court judges as an important mechanism for shaping policy. One result was an insistence by the new Bush administration that Republican senators provide it with three names of possible district court nominees rather than the traditional one. This effort to reduce senators' power resulted in a public conflict between the administration and several Republican senators, centering on a 1989 battle over a district court candidate recommended by Vermont's Senator James Jeffords. When Bush refused to nominate the candidate, senators retaliated by holding up confirmation of nominees for other states. Eventually, the administration gave in and nominated Jeffords' choice, but the battle made it clear that, as one scholar put it, "the Bush administration will not willingly surrender the appointment power to Republican senators."[13]

Even so, the administration could not eliminate the powers that senatorial courtesy provides, as a 1990 appointment indicates.[14] Conservatives strongly opposed the selection of Robert Jones to the Oregon district court because as a state judge Jones had written a 1987 opinion greatly limiting government power to regulate obscenity. But Oregon's two Republican senators jointly put forward Jones's name to the Justice Department, indicating that he was their only choice. Oregon's five House members, including two Republicans, also wrote a joint letter on behalf of Jones. Because of this strong support, combined with Jones's impressive qualifications, President Bush nominated him.

In addition to the official participants in the nomination process, a variety of interest groups also try to influence the president's choices. One important group is the American Bar Association. In contrast with the Supreme Court level, presidents typically allow the ABA judicial selection committee to rate potential nominees before they are actually chosen. But the ABA's role has declined over the past two decades, as presidents increasingly are unwilling to give its committee something like a veto power over nominations.

In contrast with the Supreme Court, people who would like to become lower-court judges routinely campaign for those positions. Indeed, according to one student of the process, "rarely is it the case that a person who has not actively sought the nomination receives it."[15] One important kind of campaigning is amassing support from people and groups that are politically significant to the administration and home-state senators. While some aspirants convey their interest indirectly, others go directly to the officials who have the greatest impact on nominations: in the month after Clinton's election in 1992, two Democratic senators heard from large numbers of people who wanted judicial appointments.[16]

President Jimmy Carter used nominating commissions for the selection of lower-court judges.[17] Carter issued an executive order establishing panels of lawyers and lay members to recommend candidates for seats on the courts of appeals. Under Carter's plan, commission members were selected by the administration and given the task of presenting three to five names to be considered for a particular judgeship. Carter also asked senators to establish nominating commissions for the district courts in their states, and ultimately such commissions were set up in most states.

The nominating commissions had some effect. They limited somewhat the freedom of both the administration and the home-state senators, and, at the appellate level, they increased the administration's power relative to that of the senators. They also reduced the power of the ABA, which could no longer claim to be the only arbiter of the qualifications of potential judges.

But in other respects the commissions had little impact. The selection of commissioners was influenced by partisan considerations, and Carter's appointees—like those from other administrations—were overwhelmingly from the president's party. Indeed, a study by Elliot Slotnick found that district judges selected through commissions differed little in their backgrounds from district judges selected during the same period without commissions. As Slotnick concluded, his study provides evidence that alteration of formal selection rules may not lead to major changes in the outcomes of the selection process.[18]

Criteria for Selection   The criteria that influence Supreme Court nominations are also important for the lower courts. Traditionally, they were given quite different weights for the lower courts, chiefly because of a general feeling that these courts were not of much consequence. The growing recognition that district courts and courts of appeals make significant policy has reduced the differences between the criteria used for these courts and for the Supreme Court, but it has not eliminated them altogether.

Political reward has always been a crucial consideration in nomination decisions: judgeships are frequently used to recognize the efforts of those who support the administration and, even more, to recompense personal and political associates of home-state senators. Indeed, the best way to become a federal judge, one Senate staff member joked, "is that you should have the foresight to be the law school roommate of a future United States senator; or, that failing, to pick a future senator for your first law partner."[19]

The joke is an enduring one because of the large element of truth it contains. Senators often seek to reward lawyers who have served in their campaigns and otherwise aided their political advancement. Presidents and Justice Department officials use nominations for similar purposes, and they have relative freedom to do so for the courts of appeals. In 1989 President Bush promoted his cousin John Walker from a New York district court to the court of appeals. According to a critic, "everyone agrees that there's no way he would have gotten the nod if he wasn't related to President Bush." However, a supporter responded that "we shouldn't get to the point where people of quality cannot be elevated because of the accident of who they're the cousin of."[20]

The pursuit of new or enhanced political support has also carried some weight in the nominating process. Although lower-court nominations are less visible than those for the Supreme Court, they too may be used to appeal to interest groups or sets of voters. The Carter administration, for example, selected unprecedented numbers of female and nonwhite judges. This record was motivated in part by the belief that enhanced diversity in the judiciary was desirable in itself, but it also reflected the desire to strengthen support for the administration among two groups that were important to it. For similar reasons, Clinton indicated during his presidential campaign that he would seek to appoint women and members of racial minority groups to judgeships.[21]

In a sense, administration deference to senators constitutes yet another kind of pursuit of political support. Some presidents go beyond the dictates of senatorial courtesy as a way of seeking goodwill. A famous example is the appointments of southern district judges by the Kennedy administration, which nominated some anti–civil rights judges in order to keep peace with powerful southern senators. Such actions have become less common because presidents are less willing to put people on the federal courts without regard for their policy views. But they have not disappeared. The Reagan administration reportedly promoted a Rhode Island district judge to the court of appeals, despite some feeling that he was too liberal, in return for the vote of Rhode Island's Republican Senator John Chafee on a defense weaponry issue.[22]

Another case of trading illustrates the complex politics of selecting judges.[23] In 1986 Senator Slade Gorton, a Republican from Washington State, proposed William Dwyer for a district court seat. The Reagan administration delayed nominating Dwyer because of his perceived liberalism. But the nomination was made after Gorton agreed to provide the decisive vote for the confirmation of Daniel Manion to the court of appeals in Chicago. Senate Democrats, angered by Gorton's vote on Manion, blocked Dwyer's confirmation at the end of 1986. Gorton's well-publicized vote for Manion also may have helped bring about his defeat in the 1986 election. In 1987 the administration renominated Dwyer, but only after Republican Senator Daniel Evans of Washington threatened to hold up other judicial nominations if Dwyer was not selected. Dwyer was then confirmed.

The qualifications of candidates have traditionally been much less important for the lower courts than for the Supreme Court. So long as the lower courts were viewed as unimportant, participants in the process thought that little harm would result if people of limited merit served on them. As late as 1974 Senator William Proxmire of Wisconsin defended a potential nominee who had come under attack by pointing out that "as a judge, he will be subject to appeals" and "he will be surrounded by some of the best judges in the country" (perhaps meaning that he would learn from them).[24]

As perceptions of the lower courts have changed, senators and administration officials have given greater attention to the qualifications of the judges they select. But it remains true that some lawyers of questionable abilities and accomplishments—people who would not be considered seriously for the Supreme Court—are placed on the district courts and courts of appeals.

The greatest change in the criteria for selecting lower-court judges is the increasing emphasis given to policy preferences. Historically, there has been wide variation in the attention that administrations gave to the views of their nominees. But ideological screening of candidates for judgeships has become standard practice in the past three decades. In the Johnson administration, efforts were made to select southern judges who had some sympathy for civil rights. President Nixon was especially concerned about criminal justice issues, and prospective nominees during his administration were scrutinized for their views about law and order. In a more general way, President Carter sought to nominate judges with liberal views.

President Reagan brought to the presidency a strong commitment to blunt what he saw as excessive judicial liberalism by appointing conservative judges. The result was, in the words of one expert, "the most self-conscious ideological selection process since the first Roosevelt Administration."[25] President Bush himself may have been less concerned with judicial ideologies, but he continued Reagan's emphasis on the selection of conservatives; the goal, according to White House counsel C. Boyden Gray, was "to shift the courts in a more conservative direction."[26] One important reason was Bush's desire to retain the support of conservative Republicans, who cared a great deal about federal court policies.[27]

Despite these painstaking efforts, the Reagan and Bush appointees may not be significantly more conservative in their judicial records than the judges appointed by earlier Republican presidents; the evidence on this question is mixed.[28] But the care taken by the two administrations ensured that their appointments would shift the ideological balance on the federal courts.

President Clinton has made it clear that ideological considerations will be important in his selection of judges as well. During his campaign, Clinton complained that Bush had "appointed judges who hold a restrictive view of constitutional rights and who favor the interests of big business over the rights of individuals," and he pledged that he would appoint only judges with "a demonstrated concern for, and commitment to, the individual rights protected by our Constitution, including the right to privacy."[29] This statement underlines the heightened role of policy preferences in the selection of judges for the lower federal courts.

Senate Confirmation The traditional confirmation process for lower-court judgeships was linked to senatorial courtesy. If home-state senators did not indicate their support for a nomination, the Judiciary Committee did not consider it. In this way, the committee enforced the requirement that the Justice Department reach agreement with the home-state senators. If a candidate did have the support of the home-state senators, the committee and the Senate confirmed the nomination automatically rather than giving it collective scrutiny; this is the other side of senatorial courtesy.

The traditional process has been modified since the late 1970s. Home-state senators of the president's party still have something like an absolute veto power, but the support of those senators no longer guarantees easy approval by the Judiciary Committee and confirmation by the Senate.

This change seems to derive partly from a general decline in senators' deference to each other and partly from the growing recognition that lower-court judgeships are important. In any case, at least some senators are now less willing to rubber-stamp the choices that an administration and the senators from another state have agreed on.

The great majority of nominations continue to go through the Senate with no difficulty; in a typical confirmation hearing, an Ohio district court nominee in 1992 faced eight minutes of questions by the two committee members who attended.[30] But some nominees receive closer scrutiny, often after interest groups have raised questions about them. The Alliance for Justice and other liberal groups played this role in the Reagan and Bush administrations, and, even before Clinton's inauguration, the conservative Free Congress Foundation announced that it would take on a similar role during his administration.[31] It has become increasingly common for votes to be cast against confirmation, and several nominations have been defeated or withdrawn in the face of likely defeat. Exhibit 4.2 describes some of these cases.

Kenneth Ryskamp was the only Bush nominee who was defeated for confirmation; his case illustrates the circumstances that can lead to such a defeat.[32] In 1991 Bush selected Ryskamp for elevation from the federal district court in Miami to the Eleventh Circuit Court of Appeals. Ryskamp drew opposition from a number of liberal groups, including the NAACP and the National Organization for Women. Opponents charged that he was hostile to litigants with civil liberties claims, that he had made racially insensitive statements as a trial judge, and that he belonged to a country club with discriminatory membership policies.

Ryskamp resigned from the country club before his Judiciary Committee hearing, and the Justice Department later pointed to his work on behalf of minority groups. But his committee testimony did not satisfy opponents, and disclosure of his remarks to a senator aroused opposition from Hispanic groups. Democratic Senator Bob Graham of Florida announced his opposition to Ryskamp, helping to sway moderate Democrats. Ultimately, the committee voted against confirmation by a 6–8 vote, entirely on party lines; the committee then could have kept the nomination alive by sending it to the floor with no recommendation, but it voted not to do so.

It is significant that only one Bush nominee lost a confirmation vote, despite Democratic control of the Senate, but other confirmations were prevented by Senate inaction. Bush had to renominate Ryskamp because an earlier nomination had been allowed to die in 1990. In 1992 the Senate took no action on more than fifty judicial nominations, largely because Democratic senators who sensed possible victory for Bill Clinton preferred that his nominees fill the vacant positions. Continued Democratic control of the Senate does not ensure confirmation for all of Clinton's nominees, but it gives him one additional advantage in the Senate.

THE SELECTION OF STATE JUDGES

The history discussed at the beginning of this chapter underlines the diversity in the formal rules for selection of state judges; state constitutions establish several different sets of procedures. This section examines those formal systems more closely, focusing on how they operate in practice.

Nominee	Year	State	Level	Charges by Opponents	Outcome
Daniel Manion	1986	Indiana	CA	Inexperience and weak skills as a lawyer, rejection of Supreme Court authority, extreme conservatism	Confirmed, 48–46
Bernard Siegan	1988	California	CA	Inexperience, extreme conservatism on constitutional issues	Defeated in committee
Robert Miller	1988	Colorado	DC	Lack of candor in responding to Judiciary Committee questionnaire	Withdrew from consideration
Vaughn Walker	1989	California	DC	Membership in all-male club, questionable litigation practices	Confirmed by voice vote
Kenneth Ryskamp	1991	Florida	CA	Racial insensitivity, hostility to civil liberties litigants	Defeated in committee
Edward Carnes	1992	Alabama	CA	Over zealous advocacy to obtain death sentences, racial insensitivity	Confirmed, 62–36

Notes: "Year" refers to year of final action on the nomination; "state" is the state of the nominee's residence; and "level" refers to the court for which the person was nominated, district court (DC) or court of appeals (CA).
Sources: Press reports

EXHIBIT 4.2 Selected Lower Court Nominations That Aroused Opposition, 1986–1992

The Formal Rules

The five selection systems used by the states may be summarized as follows:[33]

1. *Gubernatorial appointment.* In this system, as the title indicates, the governor appoints judges. In nearly every state that uses gubernatorial appointment, the governor's choice must be confirmed; usually, the confirming body is the state senate.

2. *Legislative election.* In this system the legislature elects judges; the procedures for doing so vary among the three states that retain this system.
3. *Partisan election.* Here voters choose between party nominees in a general election, with party labels indicated on the ballot. Normally, the nominees are selected through partisan primary elections.
4. *Nonpartisan election.* Under this system, voters choose between candidates in a general election, with no party labels indicated on the ballot. Usually, the top two candidates in a nonpartisan primary are placed on the general election ballot.
5. *Missouri Plan.* In this complex system, a commission is established to nominate candidates for judgeships. Most commonly, the commission includes lawyers who have been selected by their colleagues and nonlawyers who have been selected by the governor; in many states, a judge also serves. When a judgeship needs to be filled, the commission produces a short list (usually three names) of nominees, and the governor makes the appointment from this list. After the judge has served for a short time, and at periodic intervals thereafter, an election will be held in which voters decide whether or not to retain the judge; there is no opposing candidate.

Exhibit 4.3 shows the distribution of these five systems among the states. The table excludes special selection systems that many states use for a few major trial courts or for some of their minor trial courts, such as the appointment of municipal judges by mayors.

The historical patterns in the popularity of the various systems are reflected in their distribution across regions. The systems of gubernatorial appointment and election by the legislature are found almost exclusively on the eastern seaboard, among the original thirteen states. Similarly, partisan election of judges is most common in the South and Midwest, whose states were formed when this system was most popular. Because they developed relatively late, nonpartisan election and the Missouri Plan have the weakest geographical patterns.

As the summaries indicate, none of the five formal systems has only a single form. The details of the Missouri Plan, for instance, differ considerably from state to state. In addition, some states have combined features of different systems. For instance, although Ohio is classified as a nonpartisan election state, its system includes a partisan primary that precedes the nonpartisan general election.

Exhibit 4.3 shows another complication: many states use different selection systems for different courts. In Rhode Island, for example, supreme court justices are elected by the legislature, but trial judges are appointed by the governor. The special systems for minor trial courts, which are not shown in the exhibit, complicate the picture even further.

The terms of state judges can vary a good deal as well. Rhode Island gives its judges lifetime terms, and judges in Massachusetts and New Hampshire hold office until the age of seventy. Elsewhere judges have fixed terms. In many states, these terms are longer for appellate judges than they are for

Partisan Election	Nonpartisan Election	Gubernatorial Appointment	Legislative Election	Missouri Plan
Alabama	Arizona* (M)	California* (M)	Rhode	Alaska
Arkansas	California*	Delaware	Island*	Arizona*
Illinois (M)	Florida*	Maine	South	Colorado
Indiana*	Georgia	Maryland (M)	Carolina	Connecticut
Kansas*	Idaho	Massachusetts	Virginia	(M)
Mississippi	Kentucky	New		Florida*
Missouri*	Louisiana	Hampshire		Hawaii (M)
New York*	Michigan	New Jersey		Indiana*
North	(M)	Rhode Island*		Iowa
Carolina	Minnesota			Kansas*
Pennsylvania	Montana (M)			Missouri*
(M)	Nevada			Nebraska
Tennessee*	North Dakota			New Mexico
Texas	Ohio (M)			(M)
West Virginia	Oklahoma*			New York*
	Oregon			(M)
	South			Oklahoma*
	Dakota*			South
	Washington			Dakota*
	Wisconsin			Tennessee*
				Utah
				Vermont (M)
				Wyoming

Notes: The states in this table are classified according to the system they use for the regular selection of judges rather than the system for filling vacancies in the middle of terms. These systems used only for minor trial courts or for a small number of major trial judgeships are not listed. An asterisk indicates that another system is also used in that state (in such cases, both systems are listed in the table). An "M" indicates that the system used in a particular state is a significant modification of that described in the text. States that have established nominating commissions for appointments through executive order rather than through constitutional or statutory provisions are classified as gubernatorial appointment states.

Sources: *The Book of the States, 1992–93 Edition* (Lexington, Ky.: Council of State Governments, 1992), pp. 233–235; Larry Berkson, Scott Beller, and Michele Grimaldi, *Judicial Selection in the United States: A Compendium of Provisions* (Chicago: American Judicature Society, 1981); *Judicial Merit Selection: Current Status* (Chicago: American Judicature Society, 1989); state constitutions and statutes.

EXHIBIT 4.3 Formal Systems for the Selection of State Judges

trial judges. The most common period of office is six years, but some states give trial judges four-year terms, and most New York judges serve fourteen-year terms. Some states have mandatory retirement ages or ages beyond which judges cannot seek new terms.

Vacancies can occur during judges' terms due to resignation, retirement, or death. In states that do not use popular elections, such vacancies are usually filled by the same method that is ordinarily employed to select judges. But in states with elective systems, the governor generally makes interim appointments; in some of these states, the selection is made from candidates who have been nominated by a commission similar to that used in the Missouri Plan. In most states with interim appointees, the appointee must face the voters fairly soon, even if the term has not expired.

The Operation of Elective Systems

Nearly two-thirds of the states use an elective system to choose judges. The difference between partisan and nonpartisan ballots is one of several ways that formal rules for election differ. These differences in rules, as well as differences in the ways that politics operates, cause judicial elections to vary a good deal among states and even within them. Still, some general patterns do exist.

Campaigns and Voters   Although we think of judgeships as prized positions, judicial candidates often run unopposed—particularly below the supreme court level. One reason is that judgeships are *not* always attractive, particularly to lawyers whose incomes far exceed judicial salaries. Another is that, where one candidate has a great advantage, potential opponents may see no reason to run a futile campaign.

In contested judicial elections, campaigns tend to be small in scale. To take one example, in North Carolina in 1988 and 1990 the average expenditure by candidates per vote cast was 4 cents for the supreme court and 2 cents for the court of appeals; in contrast, candidates for secretary of state averaged 45 cents and candidates for governor $5.17.[34] As a result, judicial candidates often find it difficult to get their messages to voters.

Judicial candidates are also constrained by ethical rules that severely limit their discussion of policy issues, though Kentucky and Florida courts have held these rules to be so broad that they violate freedom of speech.[35] These rules stem from a fear that candidates who take positions on specific issues cannot later deal impartially with cases involving these issues. Because of the rules, candidates' speeches and materials tend to focus on such matters as career experience, endorsements by newspapers and interest groups, and family life.

The mass media could compensate for these limitations by according heavy coverage to the candidates and campaigns. But newspapers and television news programs usually concentrate on races for high executive and legislative offices, giving only occasional attention to contests for judgeships.

Because of limited campaigns and media coverage, the general rule is that voters go to the polls knowing little about the candidates. In a 1986 exit poll, for instance, the name of one judicial candidate in Houston was recognized by only 23 percent of the voters there; a Dallas candidate was recognized by only 19 percent of the local voters.[36] The problem of learning about candidates is aggravated when voters face large numbers of judicial contests, as they often do in large cities.

Lacking much information about candidates, voters make use of whatever information they can obtain. A recognizable name can provide a handy cue, so candidates who are well known usually have a considerable advantage. The same can be true of candidates who are personally unknown but who hold a familiar name. In 1990 Chief Justice Keith Callow of the Washington Supreme Court was defeated by a lawyer named Charles Johnson, who had not bothered to campaign. The winner was assisted by his sharing both first and last names with a trial judge in Seattle, though the familiar sound of a name as common as Johnson undoubtedly helped as well.[37] In 1991 two challengers to an Indiana trial judge named Donald R. Phillippe sought to enhance their chances by changing their own names to Donald R. Phillippe; the voters were spared considerable difficulty when an election board ruled that the new Phillippes had failed to meet legal requirements for getting on the ballot.[38] But it is worth noting that familiar names do not guarantee election. In 1992 a candidate named Michael J. Fox finished sixth out of seven aspirants for a judgeship in Chicago.[39]

Judicial campaigns sometimes depart from this pattern of limited activity and little substantive information, and the departures have become increasingly common in the past decade. Increased spending in some contests— more than $1 million by some supreme court candidates—has made it easier for candidates to communicate their names and messages to the voters. In turn, high levels of spending attract greater media attention to contests.

Candidates have also become more willing to skirt or directly violate the prohibitions on discussion of policy issues, thus giving voters more substantive information. Most often candidates try to associate themselves with a conservative stance on criminal justice matters. Usually, they do so subtly, as in an advertisement for a California candidate that cited endorsements from four individuals and groups associated with law enforcement and pointed out that the candidate was a former deputy district attorney.[40] Some candidates are more direct; an advertisement for an Illinois candidate in 1990 proclaimed that she would "defend our neighborhoods against the onslaught of violent criminals" and "diligently protect victims' rights."[41]

Other issues also arise in elections. Issues in personal injury law played a prominent part in campaigns for supreme court seats in Ohio in 1986 and Wisconsin in 1990. These unusually bitter contests also featured strong attacks on the candidates' qualifications and the performance of the supreme court.[42] Personal injury issues have become a permanent feature of contests for the Texas Supreme Court; they are fueled by large contributions from lawyers and other interest groups in this field. As state courts become more involved in abortion law, this issue is gaining prominence. And candidates occasionally try to appeal to voters' interest in saving money; for example, an Illinois judge proclaimed in 1990 that one of his decisions had "saved Cook County Taxpayers $2.5 million in 1989."[43]

Although issue-based appeals and contentious campaigns have become more common, it should be emphasized that they remain the exception to the rule. Especially below the supreme court level, elections with only a single candidate and contests with limited activity and controversy still predominate.

The Situation of Incumbents   The continued predominance of quiet and uncontested judicial elections is linked to the situation of incumbent judges. When incumbents in any office run for re-election, they enjoy several advantages. Voters usually know them better than their opponents, they usually come from the majority party in their state or district, and they generally can raise more campaign funds than their opponents.

Incumbent judges enjoy several additional advantages. Some lawyers are reluctant to run against sitting judges, either because they feel that a reasonably competent judge should not have to face electoral challenges or because they fear having to try cases before a judge whom they opposed unsuccessfully. For similar reasons, the organized bar and individual lawyers tend to support incumbents.

Perhaps most important, the small scale of most judicial campaigns favors incumbents. Judges may not be nearly as well known as governors or legislators, but over time their names do become familiar to many voters. In contrast, challengers often begin as unknowns, and the near-invisibility of most campaigns makes it difficult to overcome this disadvantage. In this situation, voters will be inclined to favor the candidate about whom they know a little over an opponent about whom they know nothing.

These advantages are reflected in an impressive rate of success for incumbents. Except for supreme court justices, high proportions of judges run unopposed for re-election. Over twenty-year periods, judges on the major trial courts of Ohio were opposed only 27 percent of the time, those of Michigan 26 percent of the time, and those of California only 7 percent. One scholar found that "most counties in Texas have never experienced a challenge to an incumbent" on the major trial court.[44] And judges who do face opposition win most of the time. The success rate for the Ohio and Michigan judges was more than 80 percent.[45]

Of course, some judges face strong electoral challenges, and some of these challenges are successful. In the light of their advantages, what leads incumbent judges to suffer defeats?

Several conditions can make incumbents vulnerable. Judges sometimes are caught up in political tides that are unfavorable to their political party. Occasionally, a judge will develop a reputation for incompetence, unethical conduct, or bizarre behavior. Similarly, a highly unpopular decision may arouse opposition to a judge. In 1992 eighty-one of the eighty-two superior court judges seeking re-election in Los Angeles were unopposed; the one exception drew three opponents after this judge granted probation to a grocer who had shot and killed a teenager whom she accused of shoplifting. (The judge received 51 percent of the vote and thus was re-elected without a runoff.)[46]

The growth in campaigns emphasizing policy issues primarily reflects efforts by challengers to overcome the advantages of judicial incumbents. This is particularly true in criminal justice; supreme court justices in states such as North Carolina and Louisiana have been attacked for alleged unwillingness to uphold death sentences, and trial judges frequently are charged with undue sympathy for criminal defendants. In Texas and California, organized groups seek to defeat judges whom they depict as liberals in this field. In one extreme case, in Pasadena, California, a newspaper advertisement charged that an incumbent municipal judge had never sentenced a defendant to prison; the ad did not mention the fact that municipal judges had no power to sentence defendants to prison.[47] The rise of personal injury issues in Texas in the 1980s upset a traditional pattern in which supreme court justices were re-elected in quiet campaigns.[48] Issue-based challenges to incumbents fail more often than they succeed, but their successes are one source of the occasional defeats that incumbent judges suffer. And they have contributed to a growing, if perhaps exaggerated, feeling of electoral vulnerability on the part of many judges.

Partisanship   As already suggested, partisanship can play a role in judicial elections. This role depends largely on a state's formal system. In states where the candidates' party affiliations are listed on the ballot, voters have an additional piece of information on which to base their decision. Most voters identify themselves as Democrats or Republicans, and in an election in which they have little information they tend to support their own party's candidates because they have little reason to do otherwise. As Philip L. Dubois has pointed out, judges may be more accountable in states with partisan elections, in the sense that voters can choose between judicial candidates on the basis of the general policy positions of the parties—positions that are reflected in judges' votes and opinions.[49]

Because party labels provide additional information to voters, they can complicate the positions of incumbents. A judge whose party is dominant may have little to fear from potential challengers; just as there are "safe" seats in Congress and state legislatures, so there are judicial districts in which one party ordinarily is assured of victory. But an incumbent whose party is in the minority may be vulnerable, and an unfavorable electoral tide can sweep that incumbent out of office. Thus, as Dallas became strongly Republican, Democratic trial judges became highly vulnerable to defeat; in the 1980s thirteen of twenty-one incumbent Democrats were defeated—while no Republican incumbent lost.[50]

A nonpartisan election is different, for voters generally are unaware of the candidates' party affiliations. As a result, party loyalties are less likely to compete with the incumbent's advantage. Thus fewer incumbents face opposition and suffer defeat in states that have nonpartisan elections.

Whether or not an election is officially partisan, political party organizations can give judicial contests a partisan character. The prestige and power of judgeships make them alluring prizes. As a result, in states where party organizations are strong and the political climate favorable, the parties may play important roles in the election process.

New York and Illinois, which have partisan elections for judges, are two such states.[51] In Cook County (Chicago), Democratic judicial candidates are generally chosen by the party leaders, whose endorsement virtually guarantees victory in the primary election. Because Chicago is heavily Democratic, a victory in the Democratic primary is the major requirement for winning a judgeship. In New York State, candidates for trial court judgeships are nominated in party conventions or primary elections. Where a local party organization is strong in New York, it controls the outcome in either a convention or a primary. In counties where one party dominates, the endorsement of that party's organization assures election. An incumbent from the minority party in a county is likely to suffer defeat if the other party's organization chooses to oppose the incumbent. Thus, one report concluded, "Most judges in New York are chosen by elections that are almost totally controlled by political party leaders."[52]

Interim Appointment   In nearly all states that elect judges, the governor fills vacancies between elections. These interim appointments are important because vacancies occur with some frequency and because appointees generally are successful in winning subsequent elections. As a result, at any given time a high proportion of the judges in states with elective systems will have gained their positions initially through appointments. For this reason, elective systems should be considered both elective *and* appointive.

The success of appointees in winning election is understandable: an appointed judge shares some of the advantages of long-time incumbents, and most appointees are too new to create enemies or to arouse concerted opposition. In some states, appointed judges from the minority party in their district can be vulnerable to defeat, but even in those states most newcomers hold their positions. And in other states, they do extremely well. For example, over a twenty-year period no appointee to Michigan's major trial court was defeated.[53]

In some states, appointments have become the dominant element in formally elective systems. In Minnesota, the usual pattern is for supreme court seats to be filled by interim appointments; the appointees then run for election with no opposition. A lawyer who took the unusual step of challenging an incumbent justice in 1990 was foiled when the incumbent resigned, allowing the governor to make an appointment and, under Minnesota's rules, cancel the election. When the lawyer tried to run against another incumbent in 1992, the governor sought to extend the incumbent's term by two years; the lawyer went to court, won a ruling that the governor's action was unconstitutional, and then won the election. Unusual as this sequence of events was, it does illustrate one generalization about judicial elections, the value of name recognition: the lawyer whose persistence ultimately was rewarded was Alan

Page, very well known and well liked as a former star for the Minnesota Vikings football team.[54]

The Operation of Appointive Systems

Of the three nonelective systems of judicial selection, legislative election is so rare today that it requires no further discussion. But gubernatorial appointment and the Missouri Plan are of considerable importance, the former because it is commonly used to fill vacancies in states that elect judges and the latter because of its widespread and increasing use.

Gubernatorial Appointment   Only eight states give their governors the general power to select judges. But in states with elective systems, governors choose a significant number of judges through interim appointments. As a result, a large minority of all state judges originally were selected by a governor.[55]

In making their selections, governors can consult with a wide array of individuals and groups. The views of people who are politically important to the governor are likely to receive weight. In Ohio, Republican governor George Voinovich asks the county Republican chair to nominate two or three candidates to fill a vacancy on a trial court.[56] Former California Governor George Deukmejian set up his own county-level boards to advise him on appointments; one of their jobs was to "give the governor's office the benefit of whatever information or knowledge they have as to an individual's judicial philosophy."[57]

Legislators are likely to influence the governor's choices, particularly in states where the senate must confirm nominees. In New Jersey, under a variant of senatorial courtesy in Congress, any senator from the county in which a nominee resides holds an informal veto power over the nominee's confirmation, and the governor needs to take the home-county senators' views into account in making a choice.

In some states, governors have allowed bar associations to screen potential appointees. In Mississippi, for instance, most governors have deferred to local bar associations in choosing interim appointees. These associations also exert heavy influence over judicial elections in Mississippi, and one governor characterized the state's selection of judges as "bar anointment."[58] As the popularity of the Missouri Plan has grown, some governors with appointing power have set up similar nominating commissions and agreed to select judges from the commission's nominees; this practice gives the bar a role through the inclusion of lawyers on commissions.

The criteria applied by governors in making judicial appointments fall into the same general categories as those employed by presidents. To a considerable degree, appointments are used to advance political goals, especially by serving as rewards. Most broadly, judgeships are typically reserved for members of the governor's party. Often the link between judge and governor is closer. In California, many of the judges selected by former Governor Jerry Brown and current Governor Pete Wilson had contributed money to the appointing governor's campaigns. These contributions probably helped some judges obtain their appointments, but some people who gave money already had the kinds of personal and political ties to the governor that often bring judicial appointments.[59] In any case, it is understandable that governors favor people whom they know and have come to view positively—particularly if those people had helped a governor to become governor.

The attractiveness of judgeships makes them powerful rewards to lawyer-legislators. "If there are any lawyers in the Legislature who don't want a judgeship," remarked one observer in California, "I don't know who they are."[60] With legislative term limits now operating in California and many other states, judgeships are even more attractive. Thus legislators may have an extra incentive to follow the governor's lead. On the other hand, in 1989 Governor William Donald Schaefer of Maryland appointed as judge a legislator who had been a strong critic of Schaefer, referring to him once as "Don the Con"; some observers suspected that Schaefer made the appointment to get a nettlesome opponent out of the legislature.[61]

Particularly in states where the courts play a highly visible part in policymaking, governors may seek to staff the courts with ideological allies. Thus, beginning with Ronald Reagan, recent California governors have worked hard to select judges who share their policy views. In one survey, self-described conservatives outnumbered liberals among Reagan's appointees to the major trial court by a 25–1 ratio, whereas liberals had a 7–1 advantage among the judges appointed by his Democratic successor, Jerry Brown.[62] Brown's successor, George Deukmejian, was particularly interested in selecting judges with conservative views on criminal justice issues; 65 percent of his appointees had experience as prosecutors.[63]

Governors also consider the apparent competence of potential judges, although the importance of this consideration varies a good deal by state and by level of court. Governors who voluntarily establish nominating commissions do so, at least ostensibly, to give more weight to the qualifications of candidates.

Although governors usually have full power to make interim appointments, most states with gubernatorial appointment as the regular selection method require that the governor's choices be confirmed by the state senate or, less often, another body. Few nominations fail to be confirmed, in part because governors avoid making nominations that might displease the confirming body. But the senatorial courtesy powers of New Jersey state senators have led to battles over some appointments. Until 1986 the Connecticut legislature apparently had never refused to confirm a nominee, but in that year it turned down three judges nominated to new terms by the governor, and legislative opposition caused two other nominees to withdraw.[64]

In states with gubernatorial appointment of judges, as in legislative election states, the general practice is for a judge whose term has ended and who wishes to continue in office to be given an additional term; the Connecticut defeats are among the rare exceptions to this rule. As a result, appointments to judgeships generally constitute lifetime appointments in practice.

The Missouri Plan   Nearly twenty states now use some form of the Missouri Plan as the formal selection system for at least some of their courts. As noted earlier, several states that elect judges have also established truncated Missouri Plan systems (involving commission nomination and gubernatorial appointment) to fill vacancies between elections, and a number of governors have voluntarily adopted commission nomination processes for regular or interim appointments.

Among commissioners, as we would expect, lawyers and judges predominate: a 1989 national survey of commissioners found that 59 percent were legal professionals. Nonlawyer commissioners tend to be high in socioeconomic status; most commonly, they are business executives or educators. Many were active in politics, and 37 percent of those appointed by a governor had campaigned for that governor. The great majority were white men.[65] In all these respects, commissioners are far from a random sample of the population, and nominations may reflect the perspectives of the groups that are best represented.

Partisan considerations and political conflicts do intrude into the selection of commissioners. In Missouri, for example, different segments of the bar compete over who will be chosen. Some states require a close party balance within their commissions, but in some others the overwhelming majority of lay members share the governor's party affiliation. At one time, this was true of twenty-one of the twenty-five lay commissioners in Maryland and all thirty-two in Iowa.[66]

Theoretically, a commission's decisions are to be based only on the qualifications of potential judges. Inevitably, however, other factors enter into the process. Prominent among these factors is partisanship. Because some commissioners have strong party loyalties and ties, partisanship inevitably colors their consideration of candidates. Of course, personal considerations can also play a part. "There is considerable anecdotal evidence," according to one scholar, that the process of selecting nominees in Nebraska "has been manipulated to favor friends, law partners, and even relatives."[67]

By selecting lay commissioners, the governor can influence the choice of nominees. Governors can usually achieve the results they want without direct pressure if the lay commissioners are sympathetic to the governor's goals, as many are. Several of the commissioners who responded to the 1989 survey "viewed their commissions as being controlled by gubernatorial appointees whose commission membership is a political 'thank-you' and who select whomever the governor wants."[68] But governors do not always get what they want; at one point, Mario Cuomo of New York expressed dissatisfaction with some of the lists of court of appeals nominees that he received.[69]

The governor does, of course, choose among the candidates forwarded by the commission. Where the governor's influence over the commission is sufficient, at least one nominee for each seat will be highly acceptable. (Governors may go even further; one commissioner complained that "the governor has insisted the commission present him candidates of his choice; otherwise he refuses to appoint anyone."[70]) In this situation, the governor can use court appointments to serve the same ideological and partisan goals that they serve in gubernatorial appointment states. For instance, judgeships sometimes are used as political rewards. And partisan concerns appear to play a prominent role in Missouri.[71]

In most states operating under the Missouri Plan, a judge needs to win a simple majority of votes in a retention election to remain in office. Most judges are in an excellent position to do so; in a retention election, all the ordinary advantages of incumbency are strengthened by the absence of an opposing candidate. Until recently, the results were highly favorable to judges: the overwhelming majority of judges won, and generally by large margins. For instance, 99 percent of the major trial court judges who faced retention elections between 1964 and 1984 were successful.[72]

In the past decade, judges have not done quite so well in retention elections. This change is symbolized by a few well-organized campaigns against retention. One came in California, which uses retention elections as the last stage in a modified system of gubernatorial appointment for appellate judges.[73] Over several years, conservatives became increasingly unhappy with the highly liberal state supreme court, particularly Chief Justice Rose Bird. In 1986 conservative groups mounted campaigns against Bird and two of her colleagues. These groups spent an estimated $5.5 million to defeat the three justices, while their supporters spent an estimated $2 million. The public campaigns against the justices focused on their votes against the death penalty, but large shares of the financing on both sides came from supporters and opponents of the court's liberal positions on personal injury law. Ultimately, the three justices were defeated by large margins.

Two campaigns against retention have occurred in Florida in recent years.[74] Leander Shaw in 1990 and Rosemary Barkett in 1992, each serving as chief justice at the time, drew opposition from groups that were unhappy with their support for protection of abortion rights under the state constitution and from groups that disapproved of decisions favoring criminal defendants; Barkett also faced strong opposition from the National Rifle Association. Ultimately, both Shaw and Barkett won retention, but each garnered only about 60 percent of the vote.

More important than these visible battles is a less visible trend: the frequency of negative votes has increased since the 1960s.[75] In Illinois, which requires 60 percent favorable votes for retention, a record ten out of ninety-seven trial judges lost in 1990.[76] In Missouri, the average proportion of favorable votes dropped from 82 percent in 1972 to 73 percent in 1988—and then below 60 percent in 1990. (This downward slide was halted in 1992, but that year a Missouri judge lost a retention election for the first time since 1942.[77]) Exhibit 4.4 shows the sharp decline in support for Kansas City judges in 1990. It also illustrates voters' tendency to respond to all the judges on the ballot in the same way; at each election, only a few percentage points separated the most successful and least successful judges. Nationally, that tendency is strongest in large districts and for appellate courts, where voters are less likely to know much about individual judges.[78]

Year	Number	Mean	Highest	Lowest
1984	10	74.6%	75.8%	73.3%
1986	12	70.3	71.8	67.8
1988	6	69.1	70.3	68.1
1990	19	57.6	61.4	52.4

Source: Missouri Secretary of State, *Official Manual, State of Missouri*, 1985–1986 through 1991–1992. Modeled in part on analyses in William K. Hall and Larry T. Aspin, "What Twenty Years of Judicial Retention Elections Have Told Us," *Judicature*, 70 (April–May 1987), 340–347.

EXHIBIT 4.4 Proportions of Favorable Votes for Trial Judges in Jackson County, Missouri (Kansas City), 1984–1990

The judges who do lose usually have aroused opposition from those who see their performance as substandard or who disagree strongly with their decisions. But, as the Kansas City results suggest, to a great extent the trend toward higher levels of negative voting is directed at judges in general, perhaps reflecting a decline in citizens' trust of political leaders.[79] California observers were struck by the contrast between the contentious supreme court contests of 1986 and the virtually invisible retention votes in 1990, with five justices facing no apparent opposition.[80] Yet all five received more than 30 percent negative votes, and one won by a 56–44 margin. As fewer voters are inclined to give judges automatic support, those judges who do have opposition face a greater chance of defeat than two decades ago. But it remains true that the overwhelming majority of Missouri Plan judges succeed in winning retention.

The Impact of Formal Selection Systems

How much do the various systems for choosing judges actually differ in practice? On the basis of the preceding discussion, we can look at the relationship between formal systems and the actual processes by which judges are selected. In addition, we can examine the impact of formal systems on the characteristics of the people who are selected as judges and on the behavior of judges and courts.

Effects on Selection Processes   Despite their formal differences, the various systems for judicial selection function similarly in some important respects.

First, the governor looms large in most states, regardless of which system is in operation. Even in states with judicial elections, the governor selects a good many judges by filling vacancies. Because the governor's appointees usually win subsequent elections, interim appointment gives the governor considerable power to determine the membership of the courts. In Missouri Plan states, the governor makes the final choice from a commission's list; as we have seen, the governor often has considerable influence over the list itself. "In most states, and for most judges," a California judge noted, "the path to judicial office is through the governor's door."[81]

Second, each system gives judges a fairly high level of security in office. Few incumbents are removed by the voters in states with elective systems, and even fewer in states with the Missouri Plan. In gubernatorial appointment states, governors nearly always reappoint incumbents. The level of security has declined a bit in the last decade, and judges may feel less secure than they actually are. Nevertheless, accountability tends to be limited.

Finally, all judicial selection systems are political in the sense that considerations other than the merits of prospective judges come into play. The operation of the Missouri Plan underlines this reality. After New York replaced partisan elections for its highest court with a modified Missouri Plan, one legislator complained, "I think we have brought more politics into the process . . . than we ever did when judges were elected."[82] His remark may have been an exaggeration, but it reflects the fact that no system is truly "non-political."

Of course, formal systems for choosing judges do have some effect. For example, a governor who directly appoints all judges has more power than one who only fills vacancies or one who works with nominating commissions. And voters have greater control over judges in a state that elects judges than in one where the governor or the legislature chooses them. Similarly, political parties have a better opportunity to influence the selection process in a partisan election state than in one that uses the Missouri Plan. These differences are not trivial.

Yet the ways in which states select judges are a product of their political conditions and traditions as well as their formal systems. Thus the same formal system can work quite differently from one state to another. For example, in states with partisan traditions and strong party organizations, such as New York, any formal system will be heavily influenced by partisan considerations. But in states with a nonpartisan ethos or weak party organizations, the same system will be less partisan. This produces an irony: in states where judicial selection is heavily permeated by partisanship, so that the Missouri Plan seems most attractive to reformers, the plan is least likely to minimize partisanship.

Effects on Characteristics of Judges   For those who debate methods of selecting judges, one central concern is the kinds of people who are selected. Supporters of the Missouri Plan, for instance, argue that it will strengthen the objective qualifications of judges, such as their educational attainments and legal experience.

Studies of state supreme courts from the 1960s to the 1980s suggest that the different formal systems actually produce similar mixes of judges.[83] These studies found that traits such as academic training and prior judicial experience differed little by selection system and that, as the most recent study concluded, most of the differences found in the backgrounds of justices "are due mainly to region, not selection system."[84] This does not mean that the various systems produce exactly the same results. Not surprisingly, for instance, it appears that legislators have by far the best chance to become judges in the few states in which the legislature chooses judges. (Indeed, the South Carolina legislature created a new court of appeals in 1979 and selected five legislators for the six-member court.[85]) But such differences were outweighed by similarities among the systems. And Missouri's shift from partisan elections to the Missouri Plan did not have major effects on the kinds of people selected as judges.[86]

Formal systems may have effects that have not yet been measured. For instance, the Missouri Plan might produce fewer judges who are actively involved in political party organizations. When better means to gauge the competence of judges are developed, we might find that some systems produce abler judges than others. But because the various formal systems seem to operate less differently in practice than in theory, it appears unlikely that they produce judges who differ dramatically in any significant respects.

Effects on the Behavior of Judges   Ultimately, we should be most interested in the impact of formal selection systems on the behavior of judges and the policies of courts. Advocates of a particular system often argue that it produces better justice, but not everyone agrees on what better justice actually entails. Leaving aside this question, we might expect selection systems to influence court behavior and policies for either of two reasons: the systems put different kinds of judges on the bench or they subject judges to different kinds of influences once they reach the bench.

As we have seen, there is some reason to discount the first possibility. The second possibility, however, is an intriguing one. For example, a judge who faces the voters periodically may be more responsive to public opinion than one who needs only to be reappointed. And judges who are subject to party nominations may take party interests into account in their decisions more than do judges who run in nonpartisan elections.

At present, these matters have been investigated far too little to allow firm conclusions. One possibility is that differences appear only on selected issues. For instance, the role of political parties in the selection of judges may have an impact on those issues that affect the parties' fortunes most, such as legislative redistricting. And even elected judges may pay attention to public opinion only on the most visible and controversial issues. On the other hand, such matters as the role of parties depend on the character of a state's politics, as well as on its formal selection system, and ultimately the former may have much more impact than the latter.

CONCLUSIONS

In the United States, concern about the selection of judges has focused largely on choices among formal selection systems. That focus is especially apparent in the states, which have changed their formal systems with some frequency. The concern about formal systems stems from the belief that they make a difference. As we have seen, however, this belief seems faulty in several respects.

First, the actual operation of a formal selection system often does not accord with what we would expect from its rules. Elective systems become largely appointive in practice; the Missouri Plan permits partisan politics to exert an influence.

Second, the different formal systems actually converge to a considerable extent in both their operation and their results. Chief executives play central roles in all the systems used in the United States. And systems as different in appearance as the Missouri Plan and partisan election produce similar kinds of judges.

Finally, a single formal system may work quite differently under different circumstances. The U.S. Constitution establishes the same rules for the selection of Supreme Court justices and district judges, but the two are actually selected in very different ways. President Carter and his two Republican successors established somewhat different processes for the selection of lower-court judges and chose different mixes of people.

All this does not mean that formal systems to select judges make little difference. The systems used to select judges in the United States hardly represent the full range of possible systems. Rather, in contrast with the civil service–like systems that exist in much of the world, the various American systems share an emphasis on accountability rather than judicial independence. In this sense, it is not surprising that the American systems look somewhat similar in operation and seem to produce similar results.

These similarities merit emphasis. The federal government and every state government select judges in ways that ensure a linkage between those judges and other political institutions. The results are noteworthy: a high proportion of judges are people who have been politically active and have connections with political officials, and the courts are relatively open to influence from their political environments.

Judicial selection systems, then, are significant, but in the United States their significance lies in their shared effects more than in their differences. These shared effects are explored further in the next chapter.

FOR FURTHER READING

Abraham, Henry J. *Justices and Presidents: A Political History of Appointments to the Supreme Court.* 3d ed. New York: Oxford University Press, 1992.

Bronner, Ethan. *Battle for Justice: How the Bork Nomination Shook America.* New York: W.W. Norton, 1989.

Dubois, Philip L. *From Ballot to Bench: Judicial Elections and the Quest for Accountability.* Austin: University of Texas Press, 1980.

McFeeley, Neil D. *Appointment of Judges: The Johnson Presidency*. Austin: University of Texas Press, 1987.

Phelps, Timothy M., and Helen Winternitz. *Capitol Games: Clarence Thomas, Anita Hill, and the Story of a Supreme Court Nomination*. New York: Hyperion, 1992.

Watson, Richard A., and Rondal G. Downing. *The Politics of the Bench and the Bar: Judicial Selection Under the Missouri Nonpartisan Court Plan*. New York: John Wiley, 1969.

NOTES

1. See Philip L. Dubois, *From Ballot to Bench: Judicial Elections and the Quest for Accountability* (Austin: University of Texas Press, 1980), especially ch. 1.
2. This discussion is based in part on Evan Haynes, *The Selection and Tenure of Judges* (Newark, N.J.: National Conference of Judicial Councils, 1944), chs. 2–4; and Allan Ashman and James J. Alfini, *The Key to Judicial Merit Selection: The Nominating Process* (Chicago: American Judicature Society, 1974), pp. 7–11.
3. Kermit L. Hall, "The Judiciary on Trial: State Constitutional Reform and the Rise of an Elected Judiciary, 1846–1860," *The Historian*, 44 (May 1983), 337–354.
4. Steve Williams, "Changing Patterns of Recruitment to the Tennessee Supreme Court," *Comparative State Politics*, 11 (August 1990), 36–38.
5. John Ehrlichman, *Witness to Power: The Nixon Years* (New York: Simon and Schuster, 1982), pp. 114–115.
6. David G. Savage, *Turning Right: The Making of the Rehnquist Supreme Court* (New York: John Wiley & Sons, 1992), p 136.
7. Robert Scigliano, *The Supreme Court and the Presidency* (New York: Free Press, 1971), p. 95; updated by the author.
8. Ibid., p. 111; updated by the author.
9. On the factors that shape Senate confirmation decisions, see John D. Felice and Herbert F. Weisberg, "The Changing Importance of Ideology, Party, and Region in Confirmation of Supreme Court Nominees, 1953 88," *Kentucky Law Journal*, 77 (1988–1989), 509–530; and Jeffrey A. Segal, Charles M. Cameron, and Albert D. Cover, "A Spatial Model of Roll Call Voting: Senators, Constituents, Presidents, and Interest Groups in Supreme Court Nominations," *American Journal of Political Science*, 36 (February 1992), 96–121.
10. Wayne King, "As of Now, No Hispanic Nominees for Federal Bench in New York," *New York Times*, February 15, 1991, p. A16.
11. Roger K. Lowe, "Cincinnati Woman Likely to Get Judgeship," *Columbus Dispatch*, January 11, 1991, p. 11A.
12. Neil A. Lewis, "Senate is Quick to Approve Judgeship for Former Aide," *New York Times*, November 12, 1990, p. A10.
13. Sheldon Goldman, "The Bush Imprint on the Judiciary: Carrying on a Tradition," *Judicature*, 74 (April–May 1991), 305; see Ruth Marcus, "GOP Senators, Bush Administration at Odds over Judicial Appointments," *Washington Post*, November 23, 1989, p. A25.
14. This discussion is based primarily on information provided by Professor Sheldon Goldman. See also "Inter Alia," *Family, Law and Democracy Report*, 11 (September 1989), 18–19.
15. Harold W. Chase, *Federal Judges: The Appointing Process* (Minneapolis: University of Minnesota Press, 1972), p. 29.
16. Saundra Torry, "Democrats Start Jockeying for Judgeships," *Washington Post*, December 7, 1992 (Washington Business section), p. 5.

17. Elliot E. Slotnick, "The U.S. Circuit Judge Nominating Commission," *Law and Policy Quarterly,* 1 (October 1979), 465–496; W. Gary Fowler, "A Comparison of Initial Recommendation Procedures: Judicial Selection under Reagan and Carter," *Yale Law and Policy Review,* 1 (Spring 1983), 299–356.

18. Elliot E. Slotnick, "Judicial Selection Systems and Nomination Outcomes: Does the Process Make a Difference?" *American Politics Quarterly,* 12 (April 1984), 237–238.

19. Joseph C. Goulden, *The Benchwarmers: The Private World of the Powerful Federal Judges* (New York: Weybright and Talley, 1974), p. 23.

20. Tony Mauro, "Critics Assail Bush Cousin's Nomination," *USA Today,* November 9, 1989, p. 4A.

21. Bill Clinton, "Judiciary Suffers Racial, Sexual Lack of Balance," *National Law Journal,* November 2, 1992, p. 15.

22. Aric Press, "Judging the Judges," *Newsweek,* October 14, 1985, p. 74.

23. Howard Kurtz, "Democrats Settle Score with Gorton on Judgeship," *Washington Post,* October 11, 1986, p. A10; Timothy Egan, "Judge in Seattle Finally Sworn In," *New York Times,* December 3, 1987, p. A36.

24. "The Word from Washington," *The Progressive,* 38 (April 1974), 14.

25. Ezra Bowen, "Judges with Their Minds Right," *Time Magazine,* November 4, 1985, p. 77.

26. Neil A. Lewis, "Bush Travels Reagan's Course in Naming Judges," *New York Times,* April 10, 1990, p. A1.

27. See Joan Biskupic, "Bush Boosts Bench Strength of Conservative Judges," *Congressional Quarterly Weekly Report,* January 19, 1991, p. 174.

28. See Timothy B. Tomasi and Jess A. Velona, "All the President's Men? A Study of Ronald Reagan's Appointments to the U.S. Courts of Appeals," *Columbia Law Review,* 87 (May 1987), 766–793.

29. Clinton, "Judiciary Suffers Lack of Balance," pp. 15–16.

30. Roger K. Lowe, "U.S. Judge Nominee Has Easy Time Before Panel," *Columbus Dispatch,* January 31, 1992, p. 3C.

31. "Judge-Watching," *National Law Journal,* December 7, 1992, p. 35.

32. See Ruth Marcus, "Liberal-Conservative Slugfest Looms Over a Bush Judicial Nominee," *Washington Post,* February 20, 1991, p. A17; and Neil A. Lewis, "Committee Rejects Bush Nominee to Key Appellate Court in South," *New York Times,* April 12, 1991, pp. A1, A12.

33. This discussion of the formal rules for the selection of judges is based in part on the information in *The Book of the States, 1992–1993 Edition* (Lexington, Ky.: Council of State Governments, 1992), pp. 223–243.

34. Robert Moog, "Campaign Spending for North Carolina's Appellate Courts," *Judicature,* 76 (August–September 1992), 73.

35. American Bar Association, *Code of Judicial Conduct,* Canon 7 (B)(l)(c). That provision may be found in American Bar Association, *Model Code of Professional Responsibility and Code of Judicial Conduct, as Amended August 1980* (Chicago: American Bar Association, 1982), p. 69. The decisions are *J.C.J.D. v. R.J.C.R.,* 803 S.W.2d 953 (Ky. Sup. Ct. 1991); and *American Civil Liberties Union v. Florida Bar,* 744 F. Supp. 1094 (N.D. Fla. 1990). Decisions in other states have upheld these rules; see Randall Samborn, "Ruling Caps Campaign Rhetoric," *National Law Journal,* September 7, 1992, pp. 3, 35.

36. Johnson, "Voter Survey: Judges Unknown," *Texas Lawyer,* Nov. 10–14, 1986, at 1, 8–9. Cited in Anthony Champagne and Greg Thielemann, "Awareness of Trial Court Judges," *Judicature,* 74 (February–March 1991), 272.

37. Robb London, "For Want of Recognition, Chief Justice is Ousted," *New York Times,* September 28, 1990, p. B9

38. Gail Diane Cox, "Will the Real Phillippe Please Stand Up?" *National Law Journal,* April 8, 1991, p. 2.

39. "Judicial Contests," *Chicago Tribune,* March 18, 1992, sec. 1, p. 13.

40. "Re-Elect Superior Court Judge Donald B. Cantwell" (advertisement), *Modesto Bee,* June 4, 1990, p. A6.

41. "Ellen Napleton Roche for Judge" (advertisement), *Chicago Tribune*, March 18, 1990, sec. 1, p. 8. Two typographical errors in the advertisement were corrected in this quotation from it.

42. On the Ohio contest, see G. Alan Tarr and Mary Cornelia Aldis Porter, *State Supreme Courts in State and Nation* (New Haven: Yale University Press, 1988), pp. 172–176. On Wisconsin, see James Romenesko, "Wisconsin Court Race Gets Nasty," *National Law Journal*, April 2, 1990, pp. 3, 32; and Patrick Jasperse, "Steinmetz Open to Talks," *Milwaukee Journal*, April 4, 1990, pp. 1A, 6A.

43. "Vote for Circuit Ct. Judge John P. Tully" (advertisement), *Chicago Tribune*, March 19, 1990, sec. 1, p. 6.

44. Anthony Champagne, "The Texas Judiciary: New Developments," *Texas Bar Journal*, 52 (February 1989), 156. See also Philip L. Dubois, "Voting Cues in Nonpartisan Trial Court Elections: A Multivariate Assessment," *Law and Society Review*, 18 (1984), 399; Lawrence Baum, "The Electoral Fates of Incumbent Judges in the Ohio Court of Common Pleas," *Judicature*, 66 (April 1983), 424; Susan B. Hannah, "Competition in Michigan's Judicial Elections: Democratic Ideals vs. Judicial Realities," *Wayne Law Review*, 24 (July 1978), 1303.

45. Hannah, "Competition in Michigan's Judicial Elections," p. 1303; Baum, "Electoral Fates of Incumbent Judges," pp. 424–425.

46. Seth Mydans, "Voting on Judge's Probation for Killer," *New York Times*, June 1, 1992, p. A13; Sheryl Stolberg and Frederick M. Muir, "Judge Karlin's Win Baffles Black Leaders," *Los Angeles Times*, June 4, 1992, pp. B1, B4.

47. Gail Diane Cox, "Jerry's Judges," *National Law Journal*, May 25, 1992, p. 31.

48. Patricia Kilday Hart, "Disorder in the Court," *Texas Monthly*, March 1988, pp. 118–121; Peter Applebome, "Rubber Stamp is Gone in Texas Judicial Election," *New York Times*, October 21, 1988, p. B7.

49. Dubois, *From Ballot to Bench*, pp. 146–147.

50. Champagne, "The Texas Judiciary," p. 160.

51. On Illinois, see James Tuohy and Rob Warden, *Greylord: Justice, Chicago Style* (New York: G. P. Putnam's Sons, 1989), pp. 45–49; on New York, see New York State Commission on Government Integrity, *Becoming a Judge* (New York: Commission on Government Integrity, 1988); and Matthew L. Hickerson, "Electing Little-Known Candidates as Judges," *New York Times* (Long Island Weekly), October 20, 1991, pp. 1, 15, 20.

52. New York State Commission on Government Integrity, *Restoring the Public Trust: A Blueprint for Government Integrity* (New York: Commission on Public Integrity, 1990), p. 16.

53. Hannah, "Competition in Michigan's Elections," p. 1306.

54. Michael Abramowicz, "Page Puts on Big Rush in Minnesota Court Bid," *Washington Post*, October 24, 1992, pp. G1, G4.

55. See John Paul Ryan, Allan Ashman, Bruce D. Sales, and Sandra Shane-Du Bow, *American Trial Judges: Their Work Styles and Performance* (New York: Free Press, 1980), p. 124.

56. *Newman v. Voinovich*, 789 F. Supp. 1410, 1413 (S.D. Ohio 1992).

57. Mark Vandervelden, "If the Robe Fits . . . ," *California Lawyer*, February 1984, p. 23.

58. James J. Alfini, "Mississippi Judicial Selection: Election, Appointment, and Bar Anointment," in *Courts and Judges*, ed. James A. Cramer (Beverly Hills, Calif.: Sage Publications, 1981), p. 258.

59. Sara Fritz, "Brown's Judicial Picks Often Contributors Too," *Los Angeles Times*, April 5, 1992, pp. A1, A30; Paul Jacobs, "Judges Picked by Wilson Are Often Contributors," *Los Angeles Times*, May 17, 1992, pp. A1, A24, A25.

60. Larry Liebert, "Hoping for a Judgeship," *San Francisco Chronicle*, February 18, 1978, p. 12.

61. Robert Barnes, "Schaefer Names Foe to Judgeship," *Washington Post,* April 5, 1989, p. B5.
62. Philip L. Dubois, "State Trial Court Appointments: Does the Governor Make a Difference?" *Judicature,* 69 (June–July 1985), 25.
63. Peter Allen, "Deukmejian's Judicial Legacy," *California Lawyer,* February 1991, p. 25.
64. Richard L. Madden, "Commission Set to Recruit and Screen New Judges," *New York Times,* December 14, 1986 (Connecticut Weekly), p. 1.
65. Beth M. Henschen, Robert Moog, and Steven Davis, "Judicial Nominating Commissioners: A National Profile," *Judicature,* 73 (April–May 1990), 329–333.
66. Ashman and Alfini, *Key to Judicial Merit Selection,* p. 77.
67. Steven L. Willborn, "Off the Mark: The Nebraska Supreme Court and Judicial Nominating Commissions," *Nebraska Law Review,* 70 (Spring 1991), 300–301.
68. Henschen, Moog, and Davis, "Judicial Nominating Commissioners," p. 334.
69. David Margolick, "Challenge for Cuomo: Picking Judges," *New York Times,* December 7, 1984, p. B3.
70. Henschen, Moog, and Davis, "Judicial Nominating Commissioners," p. 334.
71. Paul Wenske, "Dissension Rocks Missouri Justices," *National Law Journal,* May 27, 1985, pp. 1, 26–28.
72. William K. Hall and Larry T. Aspin, "What Twenty Years of Judicial Retention Elections Have Told Us," *Judicature,* 70 (April–May 1987), 344.
73. This discussion of California is based in part on John H. Culver and John T. Wold, "Rose Bird and the Politics of Judicial Accountability in California," *Judicature,* 70 (August–September 1986), 81–89; and John T. Wold and John H. Culver, "The Defeat of the California Justices: The Campaign, the Electorate, and the Issue of Judicial Accountability," *Judicature,* 70 (April–May 1987), 348–355.
74. "State's Chief Justice Keeps His Seat," *Miami Herald,* November 7, 1990, p. 17A; Karen Branch, "Politics and Florida's Highest Court," *Miami Herald,* November 1, 1992, p. 6M; Andrew Blum, "Jurists, Initiatives on Ballot," *National Law Journal,* November 16, 1992, p. 31.
75. Hall and Aspin, "What Twenty Years Have Told Us," p. 344.
76. Pete Rosenbery, "Voter Discontent Blamed for Ouster," *Southern Illinoisan* (Carbondale), November 11, 1990, pp. A1, A8.
77. Jonathan M. Moses, "BCCI Creditors to Challenge Settlement," *Wall Street Journal,* December 31, 1991, p. B4; William C. Lhotka and Tim Bryant, "Missouri Judge Voted Out for 1st Time in 50 Years," *St. Louis Post-Dispatch,* November 5, 1992, p. 6C.
78. William K. Hall and Larry T. Aspin, "Distance from the Bench and Retention Voting Behavior: A Comparison of Trial Court and Appellate Court Retention Elections," *Justice System Journal,* 15 (1992), 801–813.
79. Hall and Aspin, "What Twenty Years Have Told Us."
80. Philip Hager, "No Opposition, Little Notice for 5 State Justices Up for Election," *Los Angeles Times,* November 4, 1990, pp. A3, A30.
81. Joseph R. Grodin, *In Pursuit of Justice: Reflections of a State Supreme Court Justice* (Berkeley: University of California Press, 1989), p. 3.
82. David Margolick, "Picking of Judges Assailed by Cuomo," *New York Times,* August 15, 1983, pp. A1, B8.
83. Bradley C. Canon, "The Impact of Formal Selection Processes on the Characteristics of Judges—Reconsidered," *Law and Society Review,* 6 (May 1972), 579–593; Susan P. Fino, "Similarities and Differences in the Backgrounds of State Supreme Court Justices" (Paper presented at the 1983 meeting of the Midwest Political Science Association, Chicago, Illinois); Henry R. Glick and Craig F. Emmert, "Selection Systems and Judicial Characteristics: The Recruitment of State Supreme Court Judges," *Judicature,* 70 (December–January 1987), 228–235.

84. Glick and Emmert, "Selection Systems and Judicial Characteristics," p. 235.
85. Miriam R. Krasno, "New South Carolina Court," *Judicature,* 67 (September 1983), 151.
86. Richard A. Watson and Rondal G. Downing, *The Politics of the Bench and the Bar: Judicial Selection Under the Missouri Nonpartisan Court Plan* (New York: John Wiley, 1969), pp. 205–219, 257–263, 282–286.

5

Judges

The previous chapter examines the process by which people are selected as judges. This chapter examines the judges themselves, looking at them from several perspectives.

One concern running through the chapter is the balance between freedom and constraints in the working lives of judges. Like other public officials, judges are limited in what they can do by a variety of forces. Their freedom is narrowed by legal rules, external pressures, and characteristics of the courts that they join. Although there are signs that these constraints are tightening, judges still have considerable room to put their own stamp on their work. How they do their jobs and what decisions they reach are largely products of their own individual choices; thus judges are not interchangeable.

Because it makes a difference who becomes a judge, the chapter's first section focuses on the backgrounds of federal and state judges. The second section examines the behavior of judges on the bench; here the balance between individualism and constraint is considered most directly. The final section assesses the quality of judges' performance.

JUDGES' BACKGROUNDS

There are surprisingly few formal limits on who can become a judge. The most important is the requirement in most states that all judges or those above the lowest levels be licensed as lawyers. Many states also specify a length of time that a person must be a lawyer or, in some states, actually have practiced law to be eligible for a judgeship; the longest time required is ten years.[1] In contrast, the federal Constitution does not restrict judgeships to lawyers; technically, a nonlawyer could serve on any federal court, including the Supreme Court. With the exception of some minor state courts, however, only lawyers are considered for service on either federal or state courts.

Aside from their profession, judges have another characteristic in common: at some point, each of them came to the favorable attention of the people who choose judges. In many states, the voters play a central part in choosing judges. But in the country as a whole, as we have seen, the key people in the selection of judges are public officials who appoint judges directly and political leaders who influence both candidacies and outcomes in judicial elections.

This shared characteristic provides a perspective from which to view judges' backgrounds. I examine three aspects of these backgrounds: judges' political activity, their career experiences, and their social circumstances. The most extensive data are available on federal judges, largely through the research of political scientist Sheldon Goldman; I make frequent reference to his findings on recent federal court appointees, highlighted in Exhibit 5.1. We know less about state judges, and the best studies of their characteristics were done some time ago, but those sources and others provide a sense of their backgrounds.

Political Activity

Most judges were active in politics prior to their selection. For instance, Exhibit 5.1 shows that more than 60 percent of the federal judges appointed

EXHIBIT 5.1 Selected Background Characteristics of Federal Court Appointees, 1977–1992

Characteristic	District Courts (Percentage)	Courts of Appeals (Percentage)
Political activity		
Prominent party activism	59.8%	70.8%
Member of the president's party	91.9	90.6
Career experience		
Experience as a judge	49.1	58.5
Judge on another court at the time of the		
appointment	40.6	53.2
Experience as a prosecutor	41.2	29.8
In private practice at the time of the		
appointment	46.9	27.5
Firm of 25 or more members[a]	39.0	46.8
Firm of 5–24 members[a]	39.3	44.7
Firm of 1–4 members[a]	21.7	8.5
Social background		
White	87.3	89.5
Male	87.2	87.1
Private undergraduate school	55.5	72.5
Ivy League undergraduate school[b]	12.8	19.9

[a]The percentages are of those engaged in private practice.
[b]Also included in the private undergraduate school category.
Source: Sheldon Goldman, "Bush's Judicial Legacy: The Final Imprint," *Judicature,* 76 (April–May 1993), 287, 293. Reprinted by permission from *Judicature,* the journal of the American Judicature Society.

between 1977 and 1992 had records of prominent activism in a political party, and many others undoubtedly were involved in party politics in more limited ways.[2]

This pattern reflects the need to come to the favorable attention of the people who select judges. In a judicial election, a candidate who has already been involved in politics has an easier time building an organization and often has the advantage of being well known to the voters. Even more important, however, is the role of political activity in winning the support of public officials and political leaders, who play key parts in every selection system.

These people tend to favor political activists, primarily for two reasons. First, a major goal in the selection of judges is to reward political supporters. Accordingly, those who have been allied with the selectors have the best chance to be chosen. Second, since most of the people who help to select judges are political activists themselves, most of their acquaintances are also activists. Even if the selectors were concerned only with the qualifications of potential judges, they would have the greatest confidence in people they already knew.

For both of these reasons, a considerable proportion of all judges have personal ties with the officials who help to select them, especially state judges with governors. Often these ties are close; in 1990 Governor George Deukmejian of California chose his former appointments secretary for the state supreme court, while Governor Evan Bayh of Indiana selected a supreme court justice who had served as Bayh's attorney in a case about his eligibility to become governor.[3] Once, at a meeting of a San Francisco lawyers' group, "an earnest young man" asked a member of the state supreme court "how he should conduct himself to have the best chance of securing a seat on the California Supreme Court. Justice Tobriner kindly replied that the only rule he could distill from his own experiences was that one should take care to go to high school with someone who planned to become governor."[4] In a statement that is widely quoted, a judge and novelist put the matter more succinctly: "a judge is a member of the Bar who once knew a Governor.[5]

The kinds of political activity that lead to judgeships differ somewhat depending on the level of the court. Members of the U.S. Supreme Court who participated in politics before their selection often played prominent roles in presidential campaigns. This was true of former Chief Justice Warren Burger, who provided important support to Dwight D. Eisenhower at the 1952 Republican convention, and of former Justice Byron White, who led a national volunteer organization for John F. Kennedy in 1960.

At the other end of the spectrum, state trial judges have often been party activists at what is sometimes called the clubhouse level of politics. Attorneys may work for years in unglamorous local party jobs and contribute money to party coffers in order to obtain a judicial appointment or a party nomination to a lower court. This traditionally has been true in Chicago, to take one prominent example. And in Chicago, as in other places, links to powerful political figures have often led to the bench. When Mayor Richard J. Daley (father of the current mayor, Richard M. Daley) controlled the Democratic organization, he secured a party endorsement for a lawyer named Joseph Gordon. According to one account,

Gordon, a bright and highly regarded former law professor, would have been an outstanding member of any judiciary, but that had little to do with why Daley selected him. When Daley's youngest son, William, was having trouble with his grades at John Marshall Law School, Gordon tutored him privately. For this, Daley was grateful. He expressed his gratitude by making Gordon a judge.[6]

Of course, political activity in itself hardly guarantees a person's selection as a judge, since there are far more lawyers actively involved in politics than there are judgeships. To a considerable extent, the translation of activism into a judgeship is a matter of good fortune, of being allied with someone who ends up in a position to help select judges. After all, most rising state politicians do not become governors, just as most law school roommates do not become senators.

Nevertheless, political activity greatly increases a lawyer's opportunity to make the contacts and build up the credits that can facilitate selection as a judge. And such activity, if not sufficient for selection, often is necessary. "Take a popular lawyer who has not been active in party activities," said a former Democratic chair in Buffalo; that lawyer's "chance of being a nominee for a high court position is very slight."[7]

Career Experience

Except at the very lowest levels of the judiciary, nearly all of today's judges were educated in law school. But a wide variety of career paths can lead from law school to a judgeship. Exhibit 5.2 illustrates this diversity by describing the routes taken by some state supreme court justices. As there are many ways of making useful contacts and establishing a reputation for competence, the diversity of career paths is understandable. However, certain kinds of career experiences are particularly common because they provide special advantages.

Private Practice   Like other attorneys, the great majority of judges engaged at some point in the private practice of law. Indeed, in most courts, a high proportion of the judges have come directly from private practice. One national study of major state trial courts reported the proportion to be 54 percent,[8] and, as Exhibit 5.1 shows, the proportion for the federal district courts between 1977 and 1992 was 47 percent. Another large group of judges moved from private practice into public office or lower-court judgeships before attaining their current positions.

Higher-court judges come primarily from practices that are very successful in terms of financial rewards and status. Although it is imperfect, one way to detect success in these terms is through the size of the firm in which a lawyer practices. Between 1977 and 1992, eight times as many of the practicing lawyers who were appointed to the federal courts came from firms of twenty-five or more as came from solo practice. This ratio is striking because even today about half of all the attorneys in America practice alone. And the last two lawyers who went directly from private practice to the Supreme

Ruth Ida Abrams, Massachusetts

Law degree, Harvard University, 1956
Private practice, 1957–60
Assistant district attorney, 1961–69
Assistant state attorney general, 1969–71
Special counsel, state supreme court, 1971–72
Trial judge, 1972–77
Joined supreme court in 1977

David Allen Brock, New Hampshire

Law degree, University of Michigan, 1963
Private practice, 1963–69
United States Attorney, 1969–72
Private practice, 1972–76
Special counsel to governor and executive counsel, 1974–76
Legal counsel to governor, 1976
Trial judge, 1976–78
Joined supreme court in 1978

William T. Brotherton, Jr., West Virginia

Law degree, Washington and Lee University, 1950
Private practice, 1950–84
Member, West Virginia legislature, 1952–80
Joined supreme court in 1985

James Leon Dennis, Louisiana

Law degree, Louisiana State University, 1962
Private practice, 1962–72
Trial judge, 1972–74
Court of appeals judge, 1974–75
Joined supreme court in 1975

Yvonne Kauger, Oklahoma

Medical technologist, 1959–68
Law degree, Oklahoma City University, 1969
Private practice, 1970–72
Judicial assistant, state supreme court, 1972–84
Joined supreme court in 1984

Ellen Ash Peters, Connecticut

Law degree, Yale University, 1954
Law clerk, U.S. court of appeals, 1954–55

EXHIBIT 5.2 Career Paths of Some State Supreme Court Justices Serving in the 1990s

Professor of law, Yale University, 1956–78
Joined supreme court in 1978

Thomas Lee Steffen, Nevada

Law degree, George Washington University, 1964
Private practice, 1965–82
Joined supreme court in 1982

Notes: A few pre–supreme court positions are omitted.
Source: Who's Who in American Law, 7th ed. (Wilmette, Ill.: Marquis Who's Who, 1991).

EXHIBIT 5.2 (*Continued*)

Court, Abe Fortas and Lewis Powell, were both senior partners in major law firms.

For federal judges, we have more direct information on financial success. Among the Reagan and Bush appointees, 51 percent had a net worth of at least $500,000, and 26 percent were millionaires.[9] This level of wealth reflects both the financial rewards of high-status law practice and inherited wealth.

Lower-court judges are less likely to come from elite segments of the bar—though this does not necessarily mean that they are less skilled as lawyers. State trial courts, for instance, contain a broader cross section of private practitioners than do the federal courts of appeals. In the national study of major trial courts, about 60 percent of the judges who came directly from private practice reported no specialization, a characteristic associated with solo practice and small firms.[10]

There are two reasons for this difference between higher and lower courts. First, highly successful lawyers are much less likely to seek positions in lower courts, which carry only limited power and prestige. Second, participants in the selection of judges tend to demand higher levels of qualifications, as measured by success as a lawyer, for higher courts.

Government Legal Practice   A great many attorneys practice law for the government at some point in their careers, and certainly this is true of lawyers who become judges. Some spent the first few years after law school working for the government and then moved into private practice. Others came to the bench directly from government service.

A lawyer who works for the government has an advantage in coming to the attention of people who choose judges. Thus the role of the Justice Department in selecting federal judges puts lawyers working for the department in a good position to be recognized and rewarded with a judgeship. At the state level, a prominent government lawyer such as an attorney general has the sort of visibility that helps in winning an election or obtaining an appointment to the courts. Government lawyers also have a good chance to develop the trial experience that is often deemed essential for a judge.

Criminal prosecution is the most common form of prior government service for judges. From 1977 through 1992 about 40 percent of the federal district court appointees had been prosecutors; that experience is also common, though less so, among state supreme court justices.[11] The figures reflect both the large numbers of lawyers who serve as prosecutors and the credibility of prosecutors as candidates for judgeships. This credibility stems partly from a prosecutor's advantage in projecting a "law and order" image that most voters favor.

High Government Positions   Among the judges who had been politically active, politics was usually an avocation (though often a very time-consuming one) rather than a career. But some people become judges after holding high positions in the government outside the legal realm. These positions can be a brief way station between private practice and the bench, or they can be a person's primary career.

At the state level, one path to the judiciary is from the legislature. Because state legislators are in a good position to extract appointments from governors and to win judicial elections (and in an even better position to win judgeships in states selecting judges through legislative elections), the state courts include a liberal sprinkling of former legislators. In 1980–1981, 20 percent of the state supreme court justices in the country were former legislators.[12] In contrast, federal judgeships below the Supreme Court are less attractive to members of Congress, except for those who have tired of Congress or suffered electoral defeat.

It is less common but not unknown for a chief executive to become a judge. The only president to do so was William Howard Taft, who was defeated for re-election in 1912 and became chief justice of the U.S. Supreme Court in 1921, after a strenuous campaign for the position. Price Daniel of Texas served in the U.S. Senate and then as governor for three terms. Several years later, in 1971, he was appointed to the Texas Supreme Court. In Ohio, C. William O'Neill achieved the most unusual feat of heading all three branches of state government, serving as Speaker of the Ohio House of Representatives and then as governor before he became chief justice of the Ohio Supreme Court in 1970.

The Judicial Career Ladder   In many countries, judges serve within a kind of civil service system, becoming judges early in their legal careers and progressing upward through the ranks. The system in the United States is fundamentally different. Here most judges reach the bench at middle age or later, and service on one court is not required to obtain a seat on the court above it.

Still, in both the federal and the state court systems, it is common for judges to ascend upward. One reason is the widespread feeling that service on a lower court helps to qualify a person for a higher judgeship. Besides, a prospective appointee's abilities and policy preferences can be gauged more easily from a judicial record than from most other career experiences. And, where judges are elected, prior service on a lower court can give a candidate name recognition.

The federal court system shows a fairly strong promotional pattern.[13] In recent years a large minority of the district judges came directly from other judicial positions, primarily in the state courts. (This pattern indicates that the federal courts are more attractive than their state counterparts; few judges move from federal to state courts.) In turn, about half of the new court of appeals judges rose from lower courts, primarily the district courts. At the top level, a majority of Supreme Court justices have had prior judicial service; in the past half century this service has generally been on the courts of appeals.

A similar pattern exists in many states. Of the supreme court justices serving in 1980–1981, 63 percent had served on another court. Even among judges on major trial courts, 24 percent of those serving in 1977 had risen from a minor trial court.[14]

Social Background

Whatever people accomplish in their own lives, they begin with certain characteristics they cannot control. One is their parents' social and economic status. Others are race and gender. In each of these respects, judges, like other public officials, are far from a random sample of the population.

Social and Economic Status   As a group, judges come primarily from families of higher than-average status. This pattern is an inevitable product of the advantages that relative wealth and high social status confer. A high family income helps a person to become a lawyer, most directly by making it easier to pay the costs of a college education and law school. Inherited social status affords some people an advantage in entering the most prestigious schools and law firms, as well as advancing their careers in politics and government. One San Diego municipal court judge has a father who is chief judge of the federal district court there, a brother who sits on the federal court of appeals, and a grandfather who was presiding judge of the San Diego superior court; it seems likely that these connections were of some help to the judge in reaching the municipal court.[15]

High family status is most common among judges on the highest courts. The Supreme Court in particular has been populated primarily by those from high-status backgrounds, and to a lesser extent the same is true of lower federal courts. One indicator of family status patterns among federal judges is the schools that they attended. From 1977 through 1992, 59 percent of the federal court appointees had attended private undergraduate colleges. Indeed, 14 percent of these judges had gone to Ivy League schools for their undergraduate education and 18 percent for their legal education.

As noted earlier, the high level of wealth held by many federal judges results in part from the substantial family wealth that some inherited. Whether or not they were so fortunate, most people appointed to the federal courts have achieved a comfortable financial status. The Bush appointees stood out in this respect; more than one-third were millionaires. Exaggerating somewhat, a news broadcast in a 1992 comic strip announced that "a recent study of federal judges appointed by President Bush reports that nearly all the appointees . . . are rich guys."[16]

Lower-court judges appear to be a more heterogeneous group, and in some localities there is a good deal of upward mobility into the state trial courts. It is not unusual for people from relatively poor families to make their way through law school (perhaps attending classes at night while working during the day) and then make themselves candidates for judgeships through legal work and political activity. A study of trial judges in the Baltimore and San Francisco areas found that roughly a third of them were the children of industrial wage earners and low-salaried workers.[17] By the same token, fewer judges at the lower court levels come from highly advantaged backgrounds.

In recent years more people from relatively humble backgrounds have become judges. This change has occurred because college and law school educations are more widely available and because an elite social background has become less of a prerequisite for advancement in politics and law. But individuals from high-status families continue to hold advantages that are reflected in their representation on the bench.

Race and Gender   Until recently the judiciary consisted almost entirely of white men. As late as 1977 about 96 percent of the judges on major state trial courts were white, and about 98 percent were male; more than 99 percent of the state supreme court justices in 1980–1981 were white and 97 percent male.[18] The Supreme Court was entirely white until 1967, and entirely male until 1981.

These patterns resulted from several social realities. Poverty and discrimination limited the numbers of nonwhite citizens who could obtain college and legal educations. And, largely because of admissions policies, women had a difficult time getting to law school. Furthermore, nonwhites and women who did manage to become lawyers found that many career and political opportunities were closed to them. After finishing near the top of her class at Stanford Law School in 1952, future Supreme Court Justice Sandra Day O'Connor discovered that no California law firm would offer her anything more than a secretarial position.

Women and members of racial minority groups have gained many more judgeships in recent years. Especially striking are the gains for women in the federal courts. Prior to 1977 only eight women had served on the federal district courts and courts of appeals; between 1977 and 1992, 104 women were appointed to those courts.[19] The number of women has increased substantially in state courts as well, tripling in major trial courts between 1977 and 1987 and in supreme courts between 1981 and 1991.[20] The number of black judges nearly tripled between 1970 and 1980, with the most substantial growth occurring in the federal courts; since then, the ranks of black judges have continued to expand considerably in state courts.[21]

These increases reflect the changing composition of the legal profession, reduced discrimination in the profession, the greater political power of groups representing racial minorities and women, and changing attitudes of people who select judges. Some chief executives have used appointments to increase the diversity of the judiciary; President Jimmy Carter (1977–1981) and California Governor Jerry Brown (1975–1983) stood out in this respect.[22] Appointments by Governor Rudy Perpich gave the Minnesota Supreme Court a female majority in 1991; this majority, the first ever for an appellate court, symbolized the changes that have occurred in the demography of the courts.[23]

White men continue to hold judgeships well beyond their proportion in the general population, and their numerical dominance probably will decline only at a slow and uneven pace. But the numbers of female and minority-group judges are certain to increase further, with the impact of social and political changes reinforced by changes in judicial elections. In 1991 the Supreme Court ruled that the Voting Rights Act applies to judicial elections;[24] as a result, some states are likely to change their election districts for judges to give candidates from racial minority groups a better chance to compete, and in turn more such candidates would win. The growing willingness of voters to choose female candidates, which helped women running for Congress in 1992, may also assist women who seek judgeships.[25]

The Impact of Judges' Background Characteristics

In their backgrounds, judges are unrepresentative of the general population—or even of the legal profession. This reality has a potential impact on what the courts do. People with different backgrounds tend to develop different sets of values; judges' values in turn influence the decisions that they reach on the bench.

Scholars have studied the relationships between judges' backgrounds and their decisions a good deal, comparing the behavior of judges with different backgrounds.[26] Their findings have been ambiguous and inconsistent. More than anything else, the studies caution against assuming strong connections between backgrounds and behavior on the bench. But it is possible to suggest a few links between the predominant backgrounds of judges and what the courts do.

Class, Race, and Gender   In their family backgrounds, their own careers, and their associations, most judges belong to something of an elite group in socioeconomic terms. The judiciary is also unrepresentative of the general population in its racial composition and even less representative in gender.

These characteristics are potentially significant because surveys of the general population show that opinions on policy issues differ between people of higher and lower economic status and between women and men; the differences between blacks and whites are even greater.[27] In some respects, these differences can be characterized as ideological, with whites, men, and people of higher status being relatively conservative. More broadly, however, we can understand these differences as reflecting the differences in perspective that people from different groups tend to develop.

Studies of judges' race and gender have differed in their findings about the impact of these characteristics on decisions.[28] It does appear that they have an effect on sentencing, at least in some settings. A study of Philadelphia, for instance, determined that white judges treated white defendants somewhat more leniently than black defendants in deciding whether to impose a prison sentence, while no such difference existed for black judges. In contrast, male judges in Philadelphia seemed to be relatively lenient toward female defendants, perhaps because of what has been labeled "paternalism," whereas female judges treated women and men before them more evenhandedly.[29]

We have little systematic evidence about the impact of social class, but there is some reason to conclude that the upper-status backgrounds of most judges subtly influence what they do by affecting the perspectives that they bring to cases. One example is lawsuits between business creditors and individual debtors. On the whole, as I discuss in Chapter 7, business creditors who sue individual debtors are quite successful. This success results in part from the tendency of many judges to regard the creditor as the more respectable and responsible party. In turn, this perception is related to the family backgrounds and careers of most judges, which make it easier for them to identify with the owner of a business than with a low-income debtor who lives in circumstances that are far removed from their own experience.

The impact of race, gender, and class on the courts should not be overstated; by no means do all judges share the attitudes that we associate with their groups in the general population. Still, it seems to make a difference that white men from higher-status backgrounds have been represented so heavily on the bench.

Partisanship   In studies that probe the impact of judges' background characteristics, the most consistent finding is that Democratic judges tend to reach more liberal decisions than do Republicans.[30] This finding does not necessarily mean that judges are influenced by their party loyalties. Rather, people often gravitate to one party or the other on the basis of their ideological views; where people adopt the party loyalties of their parents, as often occurs, those loyalties are likely to reflect the views that parents and children share. In other words, it is more likely that judges become Republicans because they are conservative than that they turn conservative because they are Republicans.

But judges' party loyalties can affect their behavior in a more specific way. A high proportion of judges have been actively involved in one of the parties, and their party organization often plays an important role in putting them on the bench. As a result, they are likely to feel a certain loyalty to their party. This allegiance has little relevance to the great majority of cases. But the interests of political parties can be involved in some major and controversial cases, such as disputes over election rules and conflicts between the executive and legislative branches. When these situations arise, some judges can disregard their party loyalties. Others, however, are eager to uphold the interests of their parties. For instance, most Democratic judges in Chicago have close ties with the county party organization, and many of these judges are counted on to support their party's interests in relevant cases.

Legislative redistricting is an issue of critical importance to the parties because the way that districts are drawn affects the number of seats that Republicans and Democrats win. After the 1990 census, redistricting disputes in several states went to the courts. In some states, the parties battled over whether cases should go to federal or state court, believing that the partisan balance on courts at the two levels would affect the outcome. And in some instances judges seemed to confirm this belief by deciding redistricting cases along partisan lines.

In Illinois, a new set of U.S. House districts favoring Republicans was approved by a three-judge federal district court panel composed of three Republicans.[31] State Republican leaders wanted the dispute over state legislative redistricting heard in federal court as well; the Democrats wanted the case in the state supreme court, which had a 4–3 Democratic majority. Ultimately, the case was heard by the state supreme court, which approved districts drawn up by Republicans on a legislative districting commission. The vote of approval was 4–3; six justices voted along party lines, but one Democrat voted for the Republican plan. That justice was an appointee who apparently had wanted to run for a full term on the court but was turned down by the Democratic party. Two columnists said that they didn't "know if he got mad. But he sure got even."[32]

Partisan feelings may have had a more subtle effect on two criminal cases in the federal Court of Appeals for the District of Columbia. In 1989 the court overturned the conviction of Lyn Nofziger, a former adviser to President Reagan, for violation of a federal ethics law. A year later the court overturned Oliver North's convictions growing out of the Iran-Contra scandal. The panels hearing the two cases were composed of different judges, but in each instance the decision was by a 2–1 vote, with two Reagan appointees in the majority and a Carter appointee dissenting.[33] These votes are striking because Democratic judges usually are more favorable to appeals by criminal defendants than are Republicans. Although these six judges may not have responded consciously to the link between the defendants and President Reagan, that link helps to explain their positions.

Overview   In Chapter 4, I have argued that the differences among judicial selection systems in the United States are less significant than their similarities. In this section, I have made a similar point about judicial backgrounds: although judges differ a good deal, most share some important characteristics.

The two points are related. The traits shared by most judges result in part from the systems by which they are selected. Clearly, if the United States followed the example of most other nations and chose judges through a civil service system, judges' partisan ties would be much weaker. Under such a system, judges would still be disproportionately male, white, and upper-status in background but almost surely less so than they actually are.

To a degree, then, the systems used to select judges link the courts with the patterns of economic and political power in the United States. These systems favor those whose backgrounds and personal attainments give them relatively high status; they also favor people who are connected with the holders of political power. This is one subtle but powerful way that the courts are shaped by the larger society in which they operate.

JUDGES ON THE BENCH

Today more than twenty-eight thousand people serve as judges in the United States.[34] In the work that they do, perhaps the outstanding characteristic is variation. The jobs of trial and appellate judges differ fundamentally. State and federal judges operate within different systems and hear different kinds of cases. Some judges are generalists who hear a wide range of cases, while others focus on single fields such as taxes and domestic relations. Although a majority of judges serve full-time, a large minority—primarily lay judges at the lowest levels of the state systems—are part-time. And individual courts and judges develop their own ways of operating.

All this variation makes it difficult to generalize about the work of judges on the bench. But it is possible to sketch some patterns in the job of judge, and this section considers those patterns as well as the variation.

What Judges Do

The diverse activities of judges can be separated into several categories.[35]

Adjudication   The term *adjudication* refers to formal legal decision-making, which includes research on decisions and the preparation of decisions. This activity comes most readily to mind when we think about judges, and it is at the heart of what judges do. It also consumes the largest share of most judges' work time.[36] Thus it is understandable that observers who are interested in the behavior of judges focus primarily on this area.

The form of adjudication varies in a number of respects. Perhaps most important, it looks somewhat different in trial and appellate courts. Trial court decisions are nearly always made by single judges, whereas appellate decisions are group products; even if judges do most of their work on decisions apart from their colleagues, they must ultimately reach a collective decision. The timing of decisions also differs between the levels. Trial judges frequently make and announce their decisions in open court, but appellate decisions are generally made outside the courtroom and announced later.

The most familiar decisions are those that directly resolve the merits of cases—whether a defendant is guilty or innocent, whether a lower-court decision is affirmed or reversed. But judges also make preliminary decisions on matters such as the admissibility of evidence and the dismissal of criminal charges. Often these preliminary decisions resolve cases directly or indirectly.

In trial courts, different kinds of cases have their own typical forms of adjudication.[37] Trials in major criminal and civil cases are usually lengthy and formal, whereas cases involving lower stakes may be tried and decided in speedy and routine fashion. Appellate courts may also distinguish between cases that require close judicial consideration and those that can be resolved in more summary fashion. These differences and other aspects of adjudication are examined more fully in the remaining chapters.

Negotiation   A judge's work in *negotiation* involves efforts to resolve cases without formal adjudication by encouraging settlements between parties. The great majority of cases are terminated prior to trial through such agreements, and a smaller proportion of cases are worked out between the parties at the appellate level. Settlements can occur without the judge's participation, but judges often play active roles in bringing them about.

Trial judges are more likely to involve themselves actively in negotiation of civil settlements. Opinion is divided on the legitimacy of judges' participation in plea bargaining, while there is a general consensus that their involvement in civil negotiations is appropriate. Appellate judges traditionally have not taken part in efforts to settle cases, but in recent years some courts have initiated settlement efforts.

As this discussion suggests, settlement of cases is largely a discretionary activity. Although no judge can avoid heavy involvement in adjudication, a judge can play either a great or a limited part in negotiation. The roles that judges select are influenced by such factors as court rules and time pressures (where trials take longer, for instance, judges are more likely to take active roles in settling cases),[38] but the skills and preferences of individual judges are even more important.

Administration   The administration of federal and state courts is discussed in Chapter 2, but it is worth emphasizing this part of judges' responsibilities. As the size of courts and the number of cases they handle have grown, so has the volume of administrative work needed for a court to function adequately. Support staff have increased in number, taking much of the burden of this work from judges, but supervision of the staff is itself a significant task.

Among the judges on a court, the chief judge has the primary responsibility for administration. Management of the court may consume the largest share of the chief judge's time. But no judge can escape administrative work altogether; this is particularly true of trial courts, where judges usually do most of the managing of their own caseloads. Increasingly, judges are called on to help administer court systems as a whole, but below the supreme court level only a minority of judges are actively engaged in this work.

External Relations   Most judges devote at least some of their work time to the larger political systems and communities of which they are part. These activities are of several types.

Some external relations are with the other branches of government. Judges depend on the legislature for budgetary resources, and they may work with legislators to gain support for their requests. They may also lobby governors and legislators on issues that affect them. Working through the Federal Judicial Conference, for instance, federal judges in recent years have supported proposals for additional judgeships and opposed proposals that would have brought new kinds of cases to federal court. Chief judges do the greatest part of this work, but other judges also become involved.

Beyond the government, most judges engage in what might be called general community relations. They often give talks to civic groups and interviews to the mass media. Some judges work with lawyers' groups and other organizations on matters of mutual interest, such as increasing court budgets. For elected judges, one spur to this activity is the desire to maintain and enhance electoral support; community activities are one important way to build the positive name recognition that helps incumbents gain re-election.

Judges' activities outside their courts can raise questions of propriety. Solicitation of money for charities can put undue pressure on people who worry about staying in a judge's good graces; the Code of Judicial Conduct adopted by the American Bar Association prohibits such solicitation. Involvement in civic activities, generally regarded as acceptable, may compromise the appearance of impartiality; in recent years conservative legal groups have attacked judges for activities such as serving as a trustee of the Environmental Defense Fund.[39] Elected judges participate in politics simply by campaigning for re-election, but judges have been criticized for other involvement in political groups and for assisting candidates in nonjudicial elections.[40]

The Difficulties and Rewards of Being a Judge

Like other jobs, the judge's position has both positive and negative features. The attractions and drawbacks of serving as a judge are both particularly strong.

Many Skills Required, Little Preparation   My catalogue of judges' activities suggests that a good judge must possess a diverse range of skills. Effective judicial performance requires, among other things, a good knowledge of legal rules, the capacity to run trials, a talent for negotiation, and skill in managing court operations. This is a daunting set of requirements. To meet these requirements well, a judge needs an impressive set of personal traits. Inevitably, most judges fall short in some respects.

Judges' difficulties in performing their job well are aggravated by their lack of training. In nations with a career judiciary, aspiring judges study how to carry out the work of judges. In the United States, no such preparation exists. As a result, most judges begin their work with limited knowledge about what to do on the bench. As one judge put it, "We are overnight transformed from seasoned professional to rank amateur."[41] Another judge observed that "becoming a federal judge is like being thrown into the water and being told to swim."[42]

Appellate judges are not immune to these difficulties, even if they have experience at the trial level. Indeed, some Supreme Court justices—including people who had sat on other appellate courts—have noted the difficulty they faced in mastering their jobs as justices.[43] But at least appellate judges do their work largely in private, with an opportunity to consider decisions at length before making them.

Trial judges, in contrast, sit in court proceedings more or less alone, having to preside and make rulings—often instantaneously. A judge who is unfamiliar with procedures or substantive legal rules is almost certain to suffer some embarrassments, as one account suggests: "On his first day the new judge turned to the court clerk and asked him to bring in the jurors. . . . The clerk said, 'Your Honor, you never swore in the jury commissioners. Therefore we have no jurors to bring in.' "[44]

Of course, a judge's prior experience helps determine the difficulty of the learning process. An experienced trial lawyer, for example, is usually better prepared to become a trial judge than is an office lawyer who has seldom practiced in court. But even the most experienced lawyer finds that the judge's job is quite different; it was a leading trial lawyer who forgot to swear in the jury commissioners.

Inevitably, novices on the bench turn for help to those who have more experience—other judges, members of the court staff, and lawyers who appear before them. Through this process, the perspectives and approaches of people who are already in the courts are passed on to new judges. A judge who starts off with a distaste for plea bargaining usually will come to accept it, partly because the lawyers and judges with whom that judge interacts generally accept and encourage it.[45]

In the past new judges were given very little formal assistance. One appellate judge recalled that "when I joined the court, I was left to stumble, bumble, and do injustice to other people. I was given no manual, no orientation. . . . I was abandoned."[46] Increasingly, judges are receiving formal training and written materials to aid them. Still, the task of learning how to be a judge remains difficult and largely unsystematic.

Stresses of the Job   Judges are likely to become frustrated by the gap between their abilities and training and the requirements of their position. Other characteristics of the judge's job add to its stresses.

Most fundamentally, judges have to make a large number of decisions with potentially serious consequences under less than ideal conditions. In a full trial, a judge often must hand down a series of procedural rulings with little time to consider them and with the prospect that an appellate court will find a ruling in error, perhaps overturning the trial verdict as a result. Both trial and appellate judges frequently must choose between two competing sides when it is not clear where the facts and the law point and when the decision may have enormous effects on people's lives.

It has always been true that some judges face caseloads heavier than they can manage easily, and this condition has become increasingly common as the volume of cases has grown faster than the number of judgeships. Both trial and appellate judges find themselves scrambling to dispose of cases in order to prevent unacceptable backlogs. A survey of federal trial judges documented the impact of these pressures on them. One judge, expressing a widespread feeling, reported that "I am very much behind, cannot catch up, and I am frustrated and stressed because I cannot catch up."[47]

Just as caseloads have grown, so has scrutiny of judges' work from outside the court system. Increasingly, the mass media and groups such as Mothers Against Drunk Driving observe judges at work and make criticisms when they disagree with decisions or find a judge's work deficient. In one instance, a Chicago newspaper columnist wrote two dozen columns over eighteen months about a child custody case, in part to influence its handling.[48] During the past decade electoral campaigns against judges based on their decisions have become more common. Legal changes have limited the traditional immunity of judges from lawsuits; as a result, many judges now fear the financial and personal consequences of suits against them.

Judges also have reason for more immediate fears. A federal district judge in Texas was killed in 1979, and a New York district judge in 1988; both murders resulted from their work as judges. Bombs have been sent to judges in Maryland, Minnesota, and Mississippi. And in 1990 a former mayor who had been suspended from the legal profession was charged with sending letters threatening to murder all members of the Louisiana Supreme Court.[49] In response, a few judges now carry guns on the bench. In 1992, reacting to a reported threat by a defendant, a Florida judge took out a pistol and told the defendant, "If you're going to take a shot, you better score, because I don't miss." (Reportedly, this judge was regarded by some prosecutors as "too soft on criminals.")[50] The extent of some judges' fears was suggested by the aftermath of a 1993 courthouse shooting in Dallas; within a few hours all of the city's district judges stopped hearing cases to protest what they regarded as inadequate courthouse security.[51]

Another growing source of stress is financial. It may be difficult to feel sympathy for judges on this ground when salaries in major trial courts average about $80,000 and all federal judges receive at least $129,000.[52] But judges, like other people, tend to compare themselves with people in the same profession—and there is a growing gap between the salaries of judges and the earnings of the best-paid lawyers in private practice. For many judges, this perceived gap is considerable; in a 1987 survey, two-thirds of the judges estimated that they would earn at least $50,000 more in private practice, and one-third estimated that their earnings would be at least $100,000 more.[53] When judicial salaries lag behind inflation, judges feel a financial squeeze.

We would expect all these pressures to affect judges, and one study of ninety-two judges verified this expectation. Nearly three-quarters exhibited "Type A" behavior, with strong or extreme tendencies toward stress, and very few fit into the low-stress categories. The results suggested that both judges' personalities and the characteristics of their jobs make them especially vulnerable to stress.[54] In one extreme case, a judge's widow was granted survivor's benefits under the Connecticut workers' compensation law on the ground that the pressures of the judge's job had brought about his fatal heart attack.[55]

There seems to be a growing rate of resignations from the bench, in part because judges seek less stressful and more lucrative positions in the legal profession.

Status and Power   Despite the difficulties of the judge's job and the stresses that it entails, a good many people still want to be judges. Governors and presidents who appoint judges usually find many aspirants for each position. Although some judges leave the bench because of their dissatisfaction, most remain for long periods, and state judges often work hard to win re-election. Clearly, the position of judge has powerful attractions.

One of them is the status of the job. In the courtroom, judges are generally accorded great deference by court personnel, lawyers, and other participants. "No matter what their personality," one commentator noted, "when approaching the bench," lawyers "tend to sound like Eddie Haskell of 'Leave It to Beaver' talking to June Cleaver. They compliment the judge's appearance, lavish him with honorifics, pore over his decisions, praise his erudition, double over with laughter at even his lamest jokes."[56]

Outside of court, many people give automatic respect to a person who holds the title of judge. Successful lawyers may enjoy respect and status within their own profession, but in society as a whole judges fare much better.

Along with a judge's status comes a considerable measure of power. Judges routinely make decisions that fundamentally affect the lives of individuals. Particularly in appellate courts, some decisions have broader impact on people throughout a state or the nation. Few acts by a single individual could have as much impact on a community as a federal district judge's order to desegregate a school district.

If the responsibility for such decisions sometimes creates stress, it also allows judges to make a difference, to do what they see as good. And because they *are* powerful positions, judgeships attract lawyers who enjoy the exercise of power for its own sake. The study of judges and stress mentioned earlier also found that the "most pronounced" personality trait among the judges was a need for dominance.[57] Judges may speak of the burdens of the powers they hold, such as criminal sentencing, but they frequently employ these powers with enthusiasm.

Constraints and Freedom

The discussion thus far suggests that judges feel significant constraints in choosing what to do. It also suggests that these constraints still leave them with considerable freedom to chart their own course. Both the constraints and the freedom should be considered more directly.

The constraints on judges take several forms. Perhaps the most fundamental is the expectation that judges will follow the law. This expectation, largely accepted by judges themselves, rules out some decisions that judges might otherwise want to make.

Other constraints are more concrete. Pressures from outside the courts are sometimes powerful. Today, for instance, judges' responses to criminal cases are often affected by a fear of being labeled as overly sympathetic toward criminal defendants. And judges may feel more direct pressures from inside the courts—from fellow judges, particularly at the appellate level, and from lawyers at the trial level. Increasingly, heavy caseloads also create heavy pressures, requiring that judges subordinate other goals to that of maintaining the flow of cases.

Powerful as these constraints are, however, they hardly reduce judges to the status of automatons. Indeed, on the whole it is the freedom of judges rather than the limits on their freedom that stands out. That freedom is reflected in judges' individualism—the different ways that they define and undertake their jobs.

It is easy to identify differences among judges on appellate courts, whose members often vary in their responses to the same set of cases. The divergent interpretations of the Constitution by members of the Supreme Court are heavily publicized. Receiving less attention but equally sharp are disagreements over questions of law and policy among members of some federal courts of appeals and state supreme courts.

Judges' individualism may have even greater impact at the trial level. Trial judges typically operate on their own, setting their work schedules, presiding over proceedings in their own fashion, and reaching decisions by themselves. Within boundaries that usually are fairly loose, they can act as they see fit. Some judges work punishing hours, while others minimize their time on the job. One judge runs a tight and efficient courtroom; another presides in a more relaxed manner. Most important, different judges adopt different interpretations of the law, so that the law in effect can vary considerably from one courtroom to another down the hall.

The widespread practice of forum-shopping, discussed in Chapter 2, directly reflects judges' individualism. Lawyers try to get their cases before one judge or one court rather than another, because their observations tell them that judges and courts differ in their behavior and decisional tendencies.

Nowhere is judges' individualism more striking than in the federal district courts. Cases that raise significant policy issues often come to the district courts, whose highly independent judges respond to them in their own ways. As a result, as one observer has said, "probably no other courts in the nation invite the same degree of personal quirkiness in the judges who run them as the United States District Courts."[58] Exhibit 5.3 illustrates that point by describing several district judges who have made a mark during their time on the bench. These judges should serve as a reminder of the more general point: because of judges' freedom, it can make a great deal of difference what kind of person holds a judgeship.

How does the freedom of judges compare with that of other public officials? There is no simple answer because different policy makers are under different combinations of constraints. Perhaps more important than any differences are the similarities: judges, legislators, and bureaucrats all face significant constraints, but all bring to their work individual traits that affect the choices they make.

Harold H. Greene, District of Columbia

Since 1981 Greene has handled the antitrust suit by the federal government against the American Telephone and Telegraph Company. In this position, he has presided over the restructuring of the telephone industry. He approved the 1982 agreements that split up AT&T, and since that time he has ruled on a number of issues concerning the rights of the regional "Baby Bell" companies that resulted from the 1982 split-up. He has allowed the regional companies to engage in some new activities, in part because of a decision by the court of appeals above him, but prohibited other activities such as providing long-distance services and manufacturing telephone equipment. Had a different judge handled these cases, the structure of the telephone industry today could be quite different.

W. Brevard Hand, Southern District of Alabama

During the 1980s Hand played a distinctive role on issues involving religion and the schools. In 1983 he ruled that Alabama's law authorizing school prayer did not violate the Constitution, holding that the Supreme Court had "erred" in its rulings on this issue and that the First Amendment's prohibition on the establishment of religion did not apply to the states. That decision was overturned. Hand then helped to restructure the prayer case into one in which textbooks in the state's public schools were challenged for promoting secular humanism. In 1987 he ruled that forty-four texts in history, social studies, and home economics promoted secular humanism as a religion and could not be used. That decision too was reversed on appeal.

William Wayne Justice, Eastern District of Texas

Justice has stood out for his decisions in a wide array of "institutional reform" litigation challenging the legality of practices by public institutions. His rulings on the Texas prison system in the 1980s required massive changes in the operation of the system and conditions for prisoners. He also has made major rulings on such matters as statewide school desegregation, rights of juveniles in reform schools, and bilingual education. Justice stands out so much from other Texas federal judges in his approach to institutional reform that litigants have gone to considerable efforts to get cases before him or away from him. Because of his rulings, some observers have regarded Justice as the most powerful public official in Texas.

Leonard B. Sand, Southern District of New York

In 1980 the federal government and the National Association for the Advancement of Colored People brought a lawsuit challenging racial segregation in housing and education in Yonkers, N.Y. Sand ruled that the city had promoted segregation, and in 1986 he ordered as a remedy that one thousand units of low- and medium-income housing be built in predominantly white neighborhoods. After appeals and negotiation, the city council refused to carry out the remedy. Using his contempt powers as leverage, Sand secured

EXHIBIT 5.3 Selective Profiles of Some Federal District Judges

compliance from the city and thus brought about a major change in public policy and life in Yonkers.

Sources: Press reports; *Almanac of the Federal Judiciary* (Englewood Cliffs, N.J.: Prentice Hall Law & Business, 1992); Frank R. Kemerer, *William Wayne Justice: A Judicial Biography* (Austin: University of Texas Press, 1991).

EXHIBIT 5.3 (*Continued*)

THE QUALITY OF JUDICIAL PERFORMANCE

Judges routinely make decisions that affect the lives of individuals. Taken together, these decisions have a considerable impact on American society as a whole. Thus the quality of judges' performance is a matter of great importance; if that performance is deficient, the consequences may be disastrous. John Marshall, chief justice of the Supreme Court in the early nineteenth century, put the matter in dramatic terms: "The greatest scourge an angry Heaven ever inflicted upon an ungrateful and a sinning people, was an ignorant, a corrupt, or a dependent Judiciary."[59]

It is very difficult to assess the performance of American judges as a group. For one thing, observers cannot agree on the criteria for assessment and how to apply those criteria. For another, there are so many judges serving across the country that even active trial lawyers can have only a partial sense of the overall level of performance.

The evidence that we do have on this level of performance is not entirely consistent. Not surprisingly, judges have a high opinion of their own work; in a survey of three thousand state trial judges, 85 percent rated themselves as excellent or above average at adjudication, while one-tenth of 1 percent saw themselves as below average or poor.[60] It is more significant that local polls of lawyers usually produce positive ratings for most judges, a sign that the average level of performance is at least adequate. Yet lawyers may be inclined to give judges the benefit of the doubt. After a massive corruption scandal arose in the Chicago courts, columnist Mike Royko noted that "of all the pocket-stuffing judges in the Greylord scandal, only one was ever rated as 'not qualified' by the Chicago Bar Association. That's a feeble average. If lawyers who rate judges were horse players, they'd be broke by the third race."[61] As I will discuss shortly, lawyers do harbor some doubts about the general level of competence in the judiciary. And some commentators who have observed many judges argue that judicial deficiencies are widespread.

The one safe conclusion is that judges vary tremendously in their performance, from those who would rate highly on every criterion to those whose work is far below an acceptable level. It seems likely that most judges carry out their jobs at least reasonably well, but it also appears that a significant minority display major deficiencies. Because such deficiencies are so troubling, it will be useful to focus on them—while keeping in mind that inadequate judges are not representative of the judiciary as a whole.

Judicial Deficiencies

Of the problems in the performance of some judges that observers have cited, some categories stand out as especially important: general lack of competence, insufficient commitment to the job, tyrannical behavior, and favoritism and corruption.

Inadequate Competence   Competence refers to a judge's general capability to handle the job effectively. Competence is difficult to define and to measure, and this difficulty is reflected in frequent disagreements among lawyers about the quality of specific judges. In 1990, for instance, a Chicago judge was rated by three lawyers' groups as a potential state supreme court justice; one group found him exceptionally well qualified, another qualified, and the third unqualified.[62]

On the basis of lawyers' observations, there is reason to think that incompetence is a problem in the judiciary. In a 1982 poll of American Bar Association members, a 51 percent majority agreed with the proposition that a significant proportion of judges are not qualified to preside over serious cases, and only 39 percent disagreed.[63]

Much of this criticism focuses on nonlawyer judges, who remain fairly common at the lowest levels of the judiciary, serving as justices of the peace and in similar positions. Some states have prohibited judicial service by nonlawyers, but others continue to rely heavily on them. In the view of many lawyers, lay judges are incompetent almost by definition. Undoubtedly, there is some basis for this view; some lay justices of the peace clearly lack the skills needed to do their jobs. Before California barred nonlawyers from judgeships, one California justice of the peace confessed that "I don't know anything more about the law than a hog does about the Fourth of July."[64]

But the incompetence of nonlawyer judges has probably been exaggerated, in part because justices of the peace have become such familiar figures in American folklore. (It seems unlikely, for instance, that there really was a Texas justice of the peace who determined fines by leafing randomly through a Sears catalogue.[65]) Marie Provine, herself a former town justice in New York (perhaps the only person with both a law degree and a Ph.D. to serve in that position), concluded from an extensive study that lay judges differ little in their behavior from lawyers serving on the same courts. On the basis of her efforts to estimate judges' levels of competence, Provine argued that "lay persons are no less competent than lawyers as lower-court judges.[66]

Of course, admission to the bar does not guarantee competence as a judge any more than it guarantees competence as an attorney. Even successful lawyers may perform poorly as judges for a period of time while they learn the task of judging. And, inexperience aside, some lawyers simply lack the skills the job of judge demands. For this reason, criticisms of judicial competence extend far beyond the ranks of nonlawyer judges in the lower courts. Indeed, lawyer judges have been known to engage in behavior that rivals the worst excesses ascribed to lay judges. One Oregon judge apparently based several decisions in traffic cases on the flip of a coin, and a rural Maryland judge told a defendant that his fate would rest on the judge's success in shooting a paper clip into a Styrofoam cup.[67]

The competence of some judges is affected by severe illnesses, physical injuries, and the loss of sight or hearing. All of these conditions are relatively common among the elderly; this is a significant fact because the attractions of the job keep many judges on the bench even after they reach ordinary retirement age. Some older judges perform quite effectively, but the performance of others declines with age, sometimes to levels that are clearly unacceptable.

Thus, even if the average level of competence for judges is high, not all judges perform as competently as we would like. And the restriction of judgeships to lawyers would not eliminate this problem.

Insufficient Commitment   Along with its other effects, judges' relative freedom from direct supervision creates a temptation to give the job something less than a full commitment. Indeed, there is a widespread perception that many judges fail to work full-time.

In part, this perception rests on a misunderstanding: that a judge who is not in a courtroom is not working. Still, there is evidence that more than a few judges succumb to the temptation to keep short hours. In his annual report to the state bar in 1989, the North Carolina chief justice said that "I hear that in some districts, judges may be hard to find on Fridays"; the response was "knowing laughter from the lawyers."[68] In 1990 a reporter who had helped investigate the schedules of Massachusetts judges concluded that "the work force breaks down into two groups—judges who care enough to work a full day and those who don't." Focusing on the latter, he suggested that "The unspoken motto of the court system might well be: Get it done in the morning or put it off to another day." Later that year the state's chief justice penalized five judges for failing to work full days.[69]

To the extent that judges fail to work full days, they are likely to increase backlogs of cases and aggravate time pressures on the courts. Not only are cases decided later than they might be, but the delays create additional incentives to dispose of cases through means that require relatively little time. Thus not only the timing of justice is affected but its substance as well.

Tyrannical Behavior   A judge who is inclined to act in a tyrannical fashion has considerable freedom to do so. Especially at the trial level, individual judges have great power to affect people's lives with their rulings. And in their courtrooms they are masters, generally accorded great deference by the people who come before them and who work with them. Inevitably, some judges succumb to the temptation to abuse this power and deference by treating people with disrespect, compelling submission from them, and punishing those who have displeased them.

One form of this behavior is abuse of attorneys. Judges sometimes treat lawyers with disdain or prejudice. To take one example, a number of reports have documented the frequency of such behavior toward female attorneys, symbolized by a Pittsburgh federal judge's insistence—backed by a threat of jailing—that a lawyer use her husband's last name.[70] Lawyers typically refrain from complaining about such conduct because of fear that they will jeopardize the position of present and future clients before that judge.

Perhaps the greatest temptation for a tyrannical judge is misuse of powers that a judge holds, particularly the power to hold people in contempt of court. Some judges have used these powers in clearly illegitimate ways, as the following examples indicate:

- A California judge refused a criminal defendant's request to say something. When the defendant asked, "How come?", the judge held him in contempt of court."[71]
- A Washington, D.C., judge discovered that a defendant awaiting trial had fallen asleep in court. For this lapse, he not only sentenced the defendant to thirty days in jail but also gave the same sentence to a nonsleeping codefendant. When the codefendant protested, the judge declared, "You are guilty by association."[72]
- A federal judge in Los Angeles found that two lawyers appearing before him had not complied with the rules for admission to practice in his district. He fined them $6,200 and threatened to put them in leg irons.[73]
- An Illinois judge accused a student on a school field trip of creating a disturbance in his courtroom and ordered that the student be taken into custody. The student was held for forty-five minutes, and during part of that period he was handcuffed to a chair in the judge's chambers. (The state disciplinary board for judges later ruled that there had been no disturbance and censured the judge.)[74]
- After a beeper went off in a Houston courtroom, the judge asked that the person with the offending beeper confess to possessing it. When no one came forward, the judge ordered all forty people in the courtroom to remain there. After three hours the judge allowed people to leave once they denied knowing who owned the beeper.[75]

Although actions such as these might be isolated incidents in a judge's work, they are often part of a broader pattern of behavior. That some judges behave in this fashion may not be surprising, but the behavior represents a serious problem.

Favoritism and Corruption   Perhaps the most important quality of a good judge is impartiality between the parties. Perfect impartiality is impossible because all judges hold a set of views that incline them in favor of some litigants and against others. But in some instances, judges have such intense prejudices that they cannot give certain kinds of litigants a fair trial. There are judges, for instance, who approach criminal cases with a strong presumption that the defendant is guilty; one example may have been the judge who told a defendant's attorney that it was impossible "for anyone to believe that, if he was innocent, he was sitting there" as defendant. "There would be no need for a trial."[76]

Some judges succumb to the temptation to favor their own interests or those of friends in their decisions. In one instance, a New Mexico judge sentenced people convicted of drunk driving to a "Driving-While-Intoxicated" school that he had established. In another, an Indiana judge gave an unusually heavy sentence for a bad check charge; the defendant was a record producer who was in conflict with the judge over release of a record in which the judge had a financial interest.[77]

Another possible source of favoritism for certain litigants is the judge's political self-interest. As noted earlier, judges may be inclined to favor their political party in order to maintain a critical source of support. As campaign contributions to judges grow, some observers are disturbed by judges' ruling in cases where contributors are litigants or lawyers.[78] And in other situations, judges have seemed unduly favorable to people who were politically important to them. In Boston municipal court, there is evidence that four state legislators with long tenure and two other politically connected attorneys enjoyed extraordinary success before three judges who ended up handling most of their cases.[79] Similarly, party-connected people have a great advantage when they come before certain judges. The extent of this advantage is suggested by a story that one Chicago lawyer insisted was true.

> This particular judge in one of the state courts was preparing to hear a case that was going to trial. The attorneys for the two sides walked into court together and sat down in front of him. Both were heavies in the Democratic party. The judge paled, and was clearly unsure of exactly what to do about it. Well, he thought about it for a while, and finally he called both sides up to the bench. He told them, "Gentlemen, there's only one way to resolve this. Where the clout is equal, the law must prevail. Let's try the case."[80]

The kinds of political favoritism alleged in these cases involve at least the appearance of corruption. One step further is outright bribery, the direct selling of decisions. It is impossible to estimate the frequency with which judges accept bribes, but two conclusions seem safe: this kind of corruption touches only a small minority of judges, but it cannot be called rare.

From time to time, bribery of individual judges is disclosed. Beyond these individual cases, in the past few years there has been evidence of widespread corruption in some court systems. The most dramatic example is Chicago, where an FBI investigation of the courts (called "Operation Greylord") produced more than eighty convictions of lawyers and court personnel, including fifteen judges.[81] One judge who participated in the investigation speculated that as many as one-eighth of the judges in Cook County (encompassing Chicago and some of its suburbs) might be dishonest.[82] A separate federal investigation of corruption in Chicago produced evidence of bribery in many cases, and one of the highest-ranking judges in the county court system was convicted of bribery in 1991.[83] In that year four Miami judges were indicted in a federal investigation of court corruption called "Operation Clean Broom"; one, charged with taking more than $80,000 in bribes from undercover agents, pleaded guilty to racketeering.[84]

Allegations of widespread judicial corruption are not just a recent phenomenon, as indicated by an 1859 incident involving Chief Justice David Terry of the California Supreme Court.

> Senator David C. Broderick had at one time been heard to say that Terry was the only honest justice on the court; it was his retraction of that statement as applicable to Terry that prompted Terry's challenge [to a duel]. Broderick's gun misfired—there were some who said that Terry knew it would—and Terry's shot laid him low. Terry resigned from the court after criminal charges were filed against him, but he managed to obtain an acquittal from a jury when his motion for change of venue was granted to Marin County, across the Golden Gate from San Francisco, and the witnesses for the prosecution, delayed by stormy seas, failed to appear in time for the trial.[85]

Improving the Performance of Judges

I should emphasize again that a discussion of deficiencies in judicial performance gives a distorted picture of the general quality of judges. The negative examples that I have described could be offset with a good many examples of judges who do well in all respects. Still, it is clear that significant numbers of judges display inadequacies in their work. Several proposals have been put forward to remedy these inadequacies and to improve the general quality of judging; some have been widely adopted. These proposals fall into three categories: selecting better judges, removing inadequate judges, and improving the performance of sitting judges.

Selecting Better Judges   The centerpiece of the effort to select better judges is the Missouri Plan, the complex system advocated by several groups. Advocates of the plan see its nominating commissions as a device to screen out less-qualified candidates. In recent years an increasing number of states have chosen this solution, either in its original form or with modifications.

As suggested in Chapter 4, it is uncertain whether the Missouri Plan actually affects the quality of judges. According to the available evidence, the background characteristics of Missouri Plan judges, including those related to their qualifications, are similar to the characteristics of judges selected under other systems. Yet in surveys taken in the 1960s most Missouri lawyers indicated that the plan had raised the quality of the state's judiciary.[86] Although this finding is significant, it seems unlikely that the institution of the Missouri Plan would affect the quality of judges in any dramatic way. As we have seen, criteria other than qualifications affect the selection of judges under the Missouri Plan. Moreover, it is not clear that the performance of judges can be predicted very well from their records prior to their selection.

Another approach is to raise judicial salaries so that good judges will have a greater incentive to remain on the bench and good prospective judges will be more interested in serving. As the salaries and fringe benefits of judges have fallen further behind those earned by successful private practitioners, this approach has gained increasing support.[87] But it is uncertain whether better compensation actually would improve the quality of the judiciary significantly; judgeships would be more attractive, but to less competent people as well as to the more competent. In any case, it has proved very difficult to secure legislative approval for major increases in judicial salaries; if inadequate compensation does weaken the quality of the judiciary, that problem is likely to continue.

Removing Inadequate Judges   If it is impossible to ensure that only good judges will be put on the bench, then an obvious remedy is to remove judges whose performance proves to be inadequate. As Exhibit 5.4 shows, a number of removal methods exist.

The simplest of these methods is a refusal to grant a judge a new term in office. In practice, this approach works only imperfectly. In states whose governors appoint judges, sitting judges are reappointed almost automatically. In states that use regular elections or retention elections, the voters generally have only limited information about a judge's performance, and incumbents have an excellent chance of winning, no matter how well or how badly

EXHIBIT 5.4 Selected Methods to Remove Judges from Office

Method	Where Available	Frequency of Use[a]
Defeat in regular election	About ⅗ of states[b]	A
Defeat in retention election	About ⅖ of states[b]	B
Recall by voters	A few states	C
Non-reappointment by governor	About ⅙ of states[b]	C
Impeachment by legislature	Federal; nearly all states	C
Legislative "address"	About ⅓ of states	C
Disciplinary action	All states	B
Compulsory retirement for disability	Nearly all states	B

[a] "A" means used with some frequency, "B" means used occasionally, "C" means almost never used.
[b] These three categories add up to more than 100 percent because some states use two different methods to select judges.
Sources: Marvin Comisky and Philip C. Patterson, *The Judiciary—Selection, Compensation, Ethics, and Discipline* (New York: Quorum Books, 1987), pp. 149–232; other sources.

they have performed. And most defeats of incumbents are for reasons that have little to do with the quality of their performance on the bench.

Still, on occasion, a judge's bad performance is well publicized and results in an electoral defeat. In 1988, for instance, a Chicago judge, Arthur Cieslik, was criticized for allegedly tyrannical behavior: in the words of one editorial, "he thinks he has the right to insult and humiliate attorneys and defendants who appear before him, particularly if they are women or minorities."[88] With the opposition of nearly all the groups that made endorsements, Judge Cieslik lost his retention election—though even with this strong opposition he would have won except for the unusual requirement in Illinois of a 60 percent majority for retention.

Federal judges and those in nearly all states are subject to impeachment proceedings. The procedure generally used is that judges (and other public officials) can be removed if impeached (in effect, charged with an offense) by the lower house of the legislature and convicted by the upper house. With few exceptions, legislators seriously consider impeachment only where corruption or other criminal offenses are alleged, so that it is inapplicable to problems such as illness and tyrannical behavior. Because the impeachment procedure is so extreme and so unwieldy, it is not always employed even where there are serious allegations of criminal conduct.

The use of the impeachment power in practice can be illustrated with its history at the federal level. The Constitution provides for impeachment in cases of "treason, bribery, or other high crimes and misdemeanors,"[89] with a House majority required for impeachment and a two-thirds Senate majority required for conviction and removal from office. But from 1789 through 1936 only nine federal judges were impeached, and only four were convicted by the Senate (a fifth resigned).[90] After 1936 a half century passed with no impeachments.

Since then, however, impeachment has revived. In 1987 Congress removed Nevada District Judge Harry Claiborne, who had been convicted of two counts of tax evasion in court. And in 1989 two other district judges were removed: Walter Nixon of Mississippi, for perjury, and Alcee Hastings of Florida, for bribery and related offenses. The Senate limited the burdens imposed on senators by these cases through the device of having committees rather than the full Senate hear the evidence; Judge Nixon challenged this procedure as unconstitutional, but the Supreme Court in 1993 held that this was not a question for the courts to settle.[91] In 1992 Judge Hastings was elected to Congress, though there was some question about whether he was eligible to serve after his conviction.

Faced with the limitations of other methods, since 1960 every state has adopted a new structure with which to investigate and act on complaints against judges. This is the judicial conduct commission, an agency within the judicial branch.[92] People can make complaints against judges to the commission (which usually includes judges, lawyers, and lay members) on such grounds as misconduct in office and failure to perform judicial duties.

Typically, the judicial conduct commission screens complaints, investigates those that have possible merit, and recommends disciplinary action to the state supreme court. Such action can take several forms, ranging from private admonition to removal or retirement. In assessing judges' behavior and considering sanctions, most commissions are guided by their state's version of the Code of Judicial Conduct, developed by the American Bar Association.

Most complaints are dismissed without investigation, but a significant number result in some form of discipline. In one recent year about one hundred state judges received a private sanction, sixty were publicly censured or reprimanded, eight were suspended from office, and fifteen were removed altogether. Another ninety judges resigned or retired after complaints were made against them.[93] Judges have been removed from office for reasons that include criminal convictions, favoritism toward certain litigants on the basis of personal ties, financial improprieties, and misuse of the contempt power and other forms of abusive behavior.[94]

The vigor of judicial conduct commissions varies a good deal among the states. New York's well-funded Commission on Judicial Conduct stands out for the extent of its activity and the frequency with which it imposes sanctions on judges.[95] In contrast, many other commissions are regarded as weak, limited in resources to investigate complaints, and reluctant to take strong action against judges who engage in serious misconduct. In 1991 the Connecticut legislature eliminated its state commission; one member involved in the decision said that the legislature sought to eliminate ineffective programs, "and there is probably no better example of an inefficient, do-nothing program than the activities of the Judicial Review Council."[96]

The federal courts do not have an equivalent system. But Congress in 1980 gave the judicial councils of the circuits the power to act as judicial conduct commissions for federal judges. Congress did not allow the councils to remove judges from office, chiefly because of doubts that such action would be constitutionally acceptable. But a council can temporarily order that no further cases be assigned to a judge, and it can recommend that Congress consider impeachment. The circuit council for the Eleventh Circuit recommended impeachment in the case of Alcee Hastings; this action, and its approval by the Federal Judicial Conference, spurred Congress to impeach and convict Hastings. The recommendation was controversial because Hastings had been acquitted of criminal charges; the circuit council made an independent examination of the evidence and concluded that Hastings had lied and used fabricated documents in his trial.[97]

Improving Sitting Judges   Thus the methods to select judges and those to remove inadequate judges are imperfect. For the most part, we have to live with the judges we have: a set of people whose performance levels vary considerably. This reality has become increasingly clear to people who care about the quality of the judiciary. As a result, more attention has been given to improving the work of those who serve on the bench.

One form of these efforts is organized educational programs. The Federal Judicial Center conducts such programs for federal judges. Nearly all the states now provide some kind of training for their judges, and there are also several national educational programs. The largest of the national programs is the National Judicial College in Reno, Nevada, established in 1963; its sessions are now attended by more than fifteen hundred judges a year.[98] Only a few states require training for all their judges, but a large minority have such requirements for nonlawyer judges and those who serve on specialized courts. Such programs undoubtedly improve the skills of most judges who participate in them, but their overall impact is difficult to assess.

Some effort has also been made to provide help for sitting judges who are identified as having problems. Indeed, one function of the state conduct commissions is to warn judges of deficiencies that need correction, though there is no guarantee that judges will be able and willing to act on such warnings. In addition, some states have instituted programs to help judges who suffer from alcoholism and psychological problems.

Attempts to improve the performance of sitting judges, like efforts to select good judges and remove bad ones, have significant limitations. Inevitably, some of the judges whose performance is most deficient will be least willing to try to improve their work. And even judges who want to do better may be limited in their capacity to improve. Thus we will continue to have some judges who perform poorly, just as we have others who meet the highest standards.

CONCLUSIONS

This chapter has pointed to some generalizations about judges. For instance, certain background characteristics are widely shared; in turn, these characteristics help to shape patterns of judicial behavior and court policy. To take another example, most judges face the same kinds of stresses in their jobs.

On the whole, however, differences among judges stand out more than similarities. Their values, their competence, and the ways that they approach their jobs all vary a great deal. Therefore, it does make a difference which individual sits on the bench, and the amount of energy devoted to the selection of judges is quite understandable. Heated election campaigns for state judgeships and bitter battles over confirmation of Supreme Court justices, still unusual but more common in recent years, reflect a growing awareness that individual judges make a difference.

Thus far I have discussed judges' work only in general terms. The remaining chapters look more closely at judges as decision-makers, at the individual characteristics and other forces that shape their behavior, and at the influence that their decisions exert.

FOR FURTHER READING

Bass, Jack. *Taming the Storm: The Life and Times of Judge Frank M. Johnson, Jr., and the South's Fight Over Civil Rights*. New York: Doubleday, 1993.

Kemerer, Frank R. *William Wayne Justice: A Judicial Biography*. Austin: University of Texas Press, 1991.

Provine, Doris Marie. *Judging Credentials: Nonlawyer Judges and the Politics of Professionalism*. Chicago: University of Chicago Press, 1986.

Ryan, John Paul, Allan Ashman, Bruce D. Sales, and Sandra Shane-Du Bow. *American Trial Judges: Their Work Styles and Performance*. New York: Free Press, 1980.

Schmidhauser, John R. *Judges and Justices: The Federal Appellate Judiciary*. Boston: Little, Brown, 1979.

Tuohy, James, and Rob Warden, *Greylord: Justice, Chicago Style*. New York: G. P. Putnam's Sons, 1989.

NOTES

1. *The Book of the States, 1992–93 Edition* (Lexington, Ky.: Council of State Governments, 1992), pp. 231–232.
2. All statistics on federal judges appointed between 1977 and 1992 are calculated from data in Sheldon Goldman. "Bush's Judicial Legacy: The Final Imprint," *Judicature*, 76 (April–May 1993), 282—297. These data are based solely on appointments to the district courts and courts of appeals.
3. Clyde Leland, "Joining the Court He Helped Change," *California Lawyer*, 10 (September 1990), 25; "Bayh Chooses His Own Lawyer for Court," *Chicago Tribune*, November 21, 1990, sec. 1, p. 3.
4. David Balabanian, "Justice Was More than His Title," *California Law Review*, 70 (July 1982), 880.
5. Curtis Bok, *Backbone of the Herring* (New York: Alfred A. Knopf, 1941), p. 3.
6. James Tuohy and Rob Warden, *Greylord: Justice, Chicago Style* (New York: G. P. Putnam's Sons, 1989), p. 47.
7. Charles Anzalone, "Candidates in Pursuit of a Judgeship Must Learn Rules of the Game," *Buffalo News*, March 18, 1990, p. B1.
8. John Paul Ryan, Allan Ashman, Bruce D. Sales, and Sandra Shane-Du Bow, *American Trial Judges: Their Work Styles and Performance* (New York: Free Press, 1980), p. 125.
9. Goldman, "Bush's Judicial Legacy," 287, 293.
10. Ryan et al., *American Trial Judges*, p. 125.
11. Susan P. Fino, *The Role of State Supreme Courts in the New Judicial Federalism* (New York: Greenwood Press, 1987), p. 52; Henry R. Glick and Craig F. Emmert, "Stability and Change: Characteristics of State Supreme Court Justices," *Judicature*, 70 (August–September 1986), 108.
12. Glick and Emmert, "Stability and Change," 108.
13. Goldman, "Bush's Judicial Legacy"; Lawrence Baum, *The Supreme Court*, 4th ed. (Washington, D.C.: CQ Press, 1992), pp. 56–58.
14. Glick and Emmert, "Stability and Change," p. 108; Ryan et al., *American Trial Judges*, p. 125.
15. "A Chip Off the Old Bench," *California Lawyer*, 8 (December 1988), p. 122.
16. "Sylvia," *Chicago Tribune*, February 12, 1992, sec. 5, p. 8.
17. Joel S. Ish, "Trial Judges: Their Recruitment, Backgrounds and Role Perceptions" (Paper presented at the 1975 meeting of the American Political Science Association in San Francisco, California), 4–6.
18. Ryan et al., *American Trial Judges*, p. 128; Glick and Emmert, "Stability and Change," p. 108.
19. Beverly Blair Cook, "Women Judges in the Opportunity Structure," in *Women, The Courts, and Equality*, ed. Laura L. Crites and Winifred L. Hepperle (Beverly

Hills, Calif.: Sage Publications, 1987), pp. 146–149; Goldman, "Bush's Judicial Legacy."

20. For major trial courts, data are from Elaine Martin, "Views From the State Bench: Gender Roles and Judicial Roles," in *Women in Politics: Outsiders or Insiders?* ed. Lois Lovelace Duke (Englewood Cliffs, N.J.: Prentice Hall, 1993), p. 177. For supreme courts, the 1980–1981 figure is from Glick and Emmert, "Stability and Change," p. 108; the 1991 figure has been calculated from rosters in James R. Hoffman, ed., *The American Bench: Judges of the Nation* (Sacramento Calif.: Forster-Long, 1991).

21. Gerald David Jaynes and Robin M. Williams, Jr., eds., *A Common Destiny: Blacks and American Society* (Washington, D.C.: National Academy Press, 1989), p. 243.

22. Sheldon Goldman, "Reaganizing the Judiciary: The First Term Appointments," *Judicature*, 68 (April–May 1985), 319, 325; Gail Diane Cox, "Jerry's Judges," *National Law Journal*, May 25, 1992, pp. 1, 30–31.

23. David Margolick, "Women's Milestone: Majority on Minnesota Court," *New York Times*, February 22, 1991, p. B10.

24. *Chisom v. Roemer*, 115 L. Ed. 2d 348 (1991).

25. See Frank Burgos, "Dem Women Hold Court in Circuit Judge Races," *Chicago Sun Times*, March 19, 1992, p. 6.

26. See, for instance, Sheldon Goldman, "Voting Behavior on the United States Courts of Appeals Revisited," *American Political Science Review*, 69 (June 1975), 491–506; C. Neal Tate and Roger Handberg, "Time Binding and Theory Building in Personal Attribute Models of Supreme Court Voting Behavior, 1916–88," *American Journal of Political Science*, 35 (May 1991), 460–480; and Martha A. Myers, "Social Background and the Sentencing Behavior of Judges," *Criminology*, 26 (November 1988), 649–675.

27. See Howard Schumann, Charlotte Steeh, and Lawrence Bobo, *Racial Attitudes in America: Trends and Interpretations* (Cambridge: Harvard University Press, 1985); Carol M. Mueller, ed., *The Politics of the Gender Gap* (Beverly Hills, Calif.: Sage Publications, 1988); and Robert S. Erikson, Norman R. Luttbeg, and Kent L. Tedin, *American Public Opinion: Its Origins, Content, and Impact*, 2d ed. (New York: John Wiley and Sons, 1980).

28. See Thomas G. Walker and Deborah J. Barrow, "The Diversification of the Federal Bench: Policy and Process Ramifications," *Journal of Politics*, 47 (May 1985), 596–617; and David W. Allen and Diane E. Wall, "The Behavior of Women State Supreme Court Justices: Are They Tokens or Outsiders?" *Justice System Journal*, 12 (Fall 1987), 232–245.

29. Susan Welch, Michael Combs, and John Gruhl, "Do Black Judges Make a Difference?" *American Journal of Political Science*, 32 (February 1988), 126–136; John Gruhl, Cassia Spohn, and Susan Welch, "Women as Policymakers: The Case of Trial Judges," *American Journal of Political Science*, 25 (May 1981), 308–322.

30. Stuart Nagel, "Political Party Affiliation and Judges' Decisions," *American Political Science Review*, 55 (December 1961), 844–850; Goldman, "Voting Behavior on the Courts of Appeals," 496–498.

31. On redistricting in Illinois, see Edward Walsh, "Reagan-Appointed Judges Approve Illinois Redistricting Favoring GOP," *Washington Post*, November 8, 1991, p. A20; Thomas Hardy, "GOP Argues Remap Should Be Given to Federal Court," *Chicago Tribune*, December 17, 1991, sec. 1, p. 3; and William Grady and Thomas Hardy, "Court OKs GOP's Remap," *Chicago Tribune*, January 11, 1992, sec. 1, pp. 1–2.

32. O'Malley and Collin, "Inc.," *Chicago Tribune*, January 13, 1992, sec. 1, p. 12.

33. Martin Tolchin, "Court Overturns Guilty Verdict in Nofziger Case," *New York Times*, June 28, 1989, pp. 1, 10; George Lardner Jr., "North's Iran-Contra Convictions Set Aside by Split Appeals Court," *Washington Post*, July 21, 1990, pp. A1, A10.

34. By one count, there were 27,559 trial judges in 1990. Court Statistics Project, *State Court Caseload Statistics: Annual Report 1990* (Williamsburg, Va.: National

Center for State Courts, 1992), p. 10. Data in the same source yield an estimate of about 1,200 appellate judges.

35. This list of categories is adapted from a list in Ryan et al., *American Trial Judges*, pp. 6–7, and some of the material in this subsection was drawn from that source.
36. On trial judges, see ibid., p. 39.
37. See Cornelius M. Kerwin, Thomas Henderson, and Carl Baar, "Adjudicatory Processes and the Organization of Trial Courts," *Judicature*, 70 (August–September 1986), 99–106.
38. Ryan et al., *American Trial Judges*, p. 186.
39. Harriet Chiang, "Conservative Group Wants Judge's Ouster," *San Francisco Chronicle*, November 22, 1991, p. A21.
40. Jennifer L. Machlin, "Judges and Politics," *California Lawyer*, 9 (October 1989), p. 122.
41. Judith S. Kaye, "My 'Freshman Years' on the Court of Appeals," *Judicature*, 70 (October–November 1986), 166.
42. Robert Carp and Russell Wheeler, "Sink or Swim: The Socialization of a Federal District Judge," *Journal of Public Law*, 21 (1972), 374.
43. See Albert P. Melone, "Revisiting the Freshman Effect Hypothesis: The First Two Terms of Justice Anthony Kennedy," *Judicature*, 74 (June–July 1990), 6.
44. Michael Bowker, "Basic Training for the Bench," *California Lawyer*, 7 (November 1987), 42.
45. Milton Heumann, *Plea Bargaining: The Experiences of Prosecutors, Judges, and Defense Attorneys* (Chicago: University of Chicago Press, 1977), ch. 6.
46. Stephen L. Wasby, " 'Into the Soup?:' The Acclimation of Ninth Circuit Appellate Judges," *Judicature,* 73 (June–July 1989), 10.
47. Lauren K. Robel, "Caseload and Judging: Judicial Adaptations to Caseload," *Brigham Young University Law Review* (1990), 11.
48. See, for instance, Bob Greene, "Sarah Gets a New Chance for Justice," *Chicago Tribune*, February 17, 1991, sec. 5, p. 1.
49. Chuck Shepherd, "News of the Weird," *San Jose Mercury News*, June 10, 1990, p. 2L.
50. Colman McCarthy, "The Perils of Packing a Gun," *Washington Post*, June 6, 1992, p. A23.
51. Roberto Suro, "Husband Shoots 2 and Himself in Dallas Court," *New York Times*, January 20, 1993, p. A14.
52. "What Lawyers Earn," *National Law Journal*, April 27, 1992, p. S5.
53. "The View from the Bench," *National Law Journal*, August 10, 1987, p. S4.
54. C. Robert Showalter and Daniel A. Martell, "Personality, Stress and Health in American Judges," *Judicature*, 69 (August–September 1985), 82–87.
55. David Margolick, "At the Bar," *New York Times*, April 7, 1989, p. B5.
56. David Margolick, "At the Bar," *New York Times*, January 6, 1989, p. B9.
57. Showalter and Martell, "Personality, Stress and Health," p. 85.
58. Richard Kluger, *Simple Justice: The History of Brown v. Board of Education and Black America's Struggle for Equality* (New York: Alfred A. Knopf, 1976), p. 294.
59. Quoted in *O'Donoghue v. United States*, 289 U.S. 516, 532 (1933).
60. Ryan et al., *American Trial Judges,* p. 162.
61. Mike Royko, "An Unqualified Bit of Nonsense," *Chicago Tribune*, November 4, 1986, sec. 1, p. 3.
62. William Grady, "Bar Groups Differ on Court Hopefuls," *Chicago Tribune*, February 23, 1990, sec. 1, p. 7.
63. "Law Poll," *American Bar Association Journal*, 68 (October 1982), 216.
64. Donald Dale Jackson, *Judges* (New York: Atheneum, 1974), p. 46. The quotation originally appeared in a series in the *Riverside* (California) *Press Enterprise*, December 10, 12, 1968.
65. Bennett Cerf, "A Texas Sampler," in *An Encyclopedia of Modern American Humor*, ed. Bennett Cerf (Garden City, N.Y.: Doubleday, 1954), pp. 385–386.

66. Doris Marie Provine, *Judging Credentials: Nonlawyer Judges and the Politics of Professionalism* (Chicago: University of Chicago Press, 1986), p. 166.
67. "Witnesses: Judge Tossed Coin on Cases," *Chicago Tribune*, September 29, 1991, sec. 1, p. 18; Eugene L. Meyer, "Southern Md. Justice: Judges Do Much as They Please in Rural Counties," *Washington Post*, April 24, 1980, p. A1.
68. "Never on Fridays," *National Law Journal*, November 6, 1989, p. 6.
69. John Aloysius Farrell, "Half-Day Justice," *Boston Globe*, September 23, 1990, pp. 1, 34; Paul Katzeff, "Massachusetts Judges Investigated," *National Law Journal*, October 15, 1990, p. 2.
70. "Federal Judge Apologizes in Fight Over Use of 'Ms.' " *New York Times*, July 15, 1988, p. A10. See Ricki Lewis Tannen, "Report of the Florida Supreme Court Gender Bias Study Commission," *Florida Law Review*, 42 (December 1990), 803–997; and "Utah Task Force on Gender and Justice: Report to the Utah Judicial Council," *Journal of Contemporary Law*, 16 (Fall 1990), 135–299.
71. *Kloepfer v. Commission on Judicial Performance*, 49 Cal. 3d 826, 855 (1989).
72. Jackson, *Judges*, p. 156. This story and quotation originally appeared in Harvey Katz, "Some Call It Justice," *Washingtonian*, September 1970.
73. "King of the Court," *California Lawyer*, 9 (December 1989), p. 117.
74. Bill Grady, Merrill Goozner, and John O'Brien, "Last, Least: A List of Lawyer Laurels," *Chicago Tribune*, December 26, 1989, sec. 3, p. 3; William Grady, "Judge Censured for Punishing High School Visitor in His Court," *Chicago Tribune*, December 8, 1989, sec. 3, p. 6.
75. Gary Taylor, "Jeepers, Creepers; Listen to the Beepers," *National Law Journal*, July 27, 1992, p. 51.
76. Charles M. Sevilla, *Disorder in the Court: Great Fractured Moments in Courtroom History* (New York: W. W. Norton, 1992), p. 116.
77. *In re Rainaldi*, 727 P.2d 70 (N.M. 1986); *In re Littell*, 294 N.E.2d 126 (Ind. 1973).
78. See *MacKenzie v. Super Kids Bargain Store*, 565 So. 2d 1332 (Fla. 1990).
79. Dick Lehr, "The Elite Six: Big Winners at Boston Court," *Boston Globe*, September 25, 1990, pp. 1, 10–11; Dick Lehr, "Court Has Friends on the Hill," *Boston Globe*, September 26, 1990, pp. 1, 26–27.
80. Jeffrey S. Slovak, "Working for Corporate Actors: Social Change and Elite Attitudes in Chicago," *American Bar Foundation Research Journal* (Summer 1979), 470.
81. Tuohy and Warden, *Greylord*; Bill Peterson, "Operation Greylord's Scorecard Nearly Complete," *Washington Post*, August 25, 1989, p. A5.
82. Mark Starr, "Stinging the Chicago Courts," *Newsweek*, August 22, 1983, p. 21.
83. Matt O'Connor, "Jury Plays Tape Until All Agree Shields is Guilty," *Chicago Tribune*, September 29, 1991, sec. 1, pp. 1–2.
84. Rosalind Resnick, " 'Operation Clean Broom' Strikes," *National Law Journal*, June 24, 1991, pp. 3, 43; Rosalind Resnick, "Court Broom's Sweep," *National Law Journal*, August 26, 1991, p. 2.
85. Joseph R. Grodin, *In Pursuit of Justice: Reflections of a State Supreme Court Justice* (Berkeley: University of California Press, 1989), p. 51.
86. Richard A. Watson and Rondal G. Downing, *The Politics of the Bench and the Bar: Judicial Selection under the Missouri Nonpartisan Court Plan* (New York: John Wiley, 1969), pp. 257–263, 282–286.
87. See Sheldon Goldman, "Federal Judges Are Found Not Gilty," *New York Times*, April 23, 1987, p. A27; and "There's Bad News about the Federal Judiciary," *National Law Journal*, November 28, 1988, p. 5.
88. "Voters, Kick out These Three Judges," *Chicago Tribune*, November 7, 1988, sec. 1, p. 14.
89. U.S. Constitution, art. II, sec. 4.
90. Russell R. Wheeler and A. Leo Levin, *Judicial Discipline and Removal in the United States* (Washington, D.C.: Federal Judicial Center, 1979), p. 11.
91. *Nixon v. United States*, 122 L. Ed. 2d 1 (1993).

92. Irene A. Tesitor and Dwight B. Sinks, *Judicial Conduct Organizations*, 2d ed. (Chicago: American Judicature Society, 1980).
93. "Table 1: 1989–90 Complaint Disposition," *Judicial Conduct Reporter*, 13 (Summer 1991), 2. For each state, the period covered was one year. Because of reporting methods, the figures should be taken as approximate rather than exact.
94. Yvette Begue, ed., *Judicial Discipline and Disability Digest* (January 1981–June 1986 Supplement) (Chicago: American Judicature Society, 1988).
95. Gerald Stern, "Is Judicial Discipline in New York State a Threat to Judicial Independence?" *Pace Law Review*, 7 (Winter 1987), 291–388.
96. Thomas D. Williams, "Connecticut First to Abolish Judge Panel," *National Law Journal*, October 28, 1991, p. 6.
97. Fred Strasser, "Congress Releases Hastings Report," *National Law Journal*, October 19, 1987, pp. 3, 44.
98. Jean Guccione, "Judicial College Role is Changing," *Los Angeles Daily Journal*, May 16, 1990, p. 11.

6

Trial Courts: Criminal Cases

O f all that courts do, nothing receives as much attention as the work of trial courts in criminal cases. People find criminal proceedings far more fascinating than civil cases, and criminal cases touch on the deep and widespread concern about crime.

The public that observes criminal cases often expresses dissatisfaction with their outcomes. The widespread outrage in 1992 over acquittal of four Los Angeles police officers after the videotaped beating of suspect Rodney King was an extreme example of a common phenomenon. Although people sometimes feel that defendants have been treated unfairly, it is far more common for them to conclude that the courts have been too favorable to a defendant.

The same is true of broader judgments about the courts. In particular, the use of plea bargaining and judges' sentencing decisions have been widely criticized on the ground that they allow criminals to escape with too little punishment. Politicians often charge courts and their personnel with contributing to the crime problem through undue leniency toward defendants. And those charges are widely accepted; in one survey, 90 percent of the public agreed that "a legal system that makes it too easy for criminals to delay trials and to get off easier with plea bargaining" was at least an important cause of crime.[1]

Chiefly because of such criticisms, trial courts frequently are pressured to change the ways they handle criminal cases. But judges and attorneys who participate in criminal courts often resist this pressure. The practices they use to process criminal cases reflect their own goals and interests, and they usually have strong reasons to maintain those practices. Moreover, they value for its own sake their considerable freedom to shape the criminal law in its actual operation.

This chapter examines the work of trial courts in criminal cases (for convenience, referred to here as criminal courts). I discuss their handling of cases, emphasizing the conditions and motivations that shape their practices. Efforts to "reform" criminal courts also receive attention in this chapter— particularly the impact of the reforms that are actually adopted. It should become clear that criminal courts are complex institutions, and those who seek to change them must accept and deal with this complexity.

Criminal courts are not all the same; they vary enormously. The chapter describes general patterns in their operation and differences among them. Since the great majority of criminal cases go to state courts, the focus is primarily on that level. But the discussions of processes and outcomes in the chapter take federal cases into account as well.

After a general examination of criminal courts, the chapter explores four key processes: bringing cases to court, plea bargaining, trials, and sentencing.

AN OVERVIEW OF CRIMINAL COURTS

To provide an overview of criminal courts, this section surveys three matters— types of criminal cases, participants in criminal proceedings, and procedures by which criminal cases are handled.

Types of Criminal Cases

The line between criminal and civil cases is not entirely clear-cut. In general, however, criminal cases are those in which government charges people with offenses for which they may be punished if found guilty.[2]

Congress and the state legislatures determine through statutes what acts are defined as criminal offenses. For this reason, the coverage of the criminal law should be viewed as a product of political decisions. This political character is hardly visible for offenses such as murder and robbery, which always have been treated as criminal by consensus. But such a consensus does not exist for acts such as gambling, for which the laws have varied among states and changed over time. One of the most heated national debates today is about whether abortion should be treated as a criminal offense. The number of criminal offenses tends to grow over time, as legislators react to perceptions of new problems, such as the use of computers to interfere with the operation of data systems.

The criminal and civil sides of the law overlap; a single act or incident often can lead to either type of case. A barroom fight could result in a criminal prosecution, a civil suit by one participant against another, or both. Moreover, cases that are formally criminal sometimes look more like civil proceedings. Prosecutions for writing checks with insufficient funds, for instance, often are resolved when the defendant agrees to pay restitution to the business that initiated the criminal proceeding.

The criminal statutes create three types of cases: felonies, misdemeanors, and juvenile proceedings.

Felonies   The most serious criminal offenses, those punishable with the most severe sanctions, are called felonies. Some states define felonies as offenses for which a defendant may be sentenced to death or to imprisonment in the state penitentiary (as opposed to a local jail); others, along with the federal government, define felonies as offenses for which at least one year's imprisonment is possible. Violent offenses are almost always treated as felonies, whereas relatively minor crimes, such as petty theft and gambling, are usually misdemeanors, but the line between the two categories is arbitrary and varies somewhat from state to state. Typically, felony cases are tried in the major trial courts of a state system.

Felonies constitute only a minority of criminal cases, but their seriousness gives them an importance far beyond their numbers. For that reason, and because we know the most about them, this chapter gives primary attention to felonies and thus to major trial courts.

Misdemeanors   Offenses that are not classified as felonies are misdemeanors. These cases typically go to minor trial courts in the states, and most federal misdemeanors are handled by magistrates rather than judges.

Nearly all traffic and parking offenses are classified as criminal misdemeanors, sometimes in a separate category. These cases greatly outnumber all others in the criminal courts. But because most are relatively minor in seriousness and possible sanctions, this chapter gives little attention to them.

Juvenile Offenses   Crimes allegedly committed by younger people constitute a special category, which may be called juvenile offenses. Each state has established juvenile courts, sometimes as divisions of other courts. In the handling of juvenile offenses, the goal, not fully realized in practice, is to emphasize treatment rather than punishment. Below a designated age, usually eighteen to twenty-one, defendants generally go to juvenile courts. In many states, however, juveniles who are charged with the most serious offenses can be tried in adult courts if they are older than a minimum age. Besides the criminal offenses that apply to both adults and juveniles, most states have created other offenses that apply only to juveniles, such as truancy and incorrigibility.

Participants in Criminal Courts

People in a wide range of roles take part in the work of criminal courts. The most important are those who hold three positions: judges, prosecutors, and defense attorneys.

Judges and the attorneys on each side have impact not just in their individual roles but collectively as well. The processing of cases requires frequent interaction among the three, and together they shape the ways in which cases are handled and the patterns of outcomes. Typically, the judges and lawyers who handle criminal cases do so on a regular basis; therefore, they get to know each other well and often develop close working relationships. To use two terms suggested by students of criminal courts, lawyers and judges are at the center of the "courtroom work group" and the "courthouse community."[3]

The closeness of the relationships within the community differs from court to court, based in part on the stability of the work group. Relations are likely to be most cooperative and shared understandings strongest where all the lawyers and judges are frequent rather than occasional participants in criminal cases. In general, courts in small and medium-sized counties feature closer relations among their small number of participants than do big-city courts, with their large numbers of judges and lawyers. But even in big cities, members of the work group can become familiar with each other and develop strong norms and expectations about what each participant will do. In any event, judges, prosecutors, and defense attorneys—whether or not they cooperate—are all so central to criminal cases that the actions each takes and the interactions among them are crucial to what happens in court.

Judges   Most trial judges hear criminal cases at least part of the time. On multijudge courts, some judges are assigned permanently or for long periods to hear only criminal cases.

Judges, of course, play a central role in criminal cases. Simply by presiding in court, they influence the proceedings before them. But they also make several kinds of decisions about cases. Before the trial, they determine whether there is sufficient evidence to maintain a case against a defendant; in addition, they set bail and decide whether to accept a defendant's guilty plea. In a nonjury trial, the judge decides whether to convict or acquit. And if a defendant pleads guilty or is convicted after a trial, a judge usually makes the sentencing decision.

This list of responsibilities may exaggerate the judge's importance somewhat, for, even where a judge holds the ultimate power of decision, the actual exercise of that power is influenced by prosecutors and defense attorneys. In interactions among the three work group members, judges have the advantage of higher legal status. But, as one set of commentators has suggested, the judge's "dominance in formal status does not invariably translate into actual influence."[4] Judges may even find themselves in a relatively weak position to exert control; sentencing decisions, for instance, are often constrained by plea bargaining agreements that have been reached by the prosecutor and defense attorney. Even so, judges hold significant power over the handling and outcomes of cases.

Prosecutors   In minor cases, police officers sometimes act as prosecutors, but with that exception the government is represented by attorneys in criminal cases. Prosecutors work in offices that frequently handle criminal cases and other government legal work as well.[5]

Prosecutors' offices generally follow the same geographic lines as courts. In the federal court system, for instance, each judicial district has an office of the United States Attorney as well as a district court. And where a state court serves a county, there is usually a county prosecutor's office. But in Alaska, Connecticut, and Delaware, the state attorney general is responsible for prosecution throughout the state.

The structure of a prosecutor's office varies with its workload. In state systems, a rural county may have only a single part-time prosecutor. In contrast, most metropolitan counties have large offices, with scores of full-time assistants to the chief prosecutor, and the largest offices have several hundred assistants. Larger offices often feature specialization by individual assistants in specific kinds of cases; Los Angeles County, for instance, has ten prosecutors who work on environmental crimes.[6] And in such offices, power over the handling of cases may be highly decentralized.

The official who heads a prosecutor's office in a state system may have any of several titles, most often district attorney, county attorney, or prosecuting attorney. Nearly all chief prosecutors in the states are elected, most for four-year terms. In contrast, U.S. Attorneys are appointed by the president, with Senate confirmation. At both levels, chief prosecutors are frequently active politicians, and some later seek higher positions. Many become judges. In recent years a U.S. Attorney in Pennsylvania (Dick Thornburgh) became governor and then U.S. attorney general, and a Philadelphia district attorney (Arlen Specter) became a U.S. senator.

Most often assistant prosecutors take this position shortly after graduation from law school and move on to private practice after a few years. Because of this initial inexperience and fairly rapid turnover, at any given time a significant proportion of prosecutors are still in the process of learning their jobs. But the large numbers of cases they handle reduce the time required to develop expertise.

Like judges, prosecutors make important decisions at several stages in the processing of criminal cases. Initially, they decide which cases will go to court and on what charges. Prosecutors present the government's case throughout the pretrial and trial stages, and they also make plea bargaining agreements with defendants. Finally, when defendants are convicted, the prosecutor's recommendation will usually influence the judge's sentencing decision.

These decisions give the prosecutor a power that is rivaled only by that of the judge. Arguably, in many courts the prosecutor is even more important than the judge. On the basis of his experiences, one convict concluded that "the person who runs the show is the prosecutor."[7] An instructor reminded new assistant district attorneys in New York City that "you will wield an amount of power over people's lives entirely disproportionate to your age and experience."[8]

Defense Attorneys   In the most minor cases, such as those involving routine traffic offenses, a defendant is unlikely to have an attorney. But defense attorneys are usually present in more serious cases; according to one estimate, only "25 or so" defendants each year—a very small fraction of the total—represent themselves in Cook County (Chicago) circuit court.[9]

Defense attorneys can be put into three categories: public defenders, private attorneys paid by their clients, and private attorneys who are assigned and paid by courts to represent indigent defendants. Public defenders share several characteristics with prosecutors. Generally, they work out of local offices, which are part of statewide systems in some states. Some public defenders are full-time, others part-time. Like assistant prosecutors, public defenders generally move on to private practice after a few years, so at any given time most are relatively young and many are inexperienced.

Some private attorneys handle criminal cases only occasionally, whereas others spend much or even most of their time in the criminal field. Some lawyers who do substantial work in criminal defense are both prosperous and well regarded. But criminal lawyers generally enjoy less wealth and prestige than most other attorneys because their clients are usually people who have relatively low incomes and even lower social status.[10]

Defense attorneys have less control over the processing of cases than do judges and prosecutors. But they automatically have impact as the representatives of defendants in plea bargaining and in court. Along with judges and prosecutors, they make up the core of the criminal court work group.

Other Court Personnel   Other people who work in the courts also influence the handling of cases. Courtroom clerks schedule and arrange cases, and their scheduling decisions may affect the disposition of cases by giving one side a tactical advantage. Parajudges, such as magistrates, sometimes act in place of judges, usually in minor cases and in the preliminary stages of other cases.

Probation officers also work in the courts, supervising convicted defendants who have been given probation rather than a prison sentence. Within the court, they produce presentence reports that judges use in determining their sentencing decisions.

Defendants   Defendants occupy the most ambiguous position of all the participants in court proceedings. Although defendants must approve their lawyers' decisions, including any plea bargains, they stand outside the core work group of the court, being heavily dependent upon defense attorneys for information and largely unable to control the course of events.

Defendants are not, of course, a random sample of the population. The great majority are male, a highly disproportionate number are members of racial minority groups, and they stand relatively low in socioeconomic status. Among a sample of defendants admitted to prison in 1988, 36 percent had graduated from high school and only 8 percent had any college education; both figures are less than half those for the adult population as a whole.[11] In a set of nine felony courts, from 53 percent to 90 percent of the defendants had attorneys provided by programs for the indigent.[12]

Some characteristics of most defendants, such as low education, tend to increase their dependence on their attorneys. However, many defendants have had previous experience with the criminal courts. This experience can give them considerable expertise in the workings of the courts and thus some ability to assess their lawyers' advice.

The Prosecutor's Clients   In the abstract, the prosecutor's clients are the government and the citizenry as a whole. But prosecutors have two more direct clients: law enforcement agencies and the people who bring complaints of crimes. Since police departments and other agencies make the arrests that allow criminal prosecutions, prosecutors' activities depend on the kinds of arrests police make and the quality of the evidence they gather. Police officers often are important witnesses in court as well. They also serve as a significant audience for the criminal courts, one that is inclined to be critical when it perceives leniency in the treatment of defendants.

People who make criminal complaints are generally the victims of the crimes involved. Prosecutors depend on their cooperation to make effective cases against defendants, yet victims traditionally have been excluded from decisions about the handling and disposition of their cases. In recent years, however, most states have adopted legislation giving victims fuller rights to participate in cases. Most states now allow a victim to make a statement, usually in writing, at a sentencing hearing. Several require consultation with the victim in the plea bargaining process. But studies show wide variation in the extent to which victims are actually given these statutory rights and make use of them. It is uncertain how much impact victims do have when they participate.[13]

Witnesses and Jurors   In general, law enforcement officers and complainants are the most important witnesses in trials. Of course, other people also serve as witnesses. They are not given a high priority in the concerns of courtroom professionals, who often fail to inform them about what they need to do. They may appear in court only to have their cases postponed, and repeated postponements can discourage them from reappearing which is often the goal of the defense attorney who seeks postponements.

Two sets of jurors, members of *grand juries* and *petit, or trial, juries,* also take part in criminal cases. Trial jurors (and in most states grand jurors) are chosen through methods intended to produce a fairly representative cross section of the public; one common means is a random selection from the list of registered voters. In practice, however, some types of citizens, such as those of higher socioeconomic status, are more likely to serve than others.[14]

Grand juries exist in the federal system and in most states to determine whether there is sufficient evidence to indict a defendant and thus bring the defendant to trial. Unlike trial juries, they sit continuously for a substantial period of time and hear large numbers of cases. They have little independent power, because they are guided through cases by the prosecutor and nearly always follow the prosecutor's recommendations. A New York City prosecutor reported that "even the most independent-minded grand juries were eventually numbed into unquestioningly doing our bidding."[15] A former chief judge of the New York court of appeals once said that most grand juries would "indict a ham sandwich" if the prosecutor asked them to do so.[16]

Trial juries have more impact on the outcomes of cases. In the cases that actually go to jury trials, the jury decides whether to convict the defendant and, in some states, determines the sentence for a defendant it finds guilty. Only a small proportion of criminal cases culminate in jury trials, but the handling of other cases is affected by predictions of jurors' potential behavior. For instance, if a jury would be unlikely to convict a particular defendant, perhaps because the evidence was ambiguous, the prosecutor might be inclined to drop the case or offer a relatively favorable plea bargain.

Criminal Courts and Their Environments   The judges and attorneys who handle criminal cases have considerable freedom to act on the basis of their own goals and interests. That freedom is reflected in their use of unpopular practices, such as plea bargaining. But by no means are criminal courts entirely free from external influences.

The broad impact of these influences is reflected in differences among courts. Variation among cities in prosecution and sentencing policies, for instance, can be traced in part to differences in public attitudes and patterns of political power. Political scientist Stuart A. Scheingold concluded that sympathetic treatment of black defendants in Detroit resulted from the increasing political importance of black citizens in that city, while Minneapolis courts sentenced defendants more severely in response to the values and interests of its dominant white middle class.[17]

Courts also are subject to direct influence from their environment, influence that takes a variety of forms. Judges and prosecutors may be enlisted in local campaigns to attack a growing crime problem in a particular neighborhood or to "clean up" the downtown business district. Defendants who are politically well connected may be the beneficiaries of demands for lenient treatment. In 1990 the federal government released a Cuban citizen on parole, though with severe restrictions, despite claims that he had engaged in terrorist activities against the Cuban government; pressure for his release had come from the Cuban-American community in Miami, supported by two members of Congress and a Republican leader in Miami who was also a son of President Bush.[18]

Though the courts are subject to demands to treat some defendants leniently, more common is pressure for severe treatment of specific defendants—or defendants in general. The widespread feeling that courts are too lenient is recognized by prosecutors and judges, especially those who must win re-election to retain their positions. One study found that a major reason for massive growth in the prison population over the past two decades is the "toughening practices of prosecutors and judges,"[19] and one source of these practices is public demands for stronger sanctions.

Court participants feel more direct pressure when public officials, the police, or interest groups, such as Mothers Against Drunk Driving, criticize them for alleged leniency, and sometimes they respond to this pressure. In one Maryland case, the release on bail of a teenager charged with murder resulted in a campaign by the victim's family to remove the judge; after a second judge ordered the defendant jailed, an appellate court reversed his decision on the ground that he may have been unduly influenced by the public outcry.[20] Criticism over bail reportedly had a more dramatic effect in an Alabama case:

> Repeat offender Isaac Peterson, in jail in Birmingham, Alabama, happened to have his bail hearing set for the morning . . . after district judge Jack

Montgomery had become fed up with criticism from the mayor that he sets bail too low, Peterson's bail was raised from $5,000 to $9 trillion.[21]

A Summary of Court Procedures

Criminal courts operate under laws that establish a series of formal procedures for the handling of cases. These procedures do not reflect the full reality of court action, but they serve as the framework for that action. After describing the formal procedures, I discuss informal elements of case handling that modify the formal rules.

Formal Procedures   Formal criminal court procedures differ a good deal across the country, and no general description could fit all the various systems accurately. But it is possible to provide a broad description of the stages through which cases usually go.[22] Exhibit 6.1 summarizes a typical set of procedures for felony cases, procedures that are the basis of the discussion that follows.

Court handling of felony cases usually begins with an arrest by the police. This arrest can be based on a formal complaint by a citizen, on a warrant (an authorization to arrest that is issued by a judge to the police), or on police observation of a possible crime.

The suspect makes an initial appearance in court shortly after arrest. If the arrest was made without a warrant, as is usually the case, the police must convince the judge that there is sufficient basis for holding the suspect. At the initial appearance, the suspect is informed of the criminal charges and of the applicable procedural rights. In addition, counsel may be appointed for an indigent defendant and bail is likely to be set.

The preliminary hearing or preliminary examination is the point at which the prosecution must show probable cause to believe that the defendant committed the crime indicated by the charge. To do so, the prosecutor presents evidence that the defense may then attack. If the judge finds probable cause, the defendant is held for further proceedings.

EXHIBIT 6.1 Typical Major Stages of Formal Action in Felony Cases

1. Arrest
2. Initial appearance by the defendant in court
3. Preliminary hearing or examination
4. Grand jury indictment or filing of information by the prosecutor
5. Arraignment of the defendant
6. Procedures to prepare the case for trial: discovery, motions, conference
7. Trial
8. Verdict
9. Sentencing (where defendant has been found guilty)

In federal court and in the states that retain the grand jury, the prosecutor then presents evidence to that body. On the basis of this evidence, the grand jury decides whether to indict the defendant and on what charges. In states that do not use grand juries, the prosecutor simply files what is called an information, attesting that there is sufficient evidence to try the defendant.

In states where the early stages of felony cases are handled in a minor trial court, the case now moves into a major court for arraignment. Here the defendant is formally presented with the charge or charges. The defendant can enter a plea to the charge either at the arraignment itself or at a later time.

After the arraignment, several procedures are undertaken to prepare the case for trial. The procedure of discovery allows the defendant to examine the prosecution's evidence. If the defendant does so, the prosecutor may in turn examine the defense evidence. In the federal courts and in some states, either side or the judge may initiate a pretrial conference to clarify the issues. The prosecution and defense may also make pretrial motions. For example, the defense may move to suppress evidence on the ground that the police obtained it illegally.

The last three stages of court action are the most familiar. At the trial, both sides present evidence and arguments on the issue of the defendant's guilt. After the trial, the judge or jury reaches a verdict, convicting or acquitting the defendant. If there are multiple charges against a defendant, the jury can convict on some charges and acquit on others. After the verdict, if the defendant is found guilty, the judge or jury (usually the judge) pronounces a sentence.

During a trial, the judge may intervene by granting a defense motion for acquittal if the evidence is insufficient to sustain a conviction. After the trial, on such a motion, the judge may override a conviction by the jury. (A jury acquittal cannot be overridden by the judge.) And after a conviction the judge may grant a defense motion for a new trial on the basis of a serious flaw in the original trial.

The formal procedures for misdemeanors are less extensive than those for felonies. Grand juries are not used, and other pretrial stages, such as the preliminary hearing, are often omitted. For relatively minor misdemeanors, states may dispense with the right to a jury trial.

Juvenile courts were created in the belief that younger offenders needed to be treated rather than punished; indeed, after the institution of these courts, juvenile cases were no longer defined as criminal. Some important differences between juvenile and adult courts followed from this premise. Most generally, juvenile courts were intended to be governed less fully by formal rules and procedures. Juvenile courts remain less formal than adult courts today, but this difference has been narrowed, in part because of a 1967 Supreme Court decision that gave juvenile defendants most of the procedural rights granted to adults under the Constitution.[23]

Court Procedures in Practice   This description of formal procedures gives only a partial picture of how cases are actually processed. To fill in the picture, we need to look at the ways that formal procedures work in practice. Several characteristics of case processing merit emphasis.

First, cases go through a winnowing process, in which most drop out at some point between arrest and trial. This winnowing occurs primarily in two forms. In one, cases are eliminated through a prosecutor's decision not to file charges or through dismissal, usually at the initial appearance or the preliminary hearing. For felony arrests, some of these cases reappear as misdemeanors. Exactly where cases are eliminated in a court depends largely on the point at which prosecutors have the best opportunity to screen arrests.

The other form of winnowing comes from guilty pleas by defendants. Strictly speaking, a guilty plea constitutes only a waiver of trial and any pretrial proceedings that remain when the plea is made. However, by telescoping the proceedings and terminating cases early, guilty pleas have the effect of dropping cases out of court.

The combined winnowing effect of decisions not to file charges, dismissals, and guilty pleas is overwhelming. The attrition of cases is illustrated by Figure 6.1, which is based on data from thirty jurisdictions across the United States in 1987 or 1988 (primarily counties). As the figure demonstrates, only 3 percent of the cases were actually tried in the felony court (a small proportion were tried in other courts). And as low as this figure is, it would be much lower for misdemeanor arrests.

A second important aspect of court procedure in practice is the frequent bypassing or abbreviation of the prescribed procedures. Even defendants who plead not guilty may waive some preliminary procedures, such as the pretrial hearing and the grand jury's consideration of indictment. Just as important,

FIGURE 6.1 Typical Attrition of One Hundred Felony Arrests Brought by the Police for Prosecution.

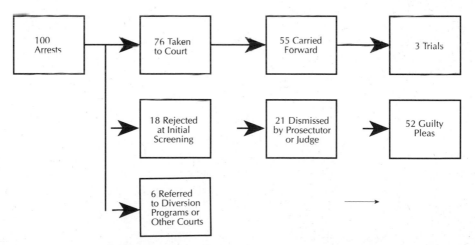

Source: Adapted from Barbara Boland, Paul Mahanna, and Ronald Sones, *The Prosecution of Felony Arrests, 1988* (Washington, D.C.: U.S. Department of Justice, 1992), p. 3. Based on data from thirty jurisdictions in either 1987 or 1988.

formal procedures may be undertaken with far more speed and less care than the rules would suggest. And "fast food justice"[24] has become speedier and more common with recent growth in court caseloads.

The most extreme abbreviation occurs in busy misdemeanor courts, which often carry out their business so rapidly that the formal stages become virtually unrecognizable. One observer of misdemeanor proceedings in New Haven, Connecticut, reported that "defendants came and went in rapid succession. While a few cases took up as much as a minute or two of the court's time—and a small handful involved the court in protracted proceedings—the overwhelming majority of cases took just a few seconds.[25]

In some big-city courtrooms, proceedings are enormously chaotic. At a conference in 1987, one Colorado judge reported on her visit to a misdemeanor court in New York City: "There were 40 million people milling around, a phone was ringing off the hook, and the public defender was shouting obscenities at the judge." A colleague from New York responded, "You must have been there on a good day."[26]

A third important procedural matter is the length of time between an arrest and the final disposition of a case. Criminal courts have both legal and practical reasons to keep this time short. The Constitution guarantees the right to a speedy trial, and Congress and many state legislatures have backed this right by setting limits on the time for disposition. Delay also penalizes defendants who are jailed prior to trial. On the other hand, delay often makes convictions more difficult as witnesses become unavailable or their memories fade.

Yet many courts, especially in big cities, face more cases than they can handle comfortably without undue delay. Judges and prosecutors must resort to a variety of measures to overcome this problem. Criminal cases are given priority over civil cases (so that civil litigants often endure very long delays before trial). And the goal of avoiding trials through dismissals and guilty pleas takes a very high priority. But delay remains a problem. In a subset of the thirty jurisdictions discussed earlier, the median time from arrest to trial was an average of about eight months. In Rhode Island, it was more than fifteen months.[27] The existence of this problem has a pervasive effect on criminal courts.

BRINGING CASES TO COURT

The large volume of criminal cases in many courts obscures a most important reality: only a small fraction of the cases that might be brought to court actually get there and last beyond the earliest stages of court action. The reasons for this phenomenon lie chiefly in the domains of the police and of prosecutors.

The Police: Making Arrests

Relatively few crimes result in arrests. Indeed, one study estimated that of every thousand serious felonies committed in the city of New York only sixty-five produced arrests.[28] And a three-state study estimated probabilities of arrest that ranged from about one in four for aggravated assaults to about one in a thousand for drug deals.[29]

Opportunities for Arrests   Most criminal offenses do not result in arrests simply because there is no opportunity to make them: the police are unable to detect a crime or apprehend a likely suspect.

Unless a crime is committed in the presence of a police officer, law enforcement agencies must rely on others to inform them of it. But even when crimes involve great injury, victims often do not make complaints to the police. A national survey in 1991 found that only 38 percent of all victims reported crimes to the police, with reporting rates generally highest for the most serious crimes.[30] For crimes that have no direct victims, such as drug sales and highway speeding, the rate of reports to police undoubtedly is very low; only through active surveillance can the police detect these kinds of offenses.

Even when the police are aware of an offense, they cannot always apprehend a suspect. When an officer observes a crime directly or when a complainant singles out a suspect who is easily located, the task is easy. But in other cases, it is usually much more difficult to identify and locate a suspect—far more difficult than detective stories would suggest. For the seven most serious criminal offenses in 1990, the proportion of offenses known to the police that were "cleared" through an arrest was only 22 percent; as with the reporting of crimes, the clearance rate was higher for more serious offenses.[31]

The Arrest Decision   When police officers identify a likely suspect, they generally make an arrest. Indeed, they often have reasons to do so even when a conviction is far from certain. For example, an arrest may seem an appropriate way to deal with an immediate problem, such as a fight, or it may allay public concern about a well-publicized crime. And more generally, police departments and individual officers are judged in part by the volume of arrests they make and the proportion of crimes they solve through arrest.

Yet there are also pressures against making every possible arrest. Police resources are often stretched thin; consequently, officers may choose not to arrest suspects in cases that appear to be relatively trivial. And reasons of policy may also militate against making arrests in particular cases. The police recognize, for instance, that the general public does not support the full enforcement of some laws; thus they seldom arrest those who are engaged in social gambling. And officers may agree not to arrest a suspect in exchange for information about criminal activity.

These kinds of judgments give the police tremendous power. Arrest in itself constitutes a kind of punishment, and it can lead to additional punishments in the criminal justice system. By the same token, a decision not to arrest ordinarily leaves a person free from possible punishment.

The Prosecutor: Charging Decisions

When a case comes to the attention of a prosecutor's office, usually through an arrest, that office must decide whether to carry the case forward or drop it. There are several points at which a prosecutor can make such a decision. In what is probably the most common pattern, prosecutors do most of their screening when they decide whether to file charges against someone who has been arrested. But in some places the police file felony charges themselves, and prosecutors then decide whether to maintain those cases in court or to dismiss them. For convenience, I refer to the prosecutor's screening of cases as the charging decision, though the screening may actually come at a later point.

The prosecutor has more choices than simply charging the suspect or dropping the case. If a suspect is to be charged, the prosecutor must also decide what charges to bring. After a felony arrest is made, one critical decision is whether to charge the suspect with a felony or reduce the case to a misdemeanor. The prosecutor may also take action other than criminal prosecution. For instance, in some cases it may seem preferable to institute a civil case against a suspect or to obtain an agreement that the suspect will provide restitution to the victim or undergo psychological treatment.

The proportion of cases in which prosecutors make and carry forward charges varies from place to place, but in most courts prosecutors screen out a high proportion of the cases that are brought to them. As Figure 6.1 shows, in one sample of jurisdictions about half the arrests were carried forward to felony court; most of the others were rejected or dismissed, chiefly by prosecutors.

Criteria for Charging Decisions   The charging decisions of prosecutors are based on many criteria, which one scholar has arranged into three categories: evidential, pragmatic, and organizational.[32]

Evidential criteria have to do with the likelihood of conviction. The question for the prosecutor is how certain a conviction seems to be in light of the available evidence. To take a case to trial and then lose it constitutes a waste of time and effort. And because prosecution puts heavy burdens on a defendant, the decision to prosecute someone who will probably be acquitted often seems unfair. Furthermore, defeats in court hurt prosecutors by lowering the winning percentage of both individual prosecutors and their offices. Defeats also weaken the prosecutor's position in plea bargaining with defense attorneys.

Studies consistently show that evidential criteria rank high in charging decisions.[33] In 1988, 45 percent of the case rejections by Portland prosecutors were for problems in the evidence; in Manhattan, the proportion was 79 percent.[34] These studies also show that conviction may be doubtful for any of several reasons. Sometimes it is simply uncertain that the defendant committed a crime, but problems may arise even when a prosecutor is confident that the defendant is guilty. A great many dismissals, for instance, result from the withdrawal of the complainant because of a relationship with the defendant, because of fear, or for some other reason. And since prosecutors are more concerned with the likelihood of a conviction than with factual guilt, a case is unlikely to go forward without a cooperative complainant.

This screening on the basis of evidential criteria helps to create an unofficial presumption of guilt in the minds of most people in the criminal courts. Knowing that prosecutors generally reject weak cases, judges and even defense attorneys often assume that if the prosecutor has chosen to carry a case forward the defendant is probably guilty and is likely to be convicted if the case goes to trial. This presumption affects the ways that cases are perceived and handled at later stages, especially in plea bargaining.

Pragmatic criteria for charging decisions involve efforts to individualize justice. Most frequently, pragmatic criteria relate to judgments about the severity of felony charges as applied to individual cases. For instance, a case may fit the legal definition of a felony but involve only minor wrongdoing, and so a prosecutor will not file a felony charge. Often the characteristics of the defendant also come into play; first offenders, for example, are likely to be treated more leniently than repeat offenders.

Aside from dropping a case, prosecutors have other alternatives from which to choose. One common choice is to charge a suspect with a misdemeanor in order to provide leniency without freeing that person from all sanctions. And, as noted earlier, noncriminal action, such as arranging restitution to the victim or psychiatric treatment for the suspect, sometimes seems appropriate. These kinds of actions can result from plea bargains, but frequently prosecutors take them on their own.

Organizational criteria for charging decisions have to do with the needs of the prosecutor's office. In one sense, all criteria for prosecution decisions have an organizational component, but some are more directly organizational than others.

One organizational concern is relationships with other policy makers and with the general public. As noted earlier, prosecutors may respond to pressures from their political environments. Especially important on a day-to-day basis is the need to maintain cooperation with law enforcement officials; one effect is that prosecutors may feel obliged to bring charges in cases that are important to the police.

Another organizational concern is the prosecutor's workload. Some offices are seriously overburdened. Even in more fortunate offices, people prefer to reduce workloads in order to ease pressures and limit the length of their workday. This concern has the effect of tightening the standards by which decisions are made to charge suspects. Thus cases that might not appear trivial in the abstract may be treated as trivial in light of the competing demands in the prosecutor's office. And reduction of a felony to a misdemeanor is especially attractive when misdemeanors are prosecuted by a different office.

Charging Decisions and the Power of Prosecutors   Just as discretion in arrest decisions gives power to the police, so too does a similar discretion in charging decisions give power to prosecutors. This power extends beyond the fates of individual suspects, for in establishing and applying criteria for prosecution the prosecutors in effect rewrite the criminal law.

Indeed, the rewriting is often formal. For instance, the federal statute dealing with bribery of bank employees was somewhat vague in its limitations on bank employees' acceptance of gifts from people with whom they do business. To provide greater clarity, the Justice Department gave U.S. Attorneys guidelines under which "occasional receipt of meals, entertainment or other gifts of modest or nominal value" should not be prosecuted.[35] Individual prosecutors' offices may develop their own guidelines, with resulting variation in policy from place to place. A study of seven U.S. Attorneys' offices found that each office prosecuted certain offenses only if at least a minimum amount of money was involved, but the minimum varied a good deal—from $500 to $5,000 for bank fraud, embezzlement, and the interstate transportation of stolen property.[36]

Such guidelines, as well as prosecution decisions in individual cases, reflect the attitudes of prosecutors, along with the pressures that they may feel. Thus prosecution policies are likely to change as social values change. Until recently, for example, most prosecutors were reluctant to bring charges in cases involving violence within the family, in part because they believed that such matters were best kept out of the criminal justice system. Today, however, many prosecutors are more willing to bring charges in such cases because of a growing belief that criminal sanctions against family violence are needed.

The power that flows from charging decisions is illustrated by the efforts of the Justice Department in the late 1980s and early 1990s to attack allegedly obscene material. Federal prosecutors engaged in forum-shopping, bringing prosecutions in relatively conservative states in order to increase the chances for convictions. In one instance, the FBI created a fake film distributorship in Oklahoma to lure a California firm into sending videos there. The Justice Department also established a policy of prosecuting obscenity defendants in multiple federal districts to drive them out of business. And federal prosecutors in Virginia initiated the practice of charging obscenity defendants under the federal racketeering laws, which provide for severe sanctions, including the forfeiture of defendants' financial assets. Although the multiple-prosecution strategy was declared illegal by two federal courts, the prosecution campaign had considerable effect.[37]

Prosecutors are often attacked for allegedly abusing their charging powers. Both federal and state prosecutors, for instance, are frequently suspected of "political" motivations—particularly an eagerness to prosecute political opponents and a reluctance to prosecute friends and allies. For example, some people accused the U.S. Attorney in Washington, D.C., of engaging in a long campaign to attack Mayor Marion Barry through prosecutions of his allies and acquaintances and, ultimately, through a set of drug-related charges against Barry himself.[38] Such attacks are reminders of the discretion involved in charging decisions, as well as the power that flows from that discretion.

PLEA BARGAINING

Every criminal defendant must choose whether to plead guilty or not guilty. Typically, at least in serious cases, the defendant initially pleads not guilty;

the choice then is whether to change the plea to guilty at some point before trial. (Occasionally, a defendant pleads *nolo contendere,* or no contest. This plea, like a guilty plea, waives the right to trial, but it does not constitute an admission of guilt.)

In most courts, the great majority of felony cases carried forward by the prosecutor are resolved through guilty pleas. This means that convictions generally result from guilty pleas rather than trials. In a sample of ten felony courts in 1988, the lowest proportion of convictions based on guilty pleas was in Portland, at 83 percent; in six of the courts, the proportion was over 95 percent.[39] And guilty pleas are even more dominant in most misdemeanor courts. In 1989, 173,000 misdemeanor cases were filed in Los Angeles; about 800 were tried.[40]

A defendant may plead guilty for a variety of reasons. In minor cases, for instance, the likely penalty may be so light that it would not be worth the expense and trouble of going to trial. But the most common reason is that the defendant expects to receive a more favorable sentence by pleading guilty rather than being convicted at trial.

This expectation may be based on an explicit agreement with the prosecutor or, less often, with the judge. In such an agreement, the defendant is promised benefits related to the sentence in exchange for a guilty plea. Alternatively, there is no explicit agreement, but the defendant still perceives that a guilty plea will produce a more advantageous sentence. This calculation, sometimes called an implicit bargain, is especially common in misdemeanor cases.

We can define plea bargaining to include only explicit bargains or to encompass implicit bargains as well. The question of definition is more than a technical matter, as it affects our judgments about such significant issues as the potential for elimination of plea bargaining. For most purposes, I think it is appropriate to use the broader definition, because a defendant who pleads guilty in the belief that a more favorable sentence will result is in effect making a bargain. And when prosecutors and judges give signals that guilty pleas indeed are rewarded, as they often do, it is not just the defendant who perceives that a bargain is occurring. In any case, most plea bargains in felony cases are explicit.

The practice of plea bargaining affects every aspect of the adjudication of felony cases. The handling of cases in their early stages is influenced by the expectation of bargaining, and the existence of a bargain constrains judges in their sentencing decisions. And the knowledge that a case was *not* settled by a bargain can influence its handling; judges, for instance, often impose heavier sentences on defendants who refused to plead guilty and were convicted at trial.

Forms of Plea Bargaining

The implicit bargain represents one form of plea bargaining.[41] Explicit plea bargains take a variety of forms, which can be placed in three categories. Exhibit 6.2 presents some basic characteristics of each type of plea bargaining.

Type	Primary Bargainer with Defense	Constraint on Judge's Power?	Certainty of Sentence
Charge bargain	Prosecutor	Yes	Variable
Prosecutor's sentence bargain	Prosecutor	·Yes	Moderate
Judge's sentence bargain	Judge	No	Very high
Implicit bargain	None	No	Very low

Source: Based primarily on John F. Padgett, "The Emergent Organization of Plea Bargaining," *American Journal of Sociology,* 90 (January 1985), 756–760.

EXHIBIT 6.2 Characteristics of Major Types of Plea Bargaining

The first is the *charge bargain,* in which the prosecutor reduces the defendant's potential sentence liability by reducing the package of charges. This reduction may be horizontal, with the number of multiple charges for an offense such as burglary being reduced in exchange for a guilty plea to the remaining charges. Or the reduction may be vertical, with the highest charges dropped in exchange for a guilty plea to lesser ones. The latter may be charges already in existence or new ones brought in as substitutes.[42] Reduction of felony charges to a misdemeanor is especially common. Police officers and prosecutors sometimes set the stage for charge bargains by "overcharging" defendants initially—bringing some charges that they have little intention of carrying forward.

Because the defendant's sentence liability is reduced in order to make a guilty plea attractive, the charges to which a defendant pleads guilty may bear little relationship to the original charges or even to the actual offense. Indeed, according to one commentator, "it is no oversimplification to say that courthouse personnel first decide what a defendant's punishment shall be and then hunt around to find a charge that is consistent with their decision."[43] In New York City, shoplifting and assault often are reduced to disorderly conduct, and assault may become harassment.[44] Armed robbery frequently turns into unarmed robbery, a process known as "swallowing the gun." Some years ago a Wisconsin prosecutor who reduced an auto speeding charge to driving the wrong way on a one-way street was embarrassed by the discovery that his town had no one-way streets.[45]

The second category is the *prosecutor's sentence bargain.* Here the prosecutor gives the defendant some assurance about the sentence that a judge will hand down. Most commonly, the prosecutor agrees to recommend a particular sentence, with the expectation that the judge will follow that recommendation. The judge, however, is not obliged to do so, and judges sometimes reject bargains where they deem the terms to be inadequate; in one well publicized instance in 1991, an Alaska federal judge rejected the initial plea bargain between the Justice Department and the Exxon Corporation over the oil spill in Prince William Sound.[46] Some sentence bargains involve less direct concessions by the prosecutor, such as an agreement to make no sentence recommendation. Until recently, plea bargains in one Maryland county featured a practice in which prosecutors offered a list of three judges to take the plea and hand down a sentence; defense lawyers would choose from the list or suggest a different judge.[47]

The final category is the *judge's sentence bargain*. A judge may indicate the likely sentence that would follow a guilty plea, and the defendant pleads guilty on the assumption that this sentence will actually be imposed. This is almost surely the least common form of bargaining in felony cases, and its legitimacy is not fully accepted; in one 1991 opinion, the Massachusetts Supreme Court sought "to remind judges that they are not to participate as active negotiators in plea bargaining discussions."[48] A failed bargaining session in 1992, described in Exhibit 6.3, suggests that not all judges have complied with this ruling. In any case, judicial sentence bargaining flourishes in New York City. Special courtrooms have been set up in New York for judges to achieve plea bargains in drug cases by working directly with defense attorneys and prosecutors.[49]

Multiple forms of bargains sometimes are combined in a particular case; for instance, a prosecutor may reduce the charges against a defendant and offer to recommend a particular sentence in exchange for a guilty plea. Each courthouse community develops its own practices, with different kinds of bargains dominant in different places.

The Bargaining Process

The process of plea bargaining varies as much as its form. Much of that variation stems from the different forms themselves, which determine

EXHIBIT 6.3 An Unsuccessful Effort at Sentence Bargaining

Bruce Damon, attempting to work a plea bargain in February to charges that he knocked off a bank in Whitman, Mass., argued to the judge that the 8-to-15-year term suggested by the prosecutor was way too long. First of all, Damon said, when he robbed a bank in 1987, he only got 3-to-5. Second, he said, citing an article from the Brockton Enterprise newspaper, the bank had enjoyed record earnings despite the robbery and expected to do well in 1992, also. Said Damon, "I didn't hurt this bank at all." When the judge asked Damon if he would rob banks again if he were free, Damon replied, "I'd like to plead the Fifth Amendment on that." The judge refused to accept the plea and scheduled Damon for trial.

Source: Quoted from Chuck Shepherd, "News of the Weird," *Funny Times*, July 1992, p. 21.

whether the defendant and defense attorney negotiate primarily with the prosecutor or with the judge—or, in the case of implicit bargaining, reach a decision to plead guilty without any negotiation. Defense attorneys usually bargain on behalf of their clients; however, in cases involving minor misdemeanors, defendants are often unrepresented and negotiate or choose to plead guilty on their own. Plea bargaining usually occurs shortly before the trial is scheduled to begin, but it can come earlier or even later. One Virginia murder defendant agreed to a sentence of forty years even while, as it turned out, the jury was in the process of acquitting him.[50]

In each court, routines develop for the initiation and transaction of bargains. In some places, prosecutors "hold court" prior to court sessions in order to negotiate with attorneys who have cases scheduled for trial that day. Some courts use pretrial conferences as a forum for bargaining. The prosecutor and defense attorney may go through a case file together to determine an appropriate bargain.

To a considerable extent, there is also a routine to the *terms* of plea bargains. Although every criminal case might be regarded as unique in some respects, basic patterns recur; members of the courtroom work group become accustomed to the most common forms of offenses, such as burglary and assault. For these "normal crimes," as one scholar has called them,[51] standard terms of bargains—"going rates"—are likely to develop. These standard terms can then be adjusted for special circumstances in cases.

The terms of bargains are likely to be quite standardized in misdemeanor cases, and political scientist Malcolm Feeley has argued that we should adjust our image of plea bargaining to reflect that reality:

> Discussions of plea bargaining often conjure up images of a Middle Eastern bazaar, in which each transaction appears as a new and distinct encounter, unencumbered by precedent or past association. Every interchange involves higgling and haggling anew, in an effort to obtain the best possible deal. The reality of American lower courts is different. They are more akin to modern supermarkets, in which prices for various commodities have been clearly established and labeled in advance. . . . To the extent that there is any negotiation at all, it usually focuses on the nature of the case, and the establishment of relevant "facts."[52]

Although Feeley focused on misdemeanor courts, bargaining in felony courts also follows the supermarket model to a degree.[53]

Both the going rates and the terms of bargains in specific cases reflect multiple factors. One of them is the participants' sense of justice and fairness, as applied to a specific offense and defendant. Perhaps more fundamental is the bargaining power of the participants, which rests largely on their estimates of what would happen if a case went to trial. Thus one important consideration is the estimated likelihood of conviction after a trial. Federal prosecutors usually have very strong cases because they carefully screen out the weaker ones; partly for this reason, they need to yield relatively little in exchange for guilty pleas.[54] Similarly, when the sentence will be handed down by a judge who tends to be severe, the prosecutor's position is strengthened. Other considerations also can affect bargaining power. Heavy caseloads, for instance, put prosecutors and judges under pressure to dispose of cases quickly and thus give the defense additional leverage.

Explaining the Prevalence of Plea Bargaining

Why is plea bargaining so common? Perhaps the best explanation lies in the motivations of those who participate in plea bargaining.

Saving Time   One basic motivation for plea bargaining is the desire of lawyers and judges to save time. Of course, time is required to reach bargains and ratify them in court, but trials ordinarily require even more time—especially jury trials in serious cases. This difference is fundamental to plea bargaining. Indeed, historical research suggests that bargaining became popular partly because trials became more time-consuming.[55]

Judges and full-time prosecutors and public defenders gain obvious advantages from reducing the time required to dispose of cases. Plea bargaining allows them to work shorter days, handle more cases in the same workday, or achieve some combination of the two.

Part-time prosecutors and private defense attorneys gain financially from speedy disposal of cases. The less time that part-time prosecutors devote to their public duties, the more they can devote to their private practices. And for private defense attorneys, quick turnover of cases is the most profitable mode of practice. Ordinarily, the attorney's fee—whether paid by the client or by the court—will not increase enough to pay for the extra time required to try a case rather than to avoid trial through a guilty plea.

Where there are heavy caseload pressures on judges, prosecutors, and public defenders, the incentive to dispose of cases quickly is especially strong. Indeed, in some cities it would be impossible to hold full-dress trials in more than a small proportion of cases; hence plea bargaining, or some equivalent, is necessary to avoid complete chaos. This need was symbolized by a three-week period of 1991 in which members of the courtroom community in Brooklyn worked systematically to cut back on an overwhelming backlog of criminal cases through plea bargaining.[56]

But an interest in speed is not confined to courts with burdensome caseloads. As one scholar put it, "regardless of caseload, there will always be *too many cases* for many of the participants in the system, since most of them have a strong interest in being some place other than in court."[57] Some prosecutors in Chicago reportedly like to end proceedings early on summer days so that they can escape to Wrigley Field for baseball games. And judges too may be interested in such escapes; a few years ago trial days in a major federal criminal case were abbreviated so that the judge could enjoy his afternoon golf games.[58]

Thus, contrary to widespread belief, plea bargaining is not a recent response to growing caseloads in big-city courts. Rather, it was common decades ago, when courts generally were less burdened. And it is common not just in cities but also in suburban and rural courts, whose caseload pressures are relatively light.[59]

Achieving Desirable Results   For its participants, plea bargaining serves purposes that go beyond speed. Most important, plea bargains are a means for both the prosecution and the defense to secure acceptable results in cases, thus eliminating the possibility of highly undesirable outcomes.

In a plea bargain, the prosecutor gains a guaranteed conviction. Any case that goes to court carries at least the risk of an acquittal, and some carry a substantial risk. By eliminating this risk, a plea bargain helps to build high winning percentages for the individual prosecutor and the prosecutor's office. And by reaching bargains and helping to set their terms, prosecutors can also bring about what they see as appropriate outcomes in terms of the kinds of sanctions that defendants receive.

On the other side, the defense attorney and the defendant gain what they perceive as advantages in sentencing. Virtually all the participants in the criminal courts assume that, all else being equal, a defendant who pleads guilty will receive a lighter sentence than one who has been convicted at trial. Indeed, some judges announce such a policy openly. A California judge sentenced a drunk driving defendant to thirty days in jail after a jury trial; earlier the defendant had turned down the judge's proposed plea bargain that would have involved no jail time. The judge then told the press that his sentence was meant to discourage jury trials and that "there had to be some incentive not to go to trial."[60] According to a reporter, a New York City judge made the same point in a different way:

> Once, three young men who made their living by robbing people in the subway spurned the deal they were offered by the arraigning judge. They went all the way to trial, and got convicted. Seeing what a menace to society they were, the trial judge gave them 5-to-15 years in prison. "How can you do that?" cried one of the defendants. "The judge downstairs offered us a year!"
>
> The trial judge replied: "At one time I could have bought Xerox at three dollars a share. I missed the market, and so did you."[61]

The primary rationale for rewarding defendants who plead guilty is that they aid the court in processing cases quickly. As one Chicago judge remarked of a defendant who might go to trial, "he takes some of my time—I take some of his."[62] Another rationale is that defendants who plead guilty have taken responsibility for their offenses rather than hoping for a lucky acquittal. The defendant who has cause for going to trial may not be punished, but others can expect to pay for their trials.

Among studies designed to measure the impact of guilty pleas on the severity of sentences, there is some disagreement in findings. But most of the evidence supports the perception that defendants who plead guilty are rewarded at sentencing—at least in comparison with defendants who are convicted in jury (rather than bench) trials.[63] Quite aside from whatever actual rewards exist, a plea bargain generally eliminates the risk that a judge

seemed to encourage implicit plea bargaining by giving lighter sentences to defendants who pleaded guilty. But an increase in trials produced a backlog of cases, so that additional judges had to hear criminal cases, and not all these judges were committed to the ban on plea bargaining. Covert bargaining by assistant prosecutors also increased. Thus the prohibitions reduced plea bargaining and made it less open, but they hardly caused it to disappear.

Most other attempts to abolish bargaining have enjoyed only limited success: they often reduce the incidence of bargaining, decrease its visibility, and change its form, but they do not eliminate it, and it frequently enjoys a resurgence over time. In Los Angeles, to take one example, bargaining was standard practice in 1990 despite a 1982 California voter initiative that was designed to curtail plea bargaining sharply.[83]

Recent efforts to reduce judges' sentencing discretion are discussed later in the chapter. But it should be noted that these efforts have neither eliminated nor, it appears, even reduced plea bargaining. Rather, bargaining practices have been maintained or adapted to fit new sentencing rules.[84]

Thus it appears that plea bargaining is very difficult to eliminate, especially if we define it to include implicit bargaining. And courts that operate with relatively low rates of guilty pleas typically do so through the standard use of short bench trials, which achieve some of the same goals as plea bargaining for lawyers and judges. This fact underlines the lesson that people who participate in criminal courts shape court practices on the basis of their incentives, and efforts to change these practices must take this reality into account.

CRIMINAL TRIALS

Of all the activities in criminal courts, trials receive the most attention. In one sense this attention is undeserved, because only a relatively small minority of felony cases and an even smaller minority of misdemeanor cases are actually tried. Yet trials are an important part of the work of criminal courts. First of all, many cases—including a disproportionate number of the most serious ones—do go to trial. Trials also set standards for other court processes; decisions by prosecutors on whether to bring charges and the terms of plea bargains are both based largely on estimates of what would happen at trial.

Trials merit attention for another reason as well. Much of the criticism of plea bargaining is based on a belief that trials are a better means to resolve the issue of guilt. But comparison of trials and bargains is often based on an idealized version of the criminal trial; instead, it needs to be based on trials as they actually operate. For that reason, this section focuses primarily on the effectiveness of trials in reaching decisions about guilt and innocence.

The Trial Process

Under the Constitution and Supreme Court decisions, a criminal defendant has the right to a jury trial in cases in which imprisonment of more than six months is possible. Most defendants opt for jury trials, though the proportion of bench trials before judges varies a good deal from place to place. Bench trials are more common in less serious cases.

In jury trials, the first important step is the selection of the jury. Federal courts and some states use twelve-member juries, while other states use smaller numbers. Jury selection centers on the voir dire, in which either the lawyers or the judge questions prospective jurors about matters deemed relevant to the trial. A lawyer may ask that the judge dismiss a juror for cause if possible prejudice has been established. Each side also has a certain number of peremptory challenges, which are used to dismiss a juror without showing cause.

In well-publicized cases, such as the trial of Manuel Noriega in Florida, it may be difficult to find a sufficient number of unbiased jurors. In extreme situations, a judge may order a change of venue—that is, a change to another location—where knowledge of a case is more limited or emotions do not run as high, but such action is rare; the 1991 change of venue in the case of four police officers accused of beating Rodney King was the first granted in Los Angeles in nearly twenty years.[85]

At the start of a jury trial, each attorney may make an opening statement. The prosecutor then presents evidence, primarily through testimony by witnesses; the defense attorney may cross-examine these witnesses. After the prosecution has presented its case, the defense offers its own case in the same manner. Throughout this process, the attorneys may make motions and object to questions or the introduction of other evidence, and the judge rules on these matters. The trial ends with closing arguments by attorneys for each side.

After the closing arguments, the judge instructs the jury on the legal rules that are relevant to the decision. The jury then retires to discuss the case and reach a verdict. (In all but a few states, a unanimous vote is required in criminal cases.) Finally, the jury's verdict is announced. If the jury cannot reach a decision, it will be dismissed and a mistrial declared. The prosecutor can then initiate a retrial.

Bench trials are generally simpler, briefer, and less formal than jury trials because procedures used to select jurors and to aid them in reaching a decision are absent. This difference is highlighted by the extreme example, the speedy bench trials of routine traffic offenses in misdemeanor courts. But both jury and bench trials tend to be brief; even in federal court, where trials are relatively formal and lengthy, most criminal cases in 1991 required only one or two days to try.[86] Some trials extend over several months, but they are very much exceptions to the rule.

The Effectiveness of Trial Decision-Making

How effectively do trials operate to produce correct judgments about guilt or innocence? The concept of a correct judgment is a slippery one. In every case, there is a factual reality and a set of applicable legal rules. Occasionally, the law and the facts combine in such a way as to leave the correct verdict uncertain. But in most cases, a decision-maker who was omniscient, learned, and objective would invariably reach the correct verdict. The issue here is the extent to which real judges and juries, functioning in real trials, can reach correct verdicts.

Decision-Making in Trials   Judges and juries decide cases on the basis of the information they are given. In practice, this information is often both incomplete and inaccurate.

Incomplete information is a widespread problem. In some cases, important evidence may not exist; for instance, there might be no witnesses to a burglary. Witnesses or physical evidence that do exist may go undiscovered. And other evidence may not get to court because of logistic problems.

Witnesses, the primary sources of information in most cases, illustrate the problem of inaccuracy. People are far from perfect in their capacities to perceive, recall, and relate what they have seen and heard. The identification of suspects is especially prone to error. In one experiment, a film of a mugging and a subsequent six-person lineup were shown on a television news program. Of the viewers who called in their identifications after the program, choosing among the six suspects or rejecting all six, 14.1 percent were accurate— about the proportion that could be expected solely on the basis of chance.[87] Difficulties in identification may help defendants; in a federal arson case, after one witness identified the defense attorney as the perpetrator and another witness pointed to the U.S. marshal, the defendant—not surprisingly—was acquitted.[88] On the other side, one expert has concluded that "faulty eyewitness testimony, in my opinion, is the major cause of wrongful conviction in this country."[89]

Thus a judge or juror may be handicapped by inadequate information. Processing that information to reach a verdict adds further difficulties. First of all, jurors and judges are, in effect, the witnesses of trials, and their recollections too may be both incomplete and inaccurate.

In addition, the judge or jury must analyze the evidence to choose the most credible version of the facts. In some trials, this process is fairly easy, because there is only one credible version. But in trials where several interpretations of the facts are possible, the choice may be exceedingly difficult. For instance, assessing the truthfulness of witnesses is often one critical part of the task. Such assessments are highly prone to error. Summarizing the relevant research, one scholar said that "decisions about whether a statement is the truth or a lie are made about as well as if one were tossing a coin."[90]

For all these reasons, a judge or jury is likely to do a highly imperfect job of ascertaining the relevant facts. Jerome Frank, a legal scholar and judge, summarized this imperfection bluntly: "Facts are guesses."[91]

Finally, the judge or juror must apply legal rules to the facts—rules that frequently are ambiguous and difficult to apply. Perhaps most important, it is necessary to determine whether the defendant is guilty beyond a reasonable doubt, but the meaning of "reasonable doubt" is murky, and one federal court has ruled that a judge need not provide jurors with a definition of the term.[92]

And judges' instructions to jurors on the law are often very difficult to understand—or, as one judge put it, "most jurors cannot understand the pompous language thrust on them by the legal caste."[93] In 1992 a federal magistrate in Chicago recommended that a defendant be resentenced because a study had shown that most jurors did not understand the standard jury instructions in death penalty cases.[94]

A decision-making task of high difficulty and ambiguity, such as the task faced by judges and juries in close cases, provides fertile ground for irrelevant information to influence judgments. "In a trial-advocacy lecture," one prosecutor reported, "we were warned never to ask jurors after a trial how they had reached their verdict. Their answers would be too disturbingly unrelated to the facts."[95]

The Impact of the Adversary System   The problems that have just been identified need to be put in the context of the *adversary system,* in which two sides contest at trial, because this system is designed to minimize such problems. Ideally, the trial operates as a kind of marketplace of ideas: if each side presents the strongest possible case, the truth will emerge from the confrontation of those cases.

Unquestionably, the adversary system in practice goes some distance toward meeting this ideal. For instance, the desire of prosecutors and defense attorneys to win cases gives them an incentive to ferret out relevant information. However, the clash between the two sides cannot eliminate the inherent difficulty of reaching a correct verdict, and one or both sides may be incapable of presenting anything resembling the strongest possible cases.

Moreover, the adversary system has negative as well as positive effects. The desire to make a strong case can cause an attorney to obscure the facts rather than illuminate them, to increase prejudice rather than reduce it. Each side, after all, is not fighting for the truth to emerge; it is fighting to win.

This problem is illustrated by jury selection, in which lawyers work hard to obtain jurors who are inclined to support their side. As one attorney put it, "If we can't get a jury which is biased in our favor, or at least a jury which is biased against [the other side], we will accept an impartial jury."[96]

Another example is the defendant's appearance. Defense lawyers often take care to make their clients look respectable and sympathetic. Thus a defendant whom a reporter described as "a menacing-looking young man with long unkempt hair and a shaggy beard" was transformed at his trial into someone "clean-shaven and dressed in summer-weight Ivy League clothes."[97] And the public defender's office in West Palm Beach, Florida, outfits clients from its "PD Boutique," which includes designer suits.[98] This tactic is understandable, but it has nothing to do with the facts of a case.

The adversary system also affects the testimony of witnesses. Not surprisingly, attorneys prepare witnesses to testify in the manner that will be most favorable to their side. Feeling a stake in the outcome, witnesses generally go along. For instance, expert witnesses generally act as advocates for the side that hires them. This was true of a psychiatrist who testified for the defense against an injured worker; the psychiatrist differed from most experts only in his candor. Asked whether the worker was a "malingerer," the psychiatrist replied, "I wouldn't be testifying if I didn't think so, unless I was on the other side, then it would be a post traumatic condition."[99]

Ideally, cross-examination serves to bring the truth to light, but in practice it may create additional problems. According to Judge Rudolph Gerber, "cross-examination by harassment is one of the greatest impediments to the truth. An all-too-frequent occurrence . . . is the use of insult and innuendo to obscure the truth by obstructing its mouthpiece—the witness."[100]

The adversary system is especially problematic when one side has an advantage over the other in the ability to make its case effectively. One source of such an advantage, of course, is the quality of the attorneys on the two sides. The aphorism that a jury has the job of deciding which side had the better lawyer exaggerates but highlights an important reality: advocacy skills can make a critical difference.

Just as important, one side may have a better opportunity to prepare the case for a trial, a difference that often reflects economics. A prosecutor may have more time and resources to develop a strong case than an overburdened public defender. On the other hand, the rare defendant with access to large sums of money can afford preparations that go well beyond what any prosecutor could undertake. Of course, the side with the more skilled attorneys and the greater resources for trial preparation does not always win, but it gains advantages that can prove decisive.

Judges and Juries as Decision-Makers   Thus far I have not distinguished between judges and juries as trial decision-makers. Yet we might expect the two to behave somewhat differently; indeed, there has been a long historical debate over the relative merits of judges and juries.

There are several issues in this debate. Critics of juries argue that their lack of experience and expertise puts them at a great disadvantage in assessing the facts of a case and applying the law. This disadvantage has been aggravated by traditional prohibitions on note taking and questioning of witnesses, prohibitions that are beginning to break down. Critics also argue that when the law conflicts with a decision-maker's personal sense of justice a juror is less capable than a judge of adhering to that law. On the other side, supporters of juries see a virtue both in their freshness—unlike many judges, they have not built up an assumption that defendants are guilty—and in their independence from the obligations and pressures that judges may feel.

We have little systematic evidence with which to test these arguments. We do know a good deal about the factors that affect jury behavior.[101] One major theme of the research is that jurors in effect modify the law to fit their own sense of equity. They resist convicting defendants under unpopular laws, take the victim's conduct into account in judging the defendant, and consider whether what they perceive to be the potential punishment for an offense is more than a defendant merits. Another theme is that jurors are sometimes swayed by irrelevant or even illegitimate considerations, such as racial bias. As both these themes suggest, the social and political attitudes of jurors can have considerable impact on their verdicts.

The existing research, however, does not tell us much about the extent to which judges differ from juries in these respects. In one study from the 1950s, judges were asked to compare jury verdicts with those that the judges themselves would have reached.[102] There was a 22 percent rate of disagreement, which the judges ascribed chiefly to jury departures from the law that no judge would have made. Yet these determinations were made by judges who had disagreed with the juries—not necessarily the most objective observers.

This study found that juries were considerably more likely to acquit than were judges. More recently, the conviction rate in jury trials seems to have risen substantially, and there is some evidence that juries now are at least as likely to convict as judges. Political scientist James P. Levine has argued that this change in jury behavior reflects increased public concern about crime.[103] And, because of changing attitudes, jurors today may be more willing to convict for some offenses that traditionally had high acquittal rates in jury trials—most notably drunken driving and sexual assault.[104]

These findings do not provide a clear picture of the relative merits of judges and juries. There is some evidence that juries have greater deficiencies as decision-makers. But, as suggested earlier, jurors' "amateur" status may have its advantages. And research in social psychology suggests that a multimember body has real strengths in reaching decisions in comparison with a single person. Those strengths may be illustrated by the admittedly unrepresentative case described in Exhibit 6.4. In any event, evidence that takes into account the different mixes of cases heard by judges and juries remains too limited to allow firm judgments.

Some Concluding Thoughts on Criminal Trials   The journalist H. L. Mencken once defined a courtroom as "a place where Jesus Christ and Judas Iscariot would be equals, with the betting odds in favor of Judas."[105] Mencken's exaggeration was meant to underline the very real imperfections of trials as means to reach the correct judgments—imperfections reflected in the occurrence of clearly mistaken verdicts in some cases.[106]

In assessing the impact of these imperfections, we should make a distinction between clear cases and close cases. In a good many trials, the facts and the law are such that one result is virtually guaranteed, and all the imperfections of trials are unlikely to have any effect. In many other cases, however, there is enough uncertainty that the process can have an effect and the wrong verdict may be reached.

The realities of trials should be taken into account in assessing other methods for resolving cases, especially plea bargaining. The weaknesses of plea bargaining must be balanced against the weaknesses of trials, and certainly neither should be idealized. It is a mistake to criticize plea bargaining in comparison with an ideal trial process that always produces the correct verdict. But it is also a mistake to prefer plea bargaining on the ground that it avoids the imperfections of the criminal trial. Since some of the same weaknesses affect both and since trials set standards by which plea bargains are negotiated, the two processes differ less in result than they do in form.

A criminal defense lawyer is making his closing argument to the jury. His client is accused of murder, but the body of the victim has never been found. He dramatically withdraws his pocket watch and announces to the jury, "Ladies and gentlemen, I have some astounding news. We have found the supposed victim of this murder alive and well, and, in exactly one minute, he will walk through that door into this courtroom."

A hushed silence falls over the courtroom, as everyone waits for the momentous entry. Nothing happens.

The lawyer then says, "The mere fact that you were watching that door, expecting the victim to walk into this courtroom, suggests that you have a reasonable doubt whether a murder was committed." Pleased with the impact of the stunt, he then sits down to await an acquittal.

The jury is instructed, files out and files back in 10 minutes later with a verdict finding the defendant guilty. Following the proceedings, the astounded lawyer chases after the jury foreman to find out what went wrong. "How could you convict?" he asks. "You were all watching the door!"

The foreman explains, "Most of us were watching the door. But one of us was watching the defendant, and he wasn't watching the door."

Source: Quoted from Rodney R. Jones, Charles M. Sevilla, and Gerald F. Uelman, *Disorderly Conduct: Verbatim Excerpts from Actual Cases* (New York: W. W. Norton, 1987), p. 143.

EXHIBIT 6.4 A Case of an Effective Jury

SENTENCING DECISIONS

Most cases that prosecutors carry forward result in convictions, either through guilty verdicts or through guilty pleas. For defendants who are convicted, sentencing is the ultimate court decision that helps determine their fate. From the perspective of society as a whole, sentencing decisions largely determine the pattern of sanctions that actually operates in the criminal justice system.

Formal sentencing power lies primarily with trial judges. Except for cases involving a possible death sentence, only six southern and border states provide for sentencing by juries. Even in those states, juries generally set sentences only in the small minority of cases involving jury trials, and judges have some power to revise jury recommendations for sentences. An increasing number of states and the federal government allow some appeals of judges' sentences,[107] but it remains the general rule that sentences cannot be appealed if they are consistent with the applicable statutes.

Sentencing Systems

Congress and the state legislatures each select their own statutory systems for sentencing. The most important difference among these systems is in the amount of discretion that is lodged with two decision-makers, the sentencing judge and the parole board that sets the release dates for prisoners.[108]

For most of this century, American sentencing systems typically granted broad discretion to judges. They could impose a variety of sanctions, including prison or jail, fines, probation, community service, and restitution. If judges did impose a prison sentence, they were given a wide range of sentence lengths from which to choose for any specific offense.

Most states retain the essential features of these "high-discretion" systems today. In Alabama, for example, a defendant who is convicted of a Class A felony, such as the most serious arsons and burglaries, can receive a prison sentence of ten years to life. Alternatively, a judge can usually impose probation, under which defendants are free from imprisonment but generally must accept a degree of supervision and some restriction on their activities. In reality, then, the possible sentence for an offense can range from life in prison to no prison time at all. The actual range is not as great as it appears because parole systems usually shorten actual prison sentences, but it is still quite considerable.

The freedom that judges have in high-discretion systems is also reflected in the range of alternative sentences and conditions for probation that they can impose. The list in Exhibit 6.5 suggests how far judges' freedom extends

EXHIBIT 6.5 Examples of Unusual Sentences and Conditions of Probation Imposed Upon Convicted Defendants

Offense	Sentence or Condition
Multiple speeding tickets	Driving only American-built cars
Cocaine possession	Reading and reporting on five novels (including *Crime and Punishment*)
Theft of two six-packs of beer	Wearing a T-shirt reading "My Record and Two Six-Packs Equal Four Years"
Burglary of a house	Letting victims come to the defendant's home and take any items they want
Hitting a police officer	Writing "people do not have to put up with a jerk like me" 100 times a day in jail

Sources: "Drive U.S. Cars (and Sensibly), Judge Says," *New York Times,* January 31, 1992, p. A13; "It Was a Novel Sentence," *Columbus Dispatch,* October 15, 1989, p. 2F; Lynn Weisberg, "Latter-Day Scarlet Letter," *National Law Journal,* March 5, 1990, p. 59; "Pick One From Defendant A, One From Defendant B," *National Law Journal,* October 21, 1991, p. 47; "Man Sentenced to Sentences," *National Law Journal,* November 21, 1988, p. 51.

by describing some examples of unusual requirements that judges have imposed on defendants.

In recent years many states and the federal government have amended their sentencing systems to reduce the discretion of judges. (The federal government and about a dozen states have also eliminated parole, effectively giving judges *more* control over a defendant's length of imprisonment.) One approach, exemplified by California, is to narrow substantially the range of permissible sentences. For each offense, the California legislature laid down a preferred length of imprisonment, along with slightly higher and lower terms that the judge can impose if there are aggravating or mitigating circumstances. Sentences may also be increased on the basis of a defendant's prior record and the character of the criminal act itself. In most cases, too, the judge retains the option of substituting probation for a prison sentence.

A second approach is to establish guidelines for sentences but to allow judges to depart from these guidelines if they provide a justification. Sentences outside the guidelines can be appealed. Minnesota, the state of Washington, and the federal government have all taken this approach. A variant is to set up voluntary guidelines for use by judges who wish to follow them, with no right of appeal from sentences that do not adhere to the guidelines. This kind of system has been adopted in Massachusetts and Maryland, as well as in many localities.

A more limited approach, adopted by nearly every state, is to set mandatory minimum sentences for certain specific offenses. Michigan requires an additional two-year prison term for the possession of a gun while committing a felony, and New York mandates prison sentences for narcotics offenses. Both these laws, like similar laws in many other states, are efforts to reduce sentencing discretion selectively within high-discretion systems.

The Sentencing Process

The process by which judges impose sentences varies, particularly in its timing. Sometimes, particularly in misdemeanor cases, the sentence is handed down immediately after the trial or the acceptance of a guilty plea. But in felony cases, sentencing generally follows a sentencing hearing, which is held at a later date after the trial.

Before the hearing, the judge usually receives a presentence report that has been compiled by a probation officer. This report contains background information on the defendant, including such matters as prior criminal record and family situation. The report usually recommends whether to impose a prison sentence or probation and sometimes makes a more specific sentence recommendation.

At the hearing itself, the judge usually hears from both the prosecutor and the defense attorney. Defendants are generally allowed to speak and sometimes do so; in some states, the victim of the defendant's crime also may speak. After these presentations, the judge usually imposes the sentence immediately. The judge may offer a brief oral justification of the sentence, but anything more extensive or more formal is unusual.

Sentencing Choices: A First Look

As we have seen, most states give judges a great deal of discretion in choosing sentences. Even in states that limit discretion severely, such as California, judges make significant choices. How do they go about making these choices?

To begin with, a judge's real options in any specific case are often considerably narrower than the applicable statute suggests. First of all, a judge develops a view as to the sentences that are appropriate under common circumstances; often the judge does so in conjunction with lawyers and other judges. In sentencing, as in plea bargaining, going rates develop for normal crimes.

In addition, the judge's sentence in a specific case is influenced by other members of the work group. Probation officers have some impact with their reports and recommendations. Indeed, the current federal sentencing system gives considerable importance to the framing of facts in presentence reports by probation officers. Prosecutors are especially important; often their recommendations carry great weight with judges, especially when a sentence bargain has been reached. In such cases, although there is no compulsion to accept the prosecutor's recommendation, a judge who supports plea bargaining almost invariably does so. Thus it is not surprising that prosecutors sometimes think of themselves as the sentencers. One New York City prosecutor reportedly told a judge that, if the defendant accepted a bargain immediately, "I'll give him a year." The judge bristled at having his authority usurped—and then gave the defendant a one-year sentence.[109]

People outside the work group also seek to influence the sentence in some cases. Judges may receive letters in behalf of a defendant, sometimes from prominent people. In 1990 the federal judge who was to sentence financier Michael Milken for securities fraud and other offenses received several hundred letters arguing for leniency; among the writers were a California judge, Los Angeles police chief Daryl Gates, and Monty Hall, former host of the television show "Let's Make a Deal."[110] Police officers often attempt to exert some pressure on sentencing judges. In one New York City case, in which a defendant had wounded several police officers in a gun battle but was convicted only of illegal gun possession, a thousand police officers paraded around the courtroom for almost two hours in a demonstration demanding the maximum sentence.[111] Undoubtedly, these efforts sometimes affect the judge's decision in a specific case. More generally, many judges feel some pressure to give heavy sentences in order to protect themselves from public criticism and possible electoral defeat.

Significant as all these influences are, judges still have considerable control over sentences. Judges themselves help to determine the going rates for particular offenses. The recommendations of other participants and the terms of sentence bargains constrain judges less than it might appear because both are tailored in part to fit a judge's preferences. Judges, after all, are free to reject recommendations and bargains that they find unacceptable. Besides, there are many cases in which no going rate applies and in which no sentence bargain has been reached. In such cases, judges often have wide ranges from which to choose in practice as well as by law. Finally, only in a small minority of cases do judges feel pressures from outside the court system that are too strong to resist.

Certainly, judges must make choices, and the task of choosing among alternative sentences is difficult. Sentences can be used to serve any of several goals, including *retribution* (giving offenders their "just deserts"), *general deterrence* (discouraging other people from committing crimes), *rehabilitation* (changing the attitudes and capabilities of offenders so that they will not commit more crimes), and *incapacitation* (confining offenders so they cannot commit crimes outside of prison). A judge may support several of these goals but find that they point in different directions. Furthermore, it is often unclear what kind of sentence best serves a goal such as rehabilitation, especially when the judge has limited information about the defendant. In addition, such practical problems as prison overcrowding and poor probation services make some possible sentences less attractive. As a result, judges may feel that they are only choosing among a set of bad alternatives.

If judges are unhappy with their alternatives, many observers of the courts have been unhappy with the choices that judges make. Some of this feeling relates to the general severity or leniency of sentencing. This issue is difficult to assess, because people differ considerably in their views about how severe sentences should be. Two other issues, both fundamental to sentencing, are more amenable to evaluation: the criteria on which sentences are based and the consistency with which they are meted out.[112]

Criteria for Sentences

Judges can base their sentencing decisions on many criteria, either consciously or unconsciously; these criteria include attributes of both the criminal offense and the defendant. Some of these attributes, such as the seriousness of the offense and the defendant's criminal record, are generally regarded as legitimate bases for decisions. Others, such as the race and economic status of the defendant, are almost universally regarded as illegitimate. Still others, such as the defendant's employment status and family situation, are subjects of disagreement.

One critical issue in sentencing is the relative importance of legitimate and illegitimate criteria. Although the evidence on this issue is incomplete and ambiguous, we have considerable information about the impact of some criteria.

Seriousness of the Offense and the Defendant's Prior Record   Most people would agree that sentences should be based primarily on the seriousness of the offense and the defendant's prior criminal record. The research on sentencing indicates that most of the variation in the severity of sentences can in fact be explained by these factors, especially by the seriousness of the offense.[113] Exhibit 6.6 illustrates the significance of the offense in determining whether defendants go to prison and the length of their prison sentences,

Offense	Pct. Sentenced to Prison or Jail	Mean Maximum Sentence for Persons Sentenced to Prison or Jail
Murder	95%	226 months
Rape	87	146
Robbery	89	100
Aggravated assault	72	59
Burglary	75	56
Drug trafficking	71	41
Larceny	65	33

Notes: Death sentences treated as sentences to prison, but death sentences and life in prison not included in mean sentence lengths. "Murder" includes non-negligent manslaughter, "larceny" includes auto theft.
Source: Patrick A. Langan and John M. Dawson, *Felony Sentences in State Courts, 1988* (Washington, D.C.: U.S. Department of Justice, 1990), pp. 2–3.

EXHIBIT 6.6 Sentences Imposed by State Courts in 300 Counties for Felony Offenses, 1988

though there might be disagreement about whether the offenses are in the appropriate order.

The importance of these two factors is not surprising. Sentencing statutes virtually guarantee a strong relationship between the seriousness of offenses and the severity of sentences by setting different ranges for different offenses. The effects of these statutory ranges are reinforced by the consensus among judges and other members of the courtroom work group that more serious offenses call for stronger sanctions. Some legislatures have also established sentencing penalties based on defendants' prior records; even where they have not, agreement in the courtroom on the relevance of this factor ensures that it will be important.

The significance of this finding should not be overstated, for there is a good deal of variation in the severity of sentences that cannot be explained by offense seriousness and prior record. If illegitimate criteria such as race have an impact on sentences—even an impact overshadowed by that of legitimate criteria—then a serious problem exists.

Race and Economic Status   For those who fear that illegitimate criteria influence sentences, the primary concerns have been race and economic status. Actually, concerns about discrimination by race and wealth extend to every stage of the criminal justice process, from arrest to release from prison. It is widely believed, both by experts and by the general public, that racial prejudice and the advantages of high economic status produce disparities in the treatment of different groups throughout the process. Hence an examination of sentencing addresses only one part of the issue of discrimination in the criminal justice system.

Some trial judges openly express prejudice against nonwhite defendants, and this prejudice undoubtedly affects their sentencing decisions. But concerted research has not produced any consensus about the overall impact of the defendant's race on sentencing. Most recent studies have sought to isolate the impact of the defendant's race by controlling for other factors that may influence sentences. Some studies have found significant racial discrimination, while others have not. At least in part, these differences reflect differences in actual sentencing practices. Discrimination appears to exist in some places, for some types of crimes, and for some judges, but not universally.[114]

Discrimination may be related to the race of the victim as well as to that of the defendant. This issue has been studied most intensively for capital punishment; in several states it appears that people who have been convicted of murdering whites are more likely to receive the death penalty than those convicted of murdering blacks, even if other factors relevant to the sentence are taken into account.[115] Though the evidence on non—death sentences is limited, it also provides support for the conclusion that crimes with white victims are punished more severely.[116]

On the economic status of defendants, researchers have tried to determine whether relatively poor people tend to receive heavier sentences than higher-status defendants. But, as with racial discrimination, studies of this issue have produced inconsistent findings.[117]

Perhaps a more important issue concerning economic status and sentencing decisions is the treatment of *white-collar crime*. The concept of white-collar crime is difficult to define, but it generally refers to offenses "committed by nonphysical means and by concealment and guile" for economic gain.[118] These offenses, such as embezzlement, mail fraud, income tax fraud, and forgery, are more likely than most other crimes to be committed by people of high socioeconomic status. Corporations can also be charged with white-collar crimes such as price fixing.

Defendants and potential defendants in white-collar cases enjoy potential advantages in all stages of the criminal justice process, based in part on their economic resources and high social status.[119] These advantages are symbolized by the successful lobbying by large businesses in 1990–1991 to obtain favorable sentencing rules for federal crimes committed by corporations. As one commentator pointed out, such groups as "drug smugglers" and "bank robbers" were not in a position to engage in such lobbying.[120]

Critics charge that the advantages of white-collar defendants extend to sentencing—that judges treat them with undue leniency, especially if they are well respected or hold high positions. These critics point to cases such as those involving a financier who was convicted of $1.2 million in tax evasion and a banker who looted his company of millions of dollars, neither of whom went to prison; the banker was required only to pay a fine of $30,000 over twenty-five years.[121] To some extent, such sentences can be explained by the high socioeconomic status of judges themselves, which makes them sympathetic toward defendants with similar backgrounds. As one federal judge said: "Probably the most important factor in sentencing in cases of white-collar crime is the empathy factor. Most of the judges in this district are white and middle-class. When they see a white-collar defendant they no doubt say to themselves, 'There, but for the grace of God, go I.' "[122]

The available data indicate that, on the whole, individuals convicted of white-collar crimes receive lighter sentences than those convicted of other crimes.[123] This difference is difficult to interpret because it might result chiefly from factors other than judicial favoritism. For example, white-collar crime by definition involves no violence, and its perpetrators usually have no prior record and appear to be good candidates for rehabilitation. Judges and others generally consider leniency to be appropriate when these conditions exist.

In recent years there have been some signs that prosecutors are more willing to bring cases and that judges are more willing to impose significant sanctions on prominent white-collar offenders.[124] For instance, New York hotel owner Leona Helmsley was sentenced to four years in prison and fined $1.7 million for tax fraud; savings and loan owner Charles Keating was sentenced to ten years for securities fraud.[125] But critics continue to argue that white-collar crime is treated with undue leniency. "The more you steal, the less time you do," says Ralph Nader, "as long as you do it on the 20th floor."[126] In part, different perceptions of sentencing in white-collar cases reflect disagreements about the appropriate severity of sanctions in such cases.

Consistency in Sentencing

The issue of consistency in sentencing focuses on the question of whether cases with the same characteristics end with the same sentences. Inconsistencies can arise at three levels. First, patterns of sentencing may differ among courts. Second, judges in the same court may adopt different sentencing practices. And third, an individual judge may operate with no firm standards, dispensing different sentences in similar cases.

The severity of sentencing varies considerably from place to place, based partly on differences in state laws and partly on the characteristics of particular courts and localities.[127] Many people regard such variation as appropriate. But variation within a single court, either among several judges or in a single judge's decisions, is difficult to justify.

We do not have a clear picture of the degree of sentencing consistency within courts. It does appear that the development of going rates in sentencing for particular crimes produces considerable uniformity in the treatment of similar cases. But it also appears that a good deal of inconsistency develops despite the existence of these informal standards.

Variation Among Judges   Some sentencing variation among judges on the same court seems inevitable. Judges do not approach sentencing with the same premises; one survey of federal district judges found fundamental disagreements about the importance of various goals for sentencing.[128] And even judges who share the same premises cannot be expected to apply them in identical ways.

Lawyers who handle criminal cases are particularly aware of sentencing differences among judges, both in general severity and in their responses to particular crimes or types of defendants. Thus, when defendants in a New York federal court had some opportunity to choose the judge who would sentence them after a guilty plea, so many preferred one judge "that they almost needed a reservation."[129]

Comparisons of sentences by different judges support these perceptions. Especially significant are studies in which several judges proposed sentences in the same cases. One study of federal judges in New York and Chicago drew data from sentencing councils in which judges recommend sentences in pending cases. The study found that a group of three judges who independently assessed the same cases agreed on whether to impose a prison sentence only 70 percent of the time. When the three judges did agree that a defendant should be given a prison term, they agreed on the length of the term only about 10 percent of the time.[130] These results provide strong evidence that the identity of the sentencing judge in a case can make a considerable difference.

Inconsistent Judges   A few years ago a District of Columbia judge advised a group of new public defenders, "Don't go before me at the end of the day. And Friday afternoon is a poor time to have anybody sentenced." A member of his audience later offered his own observations: "Sometimes a trend sweeps through the courthouse and all the judges start hitting harder, as when a high-profile murder has aroused the community; at other times, they all lighten up—around Christmas, for instance."[131]

These assessments suggest that even an individual judge may not be consistent in responses to similar cases. It is impossible to measure such disparities systematically because differences in a judge's treatment of two defendants may actually be based on subtle but relevant differences between the two cases. Yet inconsistencies in a judge's sentences seem almost inevitable; when asked to apply abstract and often conflicting goals, judges—or anyone else—will find it difficult to do so consistently.

This difficulty is suggested by the behavior of another District of Columbia judge. In the same month the judge sentenced two people who were convicted of carrying a gun without a license, both with previous related convictions. One defendant received probation, while the other was given a sentence of fifteen years to life in prison. In explaining the difference in these sentences, the judge merely cited his "gut reaction" to the two defendants.[132] We might criticize the judge for his sentences, yet he was probably doing his best to assess the two defendants' prospects for rehabilitation. Whatever his motives, most people would regard the result as unfortunate, and it illustrates the sentencing inconsistencies that can arise in practice.

Sentencing Reform Through New Systems

The available evidence points to a mixed evaluation of judges' sentencing practices. On the positive side, most judges seem to have used their discretion well in some respects, giving the greatest weight to factors that most people regard as legitimate. On the negative side, illegitimate factors sometimes affect sentences, and inconsistency seems to be a widespread problem.

Other criticisms of sentencing systems and practices have arisen as well. Criminologists and others have become disillusioned with the goal of rehabilitation and the resulting emphasis on individualized justice. This disillusion has led to greater concern with retribution and general deterrence, goals that point toward more uniform sentencing for particular crimes. And conservatives argue that judges introduce too much leniency into the criminal law through their sentencing decisions.

These criticisms differ in their implications, but each leads to an interest in reducing the sentencing discretion of judges. As noted earlier, the result has been a widespread alteration of sentencing systems to channel or limit judicial discretion by reducing the range of possible sentences, setting up sentencing guidelines, or creating mandatory minimum sentences for certain offenses.

In practice, most judges and attorneys prefer wide sentencing latitude as a means to achieve what they regard as good results and to maintain a basis for plea bargaining. As a result, they have incentives to use whatever leeway new sentencing rules provide to maintain this latitude.

Not surprisingly, voluntary sentencing guidelines seem to have only limited effects. Reportedly, in Denver and Philadelphia "few judges made significant efforts to comply with the guidelines."[133]

Systems that narrow the range of possible sentences for an offense (as in California) or that require judges to justify departures from guidelines (as in Florida and Minnesota) would seem likely to reduce sentence variation substantially. Yet even the California system leaves judges with considerable leeway, and prosecutors retain discretion in setting the initial charges and bargaining over those charges. Consequently, these new systems have had mixed effects. Literal compliance with sentencing rules is high, but variation in sentences for specific offenses declined less than might have been expected. Reports suggest that guidelines had greater effect in Florida than in Minnesota, perhaps because Florida appellate courts have been aggressive in overturning sentences that depart from the guidelines.[134] In California, according to one study, there was "no compelling evidence of substantial changes in sentence outcomes."[135]

Mandatory minimum sentences for specific offenses introduce a degree of compulsion, particularly where judges are not allowed to make exceptions. But sometimes judges simply impose a sentence that is more lenient than the minimum required by the law; such noncompliance was found to be common for drunk-driving laws in Indiana and New Mexico.[136] For their part, prosecutors can refuse to charge a defendant with an offense for which there is a mandatory sentence, as they apparently do most of the time under the New York gun possession law.[137]

Congress has made two major changes in the federal sentencing system during the last decade, and together they have had a greater impact than many of the changes in state systems. One change is the establishment of mandatory minimum sentences for more than sixty federal offenses since 1984.[138] While most of these provisions have never been used, four (three involving drug offenses) have been employed a good deal. And in 1984 Congress created the U.S. Sentencing Commission to write rules for federal sentencing that would narrow judges' discretion substantially. A detailed and complex set of rules became effective in 1987, and a number of amendments have been added since then. The basic structure of the rules is summarized in Exhibit 6.7.

Because these two changes are intertwined, the impact of each is particularly difficult to ascertain. But it is possible to reach some tentative conclusions on the basis of the experience thus far.[139]

EXHIBIT 6.7 A Summary of Federal Sentencing Rules Under the Sentencing Reform Act of 1984

1. In imposing a sentence, a district judge must consider the guidelines of the Sentencing Commission, a body established by the statute. Under these guidelines, the possible sentence ranges are based on 43 offense level categories (determined from the offense, adjusted for factors such as the type of victim and the defendant's role in the offense) and six criminal history categories (determined primarily from the number and characteristics of past convictions). For each combination of offense and criminal history categories, a range of possible imprisonment lengths (for instance, 57 to 71 months) is indicated. Other guidelines indicate when probation may be substituted for a prison sentence and the amounts of monetary fines appropriate for each offense level.

2. In each case the judge must impose a sentence within the range established by the Sentencing Commission unless the judge finds a relevant aggravating or mitigating circumstance that the Commission did not adequately take into account. Not ordinarily relevant are such personal characteristics as age, education, employment record, and family and community ties; never relevant are race, sex, religion, and socio-economic status. A judge can depart from the guidelines if the prosecution states that the defendant has provided substantial assistance in the investigation or prosecution of another offender.

3. If the sentence is above the range established by the Sentencing Commission, the defendant may appeal the sentence; if it is below the range, the prosecution may appeal. If the court of appeals finds that the sentence is unreasonable, it may return the case to the district judge for resentencing or amend the sentence itself.

Sources: United States Code, Title 18; United States Sentencing Commission, Federal Sentencing Guideline Manual, 1991 Edition (Saint Paul, Minn.: West Publishing Co., 1990).

First, the changes seem to have reduced considerably judges' discretion over sentences. Sentences fall within the range established by the Sentencing Commission in the great majority of cases, both because of the relative tightness of the rules and because deviating sentences can be appealed and overturned if they have insufficient justification.[140] However, judges have complained a good deal about the constraints imposed on them by the Commission rules and the mandatory minimums. Indeed, a San Diego judge cited his unhappiness with the commission rules as a major factor in his 1990 resignation, and a Spokane judge stopped taking criminal cases in 1991.[141] In 1992 a respected district judge in New York criticized the guidelines and argued that they were not actually binding on sentencing judges.[142]

Second, the power lost by judges has shifted primarily to prosecutors. Since charges against defendants translate more directly into sentences than in the past, prosecutors' original charges and charge bargains gain much greater impact. Under the commission rules, prosecutors can have considerable effect through their reporting of case-related facts to judges, particularly the assistance that defendants have provided with other cases. Most sentences departing from the commission's range actually result from prosecutors' motions based on "substantial assistance" by defendants.[143] One commentator said flatly that "prosecutors—not judges—now hold the power over sentencing."[144]

Third, the adoption of tighter rules for sentencing does not necessarily eliminate inconsistency or arbitrariness. While judges' decisions have become more consistent in relation to the cases presented to them, some inconsistency remains. Additional inconsistency can arise through prosecutors' decisions about which cases to present and in what form. As a result, to take one important example, racial discrimination may continue to exist.[145]

Furthermore, statutes and sentencing rules themselves may incorporate arbitrary features. In the drug area, for instance, drug "kingpins" can come out better than small-time violators because they have more information with which to assist prosecutors and the sentencing rules give weight to this consideration. And one mandatory minimum sentence provision, as interpreted by the Supreme Court, causes sentences for trafficking in LSD to vary by many years depending on the weight of the medium (such as blotter paper) in which the drug is carried.[146]

Most of what we know about state efforts to change judicial sentencing practices suggests the difficulties of securing such changes. The federal experience thus far indicates that these practices *can* be changed. But it also shows that altering judges' behavior does not necessarily eliminate problems in sentencing.

CONCLUSIONS

The widespread effort to change sentencing practices reflects a broader concern about the handling of criminal cases. Nearly everyone is unhappy with some aspects of what criminal courts do; therefore, attempts at reform are common.

Those who engage in reform often ignore the realities of criminal courts. What courts do largely reflects the goals and needs of people in the courthouse community. So long as these goals and needs remain the same, efforts to alter court practices significantly will face resistance. This is certainly true of attempts to eliminate plea bargaining and to change sentencing patterns.

These attempts have not always failed. New sentencing rules, for instance, have had considerable impact in the federal courts. Even such successes, however, are likely to be less than total. And major changes in one element of the work of criminal courts are likely to affect other elements of their work in unexpected—and perhaps undesired—ways.

Thus an understanding of criminal courts is useful for reasons other than mere curiosity. With this understanding, one can do a better job of evaluating both current practices and proposed alternatives. The lesson is not that we should be satisfied with the current workings of the criminal courts. Rather, we should be careful and realistic in considering what should be changed and how the changes should be made. Otherwise the effects of reforms are most unlikely to meet our expectations.

FOR FURTHER READING

Baldus, David C., George Woodworth, and Charles A. Pulaski, Jr., *Equal Justice and the Death Penalty: A Legal and Empirical Analysis.* Boston: Northeastern University Press, 1990.

Griset, Pamela. *Determinate Sentencing: The Promise and the Reality of Retributive Justice.* Albany: State University of New York Press, 1991.

Hastie, Reid, Steven D. Penrod, and Nancy Pennington, *Inside the Jury.* Cambridge, Mass.: Harvard University Press, 1983.

Scheingold, Stuart A. *The Politics of Law and Order: Street Crime and Public Policy.* New York: Longman, 1984.

von Hirsch, Andrew, Kay A. Knapp, and Michael Tonry, eds. *The Sentencing Commission and Its Guidelines.* Boston: Northeastern University Press, 1987.

Wheeler, Stanton, Kenneth Mann, and Austin Sarat. *Sitting in Judgment: The Sentencing of White-Collar Criminals.* New Haven, Conn.: Yale University Press, 1988.

NOTES

1. "The NLJ/Lexis Poll: A Sampler of Questions," *National Law Journal,* August 7, 1989, p. S17.
2. See Henry J. Abraham, *The Judicial Process,* 5th ed. (New York: Oxford University Press, 1986), p. 21.
3. On "work groups," see James Eisenstein and Herbert Jacob, *Felony Justice: An Organizational Analysis of Criminal Courts* (Boston: Little, Brown, 1977), ch.

2. On "courthouse communities," see Peter F. Nardulli, James Eisenstein, and Roy B. Flemming, *The Tenor of Justice: Criminal Courts and the Guilty Plea Process* (Urbana: University of Illinois Press, 1988), ch. 5.

4. James Eisenstein, Roy B. Flemming, and Peter F. Nardulli, *The Contours of Justice: Communities and Their Courts* (Boston: Little, Brown, 1988), p. 37.

5. This discussion is based in part on John M. Dawson, *Prosecutors in State Courts, 1990* (Washington, D.C.: U.S. Department of Justice, 1992).

6. Pamela Feinsilber, "Defending Mother Earth," *California Lawyer,* 10 (June 1990), p. 17.

7. Jonathan Casper, *American Criminal Justice: The Defendant's Perspective* (Englewood Cliffs, N.J.: Prentice-Hall, 1972), p. 135.

8. David Heilbroner, *Rough Justice: Days and Nights of a Young D.A.* (New York: Pantheon Books, 1990), pp. 18–19.

9. Terry Wilson, "Defendants Fight Odds as Own Lawyers," *Chicago Tribune,* June 14, 1992, sec. 2, p. 1.

10. John P. Heinz and Edward O. Laumann, *Chicago Lawyers: The Social Structure of the Bar* (New York: Russell Sage Foundation, 1982), pp. 319–333.

11. Craig Perkins and Darrell K. Gilliard, *National Corrections Reporting Program, 1988* (Washington, D.C.: U.S. Department of Justice, 1992), p. 9.

12. Roger A. Hanson, Brian J. Ostrom, William E. Hewitt, and Christopher Lomvardias, *Indigent Defenders Get the Job Done and Done Well* (Williamsburg, Va.: National Center for State Courts, 1992), p. 14.

13. Donald J. Hall, "Victims' Voices in Criminal Court: The Need for Restraint," *American Criminal Law Review,* 28 (Fall 1991), 238–248.

14. Hayward R. Alker, Jr., Carl Hosticka, and Michael Mitchell, "Jury Selection as a Biased Social Process," *Law and Society Review,* 11 (Fall 1976), 9–41; David Kairys, Joseph B. Kadane, and John P. Lehoczky, "Jury Representativeness: A Mandate for Multiple Source Lists," *California Law Review,* 65 (July 1977), 776–827.

15. Heilbroner, *Rough Justice,* p. 249.

16. Maurice Carroll, "Wachtler Urges Legislators to Approve Court Changes," *New York Times,* April 23, 1985, p. B2.

17. Stuart A. Scheingold, *The Politics of Law and Order: Street Crime and Public Policy* (New York: Longman, 1984), p. 191. Scheingold was reinterpreting the findings of other studies of criminal courts.

18. James LeMoyne, "Cuban Leading Anti-Castro Drive Is Freed by Government in Miami," *New York Times,* July 18, 1990, pp. A1, A9.

19. Patrick A. Langan, "America's Soaring Prison Population," *Science,* 251 (March 29, 1991), 1572.

20. Paul Duggan, "Bond Reinstated for P.G. Slaying Suspect," *Washington Post,* August 17, 1990, p. D3.

21. Chuck Shepherd, "News of the Weird," *The Reader* (Chicago), May 10, 1991, sec. 3, p. 51.

22. Sources of information for this description include William P. McLauchlan, *American Legal Processes* (New York: John Wiley and Sons, 1977), pp. 105–123; David W. Neubauer, *America's Courts and the Criminal Justice System,* 3d ed. (Monterey, Calif.: Brooks/Cole Publishing, 1988), pp. 26–34; and Barbara Boland, Paul Mahanna, and Ronald Sones, *The Prosecution of Felony Arrests, 1988* (Washington, D.C.: U.S. Department of Justice, 1992), pp. 3–9.

23. *In re Gault,* 387 U.S.1 (1967).

24. Deborah Nelson, "Juvenile Injustice," *Chicago Sun Times,* March 22, 1992, p. 1.

25. Malcolm M. Feeley, *The Process Is the Punishment: Handling Cases in a Lower Court* (New York: Russell Sage Foundation, 1979), p. 11.

26. David Burnham, "Confidentiality, Public Access to Records Examined at Judicial Conduct Conference," *Judicature,* 70 (December–January 1987), 246.

27. Boland, Mahanna, and Sones, *Prosecution of Felony Arrests, 1988,* p. 9.
28. Hans Zeisel, *The Limits of Law Enforcement* (Chicago: University of Chicago Press, 1982), p. 18.
29. Joan Petersilia, *Racial Disparities in the Criminal Justice System* (Santa Monica, Calif.: Rand Corporation, 1983), p. 45.
30. Lisa D. Bastian, *Criminal Victimization 1991* (Washington, D.C.: U.S. Department of Justice, 1992), p. 5.
31. Timothy J. Flanagan and Kathleen Maguire, eds., *Sourcebook of Criminal Justice Statistics—1991* (Washington, D.C.: U.S. Department of Justice, 1992), p. 462.
32. George F. Cole, *American System of Criminal Justice,* 5th ed. (North Scituate, Mass.: Duxbury Press, 1975), pp. 323–326.
33. Zeisel, *Limits of Law Enforcement,* pp. 111–112; Richard S. Frase, "The Decision to File Federal Criminal Charges: A Quantitative Study of Prosecutorial Discretion," *University of Chicago Law Review,* 47 (1980), 263–265; Celesta A. Albonetti, "Prosecutorial Discretion: The Effects of Uncertainty," *Law and Society Review,* 21 (1987), 291–313.
34. Boland, Mahanna, and Sones, *Prosecution of Felony Arrests, 1988,* pp. 35–36. These proportions include what are classified as "witness" reasons.
35. Donald K. White, "When Cookies Are OK and VCRs Are a Crime," *San Francisco Chronicle,* August 21, 1985, p. 28.
36. United States Comptroller General, *Greater Oversight and Uniformity Needed in U.S. Attorneys' Prosecutive Policies,* General Accounting Office Report GAO/GGD 83–11 (1982), p. 8.
37. "Justice's Pornography War Suffers a Setback," *National Law Journal,* June 15, 1992, pp. 5, 25; Julie DelCour, "Oklahoma Is Theater for an X-Rated Trial," *National Law Journal,* August 12, 1991, p. 8; Robert F. Howe, "U.S. Prosecutors in Va. Said to Be Targeting Soft Porn Distributors," *Washington Post,* June 5, 1992, p. D3. The decisions were *P.H.E., Inc. v. U.S. Department of Justice,* 743 F. Supp. 15 (D.D.C. 1990); and *United States v. P.H.E., Inc.,* 965 F.2d 848 (10th Cir. 1992).
38. Barton Gellman, "For the U.S. Attorney, Life Goes On," *Washington Post,* August 14, 1990, p. A7.
39. Boland, Mahanna, and Sones, *Prosecution of Felony Arrests, 1988,* pp. 24–29.
40. David Freed, "Plea Bargaining Becomes the Currency of the Courts," *Los Angeles Times,* December 20, 1990, p. A42.
41. This discussion of forms of plea bargaining is based in part on John F. Padgett, "The Emergent Organization of Plea Bargaining," *American Journal of Sociology,* 90 (January 1985), 753–800.
42. Alfred Blumstein, Jacqueline Cohen, Susan E. Martin, and Michael H. Tonry, eds., *Research on Sentencing: The Search for Reform,* 2 vols. (Washington, D.C.: National Academy Press, 1983), I, 43.
43. Donald R. Cressey, "Doing Justice," *The Center Magazine,* 10 (January/February 1977), 23.
44. E. R. Shipp, "How the Criminal Court Fails: 8 Crucial Areas," *New York Times,* June 30, 1983, p. B4.
45. Donald J. Newman, *Conviction: The Determination of Guilt or Innocence Without Trial* (Boston: Little, Brown, 1966), p. 182.
46. "Judge Rejects $100 Million Fine For Exxon in Oil Spill as Too Low," *New York Times,* April 25, 1991, pp. A1, A9.
47. Veronica T. Jennings, "Montgomery Changes Plea Rules," *Washington Post,* December 31, 1990, pp. B1, B2.
48. *Commonwealth v. Gordon,* 574 N.E.2d 974, 976 n. 3 (Mass. 1991).
49. Howard Kurtz, "In New York Courts, Next Drug Plea, Please," *Washington Post,* October 8, 1988, pp. A1, A16.
50. Don Nunes, "Acquitted Defendant Faces Years in Prison," *Washington Post,* August 20, 1982, pp. A1, A10.

51. David Sudnow, "Normal Crimes: Sociological Features of the Penal Code in a Public Defender's Office," *Social Problems,* 12 (Winter 1965), 255–276.

52. Malcolm Feeley, "Pleading Guilty in Lower Courts," *Law and Society Review,* 13 (Winter 1979), 462.

53. See Nardulli, Eisenstein, and Flemming, *The Tenor of Justice,* especially ch. 8.

54. James Eisenstein, *Counsel for the United States: U.S. Attorneys in the Political and Legal Systems* (Baltimore: Johns Hopkins University Press, 1978), pp. 178–182.

55. John H. Langbein, "Understanding the Short History of Plea Bargaining," *Law & Society Review,* 13 (Winter 1979), 261–272.

56. Robert D. McFadden, "Rush of Pleas Clears Brooklyn Cases," *New York Times,* October 19, 1991, p. A27.

57. Feeley, *Process Is the Punishment,* p. 272 (emphasis in original).

58. Both of these observations are based on personal communications to the author.

59. Relevant comparative and historical evidence can be found in Milton Heumann, *Plea Bargaining: The Experiences of Prosecutors, Judges, and Defense Attorneys* (Chicago: University of Chicago Press, 1978), pp. 24–33; Feeley, *Process Is the Punishment,* ch. 8; and Lawrence M. Friedman, "Plea Bargaining in Historical Perspective," *Law and Society Review,* 13 (Winter 1979), 247–259.

60. *Ryan v. Commission on Judicial Performance,* 754 P.2d 724, 733 (Calif. 1988).

61. Timothy Crouse, "Plea Bargains: Making a Sweet Deal with Justice," *The Village Voice,* January 17, 1977, p. 21.

62. Albert W. Alschuler, "The Trial Judge's Role in Plea Bargaining, Part I," *Columbia Law Review,* 76 (November 1976), 1089.

63. David Brereton and Jonathan D. Casper, "Does It Pay to Plead Guilty? Differential Sentencing and the Functioning of Criminal Courts," *Law and Society Review,* 16 (1982), 45–70; Thomas M. Uhlman and Darlene N. Walker, " 'He Takes Some of My Time; I Take Some of His': An Analysis of Judicial Sentencing Patterns in Jury Cases," *Law and Society Review,* 14 (Winter 1980), 323–341; Nardulli, Eisenstein, and Flemming, *Tenor of Justice,* pp. 244–245.

64. Martin Berg, "Playing the Chaos Game," *California Lawyer,* 12 (August 1992), p. 37.

65. Heumann, *Plea Bargaining,* p. 71.

66. Jonathan Barzilay, "The D.A.'s Right Arms," *New York Times Magazine,* November 27, 1983, p. 121.

67. See Heumann, *Plea Bargaining.*

68. Eisenstein, Flemming, and Nardulli, *The Contours of Justice,* p. 31.

69. Sources of information for this discussion include Lynn Mather, *Plea Bargaining or Trial?: The Process of Criminal-Case Disposition* (Lexington, Mass.: Lexington Books, 1979), pp. 142–144; and David W. Neubauer, *Criminal Justice in Middle America* (Morristown, N.J.: General Learning Press, 1974), pp. 286–287.

70. David Pritchard, "Homicide and Bargained Justice: The Agenda-Setting Effect of Crime News on Prosecutors," *Public Opinion Quarterly,* 50 (Summer 1986), 143–159.

71. Felicity Barringer, "Abortion Foes Clog Vermont Courts," *New York Times,* May 7, 1990, p. A9; Steven Pressman, "Cyrus Zal, Missionary-at-Law," *California Lawyer,* 10 (March 1990), pp. 17–18, 104–106.

72. See Stephen J. Schulhofer, "Is Plea Bargaining Inevitable?" *Harvard Law Review,* 97 (March 1984), 1037–1107. The figure for Philadelphia is on p. 1096.

73. Mather, *Plea Bargaining or Trial?,* pp. 55–56.

74. Ibid., p. 55.

75. Schulhofer, "Is Plea Bargaining Inevitable?"

76. Uhlman and Walker, "He Takes Some of My Time," pp. 323–341.

77. Dan Beyers, "Widow of Slain Md. Trooper Calls Plea Bargain 'Appalling,' " *Washington Post,* January 28, 1992, p. B2.

78. James Mills, *On the Edge* (New York: Doubleday, 1975), p. 132.

79. David Silverman and Jerry Thomas, "Lake Gets Tough on Criminals," *Chicago Tribune,* August 23, 1991, sec. 2, p. 1.

80. "Remarks to United States Attorneys," *Weekly Compilation of Presidential Documents,* 25 (June 19, 1989), 917.

81. Michael L. Rubinstein, Stevens H. Clarke, and Teresa J. White, *Alaska Bans Plea Bargaining* (Washington, D.C.: U.S. Department of Justice, 1980); Teresa White Carns and John A. Kruse, "Alaska's Ban on Plea Bargaining Reevaluated," *Judicature,* 75 (April–May 1992), 310–317.

82. Robert A. Weninger, "The Abolition of Plea Bargaining: A Case Study of El Paso County, Texas," *UCLA Law Review,* 35 (December 1987), 265–313.

83. Freed, "Plea Bargaining Becomes the Currency," pp. A1, A42–A44.

84. See Jacqueline Cohen and Michael H. Tonry, "Sentencing Reforms and Their Impacts," in Blumstein et al., eds., *Research on Sentencing,* II, 368–380.

85. Ted Rohrlich, "Venue Victory for Officers in King Beating Is a Rarity," *Los Angeles Times,* July 25, 1991, p. A1.

86. *Annual Report of the Director of Administrative Office of the United States Courts, 1991* (Washington, D.C.: U.S. Government Printing Office, 1992), p. 217.

87. Robert Buckhout, "Nearly 2000 Witnesses Can Be Wrong," *Social Action and the Law,* 2 (1975), 7, reported in Elizabeth F. Loftus, *Eyewitness Testimony* (Cambridge, Mass.: Harvard University Press, 1979), p. 135.

88. Andrew Gottesman, "Asking Witness to Point Out Suspect Can Court Embarrassment," *Chicago Tribune,* July 19, 1992, sec. 2, p. 1.

89. Warren E. Leary, "New Methods Unlock Witnesses' Memories," *New York Times,* November 15, 1988, p. C15. See Elizabeth Loftus and Katherine Ketcham, *Witness for the Defense: The Accused, the Eyewitness, and the Expert Who Puts Memory on Trial* (New York: St. Martin's Press, 1991).

90. Michael J. Saks, "Enhancing and Restraining Accuracy in Adjudication," *Law and Contemporary Problems,* 51 (Autumn 1988), 263.

91. Jerome Frank, *Courts on Trial: Myth and Reality in American Justice* (Princeton, N.J.: Princeton University Press, 1949), ch. 3.

92. *United States v. Littlefield,* 840 F.2d 143, 146–147 (1st Cir. 1988).

93. Rudolph J. Gerber, *Lawyers, Courts, and Professionalism: The Agenda for Reform* (New York: Greenwood Press, 1989), p. 81.

94. Marcia Coyle, "Door Cracks Open to More Death Challenges," *National Law Journal,* August 3, 1992, p. 5.

95. Heilbroner, *Rough Justice,* p. 95.

96. *For the Defense,* January 1988, p. 14; quoted in Gerber, *Lawyers, Courts, and Professionalism,* p. 114.

97. Calvin Trillin, *U.S. Journal* (New York: E. P. Dutton, 1971), pp. 25, 32.

98. "It's Not a Crime to Appear Well-Dressed, Defendants Facing Trial in Palm Beach Contend," *Chicago Tribune,* April 15, 1990, sec. 1, p. 12.

99. *Ladner v. Higgins,* 71 So. 2d 242, 244 (La. Ct. of Appeals 1954). The case is noted in Charles M. Sevilla, *Disorder in the Court: Great Fractured Moments in Courtroom History* (New York: W. W. Norton, 1992), p. 81. See also Anthony Champagne, Daniel Shuman, and Elizabeth Whitaker, "Expert Witnesses in the Courts: An Empirical Examination," *Judicature,* 76 (June–July 1992), 7.

100. Gerber, *Lawyers, Courts, and Professionalism,* p. 111.

101. This evidence is summarized well in James P. Levine, *Juries and Politics* (Pacific Grove, Calif.: Brooks/Cole, 1992), chs. 4–8.

102. Harry Kalven, Jr., and Hans Zeisel, *The American Jury* (Boston: Little, Brown, 1966).

103. Levine, *Juries and Politics,* pp. 123–127. On judge-jury differences, see Martha Myers, "Judges, Juries, and the Decision to Convict," *Journal of Criminal Justice,* 9 (1981), 289–303.

104. See Kalven and Zeisel, *The American Jury,* pp. 249–254, 293–296. I am grateful to an anonymous reviewer of the manuscript for this book for pointing out this possibility.

105. H. L. Mencken, *A Mencken Chrestomathy* (New York: Alfred A. Knopf, 1949), p. 623.

106. Martin Yant, *Presumed Guilty: When Innocent People Are Wrongly Convicted* (Buffalo, N.Y.: Prometheus Books, 1991); Hugo Adam Bedau and Michael L. Radelet, "Miscarriages of Justice in Potentially Capital Cases," *Stanford Law Review,* 40 (November 1987), 21–179.

107. See Susanne Di Pietro, "The Development of Appellate Sentence Review in Alaska," *Judicature,* 75 (October–November 1991), 143–153.

108. Sources of information for this discussion of sentencing systems include Blumstein et al., *Research on Sentencing,* I, chs. 1, 3.

109. Mills, *On the Edge,* p. 136.

110. Scot J. Paltrow, "They Like Mike," *Los Angeles Times,* September 11, 1990, pp. D1, D9.

111. William G. Blair, "Larry Davis Gets 5 to 15 Years for Conviction on Weapons," *New York Times,* December 16, 1988, pp. A1, B5.

112. See Blumstein et al., *Research on Sentencing,* I, 72–75.

113. Ibid., I, 83–87; Martha A. Myers and Susette M. Talarico, *The Social Contexts of Criminal Sentencing* (New York: Springer-Verlag, 1987), p. 81.

114. Martha A. Myers and Susette M. Talarico, "The Social Contexts of Racial Discrimination in Sentencing," *Social Problems,* 33 (February 1986), 236–251; Stephen Klein, Joan Petersilia, and Susan Turner, "Race and Imprisonment Decisions in California," *Science,* 247 (February 16, 1990), 812–816.

115. David C. Baldus, George Woodworth, and Charles A. Pulaski, Jr., *Equal Justice and the Death Penalty: A Legal and Empirical Analysis* (Boston: Northeastern University Press, 1990); Samuel R. Gross and Robert Mauro, *Death and Discrimination: Racial Disparities in Capital Sentencing* (Boston: Northeastern University Press, 1989).

116. Ruth Marcus, "Racial Bias Widely Seen in Criminal Justice System," *Washington Post,* May 12, 1992, p. A4.

117. Stevens H. Clarke and Gary G. Koch, "The Influence of Income and Other Factors on Whether Criminal Defendants Go to Prison," *Law and Society Review,* 11 (Fall 1976), 57–92; Blumstein et al., *Research on Sentencing,* I, 110–114.

118. Herbert Edelhertz, *The Nature, Impact, and Prosecution of White Collar Crime* (Washington, D.C.: U.S. Department of Justice, 1970), p. 3; quoted in Stanton Wheeler, "White-Collar Crime: History of an Idea," in Sanford H. Kadish, ed., *Encyclopedia of Crime and Justice* (New York: Free Press, 1983), p. 1653.

119. Kenneth Mann, *Defending White-Collar Crime: A Portrait of Attorneys at Work* (New Haven, Conn.: Yale University Press, 1985); Jack Katz, "Legality and Equality: Plea Bargaining in the Prosecution of White-Collar and Common Crimes," *Law and Society Review,* 13 (Winter 1979), 431–459.

120. Fred Strasser, "Corporate Sentences Draw Fire," *National Law Journal,* March 12, 1990. See also John C. Coffee, Jr., "Big Corporations, Off the Hook," *Legal Times,* May 6, 1991, pp. 22, 26.

121. See, respectively, Robert Kuttner, "Why Do We Send Our White-Collar Criminals to 'Country Club' Prisons?" *Chicago Tribune,* April 13, 1988, sec. 1, p. 17; and Milton Moskowitz, "Justice Comes in Strange Patterns," *San Francisco Chronicle,* September 6, 1975, p. 29.

122. Stanton Wheeler, Kenneth Mann, and Austin Sarat, *Sitting in Judgment: The Sentencing of White-Collar Criminals* (New Haven, Conn.: Yale University Press, 1988), p. 162.

123. Bureau of Justice Statistics, *White Collar Crime* (Washington, D.C.: U.S. Department of Justice, 1987), pp. 4–5; Donald A. Manson, *Tracking Offenders: White-Collar Crime* (Washington, D.C.: U.S. Department of Justice, 1986), p. 3. See also John Hagan, Ilene H. Nagel, and Celesta Albonetti, "The Differential Sentencing of White-Collar Offenders in the Federal Courts," *American Sociological Review*, 45 (October 1980), 802–820.

124. Bureau of Justice Statistics, *White Collar Crime*, pp. 6–7.

125. William Glaberson, "Helmsley Gets 4-Year Term in U.S. Prison for Tax Fraud," *New York Times*, December 13, 1989, p. 19; Susan Schmidt, "Charles Keating Sentenced," *Washington Post*, April 11, 1992, pp. A1, A2.

126. Stuart Taylor, Jr., "Stiffer Sentences," *New York Times*, May 9, 1985, p. D4

127. Mark A. Cunniff, *Sentencing Outcomes in 28 Felony Courts* (Washington, D.C.: U.S. Department of Justice, 1987), Martin A. Levin, *Urban Politics and the Criminal Courts* (Chicago: University of Chicago Press, 1977).

128. Brian Forst and Charles Wellford, "Punishment and Sentencing: Developing Sentencing Guidelines Empirically from Principles of Punishment," *Rutgers Law Review*, 33 (Spring 1981), 805.

129. David Margolick, "At the Bar," *New York Times*, December 18, 1987, p. B6.

130. Shari Seidman Diamond and Hans Zeisel, "Sentencing Councils: A Study of Sentencing Disparity and Its Reduction," *University of Chicago Law Review*, 43 (Fall 1975), 118–124.

131. James S. Kunen, *"How Can You Defend Those People?" The Making of a Criminal Lawyer* (New York: Random House, 1983), pp. 37, 106.

132. Leon Dash, "Sentences Tied to 'Gut Reaction,'" *Washington Post*, June 26, 1975, p. D5.

133. Cohen and Tonry, "Sentencing Reforms," p. 417.

134. Kay A. Knapp, "What Sentencing Reform in Minnesota Has and Has Not Accomplished," *Judicature*, 68 (October–November 1984), 181–189. The quotations are from pp. 189 and 182. See also Kay A. Knapp, "Implementation of the Minnesota Guidelines: Can the Innovative Spirit Be Preserved?" in *The Sentencing Commission and Its Guidelines*, ed. Andrew von Hirsch, Kay A. Knapp, and Michael Tonry (Boston: Northeastern University Press, 1987), pp. 127–141.

135. Cohen and Tonry, "Sentencing Reforms," p. 411. See Jonathan D. Casper, David Brereton, and David Neal, *The Implementation of the California Determinate Sentencing Law* (Washington, D.C.: U.S. Department of Justice, 1982).

136. H. Laurence Ross and James P. Foley, "Judicial Disobedience of the Mandate to Imprison Drunk Drivers," *Law and Society Review*, 21 (1987), 315–323.

137. Francis J. Flaherty, "How 'Mandatory' Are Tough Gun Laws?" *National Law Journal*, February 11, 1985, p. 3.

138. United States Sentencing Commission, *Mandatory Minimum Penalties in the Federal Criminal Justice System* (Washington, D.C.: U.S. Government Printing Office, 1991).

139. U.S. Sentencing Commission, *The Federal Sentencing Guidelines* (Washington, D.C.: U.S. Government Printing Office, 1991); United States General Accounting Office, *Sentencing Guidelines: Central Questions Remain Unanswered* (Washington, D.C.: Government Printing Office, 1992); Gerald W. Heaney, "The Reality of Guidelines Sentencing: No End to Disparity," *American Criminal Law Review*, 28 (Fall 1991), 161–232; U.S. Sentencing Commission, *Mandatory Minimum Penalties*.

140. U.S. Sentencing Commission, *Annual Report 1991* (Washington, D.C., 1992), p. 133; Michael A. Collora, "Courts Depart from Guidelines, but Only in Unusual Situations," *National Law Journal*, December 17, 1990, pp. 18–20.

141. Dennis Cauchon, "The Scales of Justice May be Tipped Unfairly," *USA Today*, June 24, 1991, p. 8A.

142. *United States v. Concepcion,* 795 F. Supp. 1262, 1271–1281 (E.D.N.Y. 1992).
143. U.S. Sentencing Commission, *Annual Report 1991,* p. 133.
144. Marcia Chambers, "Prosecutors Take Charge of Sentences," *National Law Journal,* November 26, 1990, p. 13.
145. U.S. Sentencing Commission, *Mandatory Minimum Penalties,* pp. 76–82; U.S. General Accounting Office, *Sentencing Guidelines,* pp. 111–142.
146. Jim Newton, "Long LSD Prison Terms—It's All in the Packaging," *Los Angeles Times,* July 27, 1992, pp. A1, A20, A21. The decision was *Chapman v. United States,* 114 L. Ed. 2d 524 (1991).

7

Trial Courts: Civil Cases

Criminal cases, diverse as they are, constitute only one type of legal action. Everything else is civil. Thus civil cases include such issues as liability for automobile accidents, individual and corporate bankruptcy, eligibility for Social Security benefits, and custody of children.

These examples also suggest the importance of civil cases. Outcomes of these cases help determine the financial status of individuals, the structure of corporations, and the powers of government over both. And the choice whether to imprison people or allow them to remain free, which helps to give criminal cases their drama, has its analogy in civil proceedings over commitment of people to mental institutions. Taken together, civil cases have enormous impact.

The work of the courts in civil cases is less dramatic than their criminal work, but that work assuredly does not lack controversy. In recent years this has been particularly true of personal injury cases. Critics decry what they see as an abundance of ill-founded suits and unjustified monetary awards in this field.

The diversity of civil cases makes it difficult to generalize about them. Therefore, much of this chapter examines individual types of cases rather than civil cases as a whole. But the examples provide a sense of what courts do in civil cases and of the various ways in which they operate.

In discussing civil courts—shorthand for trial courts in civil cases—I give some emphasis to two general issues involving links between courts and the larger society in which they work. The first issue concerns litigation, or the use of civil courts, and its alternatives. Matters that might be taken to court can also be handled in a variety of other ways, and only a small minority of potential civil cases actually go to court. This fact is important because the outcomes of such matters may depend on whether they are resolved in court or elsewhere. Yet the possibility of litigation affects the ways in which problems are handled outside of court; much of the negotiation through which people resolve disputes occurs "in the shadow of the law."[1] Thus an examination of civil courts must look at actions and decisions outside the courts as well as within them.

The second issue concerns benefits and burdens that civil courts allocate. Court decisions affect a great many individuals and institutions. Consequently, it makes a good deal of difference who wins individual cases and who is favored by the general rules that courts establish for broad groups of cases. Litigation aimed at winning individual cases and shaping general rules often involves contention between parties of vastly unequal economic resources—for example, injured individuals and insurance companies or debtors and finance companies. In these conflicts, we would expect the side with greater resources to have a considerable advantage, and one scholar has concluded that in general "the 'haves' come out ahead" in litigation.[2] But, as this chapter shows, the relationship between economic resources and success in litigation is complicated.

AN OVERVIEW OF CIVIL COURTS

With civil cases, as with criminal cases, it is useful to begin with a general look at trial courts and their work. This section examines the purposes behind civil cases, surveys the most common types of civil cases, and discusses the participants and procedures in civil courts.

The Purposes of Civil Courts

People go to civil courts to seek *remedies*—things they are asking the courts to give them.[3] The most common remedy is *damages* to compensate for a loss. The loss may be something concrete, such as the cost of car repair after an accident, or more abstract, such as damage to a reputation resulting from a libelous publication. Closely related to damages is *restitution,* the return of something belonging to a person, such as land or corporate bonds.

Another kind of remedy is *coercion,* in which a party asks the court to require that another party either take a particular action or refrain from an action. The major form of this remedy is an injunction, in which a court can order action such as the halting of a labor strike. The final type of remedy is a *declaration* of legal rights or status, such as the termination of marriage through divorce or a ruling that a statute is unconstitutional.

For what purposes are the courts given the power to provide these remedies? Two broad goals, each tied to a general function of the courts discussed in Chapter 1, underlie this power.[4] The first is *dispute resolution:* the law offers remedies to people who have grievances in order to secure the peaceful and orderly settlement of conflicts. The second is *behavior modification:* the law imposes costs on certain kinds of behavior with the intent of discouraging that behavior.

These broad goals enjoy general acceptance, but more specific issues elicit heated disagreement. For instance, commentators today are engaged in a debate about how well courts do in resolving disputes; this debate has direct implications for policies that give people incentives either to go to court or to stay out. There is even more contention about what kinds of behavior the law should discourage and how it should do so.[5] In order to prevent drunken driving, should party hosts and bartenders be held liable for damage caused by drivers to whom they have served excessive amounts of alcohol? Should people injured by defective products be able to obtain extra, "punitive" damages if a company had acted irresponsibly in making a product, so that companies have a stronger incentive to make safe products? Not surprisingly, both issues have been the subject of considerable conflict.

These and other issues about the availability of legal remedies are resolved in part by legislatures through statutes. But the courts play a major role by interpreting these statutes, which often are ambiguous in their application to specific situations. In some areas of law, called "common law" fields, appellate courts have been primarily responsible for establishing legal rules, with legislatures intervening only to a limited degree. Thus, for example, the rules as to when people must be compensated for personal injuries have been determined chiefly by court decisions. Not surprisingly, on many issues the law varies a great deal from state to state. For instance, in some states landlords have a legal duty to provide reasonable protection against crime to their tenants, but in other states they do not.

By offering legal remedies in some cases and denying them in others, civil courts serve another function: the allocation of gains and losses. Every individual decision gives benefits and burdens to the litigants; in the aggregate, decisions on issues such as punitive damages advantage some groups in society and disadvantage others. The gains and losses that courts allocate are usually matters such as money, affecting people in direct and concrete ways. But decisions also support the values of some people and groups over others when they address issues such as civil rights or abortion.

Because courts distribute benefits and burdens, debates over the shape of the law are not simply scholarly discussions among people who are trying to serve the needs of society as a whole. Rather, groups that are affected by the scope of legal remedies work hard to help shape the law so that it will be more favorable to their own interests. In recent years, groups whose members defend against personal injury suits—including manufacturers, physicians, and insurance companies—have expended great effort to overturn court-created rules that make it easier to win these suits. Besides lobbying in state legislatures and Congress, they have contributed money to aspiring judges in order to obtain more sympathetic state supreme courts. As this example suggests, the powers of civil courts to provide remedies are the product of a political process, one that is sometimes quite contentious.

Major Types of Civil Cases

Among the wide range of cases handled by civil courts, some occur much more frequently than others. Four types of cases are the most common by far.

Contract cases arise when one party to a contract claims that the other party has violated its terms. Such cases can involve the whole array of agreements that exist in our society. Most, however, are brought by businesses against individuals on the basis of contracts for the sale or rental of goods and services or for the lending of money. In these cases, the business alleges that it has not received the money owed to it and seeks restitution in the form of direct payment or through some other means, such as the foreclosure of a mortgage on property. I refer to this kind of contract case as *debt collection*.

Personal injury, property damage, and wrongful death cases can be lumped together under the heading of *personal injury* cases, which in turn constitute the largest part of the field called tort law. In these cases, the party who has suffered a loss seeks damages in compensation. Personal injury cases typically result from accidents, which can be triggered by everything from the use of a household product to the receipt of medical care. The majority of these cases, however, arise from accidents involving motor vehicles. Some personal injury cases result from actions other than accidents, such as statements that are alleged to involve libel or slander.

Domestic relations cases involve marriage and matters related to it. Even when we leave aside the administrative function of granting marriage licenses and performing marriages, the work of the trial courts in this area is still sizable. Most of this work concerns divorce: awarding divorces, determining child custody, and allocating economic resources.

Finally, most *estate* cases concern the assets of people who have died. In these cases, courts supervise the administration of wills; they also handle the estates of people who have died without wills. In this category, too, are guardianships for people who are declared mentally incompetent to handle their own affairs.

These four types of cases all come under the heading of private law. Only a small minority of civil cases can be considered public law, which involves the government acting as government. But the number of public law cases is growing with the scope of government activity. Because public law cases are more prominent at the appellate level, they are discussed primarily in Chapters 8 and 9.

Public law cases are likely to go to federal court. But the great majority of all civil cases are handled in state courts, and this chapter—like the preceding one—focuses chiefly on the state level. The processes involved in civil litigation are similar at the state and federal levels, and I will not generally distinguish between the two sets of courts.

Participants in the Civil Courts

As in criminal courts, the most important participants in civil courts are lawyers and judges; in both settings, they constitute the core of the courtroom work group. As in the criminal courts, the closeness of the relationships among these people depends on the regularity with which a set of lawyers comes before a particular judge. Thus, in rural courts and in courts (and court divisions) with jurisdiction over a narrow range of civil cases, a judge may deal frequently with a relatively small group of lawyers. In urban courts with a broad jurisdiction, judges may encounter a much larger group of lawyers, and close working relationships are less likely to develop.

Judges   The great majority of judges spend at least part of their time hearing civil cases. Many judges sit on courts that hear only civil cases. Some specialize even more narrowly, serving permanently on courts or divisions that handle only probate, domestic relations, or bankruptcy cases.

In most respects, the powers and responsibilities of judges in civil cases are similar to those in criminal cases. One difference is the greater frequency of bench trials compared with jury trials in civil cases, a difference that increases the judge's role as a decision maker. Another difference is that judges participate in negotiations between civil parties more often than they do in plea bargaining. But, unlike criminal litigants who must await the judge's sentencing decision, civil parties who settle out of court ordinarily can determine the specific terms of the settlement themselves.

Attorneys   As in criminal cases, attorneys are usually present in civil cases with substantial stakes. In many areas of law, the lawyers who participate in cases are primarily specialists in those areas. But in common and nontechnical areas, such as estates, much of the work is done by lawyers who are not specialists. This is particularly true outside of big cities.

Some areas of law handled in civil courts resemble criminal law in the sense that a particular lawyer always represents only one of the two types of parties that contend in court. For example, in areas that pit the government against private parties, such as taxes and economic regulation, the government is represented by its own full-time employees, while private attorneys serve private parties on a permanent or case-by-case basis. And in areas that typically involve conflicts between businesses and individuals, such as debt collection and personal injury cases, the attorneys who represent businesses are a separate group from those who represent individuals. In some other areas, however, most lawyers work on both sides. For instance, a divorce lawyer is likely to represent both husbands and wives at various times.

As discussed in Chapter 3, the corporate and government clients that some lawyers serve regularly have a relatively good opportunity to scrutinize and control their lawyers' work. In contrast, the individual whom a lawyer serves only once is likely to exert less control. In this respect, individual clients in civil cases more closely resemble criminal defendants.

Parties   The contending parties in a civil case are designated as the *plaintiff* (the party that brings the suit) and the *defendant* (the party against whom the suit is brought). Civil cases often have multiple plaintiffs, defendants, or both. Under some conditions a case may be brought as a class action, in which one or more people sue on behalf of a larger set of people who share the same situation, such as consumers who allegedly have been overcharged for a product.

The parties to civil cases can be classified in a variety of ways, but three related distinctions are especially important. One is the commonsense distinction between individuals and organizations, primarily businesses and governments. A second, made by Marc Galanter, is between "one-shotters," or "those claimants who have only occasional recourse to the courts," and "repeat players . . . who are engaged in many similar litigations over time."[6] (Typical repeat players include insurance companies, finance companies, and some government agencies.) Galanter has also distinguished among litigants by their economic status, dividing them into "haves" and "have-nots." These classifications are linked, in that organizations tend to be repeat players and to have substantial economic resources, while individuals tend to be one-shotters and to possess fewer resources.

Galanter argues that the haves generally "come out ahead" in litigation.[7] One reason is that they are often repeat players, who hold a series of advantages over one-shotters. For instance, through frequent court use, they gain expertise and the opportunity to develop good relations with court personnel. Haves can also afford the best legal services. Moreover, they can structure transactions with have-nots to put themselves in a favorable position if litigation results; Exhibit 7.1 describes how this process works.

Galanter's analysis leads to predictions about the outcomes in civil cases that pit different types of parties against each other. In most debt collection cases, for example, merchants and financial institutions sue low-income individuals; in most personal injury cases, individuals sue defendants who are represented by insurance companies. Following Galanter's arguments, we

EXHIBIT 7.1 Structuring of Transactions by "Haves"

Businesses and individuals often make agreements with each other, over such matters as warranties for products and the repayment of consumer loans. Those agreements usually are on terms established by businesses, terms that give them an advantage should a legal dispute arise. The individuals involved often are unaware of these terms or feel that they have no choice but to accept them. For instance, the back of an airline ticket creates a contract in which the passenger accepts the airline's "conditions of carriage" or "terms of transportation," which may limit the passenger's rights in important ways but which are very difficult to obtain—even if a passenger should be aware of their existence.

On the Fox network television show "Studs," contestants go out on dates with each other. Each contestant must sign a contract that is designed to limit the network's liability for any mishaps that could arise. In one clause, contestants must acknowledge their responsibility to "minimize the risk of the types of harm" that might occur. The clause goes on to list examples of such risks, including "invasion of privacy," "libel," "personal injury or property damage," and "permanent disability or death." In another clause, contestants agree that, if they follow the advice given by the show's host, "this decision shall be entirely at my own risk."

Sources: Airline ticket contracts are discussed in George Albert Brown, "Flying Over the Fine Print," *National Law Journal*, August 28, 1989, pp. 13–14; the portions of the "Studs" contract quoted here are taken from "Risks of Romance," *Harper's*, March 1992, p. 24.

would expect the organizational parties in these cases—as repeat players and haves—generally to be successful. The last section of this chapter examines the evidence on these predictions.

Other Participants   Of the other participants in criminal courts, some— such as witnesses and court clerks—play similar roles in the civil courts. Police officers are far less important, although they often serve as witnesses in auto accident cases. Grand jurors and probation officers, of course, are absent altogether.

As noted earlier, trial juries are less common in civil cases than in criminal cases. When a jury does appear, its position is somewhat different from that of the criminal jury. In suits for damages, civil court juries determine the amount to be paid if they find the defendant liable; thus they exercise the equivalent of the judge's sentencing power in criminal cases. However, the trial judge has more power in civil cases to override a jury's verdict or to take a decision away from a jury.

A Summary of Court Procedures

Both formal and actual procedures for civil cases vary a good deal. The basic and most common set of procedures, which I discuss in some detail, is the one ordinarily used in suits for damages and restitution. Variants of those procedures are discussed more briefly.[a]

The Basic System   In a typical set of procedures for civil cases, as shown in Exhibit 7.2. court action begins with the filing by the plaintiff of a *complaint* in which legal allegations are made against the defendant. (For the sake of simplicity, I assume that the case has only a single plaintiff and a single defendant.) The next step is notification of the defendant, which is called *serving process*. The defendant may then file an *answer* to the complaint. This answer offers defenses to the complaint, and it may also make counterclaims

EXHIBIT 7.2 Typical Stages of the Processing of Civil Suits for Damages or Restitution

1. Filing of a complaint by the plaintiff
2. Serving of process on the defendant
3. Filing of an answer to the complaint by the defendant
4. Discovery of evidence: depositions, interrogatories, and discovery of materials
5. Pretrial conference and order
6. Trial
7. Verdict on liability and (where liability is found) the remedy
8. Post-trial motions: for a judgment notwithstanding the verdict, to set aside the verdict
9. Compliance with or enforcement of the judgment

against the plaintiff—in effect, making the plaintiff a defendant as well. The complaint and the answer are called the *pleadings*.

A series of pretrial procedures, designed to prepare the case for trial, follows the pleadings. In *discovery*, the parties gather evidence from each other, primarily in three forms. The first is *depositions*, in which the lawyer for one side questions the other party and the witnesses for the other side. The second is *interrogatories*, in which one party presents questions to the other party for more extensive written responses. The third is the *discovery of documents and other materials* held by the other party. The judge does not supervise discovery directly but settles any disputes that may arise at this stage. Discovery is intended to eliminate the surprise element at trial, but in the process it has developed its own problems. Among them are efforts by parties to wear down their opponents through extensive and costly discovery demands and abusive questioning of witnesses at depositions "that can only be compared with a medieval inquisition."[9] Because of such questioning, one federal judge said, "The transcripts of depositions are often very ugly documents."[10]

After discovery is completed, the judge may schedule a *pretrial conference* with the parties; in some courts, the conference is mandatory. During the conference, the judge seeks to clarify the issues in the case and ready it for trial. Afterward, the judge makes up a pretrial order listing the evidence that the parties will present.

Like criminal cases, civil cases can drop out along the way to trial. In some categories, such as personal injuries, the overwhelming majority do drop out. The plaintiff can dismiss the case voluntarily, either because of a decision that it is not worth pursuing or because the parties have reached a settlement out of court. For the same reasons that they welcome plea bargains in criminal cases, judges generally encourage such settlements; indeed, they often use the pretrial conference to move the parties toward an agreement.

Less often, the judge reaches a decision in the case before it comes to trial. The judge may dismiss the case because of the plaintiff's failure to pursue it adequately. Similarly, the judge may issue a *default judgment* against the defendant for failure to file an answer or to meet other procedural requirements. Either party may also ask for a *judgment on* the basis of *the pleadings*, which the judge can grant if the other party has failed to make sufficient allegations to support a case. And the judge can grant a *summary judgment* to one party on the ground that there are no genuine issues of fact and that the law compels a decision in favor of that party.

The trial itself resembles a criminal trial. As it proceeds, the plaintiff seeks to prove the defendant's liability and the appropriateness of the desired remedy. In response, the defendant may contest either or both issues; on the remedy, the question usually is the amount of money to be paid in damages if liability is found. The standard of proof for liability generally is a *preponderance of the evidence*, a standard that is easier to meet than the proof beyond a reasonable doubt required of criminal prosecutors.

During a jury trial, the judge may grant a *directed verdict* in favor of one party at the close of the other party's case, on the ground that the evidence allows only one outcome. If there is no directed verdict, the judge or jury decides the contested issues after the trial. In addition, where damages or restitution are to be provided, the amount is determined.

After a jury decision, the losing party can ask the judge for what is called *a judgment notwithstanding the verdict,* on the ground that there was insufficient basis for the jury's decision. A party can also ask the judge to set aside the verdict and order a new trial on the basis of problems in either the trial or the verdict.

If the court's judgment requires one party to provide a remedy to the other, that party may comply readily with the judgment. But if voluntary compliance does not occur, the winning party can seek enforcement of the judgment by the sheriff or another official through a variety of methods, including garnishment (a process in which an employer withholds part of the losing party's wages and turns it over to the winning party) and the forced sale of the loser's property to pay the judgment.

Cases may take a long time to go through these stages. At an extreme, a 1990 study found that litigants in Los Angeles waited an average of five years from filing to a jury trial.[11] Complex cases may take even longer to reach a resolution; in 1990 federal courts finally completed action on lawsuits that arose from a 1971 Vietnam War protest and a 1970 auto accident.[12] Recent growth in caseloads would be expected to lengthen the time for processing civil cases, especially since speedy-trial rules require courts to give higher priority to disposition of criminal cases. But at least the federal courts have had some success in keeping up with large numbers of cases.[13]

Other Sets of Procedures   In civil cases with small stakes, as in similar criminal cases, the complex formal procedures can be abbreviated considerably. This abbreviation is made official in small claims courts, which are usually special divisions of trial courts designated to hear cases where plaintiffs seek relatively small amounts of money or (in some states) such remedies as evictions. A significant proportion of all civil cases—about 20 percent in one survey of four states[14]—are heard under such small claims procedures.

Small claims courts were created to handle cases at relatively little expense to the parties and with less delay than in other civil courts. In line with these goals, small claims courts operate under specially simplified procedural rules. Pretrial procedures are shortened and simplified, and trials are held before judges with considerable informality. Often lawyers do not even participate in the proceedings; indeed, some small claims courts prohibit their appearance.

Cases in which the plaintiff seeks a coercive remedy are handled under a different set of procedures, which can be illustrated with the example of injunctions. Prior to trial the plaintiff may ask for a *temporary restraining order,* sometimes without giving notice to the defendant. Later the plaintiff may seek a *preliminary injunction,* which the defendant can contest. Both are intended to prevent the defendant from taking irreversible action, such as demolishing a building. The trial itself, in which the plaintiff seeks a permanent injunction, is held before a judge alone. In many cases, it is relatively short because much of the relevant evidence was presented in the pretrial hearings. If an injunction is awarded, it can be enforced with a motion to hold a noncomplying party in contempt of court; if a judge holds that party in contempt, the judge can impose a fine or prison sentence.

Cases involving divorces and the estates of deceased people have their own procedures as well. In both categories, most cases are uncontested: for example, nobody disputes a will, or a husband and wife both want a divorce and agree on the terms of the settlement. Such cases must go to court for approval of the uncontested action, but the hearings are generally routine and abbreviated. Of course, when divorce and estate cases are contested, they must go through adversarial proceedings before a judge.

DECIDING WHETHER TO LITIGATE

As individuals or members of organizations, people often have to decide whether to take cases to court, that is, to litigate. These decisions emerge from situations in which a person develops a grievance or recognizes an opportunity that might be handled through litigation. In such situations, people may do nothing at all, choosing to live with the grievance or to forgo the opportunity, or they may choose to take action in some form other than litigation. But they might decide to go to court, either as a first action or after trying one or more alternatives. Going to court itself involves two steps: filing a lawsuit and taking a case to trial. Although both steps are important, the second is the more decisive, for it means that the parties are putting their dispute before a court rather than settling it in another forum.

Some Types of Litigation

The considerations that influence litigation decisions and the decision process itself vary from one area of the law to another. To provide some sense of how litigation decisions are made, I explore three somewhat different areas: discrimination, personal injuries, and disputes between businesses.

Discrimination   Although discrimination cases are not among the most common, this area tells a good deal about conditions that affect whether potential cases go to court. When commentators speak of today's Americans as *litigious,* inclined to go to court whenever the opportunity arises, they sometimes use discrimination claims to illustrate their arguments. Such references have some support in reality; the number of cases brought to court on the basis of discrimination claims has grown rapidly.[15] Yet the discrimination cases that come to court constitute only a small fraction of those that might be brought. One survey identified people who felt that they had been the victims of discrimination in such areas as employment, education, or housing. Of these people, fewer than three in five complained about the matter, fewer than one in thirty hired a lawyer, and fewer than one in a hundred filed a court case.[16] In a 1990 survey, 10 percent of those who recalled an incident of employment discrimination had complained to a government agency, while 2 percent consulted an attorney or filed a lawsuit.[17]

Several factors seem to account for this record.[18] One is lack of knowledge about how to proceed in a discrimination case. Because the legal remedies are not well publicized, few people know what action they can take if they are denied an apartment or a job and feel that the denial was discriminatory. As a result, they may simply live with their grievance.

Second, it is generally difficult to get favorable legal action on discrimination complaints. Discrimination in such matters as hiring of employees and rental of housing is often hard to prove in court. Furthermore, the administrative agencies that handle discrimination problems, either by taking cases to court themselves or by helping complainants, suffer weaknesses such as limited legal powers and inadequate staffing. In turn, the difficulty of getting favorable action and adequate fees discourages lawyers from representing complainants, who often find it difficult to obtain representation.[19] And those who are charged with discrimination frequently resist complaints rather than trying to satisfy the complainant, both because they see themselves as blameless and because the prospects of unfavorable court action are limited.

Finally, seeking to redress discrimination entails costs, and these costs are especially high when the action extends to litigation. Some costs are monetary, such as paying for the services of a lawyer who will not take a case on a purely contingent basis. Other costs are psychological. To press a discrimination claim is to become involved in a conflict, to be identified as a complainer, and to live with uncertainty. Such problems are especially great when people complain of discrimination by those with whom they must continue to deal, such as employers and school administrators. In these cases, to put it mildly, a lawsuit can lead to strained relations. A successful lawsuit hardly mends such frayed connections. As two scholars have noted, in this area even more than in most others, a "victory may turn into defeat."[20]

Despite all these difficulties, people bring a good number of discrimination cases to the courts—primarily to federal courts. But, understandably, these cases are only a fraction of the cases that could be brought.

Personal Injuries   People frequently experience physical injuries or damage to their property as a result of mishaps. Any such incident that produces a significant physical injury or costly property damage might seem likely to go to court. One reason is that the party who could sue and the party who could be sued (the other driver, for example, or the manufacturer of a product) are generally strangers, thus greatly reducing the element of personal conflict.

Furthermore, most people are aware that they have legal remedies for personal injuries, and a potential plaintiff who has a strong case involving a substantial amount of money can usually find a lawyer who is willing to take the case on a contingent fee basis. Advertising by lawyers helps to publicize remedies and to identify lawyers who might take a case. Now, too, there are personal injury lawyers who regularly rush to the scene of disasters such as massive fires and airline crashes to solicit business; one of these lawyers has compared this group to a "professional tennis circuit."[21]

Considerable litigation does arise from personal injuries. Yet this litigation, like discrimination litigation, represents only a very small proportion of the cases that could have gone to court. One of the studies cited in the discussion of discrimination found that, in torts involving $1,000 or more, 3.8 percent actually resulted in court filings.[22] A study of accidental injuries that caused restricted activity or doctor visits found a 2 percent rate of filing.[23]

The processes that keep potential cases out of court differ with the type of personal injury. Automobile accidents and medical malpractice provide two contrasting examples. After auto accidents, at least a large minority of people who suffer significant physical injuries or property losses make claims against the party they see as responsible.[24] But auto accident claims ordinarily are resolved before a lawsuit is filed. (A minority of states have "no-fault" systems that restrict lawsuits for relatively minor claims based on auto accidents, but suits are the exception to the rule in other states as well.)

The potential defendant in these cases is the party that allegedly caused the injury, but any settlement or court judgment would ordinarily be paid by that party's insurance company. As a result, the claim quickly becomes one against the insurance company, which takes over for its client in handling the case. Generally, insurance companies want to settle claims quickly, in part because they prefer to reach an agreement with an injured party who has not yet hired an attorney.

Insurance companies frequently succeed in securing early agreements, largely because people who have suffered injuries or property damage also wish to settle their cases quickly. These settlements usually involve payments to the injured party, although the adjuster sometimes convinces that party to accept no payment and take no further action.

If the two sides do not reach an easy settlement and the injured party remains dissatisfied, more often than not that party will hire an attorney. In one study of bodily injury claims, 55 percent of all injured parties eventually used a lawyer.[25] Although this step escalates the conflict, it also facilitates a settlement. The lawyers who represent injured parties are usually experienced in personal injury cases; indeed, they are often specialists in that area. On the other side, the insurance company's adjusters or attorneys are also specialists. Thus, as in plea bargaining, the two sides share an understanding of how to negotiate these cases. This shared understanding is reflected in Exhibit 7.3, which shows a list of rules for the negotiation of auto accident cases that one scholar inferred from his observations. As in plea bargaining, the two sides also share a degree of agreement on the general terms for settlements of common types of cases, terms that are shaped by the participants' predictions of what would happen if the case were brought to trial.

In a substantial minority of cases, the lawyer for the injured party eventually files suit, and serious negotiations may not occur until the scheduled trial date is close. But the two sides can usually reach a mutually agreeable settlement at some point. This success is facilitated by the experience and expertise of most negotiators and by some of the same conditions that help produce successful plea bargaining. One is that both sides wish to avoid the risks of a trial—in which an insurance company might be required to pay

1. "Yield from an initial demand."—Both sides must be willing to give the other side more than they originally offered.
2. "Balance concessions."—When one side yields something, the other side must yield as well.
3. "Retractions may not be made."—Any offer is treated as binding on the person who makes it.
4. "Bargain in good faith."—The use of negotiations for purposes other than to reach an agreement, such as obtaining information to use in litigation, prevents successful negotiations.

Source: H. Laurence Ross, *Settled Out of Court: The Social Process of Insurance Claims Adjustment,* rev. 2d ed. (New York: Aldine Publishing, 1980), pp. 149–151.

EXHIBIT 7.3 Informal Rules for the Negotiation of Automobile Accident Cases Between Insurance Adjusters and Attorneys for Injured Parties

high damages or an injured party might lose and collect nothing. Another is that both insurance companies and lawyers who represent injured parties wish to avoid spending the time that is required to take cases to trial. In cases based on bodily injuries in auto accidents, a study found that 18 percent of all claims led to lawsuits, but only 1 percent of the claims actually went to trial—and half of those were settled before a verdict.[26]

The cases that do go to trial are not a representative sample of all auto accidents. Rather, as one study shows, they tend to involve conditions that make negotiated settlements relatively difficult or unattractive.[27] One example is cases in which the damages are serious but the liability issue seems favorable to the defendant. In such a case, the insurance company is likely to offer a settlement that is relatively small in comparison with the damages, and the plaintiff may see a trial as a worthy gamble on the possibility of a much bigger recovery. In very big cases, insurance company employees may be unwilling to take responsibility for a large settlement, and the costs of a trial in such cases are insignificant compared with the stakes. Thus the company may refuse to settle.

The litigation rate in medical malpractice has risen enormously in the last thirty years, but it is still low: overall, perhaps 2 percent of all instances of malpractice lead to the filing of lawsuits.[28] A New York study found that only a small minority of people who have suffered significant injuries from negligent medical care in hospitals even take initial actions that might lead to a lawsuit. (The study also found that most potential lawsuits are initiated by people who were *not* the victims of medical negligence, though the majority of these people did suffer significant injuries through medical care.)[29] And, like other kinds of cases, most malpractice litigation is settled or dropped before trial.

One reason for the low rate of malpractice suits is that many people with potential lawsuits simply take no action. They may not recognize the possibility of malpractice or know how to make a claim; alternatively, they may decide that such action is not a good idea. But lawyers also play an important screening role, typically turning down far more malpractice cases than they accept.[30] In part, that screening role reflects the difficulty of obtaining a favorable outcome in malpractice cases. People are less likely to bring cases to lawyers when their injuries are minor, and such cases are also less attractive to lawyers.

Thus medical malpractice operates differently from auto accidents. In auto accident cases, the relative rarity of litigation reflects primarily the effectiveness of negotiation in settling legal claims out of court; in malpractice, it reflects primarily the infrequency of claims. The results—at least for use of the courts—are similar.

The Business World   The potential for lawsuits between businesses is tremendous because legal issues arise almost continuously in the process of their interaction. If, for example, a manufacturer promises to deliver goods to a wholesaler by a given time and fails to do so, or the wholesaler orders goods and then cancels the order, the offended party could bring a suit for breach of contract. Or if one manufacturer initiates a process that overlaps with one that has been patented by a competitor, the competitor could sue for patent infringement.

Certainly, businesses do file a good many lawsuits against each other. Yet, as in other areas, the volume of such litigation is quite small when compared with all the situations in which litigation is possible. This difference is especially striking because large and medium-sized businesses could bear the monetary costs of litigation with relative ease. Why, then, do they not take each other to court more often?

One part of the answer lies in the disadvantages of litigation. The length of time it requires is disruptive to business operations. Its monetary costs may be affordable, but they are still unwelcome. Perhaps the most important disadvantage is that litigation would jeopardize relationships on which businesses depend. Virtually any company relies on amicable relations with other companies, particularly for buying and selling of goods and services. Such relations are unlikely to survive a lawsuit, and a firm's readiness to litigate may discourage other businesses from dealing with it. Legal scholar Stewart Macauley found that the need to maintain business relationships militated even against putting disputes over contracts in a legal context. As one purchasing agent told Macauley, "You don't read legalistic contract clauses at each other if you ever want to do business again."[31]

Another part of the answer is the existence of alternative methods to resolve disputes. Close relationships between people in firms that deal with each other facilitate informal settlements; people can work out problems without the intervention of other parties because of their mutual trust and their shared understandings about appropriate terms of settlement. Ranchers in one California county have developed norms for the handling of situations in which one rancher's cattle trespass on the land of another—norms that have little to do with the applicable legal rules.[32]

When the parties cannot settle disputes by themselves, they can turn for help to other people. The lawyers for two businesses often reach an agreement on behalf of their clients. In addition, businesses make considerable use of *mediation* (in which a mediator helps the parties reach a mutually acceptable resolution of their dispute) and *arbitration* (in which the parties turn a dispute over to an arbitrator, who imposes a binding decision on them). Mediation is especially attractive because the parties retain control over the outcome, but even arbitration provides speed, economy, and flexibility that litigation lacks. The American Arbitration Association and trade associations in specific industries provide mediation and arbitration services, and companies that work together often arrange in advance to use these services if disputes arise.

Of course, some disputes between businesses do end up in court. Litigation is more likely when two firms lack a continuing relationship and therefore have less ability and incentive to work out their differences. In some situations, usually involving direct competitors, the stakes are simply so high that the possible benefits of litigation outweigh its costs. For example, Seven-Up brought a suit for $500 million in 1992, charging that Coca-Cola was using illegal methods to convince bottlers to sell Sprite (owned by Coca-Cola) rather than Seven-Up; the potential loss of bottlers would have a serious impact on Seven-Up's sales.[33] And, as Exhibit 7.4 illustrates, valuable patents often become subjects of litigation. Perhaps the largest category of business litigation is quite different from these high-stakes cases: one business falls into financial difficulties and fails to meet its contractual obligations to another company, which sues to recover what it is owed.[34] In this situation, the company that initiates a lawsuit probably does not expect to have further dealings with the company in trouble; therefore, the suit carries some possibility of monetary benefits and little risk.

In the evolution of industries, the volume of litigation is likely to decline over time. Early in the development of an industry, typically a great many

EXHIBIT 7.4 Some Recent Lawsuits over Important Patents

Subject of Patent	Companies Involved in Suit(s)
Computer chip software	Intel, Advanced Micro Devices
Artificial human protein	Amgen, Genetics Institute
Instant cameras and film	Polaroid, Kodak
Basketball shoes	Nike, Avia
Soft cookies	Procter & Gamble, Nabisco, Keebler, Frito-Lay
The "Salad Shooter" slicer and shredder	Presto, Black & Decker

Sources: Newspaper reports.

companies struggle for a foothold. The relationships among the companies that deal with each other and their understandings with each other about appropriate business practices are weak. Furthermore, relevant legal rules may not yet be clear. As a result, it is difficult to settle disputes without litigation. In addition, litigation may be attractive as a means to gain a decisive advantage over competitors. Thus there has been a great deal of litigation in the computer industry under a wide array of laws. In recent years, for instance, the Nintendo company has been plaintiff or defendant in a variety of lawsuits in which the issues ranged from copyright infringement to breach of contract to antitrust violations.

Later on, when the industry is more stable—when there are firmer relationships between companies and better mechanisms for resolving disputes— it is both easier and more desirable to avoid litigation. Consequently, lawsuits become less common. But litigation never disappears altogether, and new sources of instability, such as changes in technology or the entry of a major new competitor, can bring companies to court more often.

The Incidence of Litigation

In each of the areas surveyed so far, litigation is substantial in absolute numbers but uncommon when compared with the number of potential cases. In this respect, these areas are typical. The study cited in the discussion of personal injuries and discrimination looked at individuals with significant grievances, generally involving $1,000 or more, across a wide range of legal areas. Only 5 percent of these grievances led to the filing of lawsuits, a substantial majority of which were settled out of court.[35] Yet civil suits are hardly rare; more than 18 million civil cases were filed in state courts in 1990.[36]

The Disadvantages of Litigation   The discussion thus far suggests why most potential cases do not go to court: litigation has several features that generally make it unattractive. Three of these features are especially important:

1. Litigation is expensive. The lawyers' services required to prepare and try a case make all but the simplest trials unaffordable for most individuals and many organizations, unless a special device such as the contingent fee is operating. Even those who can afford litigation would still prefer to avoid its costs.
2. Litigation means that the parties lose control over the outcome. In the hands of a judge or jury, a case might produce a result that is highly unfavorable to one of the parties. Thus, as with plea bargaining, it often seems far safer to reach a settlement that is at least palatable to both sides.
3. Litigation creates or exacerbates conflict between the parties. The contest element in trials pits people against each other in a very direct and serious way. For most people, this conflict is unpleasant in itself, and it often has

practical consequences as well. If the parties had a relationship before the trial—such as two neighbors or two businesses that deal with each other—it is doubtful the relationship will survive intact.

Taken together, these attributes of litigation create powerful reasons to avoid it. Justice Richard Neely of the West Virginia Supreme Court concluded that "once anyone actually sets foot in a court, any court, he is a loser—even if he comes out of the litigation a technical winner."[37] Ambrose Bierce, a nineteenth-century writer and social critic, put the matter in more vivid terms when he defined litigation as "a machine which you go into as a pig and come out of as a sausage."[38]

These statements exaggerate the disadvantages of litigation, but they give appropriate emphasis to the negative consequences of going to court. Because people generally recognize at least some of these consequences, most of the time they avoid litigation; those who do litigate, as Sally Engle Merry notes, "usually turn to court reluctantly and only as a last resort."[39]

When Litigation Is Attractive   In view of these disadvantages, the many cases that do go to court require explanation. Part of the explanation lies in conditions that reduce or negate the disadvantages.

Under some circumstances, for instance, the monetary costs of litigation are limited. In personal injury cases, the contingent fee makes it possible for many people to afford bringing a lawsuit. The streamlined procedures of small claims courts minimize the costs of bringing a case and arguing it in court.

Similarly, in some situations the conflict element in litigation is greatly reduced. Most important, there may be no relationship that would be damaged by litigation; in the United States, as one scholar puts it, "litigation tends to be between parties who are strangers."[40] In other instances, the relationship from which litigation arises may already have been destroyed before the filing of a lawsuit.

Another part of the explanation for litigation is that under some circumstances its benefits seem particularly great. First, there are people for whom the conflict or the risk involved in litigation is an attraction rather than a deterrent. In her study of family and neighborhood problems, Merry found people who gained satisfaction from suing acquaintances.

> Some plaintiffs come to use the law as an arena for manipulation and play, a place to toy with enemies and to gain strategic successes by pummeling one's opponents with legal charges and summonses. . . . Some come to regard the court as entertainment, as a place to try out dominance games with others and to see what will happen.[41]

Such litigants may direct their activity at a particular target.

> Robert Young, 44, was murdered in San Francisco in February. Cleared in the case were Susan and David Beugen, whom police initially suspected because Young had filed 18 lawsuits against the couple in the previous eight years, claiming he felt cheated after purchasing two hair salons from the couple. Susan Beugen volunteered to start a defense fund for whoever murdered Young.[42]

Other frequent litigants attack institutions rather than acquaintances. One example is the man who filed 110 federal lawsuits in two years, including a suit for "$100 zillion" against a roller-skating rink in Rockville, Maryland, that allegedly refused him admission.[43]

Second, litigation is sometimes perceived as a last resort, the only way left to deal with an intolerable situation. This is true of most divorces and personal bankruptcies. Divorce is a kind of special case: if one or both partners wish to terminate their marriage officially, they have no alternative but to go to court. Similarly, owners of companies may sue other businesses that they see as responsible for their eroding positions or impending failures. In this category are recent suits by soft drink bottlers against the Coca-Cola company and by clothing store owners against the Benetton company, each claiming that the company supplying them with products treated them unfairly and illegally.[44]

Third, people may file lawsuits simply because litigation offers very substantial benefits that cannot be obtained in other ways. One example is bankruptcy filings by corporations that are not in dire financial straits; such a company may be using bankruptcy to overturn labor contracts or to gain protection from claims by people whom its products have injured.[45] Individuals may bring personal injury suits in the hope of gaining a big settlement; sometimes these individuals have suffered no injury at all but seek to profit from fraudulent claims. An unusual example is the Alabama prisoner who arranged for his obituary to be printed in newspapers and "then sued the newspapers for defamation and intentional infliction of emotional distress."[46]

The potential benefits from litigation may be political. Interest groups such as the American Civil Liberties Union regularly engage in "political litigation" to secure court rulings that advance their policy goals; these activities are examined in the next chapter. And in recent years businesses have increasingly brought suits against people who criticized them or who took political action unfavorable to their interests. Such lawsuits are intended to punish opponents and to deter opposition in the future. George Pring and Penelope Canan, scholars who labeled these suits "SLAPPs" (Strategic Lawsuits Against Public Participation), had identified about five hundred of them as of 1992.[47] Some examples appear in Exhibit 7.5.

Alternatives to Litigation

As already suggested, whether people go to court depends in part on the availability of alternatives to litigation. In most situations of potential litigation, people do have alternatives, and a great many alternatives exist in various situations.

These alternatives differ in several ways, of which two are particularly important.[48] The first is how public they are: to what extent is the issue between the parties opened up to wider participation and scrutiny? The second is the formality of the process by which the issue is handled. These two factors overlap to some extent, in that more formal processes tend to be more

Five Illinois homeowners picketed in front of their subdivision's model homes to indicate their unhappiness about the construction of their roofs. The company that owned the subdivision sued them, seeking an injunction against the picketing and monetary damages.

A neighborhood group and individual residents of New York City circulated a letter and fought in court against the city's leasing of property to developers for a shopping mall. The mall developers countersued the group and individuals for $200 million.

A member of the city council in Seaside, California, was removed from office in a recall election. He sued a great many people for libel and slander, including one person who apparently did nothing other than sign a petition to recall him. He included several unnamed defendants, "John Does," and wrote a letter to a local newspaper in which he warned, "Be careful, John Does."

Sources: Hugh Dellios, "Builder's Suit Quiets Picketing Residents," *Chicago Tribune,* April 4, 1990, sec. 1, p. 8; George W. Pring, "SLAPPs: Strategic Lawsuits Against Public Participation," *Pace Environmental Law Review,* 7 (Fall 1989), 14; Eve Pell, "Lawsuits That Chill Local Politics," *California Lawyer,* February 1984, p. 43.

EXHIBIT 7.5 Examples of Lawsuits to Deter Political Criticism and Activity

public as well. Thus, as Figure 7.1 shows, we can list litigation and its major alternatives in the order of their "publicness" and formality.

Direct negotiation between the parties is a simple and routine means to handle legal issues. Aggrieved consumers take their complaints to store managers. A driver whose car has been damaged talks to the owner of the other car and to the owner's insurance company. Neighbors who disagree over their property line discuss the problem between themselves. This is by far the most common way in which people deal with potential court cases.

Slightly more formal is negotiation in which attorneys represent the parties. The use of lawyers widens the scope of the negotiation, particularly for individuals and businesses that do not regularly employ lawyers. Attorneys often introduce an element of legal formality into the discussion as well, and their knowledge of the law and courts means that the way in which a court would handle the issue being considered becomes more relevant to the negotiation.

Mediation and arbitration have already been discussed in the context of business disputes, but both are used in other areas as well. Mediation can be fairly informal (when, for example, parish priests and other religious authorities help individuals resolve their disputes) or more formal (as in the mediation offered by professional mediators in negotiations between labor and management). Arbitration is less common than mediation because it is more formal, with the arbitrator reaching a binding decision. However, it is used a good deal in disputes between businesses, in consumer complaints, and in labor-management relations. A program has also been established in

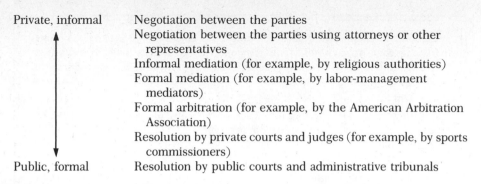

Private, informal   Negotiation between the parties

Negotiation between the parties using attorneys or other
representatives

Informal mediation (for example, by religious authorities)

Formal mediation (for example, by labor-management
mediators)

Formal arbitration (for example, by the American Arbitration
Association)

Resolution by private courts and judges (for example, by sports
commissioners)

Public, formal   Resolution by public courts and administrative tribunals

FIGURE 7.1 Litigation and Some Major Alternatives to Litigation.

Sources: Adapted from formulations in Marc Galanter, "Why the 'Haves' Come Out Ahead: Speculations on the Limits of Legal Change," *Law & Society Review,* 9 (Fall 1974), 124–135; and Austin Sarat and Joel B. Grossman, "Courts and Conflict Resolution: Problems in the Mobilization of Adjudication," *American Political Science Review,* 69 (December 1975), 1201–1208.

recent years to arbitrate disputes over claims of libel.[49] In some arbitration programs, the parties agree not to "appeal" from the arbitration judgment to a court.

A variant of arbitration is the use of private courts and judges. Some labor unions rely on tribunals to resolve disagreements within the union. The head of a professional sports league usually has the power to resolve some kinds of internal disagreements. And many big companies, such as Polaroid and General Electric, have established internal courts to hear complaints by employees.[50] One special and growing form of private court is the "rent-a-judge" system, invented in California in 1976 and increasingly used in other states. In this system, parties to disputes—often already filed in court—opt to have their cases heard privately by retired judges. Some judges work on their own, but several companies offer rent-a-judge services; as of 1991 one California company employed 160 retired judges in three states.[51]

At the furthest distance from simple two-party negotiation is the resolution of a legal issue in a court or in another government tribunal, such as an administrative court in the executive branch. Courts generally reach decisions in a fully public setting on the basis of formal procedures through the application of legal rules—a set of characteristics that distinguishes the courts at least marginally from all the alternative forums and fundamentally from most.

In recent years interest in alternatives to litigation has burgeoned, often under the heading "alternative dispute resolution." This development stems in large part from a growing recognition of the disadvantages of litigation. Interest in alternatives is reflected in the establishment of groups such as the National Institute for Dispute Resolution and in a spate of publications, including new law journals, devoted to the subject. The use of mediation and arbitration programs has increased, and many new programs have been established.

In and out of the legal community, most observers view the movement toward alternatives to litigation as a highly desirable development, one that helps people avoid the disadvantages of litigation and eases court workloads. Clearly, there is considerable support for this view. Most potential litigants are better off if they stay out of court, and the heavy use of some recently created alternatives indicates that they serve real needs.

Yet some observers express skepticism about the growing movement toward alternatives to litigation. One reason is a perception that some mediation and arbitration programs are designed to gain advantages for certain interests—particularly businesses that face consumer complaints. For instance, stock brokerage firms frequently include in their contracts with customers a clause requiring that customers take disputes with the broker to an arbitration system run by the securities industry rather than to court. Although brokerage firms might simply be motivated by the desire to save both sides money and trouble, Supreme Court Justice Harry Blackmun suggested otherwise in a 1987 opinion:

> The uniform opposition of investors to compelled arbitration and the overwhelming support of the securities industry for the process suggest that there must be *some* truth to the investors' belief that the securities industry has an advantage in a forum under its own control.[52]

It is not clear whether that advantage actually exists, but customers' lack of choice about this arrangement—compounded by a common lack of awareness that they have signed away their right to go to court—lends credence to Blackmun's suspicion.[53]

All this does not mean that the movement for alternatives to litigation is simply an effort to gain an advantage for groups that want to avoid being sued, and certainly it does not mean that litigation is necessarily preferable to such alternatives as mediation and arbitration. But the example of the securities industry is a reminder that the choice between litigation and its alternatives is not necessarily a neutral one; the benefits that result from staying out of court may not accrue equally to the two sides in a dispute.

By taking the array of potential alternatives into account, we can map out several routes to the courts. When people hold a grievance or opportunity that might be litigated, some of them go directly to court. Others employ alternatives, usually starting with those that are least public and formal and therefore least likely to share the disadvantages of litigation. After one or more alternatives fail to produce a satisfactory result—if, say, the negotiations stall or a mediator suggests an unacceptable solution—these people then go to court.

However, a much larger number of people follow paths that do not take them to court. Many people do nothing. Consumers who feel they have suffered discrimination or who find that a product is defective often simply live with their grievance. Others obtain satisfaction through some alternative to litigation, most often negotiation with the other party. Still others accept unsatisfactory outcomes from alternatives rather than taking on litigation with its negative elements; a consumer who finds a merchant unyielding in negotiations and who gets no satisfaction from mediation by the Better Business Bureau may give up at that point. Through a combination of these routes, most possible litigation never occurs.

The Impact of Government on Litigation

The discussion of litigation thus far has dealt almost entirely with the role of individuals and institutions in the private sector. However, government institutions significantly affect both the volume and the types of litigation that occur. Most directly, government agencies themselves are involved in a great many potential court cases. As a result, their conduct of these matters—particularly their willingness to go to court—has considerable impact. More broadly, courts and the other branches of government can influence private-sector litigation in a variety of ways.

First, legislative and judicial policies create and define legal remedies, thereby determining who has the right to go to court. For instance, a series of civil rights laws passed by Congress has allowed individuals to bring lawsuits for discrimination under a variety of circumstances. The Civil Rights Act of 1871 allowed people to sue for violations of their constitutional rights; largely ignored for nearly a century, it was broadened in its scope by several Supreme Court decisions and became the basis for an estimated thirty thousand federal cases each year.[54] A 1982 California law allowed police officers to bring defamation suits against people who made complaints against them; not surprisingly, officers began to bring such suits.[55]

Second, government decisions help determine the attractiveness of litigation. In recent years many state legislatures have changed legal doctrines and procedures in personal injury law in ways that are unfavorable to injured parties. For example, some states have established the rule that a manufacturer is not liable for injuries caused by a product if that product adhered to the "state of the art" when it was made. One goal of such provisions, and probably an effect, is to discourage certain kinds of personal injury suits. To take a different kind of example, establishment of small claims courts makes it easier for people to bring cases with small stakes; when the Virginia legislature created such a court in one county in 1988, the court proved so popular that it was overwhelmed with cases.[56] And judicial rules allowing monetary sanctions for the bringing of frivolous lawsuits, most notably Rule 11 of the Federal Rules of Civil Procedure, have made riskier the filing of cases that a judge might interpret as frivolous.[57]

Finally, legislatures and courts can help determine whether potential and actual cases are resolved at trial or in other ways. More and more, they encourage alternatives. Trial judges have long encouraged settlements in civil cases, and their efforts have intensified with growing caseloads. Some courts go further, providing mediators to help settle cases. In Texas and California, judges have actually agreed to reverse jury decisions as part of settlements between the parties.[58] Several legislatures have passed statutes requiring mediation or arbitration in certain kinds of cases, such as medical malpractice claims and divorce; many state and federal courts have adopted rules mandating arbitration before trial. Some courts have also strengthened the legal status of arbitration in the private sector; in 1992 the California Supreme Court ruled that an arbitration decision could not be attacked in court even if it involved a clear legal error and resulted in "substantial injustice."[59]

Because government intervenes in all these ways, it is never accurate to think of litigation as a purely private activity. Rather, individual decisions whether to litigate and the overall volume and distribution of civil cases are shaped fundamentally by government policies.

Litigation and the American Culture

Americans often are portrayed as a litigious people, eager to sue whenever the opportunity arises. Indeed, one legal scholar has argued that "we are the most litigious people in the world."[60] A prominent judge went one step further, concluding that "Americans are the most litigious nation in human history."[61]

Commentators often seize on anecdotal evidence about lawsuits to support this conclusion, and it is not difficult to find such evidence. A man sued for misconduct by the Washington, D.C., police; they had arrested him illegally, he argued, because he was on federal property—a mailbox. A Florida man sued the J. C. Penney Company for $10,000, claiming that a haircut he received at Penney's was so bad that he had to seek psychiatric help to overcome its effects. A couple in a Pittsburgh suburb sued their next-door neighbors for $2.5 million for failing to mow their lawn. A Detroit resident sued the city's two newspapers for $9 million on the ground that following their horoscope columns had done harm to his life.[62]

Yet we have seen that people in the United States avoid most opportunities to go to court; the number of civil cases is a small fraction of what it could be if Americans undertook litigation whenever they had a possible case. This fact alone suggests that Americans are not highly litigious.

The best way to explore the issue is through direct comparisons between the United States and other nations. Although truly comparable data are difficult to obtain, Marc Galanter pulled together some estimates of litigation rates for the United States and some other industrialized nations—with surprising results.[63] According to these estimates, the United States has far more cases per capita than nations such as Japan and Italy. But the American litigation rate is fairly comparable to that in some other nations, including England and Denmark. On the other hand, Robert Kagan concluded that comparable matters, especially those involving government policy, are more likely to go to court in the United States than in other industrialized democracies.[64]

To the extent that litigation is relatively common in the United States, characteristics of the American culture are not entirely responsible. Rather, legal rules and structures that encourage litigation also play a significant role.[65] The radical difference in litigation rates between the United States and Japan, often cited as evidence of cultural differences in the use of the courts, may actually result from a complex interaction between cultural values and government policies that affect use of the courts.[66] If anecdotal evidence counts for anything, it is worth citing a 1991 lawsuit that a man brought against his grandmother for throwing out his comic book collection and against his mother for failing to stop the grandmother. The lawsuit was brought in Japan.[67]

A Litigation Explosion?

"There was a time," a commentator wrote in 1989,

> when an aggrieved party was usually content to turn the other cheek or request an apology or simply tamper with the brakes of his antagonist's car—in short, to take advantage of any number of options before seeking the services of a lawyer. No longer. One tiny affront or injustice, real or imagined, and attorneys are being retained and witnesses duly sworn in before you can say "in the matter of the application of."[68]

Whether or not the United States is a particularly litigious society, this commentator is typical of many who believe the country has become more litigious in recent years. Indeed, it is common to refer to a litigation explosion. In general, that explosion is seen as centering on lawsuits by individuals, particularly suits for personal injuries.

The perception of a growth in litigiousness stems from several factors.[69] The rapid growth in the legal profession suggests that lawsuits are also increasing rapidly. Groups such as doctors, insurance companies, and local governments all complain about floods of litigation against them, and judges regularly complain about growing caseloads in their courts. The media frequently report the appearance of seemingly new types of cases, such as lawsuits by children who seek to "divorce" their parents.[70] In addition, accounts of seemingly trivial or bizarre lawsuits, such as those cited earlier, make it appear that litigation is running out of control.

These indications of growth can be deceptive. For instance, a spate of lawsuits in an area may appear unprecedented because we fail to recall similar episodes in the past. According to a sportswriter in 1992, "baseball had the dead ball era followed by the live ball era. This is the litigious era."[71] He did not realize that baseball in the early twentieth century was marked by a volume of litigation—involving players, teams, and leagues—that almost surely surpassed its volume in the 1990s.[72]

It is difficult to determine just how accurate the perceptions of an explosion actually are. One problem is that the available data on the volume of litigation are incomplete. Another problem is that the data we have are susceptible to differing interpretations. These data, however, do support some conclusions.

First, the number of civil cases has grown significantly in recent years. In the thirty-eight states for which appropriate data were available, civil cases in major trial courts grew by 24 percent between 1984 and 1990, continuing a longer-term increase in civil litigation.[73] Civil cases in the federal district courts actually declined by 18 percent between 1986 and 1991, following substantial growth in earlier years,[74] but only a small proportion of cases go to federal court.

Second, it is not clear whether this growth constitutes an explosion. A 24 percent increase every six years, sustained over time, would add enormously to the volume of cases. But when we take into account increases in population and in the interactions that create potential litigation, the resulting picture is not one of people fundamentally changing their litigation behavior. And cases are more likely to be settled out of court: the percentage of federal cases that actually reached trial dropped from 15 percent in 1940 to 4 percent in 1991.[75]

Finally, personal injury suits and other litigation by individuals do not stand out as a source of increasing litigation. In the states with adequate data, recent growth in tort filings generally has been moderate rather than precipitous.[76] Based on state data for 1984–1990, one report concluded that "the most dramatic increases in the civil caseload tended to be for real property rights cases or contract cases, not torts."[77]

Some scholars have sought to provide a broader perspective by looking at litigation trends over the course of U.S. history. They have found a tendency for litigation per capita to rise over time, but with the increases generally being moderate and with some courts having higher rates in some past periods than in recent years.[78] Summarizing these studies, one writer concluded that the thesis of "the country's growing legal dementia . . . could be true except it overlooks one salient point: It used to be worse."[79] Though not entirely conclusive, this research suggests that Americans have not developed a special inclination to litigate in the current era.

It should be noted that views about the existence of a litigation explosion are based largely on self-interest and ideological position. On one side, many people in the business community see themselves as beset by lawsuits that hurt the interests of their organizations and of society as a whole. Understandably, they emphasize the concept of a litigation explosion and the harm it does as a way of getting support for changes in legal rules that might protect them from lawsuits. On the other side, lawyers who represent individual plaintiffs and groups representing such interests as consumers see lawsuits as an important tool to protect individual rights and, in the case of lawyers, their own professional interests. Accordingly, they downplay the idea of an explosion in an effort to blunt the drive to change legal rules in unfavorable ways. More broadly, because of the interests involved, political conservatives generally conclude that a litigation explosion is occurring, while liberals deny its existence. Regardless of what the data tell us about litigation trends, the two sides will continue to disagree and battle over legal rules that favor one side or the other.

THE LITIGATION PROCESS

Whatever we conclude about the propensity of Americans to litigate, it is clear that a great many lawsuits are actually filed in court. Like criminal cases, civil cases can take many different paths; to a great extent, the path that a case takes depends on the type of litigation that it involves.[80] This section focuses on three major types of cases that generally follow different routes; the routes are summarized in Exhibit 7.6.

Pretrial Settlement and Full Trials: Personal Injuries

In some kinds of civil cases, the parties are in conflict, but they generally try to reach a settlement before trial and usually succeed. Cases in which the parties do not reach a settlement typically go to full-scale trials, often before juries. The largest category of such cases is personal injury suits.[81]

In most personal injury cases, as noted earlier, an insurance company is responsible for paying any judgment against the defendant and therefore takes charge of the defendant's case. The defendants themselves play no significant part either in negotiations or in setting strategy. One defendant in a Cincinnati dog-bite case did not know what its outcome was even a year after the case was settled; he was probably not unusual in this respect.[82]

EXHIBIT 7.6 Paths Through Court for Three Types of Civil Cases

	Personal Injury	Debt Collection	Divorce
Pretrial Stage			
Typical length of time	Lengthy	Brief	Moderate
Incidence of settlements between parties	Most cases	Some cases	Most cases
Trial Stage			
Typical length of time	Relatively lengthy	Quite brief	Quite brief
Incidence of uncontested trials	Few cases	Most cases, resulting from defaults by defendants	Most cases, resulting from agreements between parties
Post-Trial Stage			
Noncompliance with judgments	Uncommon	Common	Common

Source: Based in part on David M. Engel and Eric H. Steele, "Civil Cases and Society: Process and Order in the Civil Justice System," *American Bar Foundation Research Journal,* Spring 1979, pp. 311–317.

The filing of a personal injury lawsuit may reflect the inability of the two parties to reach an early settlement. But the filing is not a signal of failure so much as a punctuation of negotiations, an indication of seriousness by the lawyer for the injured party. Most suits eventually are settled out of court. Because of such settlements and other methods of pretrial disposition, such as dismissals, verdicts by judges or juries are unusual. A study of thirty-eight large urban trial courts found that only 5 percent of the tort cases were resolved by trial.[83]

In most respects, the negotiation process after the filing of lawsuits is similar to earlier negotiation. Because of the long period between filing and trial in most civil courts, the act of filing usually brings no urgency to the negotiations. However, as the trial date comes closer, lawyers concentrate more on efforts to reach a settlement. As Herbert Kritzer has pointed out, the prospect of trial not only shapes the terms of settlement but helps to make settlement possible.[84] When Vermont established a moratorium on civil jury trials because of budget problems, one unexpected effect was that lawyers stopped negotiating on cases.[85]

The filing of a lawsuit gives the parties additional means to test and challenge each other's positions. For example, lawyers use discovery to learn about the content and strength of the other party's case, and what they learn can affect the bargaining power of the two sides. Lawyers can also draw out the pretrial period for tactical purposes, seeking to wear down the other side.

Another frequent effect of filing is to bring the court into the settlement process. As noted earlier, judges in civil cases play an active role in encouraging settlements, primarily during pretrial conferences. These direct efforts are supplemented by broader mechanisms to encourage settlements. One example is a federal rule that gives plaintiffs an incentive to accept settlement offers by assessing court costs against a plaintiff who rejects a formal offer and then does no better at trial.[86] Another is the mandatory arbitration systems used for certain cases in some states and federal districts, some of which also provide financial incentives to the parties to accept the arbitrator's decision rather than go to trial.

Typically, negotiations are neither long nor complex. One study of federal and state cases found that in the typical tort case there were only two rounds of bargaining, and on the average lawyers spent less than three hours in negotiation. This pattern results from both the ease with which lawyers usually reach settlements and the low monetary stakes, which make it counterproductive to expend a great deal of lawyers' time to reach a settlement.[87]

Although trials are exceptions to the rule in personal injury cases, they are not rare. Indeed, the overwhelming majority of civil jury trials result from personal injuries. As in criminal law, the formality and length of trials in personal injury cases vary a great deal.

One major difference, of course, is between bench trials and jury trials. Just as criminal juries may favor defendants more than do judges, it is widely believed that civil juries are relatively sympathetic toward plaintiffs, for essentially the same reason: they tend to elevate equity—compensating people who have suffered losses—over law. But the available evidence suggests that, overall, juries differ little from judges in their support for plaintiffs.[88] And there is some evidence that jurors as a group are not particularly sympathetic toward people who bring personal injury cases, in part because business groups have sought to convince the public that such cases can have negative effects on society.[89]

The limitations of criminal trials as a mechanism to reach the truth were examined in Chapter 6. These weaknesses are also relevant to civil trials, including those in personal injury cases. In some respects, the weaknesses are more serious on the civil side. For instance, the period of time from a personal injury to a trial is usually far longer than the period from a criminal offense to a trial—a significant matter since witnesses' recollections deteriorate. Furthermore, in such areas as product liability, civil cases can involve issues of technical complexity that create special problems of understanding for both judges and juries. As in criminal law, some commentators regard juries as less capable than judges in personal injury cases. Indeed, some judges and lawyers have proposed that the right to jury trials be eliminated in some civil cases, particularly those involving highly complex issues. However, one scholar derived from the available evidence on civil and criminal cases "the unexpected conclusion that juries are one of our society's most reliable decision-making institutions."[90]

Successful personal injury plaintiffs may face two kinds of difficulties in collecting the money they have been awarded. In the small minority of cases involving uninsured defendants, who often have very low incomes, the defendant may be unwilling or unable to pay the plaintiff. This problem seldom exists in cases with businesses as defendants, but those defendants may delay payment through appeals, and payment may be reduced through the judge's modification of a jury award, a decision on appeal, or a post-trial settlement. One study of California and Illinois jury trials found that defendants in personal injury cases ultimately paid an average of 79 percent of the original amount awarded by the jury.[91]

Some personal injury cases stand out for their massive size. These cases can stem from major accidents, such as fires in public places and airline crashes. Some of the largest cases involve "toxic torts"—injuries allegedly caused by products such as the chemical dioxin and intrauterine contraceptive devices. These "cases" are often composed of many individual cases; some are consolidated through various mechanisms.

The processing of these massive cases generally looks quite different from the handling of ordinary injury cases. Settlement negotiations tend to be far more intensive, both because of the difficulty of reaching a settlement and because of the high stakes involved. In order to avoid long and costly trials, judges often make special efforts to secure settlements. In the suit brought by Vietnam veterans against chemical companies over health damage allegedly caused by the herbicide Agent Orange, federal Judge Jack Weinstein worked hard and exerted considerable pressure on both sides to settle; they ultimately signed an agreement between 3 and 4 a.m. on the day the trial was to begin.[92] In large cases, settlements often include a secrecy agreement concerning evidence discovered in the case or the monetary terms of settlement, primarily to protect defendants such as manufacturers from the use of that information in other cases. This practice has been criticized a good deal, and some states have limited the use of such agreements.[93]

When efforts to reach a settlement in massive cases fail, a trial may take considerable time. The spillage of dioxin in a train derailment resulted in an Illinois trial that lasted for three and a half years, a U.S. record. In cases with big stakes, jury verdicts are especially vulnerable to being overturned by trial or appellate judges. One lawyer who represents plaintiffs complained in 1991 that "the big cases involving big money are decided by the appeals courts"; a few months later the jury award of $16 million in the Illinois dioxin case was overturned by an appellate court.[94]

Brief Trials and Defendant Defaults: Debt Collection

Civil cases involving small amounts of money often go through pretrial stages fairly quickly, with a small proportion of settlements and little involvement on the part of the court. Trials are usually abbreviated and relatively informal, and many defendants lose by default because they fail to take the required actions before the trial or fail to appear at the trial. Most cases of this type fall in the general category of debt collection, in which businesses seek to recover money that is allegedly owed to them by individuals or seek another remedy such as eviction of a tenant. Along with landlords, businesses such as retail stores and commercial lenders bring debt collection cases with some frequency.[95]

Like other categories of cases, those involving debt collection constitute only a small portion of the total that might be filed as lawsuits. Most disputes are settled through some means other than litigation. However, creditors do file enough claims to fill a substantial portion of civil court dockets. Indeed, one study of major trial courts in three cities found that a majority of all cases filed were for debt collection.[96] Dockets in many small claims courts consist primarily of business actions to collect debts from individuals; although small claims courts were created to facilitate litigation by nonwealthy individuals, they have also provided attractive forums for business creditors.[97]

In the pretrial stage of debt collection cases, a great many defendants fail to take the necessary action to protect their positions in court. Defendants are supposed to receive a summons and then appear in court to file an answer, but in practice a good deal of slippage occurs in both these steps. A study of debtor defendants in Chicago, Detroit, and New York found that 30 percent of the defendants claimed not to have received a summons. The proportion was highest in New York, where there is considerable evidence that process servers routinely fail to perform their duty. (In one case, a New York process server swore under oath that he had served a subpoena on a person at his residence, when that person had moved to Los Angeles a month earlier.)[98] But even when people were served with a summons, only 28 percent of them appeared in court, and only 26 percent of those who appeared actually filed an answer. Altogether, then, the proportion of defendants who filed an answer in court was only 5 percent.[99]

Aside from the absence of a summons, the failure of a defendant to file an answer can result from several conditions: the debtor may not understand what is required, may fear going to court, or may feel that no effective defense is possible. The low proportions of defendants who have attorneys and the high proportions who have low incomes and limited education help to account for these conditions.

The defendant's failure to file an answer to the complaint allows the plaintiff to win a default judgment. There are several other ways in which cases can be resolved without full trials. Some defendants who have filed answers nonetheless lose default judgments because they fail to appear for the trial. The creditor may win a summary judgment based on the inadequacy of the defendant's answer, which is especially likely if the defendant has drafted that answer without a lawyer's help. Some debtors contact their creditors and reach a settlement prior to trial.

Faced with heavy caseloads, judges often make active efforts to avoid trials. Increasingly, courts that hear debt collection cases divert these cases either to mandatory or to voluntary arbitration systems. Some judges pressure litigants who appear for trial to reach settlements instead. David Caplovitz reported the following pattern in New York City:

> When the debtor does appear for a trial, he is usually summoned to the bench by the judge, who is anxious to clear his calendar, and is told to go out into the hall and work out a settlement with the plaintiff's lawyer. . . . A visitor to the civil court of New York will observe on any given day a score or more of these negotiation conferences taking place in the halls. It is this calendar-clearing practice of judges that no doubt inspired Lenny Bruce, the comedian, to observe that in the Halls of Justice, the only justice is in the halls.[100]

Some cases do go to contested trials, although the proportion is fairly small; in the study of Chicago, Detroit, and New York, discussed earlier, it was estimated to be as low as 1 percent.[101] Ordinarily, the judge conducts such a trial rather informally, without a jury, and trials usually require only part of a court day. All this is especially true of small claims courts, in which the frequent absence of attorneys further speeds proceedings; a debt collection case in a small claims court may require only a few minutes to try.

The enforcement of judgments against defendants in debt collection frequently presents a problem for victorious plaintiffs. Many debtors lack the money to pay a judgment readily, and some are unwilling to pay even if they can do so. Creditors then must resort to formal mechanisms to recover what they are owed. For example, the garnishment of wages from debtors who are employed is a common action. Despite the use of these mechanisms, many judgments simply cannot be collected. In one study of Iowa small claims courts, only 28 percent of the businesses that won cases against individuals collected all the money they were awarded, and 61 percent collected none at all.[102]

Court Ratification of Pretrial Settlements: Divorce

As noted earlier, divorce is an unusual type of litigation, in the sense that people who wish to terminate a marriage officially must file cases in court.

Traditionally, the laws of most states required not only that divorce cases go to court but also that they take the appearance of a contest; a divorce could be granted only when one spouse proved that the other was at fault under the law. Frequently, however, the spouses worked together to frame the evidence so as to prove that fault.

Because of legal changes since the late 1960s, every state now allows divorces (sometimes called dissolutions) without the showing of fault.[103] Rather, depending on the state, the party or parties seeking a divorce must simply show that the marriage has broken down irretrievably, that there are irreconcilable differences between the spouses, or that they have lived apart for a specified period of time. If only one of the spouses seeks a divorce, the other may have the right to contest it, but the new grounds make it difficult to oppose a divorce petition successfully. If the spouses agree to obtain a divorce, under some circumstances in some states they need not actually appear in court. However, many states, while allowing "no-fault" divorces, have retained the old fault-based grounds as well.

Aside from granting the divorce, the courts must deal with the economic issues of property division and alimony. Where children are involved, their custody and support must also be determined. Judges approve or disapprove agreements between the spouses on these issues and adjudicate cases in which no agreement is reached.

In perhaps 90 percent of all divorce cases, the parties reach agreement on all the issues outside of court.[104] These agreements often are achieved after long and difficult negotiation because divorce and the issues associated with it usually have enormous concrete and emotional stakes for the parties. Some states have sought to facilitate out-of-court settlement by requiring mediation between the parties; this requirement has aroused opposition from those who see mandatory mediation as advantaging the stronger partner in the marriage.[105] It is uncommon for judges to disapprove these agreements. In one sample of Wisconsin cases, for instance, judges refused to approve only one of more than three hundred agreements between the parties.[106] And the judge's scrutiny of an agreement is usually perfunctory.

This does not mean that the law and the courts have no effect on cases settled between the parties. As two legal scholars note, divorcing parents "bargain in the shadow of the law," with the strength of their positions affected by what each would get if the case went to trial.[107] Yet expectations of what would happen in court do not fully govern settlements outside of court, particularly if there seems little chance that a case actually will be contested in court. Other factors, such as the bargaining skills of the two sides, also come into play.

In the minority of cases that do go to trial, the law gives judges a great deal of discretion over issues such as alimony and child custody. Inevitably, their decisions about these issues are influenced by their personal values on such matters as the relative fitness of mothers and fathers as parents. Judges are also affected by the terms of the settlements they approve in uncontested cases, which help set their expectations as to how they should decide cases.[108] Thus, as in other areas of law, out-of-court settlements and judges' decisions affect each other in significant ways.

Noncompliance with court decrees in divorce cases is a common problem. Parents frequently violate agreements concerning custody and visitation rights, and "child-stealing" to overcome court judgments has become a highly visible phenomenon. A large proportion of people required to pay alimony or child support meet that obligation only in part or not at all, and noncompliance with that obligation becomes more common over the years after a divorce.

Efforts by courts and other government agencies to secure compliance with the terms of divorce decrees, traditionally quite weak, have increased in recent years. This is especially true of child support, as Congress and the state legislatures have adopted a number of laws to improve compliance. One example is the provision of federal law that requires deduction of child support from the paychecks of parents who are not in compliance with support orders. This legislation has not been entirely effective; in 1991 the Secretary of Health and Human Services reported that the government's level of success in collecting child support was still "abysmal."[109] It is noteworthy that some private firms now offer to track down noncompliant parents for a fee.[110]

Both noncompliance with court orders and other problems can create conflicts between the former spouses after a divorce is granted. These conflicts frequently lead one or both parties to seek court action, and several studies suggest that such action occurs in 20 percent or more of all divorces.[111] Thus divorce illustrates particularly well the fact that legal decrees may not fully resolve the problems that brought people to court.

WINNERS AND LOSERS

Political scientist Harold D. Lasswell defined politics as "who gets what, when, how."[112] In the sense of that definition, American civil trial courts are deeply enmeshed in politics. One of their main functions is the allocation of gains and losses, ranging from money to custody over children and commitments to mental institutions. Furthermore, the prospect of action by civil courts affects a much larger number of allocations that are made outside of court. Thus it is important to look at the patterns of outcomes in cases that go to court and those that might have gone to court.

Earlier in the chapter I discussed Marc Galanter's argument that "the 'haves' come out ahead"—that those who come to court with more resources than their opponents tend to prevail in court. Galanter's argument directs our attention to the relationship between resources and success, not only in cases that go to court but also in the cases that could have gone to court. The available evidence is both limited and ambiguous, but it allows some partial and tentative conclusions.

Personal Injuries

In most fields, the cases that courts actually decide are a small sample of the matters that could have gone to court; since some kinds of matters are more likely to end up in court than others, these cases are also unrepresentative of all potential cases. For that reason, we must be careful about our inferences from court decisions. This is especially true in personal injury law, where trials are relatively rare. Still, it is useful to look at what we know about jury decisions in this field, primarily from a set of studies in the first half of the 1980s.[113]

There is considerable variation in the outcomes from one type of case to another. Overall, injured parties seem to win a small majority of cases, but over a five-year period in Cook County (Chicago), the proportion of plaintiff victories varied from 72 percent for injuries at work to 49 percent for medical malpractice.[114] Similarly, the mean amount—the arithmetic average—awarded to successful plaintiffs in San Francisco during that period was $1.1 million (in 1984 dollars) in product liability cases and $131,000 in auto accidents. The mean is affected considerably by the largest verdicts; the median award was considerably smaller, $29,000, in auto accident cases.[115]

Plaintiffs are more successful in some places than in others. In the 1980–1984 period, for instance, the median amount awarded to plaintiffs in motor vehicle accidents in Los Angeles was more than twice as high as in Phoenix and more than five times as high as in Chicago.[116] Differences in state laws and jurors' attitudes help produce such differences.

There is a widespread perception among insurance companies and the groups they defend that juries have become increasingly sympathetic to injured parties. By and large, the available evidence supports this perception, particularly in "high-stakes" fields such as product liability and medical malpractice. In Cook County, in the period 1980–1984, the mean amount won by plaintiffs in jury trials, including those who won nothing, was four times what it had been in the years 1960–1964 (taking inflation into account); in San Francisco the increase was more than fivefold.[117] But these findings might be deceptive because cases during the two periods may not be comparable.[118]

Groups that represent defendants in personal injury cases have sought to reverse the perceived trend favoring plaintiffs, primarily through changes in legal rules. These groups have enjoyed some success in state legislatures. In medical malpractice, for instance, a number of states have adopted measures intended to make it more difficult for patients to bring and win lawsuits, such as reductions in the length of time after medical treatment that people are given to file suits.[119] It appears that at least some of these new rules do produce more favorable outcomes for defendants.[120] In recent years these groups have worked to obtain federal legal rules that favor their interests, but they have not yet been successful.[121]

Some studies have looked more broadly at personal injury claims, whether or not these claims result in trials. We know enough to reach some tentative conclusions about auto accidents, the most common source of personal injury cases.[122]

First, most people recover something for their injuries—through a settlement with another party, through other sources such as their own insurance, or both. But at least a substantial minority of people with serious injuries receive nothing from the other party, sometimes because they lose in court.

Second, the law has considerable effect on what people recover, even in the cases that do not go to trial. Where a defendant seems to be legally liable for an accident, the injured party is more likely to receive something in an out-of-court settlement and tends to receive a larger amount. Similarly, people with the greatest expenses for their injuries generally are entitled to recover the most under the law, if the defendant is found liable; they also receive the most when they settle out of court.

Third, despite this tendency, in an important sense those with the most serious injuries do least well. While people with minor losses frequently recover more money than they lost, thereby gaining some compensation for their nonmonetary costs, the people who are most seriously hurt typically receive only a fraction of their costs from the other party—though other sources of payment reduce this gap somewhat.[123] One reason is that minor claims have nuisance value: it is cheaper for insurance companies to offer generous settlements than to bear the costs of going to court. In contrast, people with more severe losses suffer from the opposite situation: insurance companies can discount their offers in such cases because the injured party wishes to avoid the costs of going to court to receive full compensation. Besides, the costs of a serious accident may exceed the limits on the defendant's insurance coverage.

Fourth, lawyers have dual economic effects. Injured parties who are represented by attorneys do better than unrepresented parties, presumably because of lawyers' effectiveness in bargaining and in threatening court action. But lawyers' fees take up a significant part of what clients recover, a part that averages a quarter or more of the settlement.[124]

Overall, according to one study, people injured in auto accidents recover 70 percent of their costs from some source, and about one-third of this total comes from legal claims against other parties. The 70 percent recovery is somewhat better than the 62 percent rate for all personal injuries.[125]

Personal injury claims generally pit prosperous insurance companies against individuals of varying incomes. Do insurance companies—the haves—usually come out ahead? Personal injury plaintiffs certainly hold their own in court, and they receive a good deal of money from actual and potential defendants through their insurance companies. But on the whole, payments for personal injury claims leave a considerable gap between the costs that individuals bear for accidents and their compensation for those costs. Thus the overall picture is mixed and ambiguous; it is not clear whether the haves should be viewed as successful.

Debt Collection

As noted in the discussion of debt collection litigation, defendants frequently fail to protect their rights by making necessary court appearances and taking other required actions. Consequently, creditors win a great many cases without opposition. Even when debtors do contest claims at trial, their creditors usually win.

On the whole, then, creditors do quite well in court. A study of Chicago, Detroit, and New York courts found that the debtor won only 3 percent of the time; in about 90 percent of the cases in each city, the creditor won a default judgment.[126] In a study of major trial courts in Cleveland, Milwaukee, and Baltimore, Craig Wanner found a similar success rate. Wanner also calculated that business creditors as a group recovered more money than what they originally claimed was owed to them. This seemingly impossible result is explained chiefly by court penalties against defendants for such items as interest, late-payment charges, and attorneys' fees.[127] Both studies may overstate the success of business creditors, but it is clearly very high.

However, the difficulty of actually collecting what the courts award must be taken into account. Although businesses do better than individuals in this regard, a significant proportion of money awarded to them does not get collected. This slippage is an important exception to the general effectiveness with which businesses use the courts for debt collection.

Business success in debt collection can be interpreted in quite different ways. On the one hand, we might see it as meaning simply that a set of litigants with very strong cases are able to use the courts effectively to secure their rights. According to this interpretation, consumers and borrowers agree to pay money; they fail to do so; and the courts, when requested to rule that debtors are obliged to pay, do so. Thus the courts are operating as they should in cases where there is little ambiguity about the law and the facts.

However, under another interpretation, the courts are not operating in so benign a fashion. From this perspective, business creditors have strong cases partly because they have shaped the law in their favor through lobbying in the legislature and through past advocacy in the courts and partly because they can arrange transactions so as to leave debtors with little basis for a defense. Furthermore, some debtors have potentially strong defenses under the law, but they are unable to protect their interests in the courts because of a lack of legal knowledge and access to lawyers and a lack of sympathy on the part of court personnel. In contrast, creditors develop expertise in using the courts and credibility with judges. And because of their backgrounds and experiences, many judges begin with a predisposition to favor creditors. Given all these factors, some commentators view the success of business creditors as at least partially undeserved. Indeed, one student of small claims courts referred to their "persecution and intimidation of the low-income litigant" in debt collection cases.[128]

This second interpretation fits neatly into Galanter's framework of analysis. Debt collection cases are a particularly clear example of a conflict between haves and have-nots. Business creditors enjoy all the advantages of haves, including their status as repeat players, while the defendants are primarily low-income individuals and one-shotters with limited resources and capacities to use the courts. Because of this disparity, the haves are quite successful.

People who see the success of business creditors as less than fully justified have sought to improve the position of debtors in court. They have made several kinds of proposals, many of which have been adopted to some degree. For example, federally funded legal services for the poor have given some debtors a better chance to defend themselves. Many courts have made procedural changes, such as improvements in the serving of summonses. In addition, some states have made the law more favorable to consumers and debtors. For instance, the inadequacy of goods and the failure to repair an apartment have been adopted as defenses in debt cases.

Thus far such changes have had only a limited impact because they have been insufficient to overcome the cumulative advantages of creditors over debtors. For example, even after Michigan law was changed to provide more defenses for tenants in eviction and payment cases, landlords continued to enjoy a very high level of success; the other disadvantages of tenants, such as limited access to lawyers, continued to exert an impact.[129] More far-reaching changes, both in government policy and in the organization of low-income people, might be sufficient to alter the general pattern of outcomes in debt collection cases; such changes, however, seem unlikely to occur.[130] The high rate of victories that creditors secure in court may or may not be desirable, depending on our perspective. In either case, we can expect this rate to continue.

Divorce

One important outcome of divorce proceedings is that people who want divorces usually get them; this is increasingly true since the advent of the movement toward no-fault divorce. Depending on the circumstances, the ease of divorce can favor either or both parties.

A second outcome is that mothers usually receive physical custody of children (that is, children live only or primarily with their mothers), perhaps 85 to 90 percent of the time.[131] (Although many states now encourage joint legal custody arrangements, children generally are put in the physical custody of a single parent.)[132] But since custody is seldom actually contested in court, it is difficult to judge what this percentage means in terms of winners and losers. Traditionally, courts have given preference to mothers, particularly for custody of younger children. For this reason, even a father who would like to obtain custody may not seek it. In fact, attorneys for fathers often convince their clients that a custody battle would be not only expensive and unpleasant but probably futile as well. Yet some fathers may not seek custody because they would prefer not to take that responsibility.

The economics of divorce are also complex. In most instances, if the court transferred no money from one partner to the other, the woman would be at a great disadvantage. If a woman is employed full-time when the divorce occurs, her income is likely to be considerably lower than that of her husband. Many women have part-time employment or no employment, and if they take a full-time job after a divorce, it probably will be a low-paying one. Since women are far more likely to have custody of children, they also bear the costs of their care.

To some degree, this situation is alleviated by the payment of alimony and child support. But such payments are fairly limited.[133] Alimony is awarded in less than one-fifth of all divorces, and generally it is allowed for relatively short periods. Most divorced women with custody of children are awarded child support. But the levels of child support awarded, like the levels of alimony, tend to be low. Many women entitled to child support and alimony receive only part of the amount to which they are entitled or none at all; about one-half of the women who are supposed to receive child support get the full amount due, one-quarter get a portion of what is due, and one-quarter get no payments at all.

As a result, on average, the money transferred from former husbands to former wives is insufficient to compensate for the differences in their earnings from employment and for the costs of raising children. Indeed, a number of studies have shown that—at least for the first few years after divorce—former husbands generally end up in a considerably better economic position than do former wives.[134]

When larger awards of alimony and child support are necessary to produce economic equality between the former spouses, why are they not typically made? Some observers argue that no-fault divorce laws are a major cause of this situation because they reduced the bargaining leverage and economic rights of women who were "innocent parties" in a divorce; others disagree.[135] It does appear that most divorced women end up worse off economically than their former husbands under any divorce system; in the words of one scholar, "the economic situation of women and children . . . was bad before no fault, and it continues to be bad now."[136] This situation may well stem most fundamentally from judges' reluctance to require that men pay a large share of their income in alimony and child support, which makes it very difficult for women to obtain that large share in negotiated settlements.

In the past few decades policy makers have taken some steps to improve the economic situation of divorced women. Most important, and largely as a result of federal rules, states have increased their efforts to enforce child support orders and have established guidelines for judges that tend to increase the levels of support. One study of three states found that guidelines did increase the average level of child support—by proportions ranging from 5 percent, in Colorado, to 28 percent, in Hawaii. Since the level of support had been highest in Colorado and lowest in Hawaii, the guidelines had an equalizing effect.[137]

The situation that exists now can be understood in terms of Galanter's haves and have-nots. Ordinarily, former husbands are in a better position to earn money than are their former wives, especially if the wives had left the work force during their marriage. Thus, without massive reallocations from husband to wife after divorce, the average woman will be worse off than her former husband, especially if she has children in her custody. The more limited reallocations typically made by the courts are insufficient to eliminate this gap.

An Overview

The three areas of court activity considered in this section, though quite significant, are not a representative sample of everything that civil courts do.

In particular, each is a private-law area, and I have not discussed the areas in which government plays a prominent role.

At the least, these three surveys suggest the difficulty of analyzing success in court and in matters affected by the courts. Depending on our concept of success and how we apply it, we might reach different conclusions about the success that a particular group of litigants enjoys.

The area of personal injuries is the most ambiguous. It is not entirely clear what should be the benchmark for success in negotiations and in court for people who have been injured; furthermore, the results are so mixed that any benchmark would be difficult to apply.

Divorce is also ambiguous. In divorce cases, a great deal of money is transferred from men to women, but divorced women on average seem to end up much less well off than the men. Which group is more successful in court? I would interpret the results to mean that it is former husbands who are more successful in the financial aspects of divorce, but some might disagree.

Debt collection seems clearest. Creditors have some difficulty in collecting the money that courts award them. With that exception, however, creditors appear to be highly successful in their use of the courts.

Because of the ambiguities that have been noted, as well as the gaps in our knowledge about the outcomes of litigation, some caution in assessing winners and losers is appropriate. But in one of the three areas discussed, and probably in a second, it can be said that the litigants starting out with an economic advantage generally enjoy success in court. If these three areas are fairly typical in this respect, it seems reasonable to conclude that in litigation the haves do tend to come out ahead.

CONCLUSIONS

This chapter has stressed the links between civil trial courts and American society as a whole. The discussion of winners and losers underlines the strength of these links.

The field of personal injury law illustrates the effects of courts on actions outside the judicial system. A very small proportion of injuries are the subject of court trials; the remainder are handled elsewhere. Yet the laws that courts apply and the decisions that they reach influence the resolution of claims and disputes that never come to court—because a dispute that is not resolved outside of court would be resolved on terms imposed by the courts. Although negotiated settlements certainly do not mirror court decisions perfectly, they are shaped by predictions of what would happen if cases went to court. It is through this indirect impact that the courts help allocate far more gains and losses than the number of trials suggests.

Conversely, the field of debt collection illustrates the impact of social realities on the courts. As we have seen, the outcomes of debt collection cases can be interpreted in different ways. But it is clear that creditors are far better able to defend their interests in court than are debtors. In turn, this advantage stems primarily from the differences in economic and social status between the two groups.

These kinds of links, of course, are not unique to the civil side of the law. As Chapter 6 indicates, the work of criminal courts is also linked to events and forces outside of court. But the ties between trial courts and their environments seem especially close in civil cases. Certainly, they make it clear that we can understand what courts do only in the context of the larger society in which they operate.

FOR FURTHER READING

Danzon, Patricia M. *Medical Malpractice: Theory, Evidence, and Public Policy.* Cambridge, Mass.: Harvard University Press, 1985.

Ellickson, Robert C. *Order Without Law: How Neighbors Settle Disputes.* Cambridge, Mass.: Harvard University Press, 1991.

Hensler, Deborah R., et al. *Compensation for Accidental Injuries in the United States.* Santa Monica, Calif.: Rand Corporation, 1991.

Kritzer, Herbert M. *Let's Make a Deal: Understanding the Negotiation Process in Ordinary Litigation.* Madison: University of Wisconsin Press, 1991.

Merry, Sally Engle. *Getting Justice and Getting Even: Legal Consciousness Among Working-Class Americans.* Chicago: University of Chicago Press, 1990.

Ross, H. Laurence. *Settled Out of Court: The Social Process of Insurance Claims Adjustment,* rev. 2d ed. New York: Aldine Publishing, 1980.

Sullivan, Teresa A., Elizabeth Warren, and Jay Lawrence Westbrook. *As We Forgive Our Debtors: Bankruptcy and Consumer Credit in America.* New York: Oxford University Press, 1992.

NOTES

1. Robert H. Mnookin and Lewis Kornhauser, "Bargaining in the Shadow of the Law: The Case of Divorce," *Yale Law Journal,* 88 (April 1979), 950–997.
2. Marc Galanter, "Why the 'Haves' Come Out Ahead: Speculations on the Limits of Legal Change," *Law and Society Review,* 9 (Fall 1974), 95–160.
3. Sources of information for this discussion include Dan B. Dobbs, *Handbook on the Law of Remedies* (Saint Paul: West Publishing, 1973), pp. 1–3.
4. Kenneth E. Scott, "Two Models of the Civil Process," *Stanford Law Review,* 27 (February 1975), 937–950.
5. See Peter H. Schuck, ed., *Tort Law and the Public Interest: Competition, Innovation, and Consumer Welfare* (New York: W. W. Norton, 1991).
6. Galanter, "Why the 'Haves' Come Out Ahead," p. 97.
7. Ibid., pp. 97–124.
8. The following descriptions of procedures are based in part on William P. McLauchlan, *American Legal Processes* (New York: John Wiley & Sons, 1977), ch. 3; and Mary Kay Kane, *Civil Procedure in a Nutshell,* 2d ed. (Saint Paul: West Publishing, 1985).
9. Geoffrey C. Hazard, Jr., "Depositions: Modern-Day Inquisitions," *National Law Journal,* March 14, 1988, p. 13.

10. *DF Activities Corporation v. Brown*, 851 F.2d 920, 923 (7th Cir. 1988); cited in Walter K. Olson, *The Litigation Explosion* (New York: Truman Talley Books, 1992), p. 117.

11. James S. Kakalik, Molly Selvin, and Nicholas M. Pace, *Averting Gridlock: Strategies for Reducing Civil Delay in the Los Angeles Superior Court* (Santa Monica, Calif.: Rand Corporation, 1990), p. 1.

12. Saundra Torry, "19 Years Later, Suit by Vietnam War Protesters Is Finally at Peace," *Washington Post*, November 19, 1990 (Washington Business section) p. 5; James Warren, "Books Are Closed on 1970 Case," *Chicago Tribune*, September 4, 1990, sec. 2, p. 1.

13. Terence Dungworth and Nicholas M. Pace, *Statistical Overview of Civil Litigation in the Federal Courts* (Santa Monica, Calif.: Rand Corporation, 1990), pp. 16–25.

14. Victor E. Flango, Robert T. Roper, and Mary E. Elsner, *The Business of State Trial Courts* (Williamsburg, Va.: National Center for State Courts, 1983), p. 33.

15. Paul Burstein and Kathleen Monaghan, "Equal Employment Opportunity and the Mobilization of Law," *Law and Society Review*, 20 (1986), 361.

16. Richard E. Miller and Austin Sarat, "Grievances, Claims, and Disputes: Assessing the Adversary Culture," *Law and Society Review*, 15 (1980–81), 544; Herbert M. Kritzer, Neil Vidmar, and W. A. Bogart, "To Confront Or Not to Confront: Measuring Claiming Rates in Discrimination Grievances," *Law and Society Review*, 25 (1991), 883.

17. Randall Samborn, "Many Americans Find Bias at Work," *National Law Journal*, July 16, 1990, p. 1.

18. See Kristin Bumiller, *The Civil Rights Society: The Social Construction of Victims* (Baltimore: Johns Hopkins University Press, 1988), pp. 27–28.

19. Sharon Walsh, "The Vanishing Job-Bias Lawyers," *Washington Post*, July 6, 1990, pp. C1, C2.

20. Miller and Sarat, "Grievances, Claims, and Disputes," p. 541; see George R. LaNoue and Barbara A. Lee, *Academics in Court: The Consequences of Faculty Discrimination Litigation* (Ann Arbor: University of Michigan Press, 1987), pp. 224–227.

21. Ruth Marcus, "Legal Profession Draws Criticism for Quick Response When Disaster Strikes," *Washington Post*, January 9, 1987, pp. A1, A20.

22. Miller and Sarat, "Grievances, Claims, and Disputes," p. 544.

23. Deborah R. Hensler et al., *Compensation for Accidental Injuries in the United States* (Santa Monica, Calif.: Rand Corporation, 1991), p. 122.

24. This discussion of auto accident cases draws from Miller and Sarat, "Grievances, Claims, and Disputes"; Hensler et al., *Compensation for Accidental Injuries;* All-Industry Research Advisory Council, *Compensation for Automobile Injuries in the United States* (Oak Brook, Ill.: AIRAC, 1989); and especially H. Laurence Ross, *Settled Out of Court: The Social Process of Insurance Claims Adjustment,* rev. 2d ed. (New York: Aldine Publishing, 1980).

25. All-Industry Research Advisory Council, *Compensation for Automobile Injuries,* p. 115.

26. Ibid., p. 115.

27. Ross, *Settled Out of Court,* pp. 215–224.

28. Patricia M. Danzon, *Medical Malpractice: Theory, Evidence, and Public Policy* (Cambridge, Mass.: Harvard University Press, 1985), pp. 18–29, 59–63; A. Russell Localio et al., "Relation Between Malpractice Claims and Adverse Events Due to Negligence," *New England Journal of Medicine*, 325 (July 25, 1991), 247; Michael J. Saks, "Do We Really Know Anything About the Behavior of the Tort Litigation System—And Why Not?" *University of Pennsylvania Law Review*, 140 (April 1992), 1194.

29. Harvard Medical Practice Study Group, *Patients, Doctors, and Lawyers: Medical Injury, Malpractice Litigation, and Patient Compensation in New York* (duplicated, 1990), pp. 7–1, 7–7, 7–28, 7–36; the study is also reported in Localio et al., "Relation Between Malpractice Claims."

30. Mark Crane, "Lawyers Don't Take *Every* Case," *National Law Journal*, January 25, 1988, pp. 1, 34.

31. Stewart Macauley, "Non-Contractual Relations in Business: A Preliminary Study," *American Sociological Review*, 28 (February 1963), 61.

32. Robert C. Ellickson, *Order Without Law: How Neighbors Settle Disputes* (Cambridge, Mass.: Harvard University Press, 1991), pp. 52–55.

33. "Coke Is Sued by Seven-Up," *New York Times*, February 28, 1992, p. C6.

34. Ross E. Cheit, "Patterns of Contemporary Business Litigation in Rhode Island" (Paper presented at the 1990 meeting of the Law and Society Association in Berkeley, California), pp. 36–38.

35. Miller and Sarat, "Grievances, Claims, and Disputes," p. 544; Joel B. Grossman, Herbert M. Kritzer, Kristin Bumiller, Austin Sarat, Stephen McDougal, and Richard Miller, "Dimensions of Institutional Participation: Who Uses the Courts and How?" *Journal of Politics*, 44 (February 1982), 105.

36. Court Statistics Project, *State Court Caseload Statistics: Annual Report 1990* (Williamsburg, Va.: National Center for State Courts, 1992), p. 4.

37. Richard Neely, *How Courts Govern America* (New Haven: Yale University Press, 1981), p. xiv.

38. Ambrose Bierce, *The Devil's Dictionary: A Selection of the Bitter Definitions of Ambrose Bierce* (Mount Vernon, N.Y.: Peter Pauper Press, 1958), p.37.

39. Sally Engle Merry, *Getting Justice and Getting Even: Legal Consciousness Among Working-Class Americans* (Chicago: University of Chicago Press, 1990), p. 3.

40. Marc Galanter, "Reading the Landscape of Disputes: What We Know and Don't Know (and Think We Know) About Our Allegedly Contentious and Litigious Society," *UCLA Law Review*, 31 (October 1983), 24.

41. Merry, *Getting Justice and Getting Even*, pp. 142–143.

42. Chuck Shepherd, "News of the Weird," *The Reader* (Chicago), December 20, 1991, sec. 3, p. 31.

43. Laura A. Kiernan, "Judge Bars Amateur Lawyers from U.S. Court as Nuisance," *Washington Post*, June 16, 1980, pp. C1, C3.

44. Peter Applebome, "Coke in Bitter Legal Fight Over Cost of Sweetener," *New York Times*, September 22, 1989, p. B20; Warren Brown, "Bitterness at Benetton," *Washington Post*, July 30, 1989, pp. H1, H4.

45. Kevin J. Delaney, *Strategic Bankruptcy: How Corporations and Creditors Use Chapter 11 to Their Advantage* (Berkeley: University of California Press, 1992).

46. Eric Freedman, "Non-Death Be Not Proud," *National Law Journal*, May 18, 1992, p. 47.

47. Andrew Blum, "SLAPP Suits Continue in High Gear," *National Law Journal*, May 18, 1992, p. 3.

48. See Austin Sarat and Joel B. Grossman, "Courts and Conflict Resolution: Problems in the Mobilization of Adjudication," *American Political Science Review*, 69 (December 1975), 1200–1217.

49. Roselle Wissler, Gilbert Cranberg, John Soloski, Brian Murchison, and Randall Bezanson, "Resolving Libel Cases Out of Court: How Attorneys View the Libel Dispute Resolution Program," *Judicature*, 75 (April–May 1992), 329–333.

50. David W. Ewing, *Justice on the Job: Resolving Grievances in the Nonunion Workplace* (Boston: Harvard Business School Press, 1989); Sherwood Ross, "More Companies Giving Workers Their Day in Court," *San Francisco Chronicle*, May 6, 1992, pp. D1, D2.

51. Jean Guccione, "Selling Justice," *California Lawyer*, 11 (October 1991), pp. 32–36.

52. *Shearson/American Express, Inc. v. McMahon*, 482 U.S. 220, 261 (1987) (emphasis in original).

53. U.S. General Accounting Office, *Securities Arbitration: How Investors Fare* (Washington, D.C.: General Accounting Office, 1992).

54. Linda Greenhouse, "1871 Rights Law Used for Many Cases," *New York Times*, August 26, 1988, p. B6.
55. Gary Webb, "Police Oppose Bill Shielding Complainants," *San Jose Mercury News*, August 5, 1992, p. 3B.
56. Sandra Evans, "Small Claims Court Proves Popular in Fairfax Test," *Washington Post*, November 27, 1989, p. D4.
57. See Thomas E. Willging, *The Rule 11 Sanctioning Process* (Washington, D.C.: Federal Judicial Center, 1988); and Stephen B. Burbank, *Rule 11 in Transition: The Report of the Third Circuit Task Force on Federal Rule of Civil Procedure 11* (Chicago: American Judicature Society, 1989).
58. Gail Diane Cox, "Innovation—Or Just Court Triage?" *National Law Journal*, October 5, 1992, pp. 1, 10, 11.
59. *Moncharsh v. Heily & Blase*, 832 P.2d 899, 900 (Cal. 1992).
60. Bayless Manning, "Hyperlexis: Our National Disease," *Northwestern University Law Review*, 71 (January–February 1977), 772.
61. Lois Forer, *The Death of the Law* (New York: David McKay, 1975), p. 133.
62. See, respectively, Laura Blumenfeld, "Case Dismissed! Those Loopy Lawsuits," *Washington Post*, August 30, 1991, p. C1; "Florida Man Says He Got Clipped," *Chicago Tribune*, July 28, 1991, sec. 1, p. 3. "Suit: Grass Always Longer on Other Side," *Chicago Tribune*, June 16, 1991, sec. 1, p. 18; and Debra Carr, "Lawsuit: Newspapers' Horoscopes Turn Into Horrorscope for Detroit Man," *National Law Journal*, March 23, 1992, p. 47.
63. Galanter, "Reading the Landscape of Disputes," pp. 51–61.
64. Robert A. Kagan, "Adversarial Legalism and American Government," *Journal of Policy Analysis and Management*, 10 (1991), 369–406.
65. *Ibid.*, pp. 386–397.
66. See V. Lee Hamilton and Joseph Sanders, *Everyday Justice: Responsibility and the Individual in Japan and the United States* (New Haven, Conn.: Yale University Press, 1992), pp. 186–202.
67. Chuck Shepherd, "News of the Weird," *Funny Times*, June 1992, p. 21.
68. George Kalogerakis, "Those Who Can, Sue," *Spy Magazine*, June 1989, p. 94.
69. Galanter, "Reading the Landscape of Disputes," pp. 10–11.
70. Larry Rohter, "Boy Allowed to Sue for Separation from Parents," *New York Times*, July 10, 1992, p. A12.
71. Murray Chass, "There's No Joy in Mudville? Sue for Mental Anguish," *New York Times*, August 21, 1992, p. B9.
72. Harold Seymour, *Baseball: The Golden Age* (New York: Oxford University Press, 1971).
73. Court Statistics Project, *State Court Caseload Statistics 1990*, p. 15; Thomas B. Marvell, "Caseload Growth—Past and Future Trends," *Judicature*, 71 (October–November 1987), 160.
74. *Annual Report of the Director of the Administrative Office of the United States Courts, 1991* (Washington, D.C.: Government Printing Office, 1992), p. 190; *Annual Report of the Administrative Office, 1986* (Washington, D.C.: Government Printing Office, 1987), p. 175.
75. Galanter, "Reading the Landscape of Disputes," p. 4; *Annual Report of the Administrative Office, 1991*, p. 208.
76. See Saks, "Do We Really Know Anything," 1206–1207.
77. Court Statistics Project, *State Court Caseload Statistics 1990*, p. 25.
78. Wayne McIntosh, "150 Years of Litigation and Dispute Settlement: A Court Tale," *Law and Society Review*, 15 (1980–1981), 823–848; Lawrence M. Friedman and Robert V. Percival, "A Tale of Two Courts: Litigation in Alameda and San Benito Counties," *Law and Society Review*, 10 (Winter 1976), 267–301; Stephen Daniels, "Caseload Dynamics and the Nature of Change: The Civil Business of Trial Courts in Four Illinois Counties," *Law and Society Review*, 24 (1990), 299–320.

79. William Mullen, "U.S. Seeks a Cure to Legal Dilemma," *Chicago Tribune*, July 26, 1991, sec. 1, p. 1.

80. David M. Engel and Eric H. Steele, "Civil Cases and Society: Process and Order in the Civil Justice System," *American Bar Foundation Research Journal*, Spring 1979, 307–311.

81. Sources of information for this discussion include Herbert M. Kritzer, *Let's Make a Deal: Understanding the Negotiation Process in Ordinary Litigation* (Madison: University of Wisconsin Press, 1991); Miller and Sarat, "Grievances, Claims, and Disputes"; and Ross, *Settled Out of Court*.

82. Edward A. Adams, "The System Works, But Are Clients Served?" *National Law Journal*, April 29, 1985, p. 42.

83. David B. Rottman, "Tort Litigation in the State Courts: Evidence From the Trial Court Information Network," *State Court Journal*, 14 (Fall 1990), 9.

84. Kritzer, *Let's Make a Deal*, p. 130.

85. Ted Rohrlich, "The Case of the Missing Jurors . . ." *Los Angeles Times*, May 19, 1990, p. A27.

86. *United States Code*, Title 28, Federal Rules of Civil Procedure, Rule 68.

87. Kritzer, *Let's Make a Deal*, pp. 32, 38, 65.

88. Kevin M. Clermont and Theodore Eisenberg, "Trial by Jury or Judge: Transcending Empiricism," *Cornell Law Review*, 77 (July 1992), 1124–1177.

89. Theodore Eisenberg and James A. Henderson, Jr., "Inside the Quiet Revolution in Products Liability," *UCLA Law Review*, 39 (April 1992), 791–794; Neil Vidmar, "The Unfair Criticism of Medical Malpractice Juries," *Judicature*, 76 (October–November 1992), 120–121.

90. Saks, "Do We Really Know Anything," p. 1239.

91. Michael G. Shanley and Mark A. Peterson, *Posttrial Adjustments to Jury Awards* (Santa Monica, Calif.: Rand Corporation, 1987), p. 36.

92. Peter H. Schuck, *Agent Orange on Trial: Mass Toxic Disasters in the Courts* (Cambridge, Mass.: Harvard University Press, 1986), pp. 143–167.

93. Philip L. Corboy, "Masked and Muzzled, Litigants Tell No Evil: Is This Blind Justice?" *Legal Times*, January 8, 1990, pp. 27–28.

94. Amy Dockser Marcus, "Few Large Jury Awards Survive Appeal," *Wall Street Journal*, January 28, 1991, p. B6; "Dioxin Verdict Following 3–1/2-Year Trial is Voided," *New York Times*, June 13, 1991, p. A10.

95. This discussion is based in part on David Caplovitz, *Consumers in Trouble: A Study of Debtors in Default* (New York: Free Press, 1974).

96. Craig Wanner, "The Public Ordering of Private Relations. Part One: Initiating Civil Cases in Urban Trial Courts," *Law and Society Review*, 8 (Spring 1974), 422.

97. Barbara Yngvesson and Patricia Hennessey, "Small Claims, Complex Disputes: A Review of the Small Claims Literature," *Law and Society Review*, 9 (Winter 1975), 235–243; Project, "The Iowa Small Claims Court: An Empirical Analysis," *Iowa Law Review*, 75 (January 1990), 483–488.

98. John Gregory Dunne, *Quintana and Friends* (New York: E. P. Dutton, 1978), pp. 243–244.

99. Caplovitz, *Consumers in Trouble*, p. 215.

100. Ibid., pp. 218–219.

101. Ibid., p. 220.

102. Project, "The Iowa Small Claims Court," p. 521.

103. See Herbert Jacob, *Silent Revolution: The Transformation of Divorce Law in the United States* (Chicago: University of Chicago Press, 1988).

104. Kenneth Kressel, *The Process of Divorce: How Professionals and Couples Negotiate Settlements* (New York: Basic Books, 1985), pp. 7–10.

105. Florence Hamlish Levinsohn, "Breaking Up is *Still* Hard to Do," *Chicago Tribune Magazine*, October 21, 1990, p. 23.

106. Marygold S. Melli, Howard S. Erlanger, and Elizabeth Chambliss, "The Process of Negotiation: An Exploratory Investigation in the Context of No-Fault Divorce," *Rutgers Law Review*, 40 (Summer 1988), 1145.

107. Mnookin and Kornhauser, "Bargaining in the Shadow of the Law," 968.
108. Melli, Erlanger, and Chambliss, "Process of Negotiation," p. 1147.
109. Paul Taylor, "Child Support System Called 'Abysmal,' " *Washington Post*, April 6, 1991, p. A9.
110. Sandra Evans, "Company Makes It Its Business to Get Overdue Child Support," *Washington Post*, April 13, 1992, pp. B1, B7.
111. Miller and Sarat, "Grievances, Claims, and Disputes," pp. 544–546; Kressel, *Process of Divorce*, pp. 10–13.
112. Harold D. Lasswell, *Politics: Who Gets What, When, How* (New York: P. Smith, 1950).
113. This discussion of jury decisions is based primarily on Mark A. Peterson, *Civil Juries in the 1980s: Trends in Jury Trials and Verdicts in California and Cook County, Illinois* (Santa Monica, Calif: Rand Corporation, 1987); and Stephen Daniels and Joanne Martin, "Jury Verdicts and the 'Crisis' in Civil Justice," *Justice System Journal*, 11 (Winter 1986), 321–348.
114. Peterson, *Civil Juries in the 1980s*, p. 17.
115. Ibid., p. 21.
116. Daniels and Martin, "Jury Verdicts and the 'Crisis,' " p. 340.
117. Peterson, *Civil Juries in the 1980s*, p. 35.
118. Saks, "Do We Really Know Anything," 1262–1271.
119. United States General Accounting Office, *Medical Malpractice: No Agreement on the Problems or Solutions*, GAO/HRD–86–50 (Washington, D.C.: Government Printing Office, 1986), pp. 77–82.
120. See Patricia M. Danzon, *Medical Malpractice: Theory, Evidence, and Public Policy* (Cambridge, Mass.: Harvard University Press, 1985), pp. 77–79; and Paul C. Weiler, *Medical Malpractice on Trial* (Cambridge: Harvard University Press, 1991), pp. 32–38.
121. Linda Lipsen, "The Evolution of Products Liability as a Federal Policy Issue," in *Tort Law and the Public Interest: Competition, Innovation, and Consumer Welfare*, ed. Peter H. Schuck (New York: W. W. Norton, 1991), pp. 247–271.
122. This discussion is based on several studies, including U.S. Department of Transportation, *Economic Consequences of Automobile Accident Injuries* (Washington, D.C.: Government Printing Office, 1970); Hensler et al., *Compensation for Accidental Injuries;* and All-Industry Research Advisory Council, *Compensation for Automobile Injuries*.
123. See All-Industry Research Advisory Council, *Compensation for Automobile Injuries*, pp. 31, 129.
124. See James S. Kakalik and Nicholas M. Pace, *Costs and Compensation Paid in Tort Litigation* (Santa Monica, Calif: Rand Corporation, 1986).
125. Hensler et al., *Compensation for Accidental Injuries*, pp. 105–108.
126. Caplovitz, *Consumers in Trouble*, p. 221.
127. Craig Wanner, "A Harvest of Profits: Exploring the Symbiotic Relationship Between Urban Civil Trial Courts and the Business Community" (Paper presented at the 1973 meeting of the American Political Science Association in New Orleans, Louisiana).
128. Beatrice A. Moulton, "The Persecution and Intimidation of the Low-Income Litigant as Performed by the Small Claims Court in California," *Stanford Law Review*, 21 (June 1969), 1657–1684.
129. Marilyn Miller Mosier and Richard A. Soble, "Modern Legislation, Metropolitan Court, Miniscule Results: A Study of Detroit's Landlord-Tenant Court," *Journal of Law Reform*, 7 (Fall 1973), 6–70.
130. Galanter, "Why the 'Haves' Come Out Ahead," pp. 135–151.
131. Lenore J. Weitzman and Ruth B. Dixon, "Child Custody Awards: Legal Standards and Empirical Patterns for Child Custody, Support and Visitation after Divorce," *University of California, Davis, Law Review*, 12 (Summer 1979), 471–521; Diane Shrier, Sue K. Simring, Judith R. Grief, Edith T. Shapiro, and Jacob J.

Lindenthal, "Child Custody Arrangements: A Study of Two New Jersey Counties," *Journal of Psychiatry and Law,* 17 (Spring 1989), 9–20.

132. Lenore J. Weitzman, *The Divorce Revolution* (New York: Free Press, 1985), pp. 245–258.

133. Gordon H. Lester, *Child Support and Alimony: 1987,* U.S. Bureau of the Census, Current Population Reports, Series P–23, No. 167 (Washington, D.C.: Government Printing Office, 1990); Spencer Rich, "50% Falling Short on Child Support," *Washington Post,* October 11, 1991, p. A8; U.S. Bureau of the Census, *Statistical Abstract of the United States: 1992* (Washington, D.C.: U.S. Government Printing Office, 1992), p. 372.

134. Greg J. Duncan and Saul D. Hoffman, "Economic Consequences of Marital Instability," in *Horizontal Equity, Uncertainty, and Economic Well-Being,* ed. Martin David and Timothy Smeeding (Chicago: University of Chicago Press, 1985), pp. 427–470; Suzanne Bianchi and Edith McArthur, *Family Disruption and Economic Hardship: The Short-Run Picture for Children,* U.S. Bureau of the Census, Current Population Reports, Series P–70, No. 23 (Washington, D.C.: Government Printing Office, 1991).

135. Weitzman, *The Divorce Revolution;* Herbert Jacob, "Faulting No-Fault," *American Bar Foundation Research Journal,* Fall 1986, 773–780; Susan Faludi, *Backlash: The Undeclared War Against American Women* (New York: Crown, 1991), pp. 19–25.

136. Marygold S. Melli, "Constructing a Social Problem: The Post-Divorce Plight of Women and Children," *American Bar Foundation Research Journal,* Fall 1986, 770.

137. "An Evaluation of the Impact of Child Support Guidelines," *SJI News* 2 (issue 1, 1990), 7; the study, by the Center for Policy Research, was entitled, *The Impact of Child Support Guidelines: An Empirical Assessment of Three Models.*

8

Appellate Courts: The Process

A bove the trial courts stand appellate courts, which hear and decide appeals. The final two chapters of this book focus on appellate courts. This chapter examines matters of process—how cases flow to and through appellate courts and how they are decided. Chapter 9 considers appellate courts as policy makers, discussing the policies they produce and the impact of those policies.

In both the state and federal court systems, trial and appellate courts are closely linked. Cases move back and forth between the two sets of courts, which apply the same body of law in deciding them. Yet in some important respects the appellate process differs fundamentally from the trial process. Indeed, as suggested in Chapter 1, trial and appellate courts each may resemble some nonjudicial institutions more closely than they resemble each other.

One difference between them is that judges play more central roles at the appellate level. Most cases that come to an appellate court are ultimately decided by the court—by judges—rather than settled outside of court. Although judges are influenced by other people in reaching their decisions, they are still the primary decision-makers. Thus the goals and motives of judges most directly determine what appellate courts do.

Another difference is that the participants in appellate courts give more attention to individual cases than do their counterparts in trial courts. In appellate courts, single cases are more likely to have implications that extend beyond the litigants in those cases. A contract case in a trial court probably will affect only the parties to that case, whereas a contract case in a state supreme court may be the basis for rules that affect every party to the same kind of contract. As a result, judges and others in trial courts tend to treat each case as one of many similar cases; in appellate courts, they are more likely to recognize and respond to the special importance of each individual case.

In these and other respects, however, we should distinguish between two types of appellate courts, which I call "first-level" and "second-level." First-level courts stand directly above trial courts and review their decisions. Second-level courts stand above the first-level courts and review *their* decisions. About one-quarter of the states have only a single appellate court, usually called a supreme court, that serves as a first-level court. The remaining states and the federal system have intermediate appellate courts, most often called courts of appeals, and supreme courts above them.

It is second-level appellate courts such as the U.S. Supreme Court that differ most sharply from trial courts. First-level courts—particularly intermediate appellate courts—are a little more like trial courts. And growing caseload pressures in recent years have increased their resemblance to trial courts in some ways. In response to the greater volume of appellate litigation, judges on intermediate courts have delegated significant responsibility to other court personnel, and increasingly some cases are handled in the relatively routine fashion that we associate with trial courts. In turn, these procedural changes have affected the outcomes of cases and subtly changed intermediate appellate courts as institutions.

AN OVERVIEW OF APPELLATE COURTS

We can begin our consideration of appellate courts by examining some general matters: the purposes that underlie them, their business, their major participants, and their procedures for handling appeals.

The Purposes of Appeal

Appellate courts exist, and dissatisfied litigants are permitted to appeal, to serve two general purposes.[1]

First, appellate courts can correct errors in the application of the law to individual litigants and thus serve justice. Because individual judges and juries can err, some kind of review of their judgments seems necessary so that litigants do not suffer injustice because of their mistakes.

Appellate courts enjoy some advantages in reaching the right result under the law: they often possess more information, and they can operate at a more deliberate pace. A trial judge may make a procedural ruling with little time for consideration or study in the emotional and chaotic conditions of a trial. An appellate court has the luxury of considering that ruling on the basis of extensive written briefs and oral arguments and with weeks or months to make a judgment. And because appellate decisions are made by multiple judges rather than a single one, the chance of an erroneous decision is reduced.

Second, appellate courts can help make the law clear and consistent with their decisions. Clarity and consistency are important because they allow people and their attorneys to be more certain of the legal consequences of their actions—whether a contract will be declared valid if it is challenged or whether a corporate merger might be disapproved under the antitrust laws. Clarity and consistency also serve the goal of equal justice by helping to ensure that the law will be applied in the same fashion to different cases.

One way that appellate courts reduce ambiguity and inconsistency is by resolving conflicting interpretations of the law. If federal district judges in the Sixth Circuit produce different interpretations of the federal sentencing laws, the Sixth Circuit Court of Appeals can adopt a single interpretation for them to follow. Even in the absence of a conflict, an appellate court can overturn what its members see as a lower court's mistaken interpretation of a legal provision. By correcting interpretations of the law, and by correcting its application to specific cases, appellate courts can supervise trial courts and keep them on what appellate judges see as the right path.

To some degree, there is a division of labor between first-level and second-level courts in serving these purposes. In systems with two tiers of appellate courts, the courts of appeals do most of the work of correcting perceived errors in trial court decisions; thus the supreme court can concentrate on developing and clarifying the law.

The Business of Appellate Courts

Since litigants who are dissatisfied with trial court decisions usually have the right to appeal those decisions, we would expect the business of appellate courts to mirror that of trial courts. To a great extent, this is indeed so, but for several reasons, appellate court business does not reflect trial court business perfectly.

First, the jurisdiction of appellate courts differs from that of trial courts in a few important respects. Appeals from some administrative agencies go directly to appellate courts, bypassing the trial level entirely. In most states appeals from minor trial courts go first to major trial courts, and few of these cases ever get to appellate courts. Under the constitutional prohibition of double jeopardy, the prosecution can appeal certain trial court rulings in criminal cases but not the acquittal of a defendant.

Furthermore, second-level appellate courts hold primarily discretionary rather than mandatory jurisdiction; a court is not obliged to hear a case that comes to it under its discretionary jurisdiction. Judges on these courts can thus express their preferences for certain kinds of cases by agreeing to hear them more often than others. A state supreme court, for instance, could hear large numbers of tort cases while rejecting domestic relations cases.

Third, litigants in different kinds of cases are not equally likely to appeal. Patterns of appeals are examined later in the chapter, along with the use of discretionary jurisdiction.

Finally, the content of cases is often transformed at the appellate level. The factual questions that dominate most trials are largely irrelevant to appellate courts, which generally accept the conclusions about facts of trial judges and juries. Rather, appeals from trial decisions usually emphasize issues of legal interpretation. Such issues ordinarily must be raised at the trial level to be considered on appeal, but they may receive relatively little attention in the trial court. As a result, to take a common example, a case whose trial focused on whether the defendant was the burglar of a store may be transformed on appeal into a case about the legality of a police search of the defendant's car. And broad legal issues tend to receive even greater emphasis as cases move up to second-level appellate courts.

By no means do all appeals come after trials. Many result from pretrial rulings, and in some states a criminal defendant who pleaded guilty can appeal the sentence or procedures used in the case. One study found that only one-quarter of the cases decided by the Arizona court of appeals in Phoenix resulted from trials.[2]

The Participants

Cases on appeal involve a narrower range of participants than do trials. As noted earlier, appellate court activities center on judges. Attorneys play integral roles as well. Other participants are important because they affect what judges and lawyers do: law clerks influence judges, and the parties to cases influence their attorneys.

Judges   As already noted, the importance of judges at the appellate level stems from the fact that they actually rule on most cases rather than watch cases drop out because of agreements between the parties or simply ratify those agreements. Yet in one respect individual appellate judges are less important than are trial judges. Because appellate courts almost always decide cases collectively—usually in groups of three to nine judges—the power of any single judge is diluted somewhat. Trial judges can put their individual stamp on courtroom proceedings and decisions. As a result, federal district judges in particular have made a good deal of difference by themselves. Supreme Court justices such as William Rehnquist and John Paul Stevens can also make a great deal of difference, but they do so as part of a group rather than by acting alone.

Law Clerks   Judges increasingly have the assistance of attorneys who serve as law clerks.[3] (Law clerks should not be confused with court clerks, who help to administer and manage courts.) Law clerks are especially important at the appellate level. One reason is that appellate judges are more likely to have law clerks. All federal courts and the great majority of state appellate courts provide clerks to their judges, but clerks are less common on state trial courts. Many appellate courts also have established central staffs of law clerks who carry out major functions for the court as a whole. (Members of these staffs are sometimes called staff attorneys.)

Most law clerks are recent law school graduates who take their positions for a relatively short period, often only a year. Especially at the appellate level, these short-term clerks typically are high-ranking graduates of prestigious law schools. It has become more common, however, for clerks to be hired for longer periods. This is particularly common on central staffs, but one clerk served a series of individual California Supreme Court justices for thirty-five years.[4] For the young attorneys who serve individual judges, clerkships can be considered a form of apprenticeship in which close contact between judge and clerk helps to socialize clerks and prepare them for elite positions in the legal system—including, in some instances, judgeships of their own later in life.[5]

The number of law clerks has increased in response to the growing caseloads of appellate courts. In the federal court system, Supreme Court justices are now allowed to hire four personal law clerks each; court of appeals judges are allowed three. Central staffs of clerks, which did not become common until the 1970s, now exist in each federal court of appeals and in many state appellate courts.

Caseload growth has also led judges to delegate more responsibility to clerks. The clearest example of delegation is the typical role of central staff attorneys in intermediate appellate courts. These law clerks categorize cases and perform preliminary work in those deemed to be relatively simple and straightforward—preliminary work that often extends to proposing decisions and opinions to the judges. Law clerks serving individual judges are delegated such important functions as summarizing the written materials in cases and drafting opinions.

Many judges have expressed concern about the changes in their courts that this delegation to law clerks has produced. In a survey of judges on the federal courts of appeals, 32 percent said that they sometimes relied on clerks to do work that judges should do themselves, while another 31 percent said they often or usually did so. One judge noted that "in this circuit, a judge has to turn out 150 opinions a year to stay current. It is not possible to do that without excessive reliance on the law clerks."[6]

The importance of law clerks to judges is suggested by the elaborate efforts that many federal judges undertake to hire those whom they identify as the best candidates for clerkships, efforts in which—according to one observer—"the law of the jungle reigns and badmouthing, spying and even poaching among judges is rife."[7] Chief Judge Patricia Wald of the federal court of appeals for the District of Columbia offered one explanation for this behavior:

> An excellent versus a mediocre team of clerks makes a huge difference in the judge's daily life and in her work product. Indeed, a judge sometimes decides whether to file a separate opinion or to dissent in a case based—at least in part—upon the support she can anticipate from her clerks. Or she may ask for, or beg off, responsibility for a particular opinion assignment because of the availability or nonavailability of a particular clerk to work on the case.[8]

Such statements of judges underline an important change in the operation of appellate courts—a change that is examined in more detail later in the chapter. But the shift of power from judges to law clerks should not be exaggerated. Delegation of responsibility in appellate courts remains far more limited than in many other government organizations; more than cabinet secretaries and members of Congress, appellate judges still do their own work. And judges retain the greatest control over the most important cases and decisions.

Attorneys   The great majority of parties in appellate courts are represented by attorneys. Parties that can afford to hire them nearly always do so. Indigent criminal defendants are provided with free attorneys for their first appeal from a conviction, so long as they have a right to that appeal (as they nearly always do). Indigent defendants often must petition second-level appellate courts to hear their cases without a lawyer's help, but a court that does grant a hearing will then supply an attorney to argue the case.

The attorneys who handle appeals are a mixture of appellate specialists and nonspecialists. Many of the specialists work for government. For example, appellate specialists in the U.S. Department of Justice are responsible for some federal government litigation in the courts of appeals and nearly all of the government's cases in the Supreme Court. Some states operate public defenders' offices that handle only appeals. The private sector also has some lawyers who are full or partial appellate specialists, among them attorneys who work with interest groups such as the NAACP Legal Defense Fund and the AFL-CIO.

But it is the general rule in the private sector and common in the public sector for a lawyer who has tried a case to handle it on appeal as well. One result is that a good deal of appellate work is done by lawyers with little experience at that level. Over the four terms from 1988 to 1992, the overwhelming majority of lawyers who argued cases before the Supreme Court did so only once, and occasionally a lawyer who has never even filed a petition with the Supreme Court argues a significant case before the Court.

The inexperience of many appellate lawyers is often reflected in their work. Appellate judges sometimes complain about the limited competence of the lawyers who argue before them, focusing chiefly on the nonspecialists.

At the appellate level, as in trial courts, attorneys play crucial roles in developing and presenting cases. However, their roles differ considerably between the two levels. Trial lawyers generally negotiate settlements outside of court and orchestrate the presentation of evidence at trial. In contrast, appellate lawyers do much less negotiation and, rather than orchestrate evidence, they offer legal arguments directly through written *briefs* (detailed presentations of their line of reasoning in the case) and through oral argument.

Parties   The parties to appellate cases, like the cases themselves, are quite diverse. Criminal defendants are prominent because of the large numbers of appeals in criminal prosecutions and habeas corpus cases. Government agencies appear in criminal cases and in an array of civil cases. A variety of other litigants, both individuals and institutions, are parties in appellate cases.

The parties that are represented by attorneys do not participate directly in appellate court proceedings. (Indeed, in one Supreme Court case, Justice Potter Stewart asked an attorney to verify that his reclusive client actually existed.[9]) Their roles in appellate litigation vary considerably. At one end of the continuum, some parties supervise their attorneys closely; at the other end, some are distant spectators as their lawyers develop and carry out strategies in appellate court.

A Summary of Appellate Court Procedures

Like trial procedures, appellate procedures vary among courts and types of cases. The most important distinction is between a traditional system of full appellate procedure and a collection of procedures that depart from it, primarily by abbreviating the traditional process.

The Traditional System   What I call the traditional system of appellate procedure can have either of two versions, depending on whether a court has discretionary jurisdiction over the cases to be handled. Thus, because first-level appellate courts have mostly mandatory jurisdiction and second-level courts mostly discretionary jurisdiction, they generally use different versions of the traditional procedure. (Another important difference is that intermediate appellate courts typically decide cases in three-judge panels, while supreme courts generally decide them en banc, with their full membership.) As Exhibit 8.1 shows, these two versions have much in common, and they can be discussed together.

Where a court's jurisdiction is mandatory, the process begins when one side (or, occasionally, both sides) decides to appeal a lower-court verdict or other ruling. The party who files an appeal generally must have the record of the case prepared and transmitted to the appellate court; the largest part of this record is usually a transcript of the trial proceedings. The costs of

EXHIBIT 8.1 Typical Stages of Processing in Appellate Courts (Traditional Procedures)

Mandatory Jurisdiction	Discretionary Jurisdiction
a. Filing of an appeal and brief by the appellant	a. Filing of a petition for a hearing by the petitioner
b. Submission of a brief by the appellee	b. Submission of a brief in opposition to this petition by the respondent
c. Submission of a reply brief by the appellant	c. Court decision on whether to grant a hearing
	d. Submission of additional briefs by the parties

1. Prehearing conference (in some courts)
2. Court rulings on motions by the parties (such rulings may also come at other points)
3. Oral argument by the attorneys before the court
4. Court conference to reach a tentative decision
5. Writing of opinion(s) and continuing discussion of the case
6. Announcement of the decision and opinion(s)
7. Further action by the lower court in response to the appellate decision (in most cases)

preparing both the transcript and the rest of the record make appeals expensive for those who must pay the full costs. However, these costs are waived for indigent criminal defendants.

The party making the appeal, the *appellant*, submits a written brief arguing in favor of the appellant's position. This brief generally focuses on legal issues, pointing to alleged errors by the lower court that require overturning of its decision. In opposition, the other party, the *appellee*, submits a brief supporting the lower-court decision and taking issue with the appellant's contentions. The appellant may then submit a reply brief.

In a case falling under a court's discretionary jurisdiction, these early stages take a somewhat different and more extended form. The process begins when the party dissatisfied with a lower-court decision, the petitioner, asks the appellate court to call up the case and hear it. This petition takes different legal forms in different courts. In the Supreme Court, a petitioner asks the Court to issue a *writ of certiorari* to the court that last decided the case; if the writ is issued, it requires that the record of the case be sent up to the Supreme Court. The petitioner submits a brief in support of the request for a hearing, which is accompanied by the record of the case. The other party, the *respondent*, may then submit a brief in opposition to the request.

The court then considers and rules on the petition. (Courts typically require a majority vote or a near-majority—four of nine on the U.S. Supreme Court—to accept a case.) If the petition is rejected, the court reaches no decision in the case and simply allows the lower court to make its ruling final. But if the petition is accepted, the case is called up for decision. The parties may—and generally do—submit additional briefs on the merits of the case.

From this point on, cases under mandatory and discretionary jurisdiction are treated in the same way. After all the briefs in a case are submitted, some courts allow for a conference with the parties to help prepare the case for a hearing or to promote a settlement. Whether or not the court encourages settlements, in some first-level appellate courts a large minority of cases—primarily civil cases—drop out through settlement or dismissal.[10]

Before the hearing, the court may need to rule on motions by the parties. The subjects of such motions can include requests for the release of prisoners while their appeals are pending, for permission for indigents to proceed without paying court fees, and for exceptions to the court's procedural rules.

The written materials in the case are considered by the court. The judges then hold oral argument, in which the attorneys for the two sides make presentations that highlight and supplement their briefs. The judges may interrupt these presentations to ask questions, and in some courts such interruptions are frequent. The length of the oral argument varies, but one common practice is to divide one hour equally between the two sides. Sometimes the argument is dramatic; however, as one judge has cautioned, it "is for the most part intensely boring."[11]

After the hearing, the judges meet in conference to consider the case and reach a tentative decision. Here their choice is whether to uphold, or *affirm,* the lower-court decision, or to overturn it either completely or in part. In general, a court *reverses* a decision when it overturns the decision

completely, and it *modifies* a decision by overturning the decision in part. (The court might, for example, uphold a verdict for a personal injury plaintiff but rule that the damages awarded by the trial court were too high.) A court may also *vacate,* or make void, a lower court decision; the Supreme Court sometimes uses this procedure when a recent change in the law calls into question the validity of a lower-court decision.

At some point, usually after the conference, one judge is assigned to write the opinion that will announce the court's decision and describe the reasoning on which that decision is based. This opinion has several purposes: to justify the decision to the parties and any other audience; to instruct the lower court on what to do if it must reconsider the case; and to announce the rules of law that determined this decision, rules that this court and the courts below it are bound to follow in future decisions.

The assigned judge works to produce a draft opinion for the consideration of the other judges, whose comments may cause the opinion to be modified in minor or major ways. Meanwhile, other judges may be writing and circulating alternative opinions, which reach a different result from the assigned opinion or offer different rationales for the same result. When there are multiple opinions, a process of compromise and bargaining may follow, with the judge assigned the opinion trying to win maximum support for that opinion, even as other judges with different positions seek to gain support for them. In many cases, such disagreement does not exist, but some bargaining can still occur: "you take out this sentence, or put in this footnote, and I will sign."[12]

The process of decision ends when each judge takes a final position. The court's decision is then announced, with the opinion that represents the majority being issued on the court's behalf. Judges who disagree with the court's decision in the case, in that they favored a different outcome for the parties, may cast dissenting votes. When judges dissent, one or more usually write *dissenting opinions,* in which they explain their differences with the majority. Other dissenters may sign on to one judge's dissenting opinion. Such opinions have no direct impact on the law, but they allow judges to express their views and perhaps influence future court decisions.

Sometimes judges agree with the court's decision and so vote with the majority but still cannot accept the reasoning in the majority opinion—the rules of law that the court uses to justify its decision. These judges will announce that they concur only with the decision, and they often write or sign on to *concurring opinions* that explain their position. Because the long-term impact of an appellate decision lies primarily in the rules of law that it announces, the disagreement expressed in concurring opinions often is as significant as the disagreement in dissenting opinions. In a 1992 decision, the Supreme Court was unanimous in striking down a city ordinance prohibiting "hate speech" such as cross burning, but Justice Byron White's concurring opinion vehemently disagreed with the majority's interpretation of the First Amendment.[13]

Occasionally, because of disagreement about the rationale, no opinion gains the support of a majority of judges; in this situation, there is a decision

but no authoritative interpretation of the legal issues in the case. Not all concurring opinions express disagreement, however. Even justices who agree with the majority opinion sometimes write concurring opinions to add their own views; they may, for example, give an additional reason for supporting the court's decision.

What happens after an appellate court decision depends primarily on the content of the decision. If the court affirms the lower-court decision, it notifies the lower court that it can make its ruling final. If the court overturns the lower-court decision in some form, it may make a final disposition of the case itself or direct the lower court to reach a particular final decision. Frequently, however, an appellate court that has reversed, modified, or vacated a decision sends the case back (*remands* it) to the lower court for further consideration in light of the appellate court decision and opinion; the lower court then has at least some freedom to resolve the case as it sees fit.

Alternative Procedures   Many appellate courts follow this traditional set of procedures fairly closely in at least a portion of their cases. But there have always been deviations from this model, primarily as means to expedite the processing of cases and to reduce the workload of judges. These deviations have become far more common since the 1960s; in first-level courts today, two scholars note, "the traditional appellate process exists, if at all, in most courts for only a small portion of appeals."[14] Most of the alternative procedures can be placed in three categories.

The first concerns the opportunities for arguments by the parties. Most courts have reduced the length of oral argument or, in some cases, eliminated it altogether. Of the cases decided on the merits by federal courts of appeals in 1991, oral argument was held in only 44 percent.[15] Courts with discretionary jurisdiction sometimes decide cases solely on the basis of the petition for hearing and the brief in opposition, dispensing both with further briefing and with oral argument.

The second category involves the court's decision-making process. Judges sometimes dispense with conferences to consider cases collectively, and a few courts announce some of their decisions immediately after oral argument. Some courts delegate the primary responsibility for a decision to a single judge, who is assigned the case at an early point, with other judges largely deferring to the assigned judge. An even more radical departure is delegation to nonjudges. In recent years, as we have seen, a number of courts have given central staff attorneys major responsibilities for decisions in some cases.

The final category of alternative procedures concerns the court's opinion. Decisions may be announced with no opinion. Alternatively, the court may issue an opinion that is relatively brief—sometimes so brief that it is essentially no opinion at all. Shorter opinions are often designated as *per curiam*, by the court, rather than being signed by a single judge. This form avoids individual responsibility for opinions that may not be as carefully developed as longer, signed opinions. Such practices have become quite common; in a recent period a Florida court of appeals issued an opinion in only one-third of its decisions.[16] Finally, courts can direct that opinions not be published, which means that the rules of law in those opinions are not binding in future cases. Opinions that are not intended for publication may require less care and thus less time to write.

Often these alternative procedures are used in combination. In some courts, for instance, certain cases are decided without oral argument, are given tentative decisions by central staff attorneys, and are handed down with brief unpublished per curiam opinions written primarily by staff attorneys. Many appellate courts have created two tracks, with some cases handled under a system that resembles the traditional one and others given more limited consideration and treatment.

APPEALS

With a few exceptions, cases come to appellate courts because one or more of the parties choose to bring those cases. Thus the work of appellate courts is based on the composition of appeals and petitions for hearings. For the sake of simplicity, I refer to all cases as appeals in the discussion that follows.

Factors That Affect the Decision to Appeal

In many respects, opting to appeal is similar to choosing to go to court in the first place. In both instances, people who are dissatisfied with their situation—in this case, an unfavorable court ruling—must decide whether to accept the situation or seek redress.

But there are also differences between the two decisions. Perhaps most important, appealing an adverse decision is less momentous than the original decision to litigate because the case is already in the court system and the parties have already experienced the disadvantages of going to court. This difference helps explain why a higher proportion of potential cases are filed and why cases are less likely to be settled out of court at the appellate level.

Decisions to appeal, like initial decisions to go to court, are based on many factors. But three considerations seem to be especially important: the degree of dissatisfaction with the lower court decision, the chances of success on appeal, and the monetary cost.

Dissatisfaction with a Decision   Almost nobody is happy to lose a court case. Yet the intensity of the loser's unhappiness can vary a good deal, depending chiefly on how much has been lost. A criminal defendant who was granted probation and one who was sentenced to death are likely to have very different feelings about their defeats. Similarly, the amount of money a civil defendant has lost in a trial verdict or a losing plaintiff had hoped to win conditions their reactions.

These prosaic observations suggest an obvious conclusion: litigants who have lost the most will generally appeal at the highest rates. Not surprisingly, the available evidence supports this conclusion. A California study found, for example, that the rate of criminal appeals increased with the seriousness of the offense.[17]

As a result, even appellate courts that must hear all appeals deal disproportionately with cases that have relatively large stakes. Another result is that minor trial courts, whose cases involve relatively small stakes, are generally subject to little appellate scrutiny. Finally, since the average case at the federal level involves bigger stakes, the rate of appeal there is higher than in state courts.

Chances of Success   In one survey of lawyers, by far the most important factor in deciding whether to appeal federal district court rulings was the likelihood of success on appeal.[18] This finding is not surprising. Because appellate courts are not inclined to overturn the decisions they review, ordinarily the odds are against a successful appeal. In courts with mandatory jurisdiction, the affirmance rate typically is two-thirds or higher. In some courts with discretionary jurisdiction, the odds are more than ten to one against the grant of a hearing. But the odds vary from case to case, and we would expect people to appeal most often where they see the chances of victory as relatively great.

Lawyers are important in estimating the chances of success for their clients because they usually have a much better basis for this judgment. Attorneys discourage some appeals by indicating that reversal is unlikely, but they may exaggerate the prospects for a favorable result in some cases because an appeal will bring them additional fees.

Of course, perceptions of the likelihood of success are heavily influenced by past decisions; in this way, appellate courts affect decisions whether to bring appeals. The Supreme Court's growing conservatism in recent years, for instance, has discouraged some people with civil liberties claims from bringing those claims to the Court. At the same time, prosecutors and others whose claims might appeal to conservative justices have become more willing to bring cases to the Court. And courts sometimes offer more specific invitations to potential litigants, indicating in opinions that they would look favorably on cases raising a particular legal claim.

Some appeals are brought even though the chances of success seem slim. Sometimes litigants or their attorneys simply miscalculate; at other times, the stakes are so large—a possible death penalty, for instance—that the gamble seems justified. In some cases, the appellant can win even by losing. For example, a corporation that lost in trial court and was ordered to pay substantial damages to the other party often makes money in interest by delaying the time when the damages actually must be paid. Appeals also can be used as a weapon to wear down opponents who have fewer resources for continued litigation, sometimes forcing them to accept compromise settlements or making enforcement of trial court judgments more difficult.

Financial Costs   As noted earlier, appeals generally are expensive. It is costly not only to prepare a trial record but also to compensate lawyers for their time in preparing for and presenting an appeal. Furthermore, the remand of a case after a successful appeal frequently results in a new trial, exacting additional costs from the appellant.

As a result, at least in civil cases, individuals and institutions with the most resources are the most likely to appeal. A litigant whose limited money supply has already been depleted by the costs of a trial may be reluctant to undergo the additional expense of an appeal. In contrast, litigants who are in a stronger financial position can make an appeal if the potential gains from a successful appeal or from delay are sufficient.

Personal financial resources have much less impact on criminal appeals. Most people convicted of serious crimes are indigent, and, as a result of Supreme Court rulings, the costs of a first appeal are ordinarily waived for indigent defendants. In addition, second-level courts typically allow indigent people to petition for hearings without paying the usual fees and costs for preparing the necessary materials. (In recent years, however, the Supreme Court has denied "pauper" status to several litigants on the ground that they were not really indigent.) This, of course, is another way that courts influence decisions whether to appeal.

Thus criminal appeals carry no financial costs for most defendants; in this respect, criminal defendants are freer to appeal than are large corporations. Accordingly, a defendant who has received a heavy sentence may see little reason not to appeal, whatever the chances of victory: much might be gained, and there is little harm in trying. Not surprisingly, then, a high proportion of criminal defendants appeal from defeats at trial—a far higher proportion than of those who lose civil cases.

Appeals by the Government

In deciding whether to bring appeals, government officials consider the same factors as do other litigants, but they often operate somewhat differently from most other parties. The most distinctive is the federal government, whose approach to appeals merits some attention.[19]

Decisions to appeal by the federal government are shaped by three key characteristics. First, in any given field, such as personal injuries or labor law, over time the government has a great many cases that it could appeal. Second, control over appeals is centralized. At the trial level, federal cases are filed by U.S. Attorneys' offices in each district and by federal agencies that handle their own litigation. But in the courts of appeals and the Supreme Court, cases generally cannot be filed without the authorization of the solicitor general's office within the Justice Department. Finally, while resources are not unlimited, the federal government faces fewer financial constraints in bringing appeals than do most private parties. All these characteristics enhance the government's capacity to use appeals effectively.

The number of potential appeals and the centralization of decisions to appeal make the federal government an especially good example of the "repeat player" in litigation that Marc Galanter has described; in the Supreme Court, one scholar argues, "Solicitors general are the definitive Repeat Players."[20] In deciding whether to appeal in any specific case, government lawyers can think in terms of long-term goals, as well as the outcome in that case. To put the matter another way, they have greater freedom to act strategically.

One example of strategic action is the use of selective appeals to help shape the law. The government sometimes forgoes an appeal in a tax case because the court of appeals to which the appeal would go seems unfavorable to the position of the Internal Revenue Service; instead, the government will wait for a case in a circuit whose court of appeals seems likely to be more sympathetic.

Another example of strategy is the rationing of petitions for hearings in the Supreme Court. The solicitor general's office is far more selective in asking for hearings than are private litigants as a group. This restraint allows the government generally to take only its strongest cases to the Court; one benefit is that the justices expect government petitions to be meritorious.

The federal government's repeat player status also allows its attorneys to develop expertise in handling appeals. In the Supreme Court, for instance, the preponderance of the government's legal work is handled by the small staff of attorneys in the solicitor general's office. Those lawyers gain a good deal of experience in writing briefs and arguing cases before the Court—experience that few other attorneys can match.

The skill that they develop through this experience, in combination with the government's ability to act strategically, helps to produce extraordinary success for the federal government both in getting the Court to accept its cases and in winning cases that the Court does hear. Those successes are documented in Exhibit 8.2 for one recent year.

The characteristics of the federal government are not typical of all governments. Some state governments lack centralized control over appeals. Particularly in smaller cities and counties, local governments may have too few cases to act strategically and to develop experience in their attorneys. Financial constraints on appeals also tend to be more severe at the state and local level. But many of the larger state and local governments share enough similarities with the federal government to distinguish them from most private litigants in the ways that they operate in making appeals.

Interest Groups and Litigation

Because courts are important policy makers, their decisions affect a wide range of interest groups. Inevitably, groups seek to influence those decisions.

One route is through the selection of judges; this may be the most effective way to shape a court's policies, since those policies largely reflect the attitudes of its judges. Thus groups contribute money to candidates for state judgeships and lobby senators over federal court nominations.

Interest groups can also lobby courts indirectly, through the mass media, public statements, and even demonstrations and marches. Groups on both sides of the abortion controversy have used all these methods to try to influence Supreme Court decisions.

Perhaps most common, and increasingly so, is interest group participation in litigation itself. A wide range of groups involve themselves in litigation, as

A. Granting of Petitions for Certiorari

	Federal Government Petitions[a]	Petitions from Other Parties
Petitions granted	26	93
Petitions denied	6	4559
Petitions granted as percentage of petitions filed	81%	2%

B. Decisions in Cases Heard by the Court with the Federal Government as a Party[b]

	Number	Percentage
Federal government victories	67	63%
Federal government defeats	39	37%

[a]Includes cases in which the federal government supported the petition of another party.
[b]Cases in which the results could not be classified are omitted.
Source: Data were provided by the Office of the Solicitor General, U.S. Department of Justice.

EXHIBIT 8.2 The Federal Government's Success in the Supreme Court, 1989–1990 Term

do other entities such as companies and individuals (for example, government officials) that act as interest groups at particular times.

Interest groups sometimes involve themselves in cases at the trial level, but their participation becomes increasingly common at each step up the ladder of appellate courts. One reason is that groups frequently become aware of cases and join them only at the appellate level. Another is that the kinds of cases that reach the highest courts are the most likely to attract the interest of groups because of their broad implications. And it is sometimes group efforts that allow cases to move beyond the trial level.

Interest Group Roles   Interest groups that participate in litigation can take three kinds of roles. The first is direct sponsorship of cases. Rules of *standing* require that a litigant have a direct stake in a case; therefore, an interest group ordinarily cannot file a suit in its own name. But a group can begin with a general or specific policy goal and look for potential clients whose cases could be used to advance that goal. Thus local chapters of the American Civil Liberties Union (ACLU) take complaints from individuals that their civil liberties have been violated and use some of these complaints as vehicles for lawsuits.

In the second role, groups locate a case that is already in the courts and belatedly sponsor or support one side. After a criminal defendant has been convicted at trial, for example, the NAACP Legal Defense Fund may learn that the case involves a challenge to racial discrimination in the selection of jurors, an issue with which the group is concerned. It might then offer to finance any appeals, and such financing gives the Legal Defense Fund an opportunity to shape the case so as to serve its own goals.

A group can play a third, more limited, role in a case by submitting an *amicus curiae* ("friend of the court") brief. An amicus brief is intended to supplement material provided by the litigant that the group supports in order to strengthen that party's case or to suggest a resolution of the legal issues that the group favors. The submission of an amicus brief usually requires a court's permission. An amicus brief can cost tens of thousands of dollars to prepare, but it is not as expensive as sponsoring a case and avoids the logistic difficulties of doing so.

Group Interest in Litigation   From the perspective of an interest group, government offers a number of possible forums in which to exert influence. A group will devote some of its efforts to the courts when courts provide a means to advance the group's goals. Litigation can serve interest group goals in several ways.

The most obvious way is as a means to obtain a definitive Supreme Court ruling favoring the group's position. The Public Citizen Litigation Group has helped bring and win cases to overturn the legislative veto of administrative rules and the Gramm-Rudman-Hollings "budget-balancing" law in order to maintain what it views as the appropriate separation of powers between Congress and the executive branch.[21] In recent years several groups have worked to achieve decisions that expand the rights of private property owners who are subject to government regulation.[22]

At the other end of the spectrum is litigation undertaken for tactical purposes, with little concern for judicial doctrine. Environmental groups sometimes file lawsuits against proposed projects in order to delay the projects and thus make them less feasible. In the 1980s the Southern Poverty Law Center brought a series of lawsuits against Ku Klux Klan organizations as a means to weaken the Klan financially and more generally.[23]

In between these two uses of litigation are a variety of others. One common "intermediate" type is lawsuits to strengthen and help enforce existing laws. The State Department chose not to enforce a 1989 statute prohibiting shrimp imports from countries whose fishing methods endanger sea turtles; in 1992 an environmental group brought a federal case to require enforcement of the statute.[24]

Some interest groups engage regularly in litigation, while others become involved in the courts only infrequently.[25] One reason is that the courts are more relevant to some groups than to others. Courts can do little for a farm organization that seeks increased crop subsidies, but they can do a great deal for an insurance group that seeks changes in legal rules of product liability. Another reason is that some groups see the courts as more sympathetic to their positions than the other branches, whereas others perceive the legislature and executive branch as more friendly.

For both these reasons, the most prominent interest groups in the courts between the 1940s and the 1960s were the NAACP Legal Defense Fund and the American Civil Liberties Union. The NAACP sought protection for the constitutional rights of black citizens, and so the courts were an appropriate forum; in addition, until the 1960s the Supreme Court was far more willing to support black civil rights than were Congress and the president. Similarly, the ACLU's focus on protection of civil liberties drew it to the courts, and many of its "clients"—criminal defendants, political extremists, unconventional religious groups—attracted little sympathy in the other branches.

Other groups with liberal ideological goals later developed. The NAACP Legal Defense Fund provided a model for groups representing women, Hispanics, and the disabled. Environmental groups, such as the Sierra Club, have engaged in a good deal of litigation. *Public interest law firms,* inspired by Ralph Nader, were created specifically to bring cases on issues such as employment discrimination, occupational safety, and consumer rights.

More recently, a number of new groups with conservative goals have appeared. Several conservative public interest law firms have been established since 1973; these firms litigate on a wide array of issues. Other conservative groups focus on such matters as abortion, criminal justice, and labor-management relations.[26] This conservative activity is partly a reaction to the success of liberal groups, but it has also been encouraged by the growing conservatism of the federal courts resulting from appointments by Republican presidents. With that change in the federal courts, liberal groups such as the ACLU increasingly have turned their attention elsewhere—especially to Congress and the state courts. The new conservative groups contribute to a growing diversity of groups using the courts, as illustrated by a sampling of active litigating groups, shown in Exhibit 8.3, and a sampling of groups submitting amicus briefs to one state supreme court, shown in Exhibit 8.4.

Alongside these groups, which emphasize use of the courts, are many others that engage in litigation as a relatively small part of their political activities. This category includes major economic groups, such as the U.S.

EXHIBIT 8.3 Some Interest Groups That Are Active in the Courts

---

American Civil Liberties Union. The ACLU was founded after World War I, gradually gaining a large membership (as many as 250,000 people). Throughout its history it has been heavily involved in litigation as a means to protect civil liberties, with some emphasis on freedom of expression. Over the past two decades it has established special projects to undertake litigation on issues such as women's rights and national security. The ACLU frequently participates in Supreme Court cases: in the Court's 1989–1990 term it sponsored four cases, including the challenge to Missouri's restrictions on the "right to die," and submitted amicus briefs in twenty-two other cases that the Court heard.

NAACP Legal Defense and Educational Fund. The National Association for the advancement of Colored People created a Legal Defense Fund in 1939 to focus on litigation, reflecting the organization's belief that the rights of black citizens could be advanced significantly through court decisions; the fund has since become a separate organization, with no mass membership. Under the leadership of Thurgood Marshall, it orchestrated the legal attack on school segregation, including a series of cases that resulted in major Supreme Court decisions—most important, *Brown v. Board of Education* (1954). In recent years the fund has used litigation to enforce federal laws against discrimination in voting and in employment, and it has continued its long-standing involvement in capital punishment cases based on the racial implications of the death penalty.

National Right to Work Legal Defense Fund. The Legal Defense Fund was established in 1968 by the National Right to Work Committee to litigate against rules under which employees must join labor unions or pay union fees, with a focus on unions' use of compulsory dues for political purposes. It usually learns of possible cases from employees who feel that their rights have been violated. The fund has sponsored or participated as amicus in a number of federal cases. It won a favorable ruling from the Supreme Court in a 1977 case involving the use of teachers' union dues, *Abood v. Detroit Board of Education.*

Public Citizen Litigation Group. Consumer advocate Ralph Nader helped create this organization in 1972 as a "public interest law firm." The group has brought suits on behalf of consumers on such matters as fees involved in home sales, and it has challenged limits on advertising by pharmacists and lawyers. It has also brought or supported a series of challenges to federal laws on the ground that they breached the Constitution's separation of powers among the three branches. These challenges have resulted in major Supreme Court decisions on congressional vetoes of administrative rules, the Gramm-Rudman-Hollings budget deficit reduction law, and guidelines for sentencing by federal judges.

Washington Legal Foundation. The foundation was created in 1977 as a conservative counterpart and counterbalance to liberal public interest law firms, and it grew into an organization with 200,000 members. The foundation frequently submits amicus briefs. It also sponsored Senator Barry Goldwater's lawsuit against President Carter's termination of a treaty with Taiwan and a lawsuit against John Hinckley by a secret service agent who was shot in Hinckley's attempt to assassinate President Reagan. In recent years it has challenged activities of the organized bar that foundation leaders see as supporting liberal goals.

Sources: Karen O'Connor and Lee Epstein, *Public Interest Groups: Institutional Profiles* (New York: Greenwood Press, 1989); Lee Epstein, *Conservatives in Court* (Knoxville: University of Tennessee Press, 1985); John Greenya, "Supreme Lawyers," *The Washington Lawyer,* 1 (May–June 1987), 34–51, 59; Samuel Walker, *In Defense of American Liberties: A History of the ACLU* (New York: Oxford University Press, 1990); information provided by Diane E. Weiss of the ACLU Foundation; other sources.

EXHIBIT 8.3 (*Continued*)

Pharmaceutical Manufacturers Association
Ohio Cable Television Association
Ohio Society of Certified Public Accountants
National Employment Lawyers Association
Ohio Chamber of Commerce
Ohio Municipal League
Meridian Mutual Insurance Company
International Association of Firefighters, Local Union No. 67
Ohio AFL-CIO
National Organization for Women, Ohio Chapter
City of Westerville
Clermont County Prosecutor's Office
Public Utilities Commission of Ohio
Ohio Public Defender Commission
Virginia State Board of Medicine
Western Reserve Kennel Club

EXHIBIT 8.4 A Sampling of Groups Submitting Amicus Curiae Briefs to the Ohio Supreme Court in Cases Decided in 1991

Chamber of Commerce and the AFL-CIO, whose goals and political strength lead them primarily to the executive branch and the legislature. Frequently, however, they turn to the courts to protect gains or redress losses elsewhere.

Governments can be considered interest groups when they litigate in behalf of their own interests, but they also intervene on behalf of other interests. The most significant form of such activity is the solicitor general's frequent submission of amicus briefs to the Supreme Court. The Reagan and Bush administrations used such briefs to argue for conservative positions on a number of legal issues, such as abortion and religious observances in schools.

The level of interest group activity in the courts has grown over the years, primarily because of a growing recognition that courts can serve group purposes. It remains true that interest groups take part in only a small minority of all court cases, but they have become increasingly frequent participants. The Supreme Court, for instance, receives amicus briefs in most of the cases that it considers fully. Interest group activity has also burgeoned in the state supreme courts; between 1970 and 1985 the number of cases with amicus briefs in the Illinois Supreme Court tripled, while it quadrupled in the Florida Supreme Court.[27] And even in the federal district court for Minnesota, groups were associated with the plaintiffs in a significant proportion of cases.[28]

Interest Group Influence   Most activity of interest groups in litigation is aimed at obtaining favorable judicial decisions. To what extent can groups actually bring about such decisions?

One means of influence for groups is that they can facilitate litigation that otherwise might not occur. A great many cases that raise important legal and policy questions would not arise without the aid of interest groups because no individuals have the resources and the incentives to carry such cases forward on their own. This is true, for instance, of most cases challenging school segregation, government aid to religious schools, and nonenforcement of environmental laws. Just by getting such cases to court, interest groups make a difference.

Groups also can exert influence through their argumentation, which may affect judges' perceptions of issues and therefore their positions. An amicus brief may, for example, suggest to a court a basis for its decision that might otherwise have gone unnoticed. Similarly, the lawyers who represent some interest groups may sway undecided judges with their oral arguments.

The ability of groups to influence courts in these ways is not unlimited. Monetary costs and logistic difficulties may limit the extent of a group's activity in litigation. And when groups do participate, their success depends less on the quality of their own work than on judges' predilections. On the whole, the American Civil Liberties Union has enjoyed less success in the Burger and Rehnquist Courts than it did in the Warren Court; the difference lies primarily in the Court's increased conservatism. For this reason, interest groups may not enjoy a significant advantage over other participants in litigation.[29]

The connections between interest group activities in the courts and elsewhere in government should be emphasized. Groups that want to shape policy in a particular area usually divide their efforts between the courts and the other branches, and they often work simultaneously in both. In this respect, as in others, courts are closely linked with other government institutions.

The Growth in Appeals

The total size of appellate caseloads has grown rapidly in the last few decades. Most courts now receive far more cases than they did ten or twenty years ago. Figure 8.1 illustrates this growth by showing the numbers of cases brought to the intermediate courts of appeals in Illinois and the federal system in selected years.

In part, this growth reflects increases in cases at the trial level; there are more decisions to appeal now. But it also stems from increases in the proportion of decisions that are appealed. The rise in the rate of appeal for criminal cases is particularly striking. In 1951 defendants in the federal courts appealed 14 percent of their convictions at trial, but by 1970, 54 percent of the convictions were appealed.[30] It is likely that the proportion has increased further since then.

As suggested earlier, the primary source of this change is the court decisions and legislation that have made appeals much easier for criminal defendants. Indeed, one commentator concluded that the Supreme Court's decisions assuring free counsel for indigent defendants on appeal "undoubtedly caused most of the increase" in appeals over the next two decades.[31] This conclusion underlines the impact courts can have on their own caseloads.

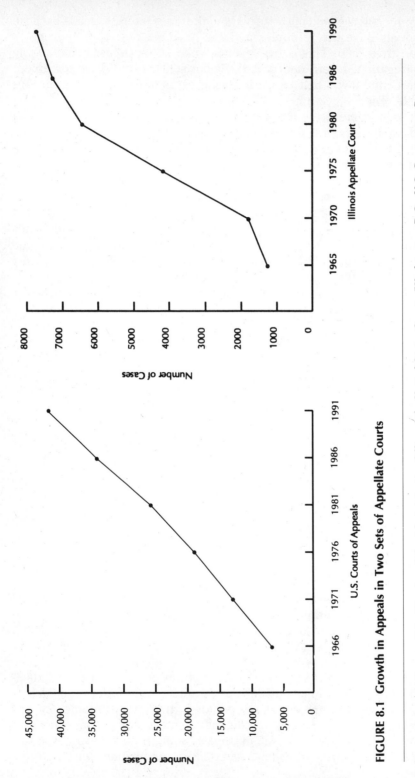

FIGURE 8.1 Growth in Appeals in Two Sets of Appellate Courts

Sources: Annual Report of the Director of the Administrative Office of the United States Courts (Washington, D.C.: U.S. Government Printing Office, various years); Administrative Office of the Illinois Courts, *Annual Report to the Supreme Court of Illinois* (Springfield: Administrative Office of the Illinois Courts, various years).

SCREENING CASES

The growth in appeals over the past few decades is an acceleration of a long-term trend: most appellate courts in most periods experience an increase in their caseloads. At different times over the last century, the caseloads of most courts reached a point at which their judges no longer felt they could give full attention to each case without creating an intolerable backlog. The primary response to this problem has been to adopt screening systems, under which some cases are selected to receive full judicial consideration, while others are handled in a more summary way.

These screening systems take two quite different forms. One involves the exercise of discretionary jurisdiction, under which some cases are given no decision at all. The other involves the selection of certain cases for abbreviated consideration by judges.

In general, different courts rely on different forms. Second-level appellate courts, which hold broad discretionary jurisdiction, screen out cases primarily by rejecting jurisdiction over them. In contrast, first-level courts, whose jurisdiction is mostly mandatory, give abbreviated consideration to some of the cases they are required to hear.

Discretionary Jurisdiction

The discretionary jurisdiction of some appellate courts is linked to the creation of appellate systems with two levels. Most supreme courts began as the only full appellate courts in their systems. Because of the belief that litigants are entitled to one appeal, most of their jurisdiction was mandatory. But as a supreme court's caseload grew and became burdensome, its justices sought relief. Congress and about three-quarters of the state legislatures responded by creating an intermediate appellate court and by giving the supreme court discretionary jurisdiction over a large share of the cases brought to it from the intermediate court. In some systems, as caseloads continued to grow, the supreme court's area of discretionary jurisdiction was later broadened to include more types of cases.

Under discretionary jurisdiction, a court can simply deny a hearing in any case that it chooses, thereby allowing the lower-court decision to become final. Furthermore, the court does not need to provide any reasons for such denials. Typically, it says only that the petition was denied, although according to legend one court sometimes responded with a longer message:

> Your case is so touching
> Your tale is sad.
> But we're too busy
> So it's too bad.[32]

A court's refusal to hear a case cannot be appealed elsewhere. (However, the U.S. Supreme Court can agree to hear a case that a state supreme court has refused to hear.) Thus courts with discretionary jurisdiction hold an impressive power to set their agendas as they see fit.

Screening Procedures Courts use a variety of procedures in deciding on requests for hearings. In general, as we would expect, the courts that receive the largest volume of cases have developed the most elaborate screening procedures.

The U.S. Supreme Court receives more petitions than any other court, currently more than five thousand each year. To deal with these petitions, it has created a two-stage screening process.[33] In the first stage, the Court identifies cases that seem to deserve closer scrutiny by putting them on its *discuss list*. Petitions for certiorari that fail to reach this list are denied without collective consideration.

The chief justice is primarily responsible for creating the discuss list, although another justice can ask that cases be added to it. In practice, at this stage the justices delegate most of the work of identifying meritorious petitions to law clerks, and most justices personally read only a small portion of the petitions and supporting materials. As of 1993 all but one of the justices pool their law clerks so that a single clerk summarizes a particular petition for all the justices who participate in the pool, after which a justice's own clerks do additional work on the petitions.

The second screening stage is consideration of the cases on the discuss list, fewer than one-third of the total. The justices vote in conference on whether to hear individual cases, usually without much discussion. As noted earlier, four votes from the nine justices are necessary to accept a case.

State supreme courts vary a good deal in their screening procedures. The procedure used by the California Supreme Court resembles the U.S. Supreme Court's process in most respects: a staff attorney prepares a "conference memo" on each petition for review for the justices and their clerks to consider, and petitions are placed on a "B-list" if no justice thinks that they deserve discussion by the court in conference. The key difference with the Supreme Court is that a majority vote—four of the seven justices—is required to accept a case.[34]

Courts differ in their propensities to accept cases; in general, those that receive the largest numbers of cases reject the largest proportions. Some cases are neither rejected nor fully accepted but receive summary decisions on the merits: in recent years the Michigan Supreme Court has rejected nearly 90 percent of what are called petitions for leave to appeal, disposed of another 8 percent through peremptory orders, and fully decided about 3 percent.[35]

Screening Criteria As we might expect, a variety of considerations influence decisions whether to accept cases. In broad terms, judges are motivated both by what they see as their court's responsibilities and by their policy goals. More specifically, several criteria appear to be important, with none dominant.[36]

One is the significance of the legal issues involved in a case. A supreme court can do the most to make the law clear and consistent, and its members can best advance their policy goals, by selecting cases with broad legal and practical significance. Ordinarily, for example, it makes little sense to accept a tort case with a narrow issue related to the facts of that case, an issue that may never arise again. But it makes a great deal of sense to accept a tort case involving general requirements for the safety of products, requirements that will be relevant to any product liability case in the future. Many petitions for hearings can be denied almost automatically because the narrowness of the issues they involve is self-evident. This does not mean that all significant cases are accepted, but those with the greatest potential impact usually gain a hearing.

Another important criterion is conflict or uncertainty in the law. Conflict can arise when two lower courts interpret a legal provision differently or when a lower court seems to depart from the supreme court's interpretation. Uncertainty can arise from an ambiguous provision of law. In practice, judges give high priority to resolving conflict and uncertainty. But as the numbers of laws and lower-court decisions proliferate, so too does the volume of legal conflicts and uncertainties. As a result, at least some supreme courts are unable to accept all the cases in which the law needs to be clarified; indeed, former Supreme Court Justice Byron White has made a frequent practice of pointing out cases that the Court rejected despite a conflict between lower courts. Nevertheless, a conflict or uncertainty on a significant issue, such as the meaning of a major tax provision or a fundamental principle of divorce law, is almost certain to gain consideration.

An impression that the lower court has made an error in the decision under review impels supreme court justices to accept certain cases. Though correction of errors is not the primary purpose of second-level courts, justices feel better about allowing a lower-court decision to stand if they think it was the right one. Thus the U.S. Supreme Court reverses lower-court decisions in most of the cases it hears, while courts without discretionary jurisdiction typically affirm in a clear majority of cases. Of course, different justices may not agree on whether a lower court erred, and their judgments are colored by their ideological predispositions. For instance, liberals are more inclined to accept cases brought by criminal defendants than are conservatives.

Judges' policy preferences may be manifested in other ways as well. For instance, they sometimes act on their predictions of what would happen if their court accepted a case. If a justice thinks that the lower court interpreted the law incorrectly but that the supreme court would still affirm the lower court, the justice might prefer to leave the decision standing rather than give it supreme court approval. This practice is so common on the U.S. Supreme Court that it has a standard label: "defensive denials."[37]

As this discussion suggests, judges frequently disagree as to whether a case should be heard. In the Supreme Court, a great many cases are accepted with only four or five votes, and sometimes justices are sufficiently unhappy with decisions to deny hearings that they announce their dissents from those decisions. A study of the Georgia Supreme Court suggests one explanation for such disagreements: different justices seem to give different weights to various criteria in deciding whether to accept a case.[38]

As these disagreements indicate, the agendas of courts with discretionary jurisdiction reflect the goals and perspectives that are dominant among their justices at a given time. As a court's membership changes, so will its case-screening decisions: it is not surprising, for instance, that the Burger and Rehnquist Courts have been more favorable to prosecutors' petitions for hearings in criminal cases than was the Warren Court.[39]

Screening of Mandatory Cases

When judges on supreme courts find their caseloads burdensome, they can seek discretionary jurisdiction. But judges on intermediate courts have no such option; their jurisdiction will remain mandatory. Working within this constraint, judges on these courts have taken several kinds of actions to cope with growing caseloads. One is to request additional judges and supporting personnel. Another is to use prehearing conferences to encourage the parties to settle.

Courts have also made staffing and procedural changes that allow them to dispose of cases with smaller expenditures of judicial time. The most important of these changes are the creation of central staffs and the regular use of abbreviated alternatives to traditional procedures. In most courts, the two innovations go together: central staff members screen cases to determine which will receive abbreviated consideration and do much of the work in the cases that are selected for that abbreviated consideration. As noted earlier, in courts that regularly use abbreviated procedures, they can become the rule rather than the exception.

Case Screening and the Use of Abbreviated Procedures   Different courts screen cases and abbreviate their consideration in different ways. But certain procedural similarities do exist, in part because courts have copied practices from each other. The approach taken by most courts follows the general lines of this model:[40]

1. After the court has received the full set of written materials in a case, these materials are routed to its central staff. Either the chief staff attorney or an individual member of the staff then reviews each case and decides tentatively whether it should receive full court consideration or more limited treatment. Cases assigned to the latter category are viewed as easy to decide, usually because the appellant seems to have a weak case. Full-consideration cases are sent to a panel of judges for a decision; in most courts, the panel usually holds oral argument in these cases. In contrast, the cases designated for abbreviated treatment are retained within the central staff for further work.
2. A staff attorney examines more fully each case that has not been sent to a panel of judges for decision. At this point, the staff member may decide that the original judgment was wrong and that the case requires full court consideration. Ordinarily, however, the staff member proceeds to write a memorandum on the case, usually with a recommendation as to how it should be decided. In many courts, the staff member also writes a brief proposed opinion for the court.

3. The cases that the staff has considered are assigned to a court panel, often a special "screening" panel, and the case materials are forwarded there as well. The judges on the panel, usually three in number, review each case individually or as a group. If any judge feels that oral argument is necessary, it can then be scheduled. Otherwise the panel considers the case and reaches a decision on the basis of the written materials. This decision is issued with an opinion, usually a brief per curiam one that is based on the staff attorney's work. This opinion usually goes unpublished.

The Impact of Case Screening and Abbreviated Procedures   Appellate courts screen mandatory cases and reach decisions through abbreviated procedures primarily to improve their efficiency. By deciding a high proportion of cases with less of its judges' time, a court potentially can dispose of more cases with the same number of judges. And screening does seem to have this impact. In the intermediate courts of Illinois and New Jersey, for example, the adoption of screening systems helped to bring about measurable increases in output.[41]

Screening may have other effects on a court and its work, some of them unintended and undesired. One concerns the quality of the court's decision-making—its capacity to reach the decisions it would make under ideal conditions, when its judges would have unlimited time to learn about the facts and law involved in a case and to consider them. Advocates of staff involvement in decisions argue that preparatory work by staff attorneys provides busy judges with a better basis for their decisions, and undoubtedly there is some truth to this claim. Yet Thomas Y. Davies concluded from his study of a California court of appeal that central staff involvement in cases is unlikely to improve the quality of decision-making; indeed, in his view the "assignment of an appeal to staff processing normally ensures that the case will be treated as 'routine' or 'frivolous,' " and so it is given relatively little scrutiny.[42] Two legal scholars with experience on appellate courts suggested that "there is a substantial risk that central staff case processing may lead to premature judgment based upon information inaccurately filtered by staff."[43]

Another possible effect is to reduce judges' control over decisions. While abbreviated procedures are designed to ensure that judges determine how cases are decided, practical realities may undermine this goal. When pressed for time, judges are strongly tempted to accept a staff attorney's analysis of a case rather than engage in the laborious task of examining and considering case materials themselves. A study of the Michigan Court of Appeals found "high levels of agreement between staff recommendations and the judges' decisions, strongly suggesting that the judges rely almost entirely on staff recommendations to reach their decisions."[44] A staff attorney on the Kansas Court of Appeals interpreted high agreement rates differently: "the judges agreed with me most often simply because they had no choice—there was only one answer possible."[45] Yet the concerns that judges themselves express about the roles of central staffs indicate that they too perceive a loss of control, and some shift of power from judges to staff members seems inevitable.

A final consequence is that staff screening may weaken the vitality of the right to appeal. Most cases to which courts give abbreviated consideration are put in this category because the appellant's case seems weak. But in light of such an initial perception and the absence of oral argument, does this mean that appellants are effectively denied the opportunity to make their case? A study of the federal Fifth Circuit Court of Appeals found that the proportion of cases in which the district court decision was affirmed increased after the introduction of screening procedures.[46] This finding suggests that such procedures can exert a subtle but significant—and perhaps troubling—impact on the outputs of the appellate courts. Yet a study of the Ninth Circuit Court of Appeals indicated that assignment of cases to screening panels did not affect the likelihood of reversal—though it did decrease the likelihood of a published opinion.[47]

This issue underlines a more general point: structural and procedural changes adopted for such seemingly neutral reasons as efficiency can affect the substance of what courts do. Judges have not adopted abbreviated procedures in order to change the patterns of the decisions that they reach; they are simply trying to keep up with their caseloads. Yet the changes they have made may be producing different outcomes for some litigants and different court policies.

DECISION-MAKING

Whether its jurisdiction is chiefly mandatory or discretionary, the heart of an appellate court's work is its decisions in the cases it hears. These decisions produce victories and defeats for individual litigants. More important, they establish rules of law that influence both future cases and activity outside the courts. This section examines the forces that shape appellate court decisions.

Perspectives on Decision-Making: An Overview

The explanations for court behavior presented in Chapter 1 suggest that judicial decisions can be explained from several perspectives: the legal perspective, which views decisions as the products of legal rules; the personal perspective, which explains decisions in terms of the judges themselves; and the environmental perspective, which emphasizes influences on judicial decisions from the larger society. The applicability of each perspective differs somewhat between first-level and second-level appellate courts.

First-Level Courts   Because first-level courts have mandatory jurisdiction, they must decide both "easy" and "difficult" cases. Judges on these courts frequently express the view that most of their cases are easy to decide because the merits clearly lie on one side. Indeed, legal scholar and Supreme Court Justice Benjamin N. Cardozo concluded that perhaps 90 percent of appeals could be decided only one way.[48]

When judges speak of easy cases, for the most part they are referring to appeals that they perceive as having little merit, so that affirmance is the obvious result. The chief judge of the federal Eighth Circuit Court of Appeals in St. Louis estimated that about one-quarter of all appeals his court receives are "frivolous."[49] A judge on a California court of appeal commented that "if 90 per cent of this stuff were in the United States Post Office, it would be classified as junk mail."[50]

These judges are saying in effect that the law is the dominant element in the decision-making performed by first-level appellate courts: in their view, most of the time only one result can be justified under the law. This belief helps judges to feel comfortable about delegating responsibility in many of the seemingly easy cases to central staffs. It also helps explain the low rates of dissent in most first-level appellate courts: in a high proportion of these cases, it would be difficult for judges to disagree about the result.

In some cases, probably more than most judges recognize, the decision is not so clear-cut and judges must exercise discretion. In doing so, they usually are not subject to much external pressure. Most first-level courts are intermediate courts, less visible to the public than the courts above or below them. Particularly at the state level, intermediate courts receive relatively little attention and thus relatively limited scrutiny from the mass media and interest groups.

This does not mean that these courts are entirely free from influence by their environment. But the influence is primarily indirect and fairly subtle. Because external pressures are relatively weak, judges' personal characteristics become especially important in shaping their judgments. And because appellate decisions are made by groups of judges, their interaction helps determine how individual proclivities are translated into collective decisions.

Second-Level Courts   Second-level courts usually have some mandatory jurisdiction; as a result, they decide some relatively easy cases. But their jurisdiction is mainly discretionary, allowing them to screen out a substantial majority of cases in which parties ask for hearings. Because there would be little point to hearing cases with obvious results, those that a court selects generally involve more difficult and arguable questions. Thus, because of case screening, existing legal rules constrain second-level courts to only a limited degree. Indeed, cases often require that courts establish new rules in order to clarify ambiguities and fill in gaps in the law.

This does not mean that the law is irrelevant to decisions in these courts. On the contrary, existing legal principles often push a court strongly toward some results and away from others; this fact helps explain why even the U.S. Supreme Court, whose members feel free to express their disagreements in public, often makes a unanimous decision. Nevertheless, the frequency of dissent both in the Supreme Court and in many state supreme courts reflects judges' freedom to interpret the law in different ways.[51]

In general, the U.S. Supreme Court and state supreme courts enjoy considerably less insulation from their environments than do intermediate appellate courts. Some supreme courts receive extensive newspaper coverage, sometimes headlines, and interest groups are often involved in cases before them. Legislators, too, pay considerable attention to the activities of supreme courts. As a result, supreme court justices feel more direct external pressure than do intermediate appellate judges. But even in supreme courts, a great many decisions, including some important ones, receive comparatively little notice. And even when supreme courts are subject to intense scrutiny, they are generally less vulnerable to external pressures than legislatures and chief executives.

Thus the law and the environment leave judges on second-level courts with considerable—though incomplete—freedom to take the directions that they wish in their decisions. As a consequence, perhaps more than in any other courts, judges' characteristics and interactions among judges determine the decisions that these courts make. For this reason, an explanation of the decisions made in most supreme courts must focus primarily on the justices themselves.

The rest of this section looks more closely at three elements in appellate court decision-making: judges' policy preferences, group processes, and the environment of courts.

Policy Preferences

In voting on cases over the course of a year, the justices on the U.S. Supreme Court divide along a variety of lines; in the various 5–4 decisions that the Court reaches, there are likely to be several different combinations of five justices who make up the majority. But this does not mean that the patterns of justices' votes are random. Rather, these patterns are fairly systematic, with certain justices taking relatively liberal positions in most cases and other justices taking more conservative positions.

As a result, there is considerable predictability as to the ways that justices line up. In 1993, if we heard that the Court had voted 7–2 against someone with a civil liberties claim, we could guess with considerable confidence that the dissenters were John Paul Stevens and Harry Blackmun. Such a guess would be accurate the overwhelming majority of the time.

Preferences, Ideology, and Decisions   What accounts for this predictability? The primary reason is that differences in the responses of justices to the same case result primarily from their preferences about the policy issues in the case. External pressures and the law may move the whole Court in one direction or the other, but disagreements among the justices stem chiefly from their views about policy. Because the preferences are fairly stable, so are the differences in interpretations of the law that they produce. Knowing that Stevens and Blackmun were the two justices who interpreted legal protections for civil liberties most broadly, we could point to them as the most likely dissenters from a ruling against a claim based on those protections.

As noted in Chapter 1, most of the policy issues that courts address can be characterized in liberal-conservative terms. And a justice who takes a liberal position on one issue is likely to take liberal positions on most others.

John Paul Stevens, for instance, has been highly supportive of a wide range of civil liberties claims; he has also supported the use of government regulatory power over business. Some other justices are less consistent in this sense, taking more liberal positions on some issues than on others, but it is quite rare for a justice to stand at the liberal end of the Court on one set of issues and at the conservative end on another.

Based on the frequency with which they cast liberal and conservative votes, the justices can be placed on a continuum ranging from the most liberal to the most conservative. Figure 8.2 shows how the members of the Court in 1993 might be placed, based on their liberal and conservative votes on civil liberties cases in the Court's 1991–1992 term. (The figure depicts the positions of the justices relative to each other, not in absolute terms; because there was no strong liberal on the Court, the continuum makes moderate liberals and moderate conservatives appear more liberal than they actually were.)

Figure 8.2 also shows the divisions between justices on the two sides in some civil liberties decisions during the term. Most divisions were consistent with the positions of the justices on the overall continuum, showing that general ideological positions are often reflected quite clearly in individual decisions. But some cases divided justices in ways that we would not predict from the continuum.

Of course, something other than policy preferences might account for the degree of consistency that exists in the ways that the Court divides, but no other explanation seems nearly as reasonable. Indeed, the general positions that justices will take on issues before the Supreme Court can usually be predicted with some accuracy as soon as they are appointed, on the basis of the preferences they have expressed up to that time.[52] Chief Justice William Rehnquist, a strong conservative on the Court since his appointment as associate justice in 1971, had established himself as very conservative during his legal and political career up to 1971.

The impact of ideology on the justices' behavior should not be exaggerated. First of all, some issues that come to the Court, such as disputes between states over their borders, do not have much ideological content. And cases involving economic issues do not have as clear an ideological content as they once did, so that they produce less systematic voting patterns than do civil liberties cases. More important, even justices with strong preferences on particular issues sometimes take positions that seem to deviate from these views, usually because their reading of the law pulls them toward these positions or because of a desire to achieve unanimity on the Court.

Yet justices' policy preferences are perhaps the most important factor influencing their behavior. As we have seen, differences among the justices stem chiefly from their preferences, and the basic direction that most justices take on the Court seems to reflect the attitudes about policy issues that they bring to the Court.

So far I have focused on the U.S. Supreme Court, but policy preferences tied to ideology influence the positions that judges take on other appellate courts as well. This is especially true of state supreme courts with discretionary

Liberal ←————————————————————————————————→ Conservative

Stevens	Blackmun	O'Connor	White	Scalia
		Souter	Rehnquist	
		Kennedy	Thomas	

Cases with Divisions That Were Entirely Consistent with the Continuum

Hudson v. McMillian (1992): Can the use of excessive physical force against a prisoner constitute cruel and unusual punishment even if the inmate does not suffer serious injury?
Yes: Stevens, Blackmun, O'Connor, Souter, Kennedy, White, Rehnquist
No: Scalia, Thomas

Medina v. California (1992): Under the due process clause of the 14th Amendment, can a state require that criminal defendants who claim incompetence to stand trial bear the burden of proof on that issue?
Yes: Scalia, Thomas, Rehnquist, White, Kennedy, Souter, O'Connor
No: Stevens, Blackmun

Lee v. Weisman (1992): Do prayers by clergy at official public school graduation ceremonies violate the Establishment Clause of the First Amendment?
Yes: Stevens, Blackmun, O'Connor, Souter, Kennedy
No: Scalia, Thomas, Rehnquist, White

Cases with Divisions That Were Partially Inconsistent with the Continuum

Wyatt v. Cole (1992): Do private parties have partial immunity from lawsuits brought for violations of rights under the Civil Rights Act of 1871?
Yes: Thomas, Rehnquist, Souter
No: Stevens, Blackmun, O'Connor, Kennedy, White, Scalia

Doggett v. United States (1992): Did an eight-and-a-half year delay between a defendant's indictment and arrest, for which the federal government was responsible, violate the defendant's right to a speedy trial?
Yes: Stevens, Blackmun, Souter, Kennedy, White
No: Thomas, Scalia, Rehnquist, O'Connor

FIGURE 8.2 Positions of 1993 Supreme Court Justices on a Liberal-Conservative Continuum in Civil Liberties Cases, with Divisions of Justices in Selected Cases

Note: The places of the justices on the continuum and the width of the distances between them are based on the numbers of liberal and conservative dissenting votes cast by each justice in civil liberties cases in the 1991–1992 term. Justices in the same position on the continuum cast about the same numbers of liberal and conservative votes in the term. Justice Thomas joined the Court after the beginning of the term; his place has been adjusted slightly to compensate for his nonparticipation in some cases.

jurisdiction, for the law is uncertain in most of the cases that they hear. It is less true of first-level appellate courts because they hear so many cases with seemingly obvious results; in such cases, judges' policy preferences can have little impact. However, the minority of cases in which ideology is relevant tend to be the most important—the ones in which the court's decision affects people other than the parties.

Indeed, there is a variety of evidence that judges' preferences influence decisions at all levels of appellate courts. For instance, as in the Supreme Court, lower-court judges who bring well-established views on legal issues to their positions typically follow the same path on the bench. A good example is Richard Posner, a noted law professor at the University of Chicago, who was appointed to the federal Court of Appeals for the Seventh Circuit. As a professor, Posner had staked out strong conservative positions on legal issues involving economic questions; as a judge, he has taken similarly conservative positions.[53]

There are some appellate courts in which judges do not seem to follow ideological lines in the positions they take. In 1990 one observer said of the Maryland Court of Appeals, the state's highest court, that "I can't think of anyone on the court who is ideological one way or the other."[54] But in general, from the Supreme Court to state intermediate courts, judges' preferences on individual issues and their overall positions on the liberal-conservative spectrum go far toward determining their behavior on the bench.

Court Policies and the Selection of Judges   It follows that the general direction of an appellate court's policies is chiefly the product of its membership. For example, a state supreme court whose members are mostly liberals is very likely to take liberal positions on most issues. The positions of federal courts of appeals on controversial issues vary with the mix of liberals and conservatives in the various circuits. Change in a court's position can be explained in similar terms. The U.S. Supreme Court has shifted a good deal in the ideological tenor of its policies over the past half century, and these shifts result chiefly from the departure of some justices and their replacement by justices with different views.

In turn, this means that the people who select judges have considerable power to shape the direction of the courts. Presidents and governors are in especially powerful positions because presidents choose federal judges with Senate confirmation and governors choose a high proportion of state judges through regular and interim appointments. Thus, given enough opportunities and sufficient care, a chief executive can have a fundamental effect on court policies.

We are most familiar with the impact some presidents have had on the Supreme Court. For example, with eight appointments, Franklin Roosevelt was largely responsible for making the Court a liberal force in American life. In turn, Richard Nixon used his four appointments to moderate the Court's liberalism.

Presidents have similar effects on the lower federal courts. Although Jimmy Carter was the first president in a century who filled no Supreme

Court vacancies, he did appoint more judges to the lower federal courts than any of his predecessors. Carter and his aides in the Justice Department selected judges with attention to their policy views, and as a result his appointments made the courts of appeals and the district courts more liberal.

The impact of Ronald Reagan and George Bush on the federal courts is particularly clear. On the Supreme Court, Reagan's elevation of William Rehnquist to chief justice in 1986 brought the Court's most conservative member into that leadership position. Reagan's three appointments of associate justices (Sandra Day O'Connor, Antonin Scalia, and Anthony Kennedy), followed by Bush's selection of David Souter and Clarence Thomas, tilted the Court in a more conservative direction.

Reagan and Bush also had a considerable effect on the courts of appeals and district courts. By the time that Bush left office in 1993, about two-thirds of all federal judges were their appointees. As a result, federal judicial policy moved substantially, though unevenly, in a conservative direction. While this movement was most visible in civil liberties law, it was also reflected in economic fields such as antitrust and environmental protection.[55]

Almost surely, most of the people whom Bill Clinton appoints to the lower courts will be liberals, so that the conservative shift in these courts will be halted and probably reversed to some degree. Clinton's impact on the Supreme Court is less certain, depending not only on his choices but also on how many vacancies appear during his tenure and which justices he replaces.

In California, supreme court appointments by Democratic Governor Jerry Brown (1975–1983) made a liberal court even more liberal in its collective point of view, resulting in doctrinal positions strongly favorable to groups such as injured people and criminal defendants. A series of appointments by Brown's Republican successor, George Deukmejian (1983–1991), created a strong conservative majority, and the court reversed its decisional tendencies in civil liberties and economic policy—overturning several of its precedents in the process. The most striking indication of the court's shift is the proportion of death sentences that it reversed: 93 percent between 1977 and 1986, as against 22 percent between 1987 and 1990.[56]

There are, of course, limits to the impact of the appointment power. Some judges disappoint the chief executives who appointed them, either because their views were misunderstood or because they changed after appointment. And even a judge who generally performs as expected will cast some votes that the judge's appointer dislikes.

These limits are reflected in the work of the Reagan and Bush appointees to the Supreme Court. The positions taken by each have been more conservative than liberal; in that sense, the appointments were successful. But some of these justices, such as O'Connor, have adopted a relatively moderate conservatism; as a result, the Court has not moved as far to the right as many observers had expected. And, even though Reagan and Bush were particularly concerned with their nominees' views on abortion, in 1992 three of their appointees (O'Connor, Kennedy, and Souter) jointly wrote the decisive opinion that maintained significant restrictions on state regulation of abortion.[57]

In the states that elect judges, voters can also change the courts' direction. In Texas and Ohio, voters in the late 1970s and early 1980s elected new supreme court justices with liberal views on issues in tort law, and the new justices brought about changes in long-standing tort doctrines. More recently, voters in those two states elected some more conservative justices, producing some policy changes in the opposite direction.

Group Processes

The classic image of an appellate court is one in which judges work closely together, discussing and arguing about decisions, drafting and redrafting opinions, until the court reaches its collective conclusion. This image suggests that group processes are quite important in shaping appellate court decisions. Although it has considerable accuracy, the image nonetheless exaggerates what might be called the group element in appellate court decisions. Some conditions work in favor of group influence on decisions, and others against it.

The group element in decisions is promoted by the desire to reach a consensus. Judges strive to produce an opinion that can be accepted by at least a majority, so that there can be an authoritative statement of legal principles by the court. Most judges also want to achieve unanimity on both the outcome of the case and the opinion of the court, for unanimity may give their decisions greater authority. Thus the members of an appellate court have an incentive to work together to reach mutually acceptable decisions and opinions.

The strong views that judges often hold on policy issues also promote the group element, for most judges want to see their views reflected in their court's decisions. Hence, particularly in cases that raise important policy questions, judges are likely to work at persuading their colleagues. Certainly, this is the case on the Supreme Court, whose members often engage in intensive efforts to influence the positions of other justices.

The group element in decisions can have an impact on what a court decides, as judges compromise over the language of an opinion or their arguments convince colleagues to change their positions. At the Supreme Court, for instance, it is common for the decision tentatively reached in conference after oral argument to become a different final decision after interaction among the justices.

The extent to which a court's decisions are actually group products depends in part on structural conditions and time pressures. One relevant structural condition is the difference between supreme courts that typically decide cases en banc, as a single group, and intermediate appellate courts that decide cases primarily in shifting panels of judges. In courts that sit en banc, the same judges work together continuously and thus develop a sense of how to work with—and persuade—each other. On large federal courts of appeals, in contrast, it is difficult for any particular set of three judges to develop the sorts of relationships and routines that facilitate effective group decision-making. The schedule of the federal Court of Appeals for the District of

Columbia, however, is arranged so that every judge sits for at least one week with every other judge each year; one member of the court has described this system as part of the court's effort to move judges toward "institutionally-minded" rather than "individualist" judging.[58]

Another structural condition is the amount of time that judges spend together. On most federal courts of appeals, judges reside and work in different cities, and on some state supreme courts the judges do most of their work in their home cities rather than in the capital. Although this separation does not preclude group interaction, it does limit such interaction.[59] In contrast, the judges on some courts work in close proximity to each other. When the Illinois Supreme Court is in session, for about six months a year, its members "work, eat and sleep in the same building, a situation that keeps them in almost constant contact."[60]

A member of the New York Court of Appeals, the state's highest court, has argued that these two structural conditions have considerable impact on her court:

> The fact that we are a nonresident, plenary bench promotes quick bonding. In Albany, we are all away from hearth and home, with a huge caseload and the same seven of us to work our way through it. Every case is a matter to be resolved in common. We spend a major part of our Albany days in conference, engaged in the sometimes bruising but miraculously solidifying process of trying to reach a consensus.[61]

The extent of a court's time pressures also influences its group life. On a court with limited pressures, judges have the freedom to spend considerable time working with colleagues to reach a decision in each case. With growing caseloads, however, judges increasingly lack that freedom. As we have seen, the heavy time pressures that exist in most appellate courts today lead judges to delegate important work to law clerks and central staff members. The same pressures also work against the long and careful deliberation that must be undertaken if decisions are truly to be group products. Today judges on many courts simply may not have the time for lengthy discussion and negotiation over their cases.

Indeed, appellate decisions sometimes take a form that is at the other extreme from a truly collective decision—in what has been called a one-judge decision.[62] In many courts, a case is assigned to one judge early in the court's consideration of it, with the implicit understanding that this judge will take primary responsibility for the decision. The other judges pay less attention to the case and generally defer to the assigned judge's view. As a result, the court's decision in some instances depends largely on the random assignment of a case to one judge rather than another. And even when a court does not use early assignment procedures, its judges may be reluctant to disagree with the position of the judge who writes the opinion in a case. "I hate to say this," one California judge conceded, "but just the workload alone may encourage one judge to agree with the others, because otherwise he or she would have to write a dissenting opinion."[63] Several judges on one federal court of appeals reported that they limited their dissents to cases in which they disagreed strongly with the majority—when they felt what one judge called "outrage"—primarily because of a lack of time.[64]

In the current Supreme Court, however, time pressures seem to have something like the opposite result. In the last two decades there has been a proliferation of concurring opinions, with justices writing an unprecedented number of individual opinions to express their own reasons for joining the majority.[65] While this proliferation may reflect interpersonal conflicts and the increased availability of clerks to draft opinions, perhaps more important are the time pressures that prevent justices from working together to iron out the differences in their positions.

As this discussion has suggested, the significance of group processes in shaping court decisions can vary. Such processes affect the decisions of some courts more than others because of differences in their structural features, time pressures, and even traditions. On any particular court, some decisions receive more collective consideration than others; even on a court with a high division of labor, judges will not defer to a single colleague on a major case involving abortion or the death penalty. In general, it is best to consider group processes as an important factor in appellate decisions, albeit one that is distinctly secondary to the preferences of individual judges.

Influence of Individual Judges   In the group processes that shape decisions, we can expect some judges to exert more influence than others. One source of special influence is the judge's position. Each court has a chief judge or chief justice who holds certain powers within the court. Particularly where the position is permanent rather than rotating among judges, it may also carry a degree of prestige. On appellate courts that divide into panels, the most senior judge on each panel generally acts as a kind of temporary chief who directs the panel's work.

The powers of chief judges vary considerably from court to court.[66] Of the various powers that some chief judges hold, among the most important is presiding over conference discussions of cases. The conference leader can formulate the alternatives to be considered and channel the discussion of those alternatives, thereby helping to move the court in a particular direction.

Also useful is the power to assign the responsibility of writing the court's opinion. On most appellate courts, assignment generally is random. But in some courts the chief judge holds this power. (In a few of these courts, including the U.S. Supreme Court, chief justices assign opinions only when they were part of the majority in the court's initial vote on a case.) By assigning an opinion to an ideological ally or writing the opinion personally, the chief judge can secure a desired rationale for the decision; by assigning the opinion to an ideologically moderate judge, the chief judge can increase the likelihood of achieving consensus.

The influence of a chief judge depends on leadership skills and on the inclinations of other judges, as well as on the formal powers of the position. Some chief justices of the Supreme Court seem to have exerted considerable influence over the Court's direction, while others have played much more limited roles. Some observers, for instance, see William Rehnquist as more influential than his predecessor Warren Burger.

Of course, judges other than the chief judge can also have a disproportionate influence on their colleagues—an influence often stemming from extraordinary legal or persuasive skills. On the Supreme Court, William Brennan (1956–1990) seemed to be an important leader because he worked effectively to build majorities for liberal positions. Indeed, Brennan's leadership has been credited with solidifying the liberal majority on the Warren Court and with achieving some victories for liberal positions in an increasingly conservative Court under Warren Burger and William Rehnquist.

Some judges, in contrast, exert little influence over their colleagues. They make no effort to sway other judges, or their personal characteristics or situations blunt their effectiveness. John Purtle, a member of the Arkansas Supreme Court from 1979 to 1990, found himself completely at odds with the other six justices because of strong ideological disagreement and their disapproval of some of his conduct on and off the bench. Purtle resigned from the court, saying that "there is no need to keep butting my head against the wall. . . . There is no likelihood that either the majority or I will change."[67]

Ultimately, however, the small size of appellate courts and panels produces a considerable equality of influence. Simply casting one vote out of nine provides a good deal of leverage in itself, and one out of three provides even more. On any court, then, influence is likely to operate in all directions.

Interpersonal Relationships   In appellate courts, as in other groups, interpersonal relations can vary from harmonious to highly conflictual. But because interaction among judges generally occurs in private, it is often difficult for people outside a court to discern the character of relationships within it.

We might take frequent disagreement in cases as evidence of internal conflict, but this is not necessarily so. High dissent rates may reflect a court's ideological lineup and its traditions rather than the relations among justices. A more meaningful sign of conflict is heated language in opinions, as illustrated by the excerpts from one case in Exhibit 8.5. But even judges who direct sharp comments at each other in their opinions may actually work well together. On the current Supreme Court, justice Antonin Scalia stands out for the frequency with which he uses strong language in his opinions to attack competing opinions, but this does not necessarily mean that Scalia is in personal conflict with the colleagues he attacks. (But in 1991 Robert Bork— denied confirmation to the Supreme Court in 1987—declared that the Court was "a snake pit.")[68]

Occasionally, though, the conflict within a court is so intense that it becomes visible even to outsiders. In the Missouri Supreme Court, one judge was attacked by two colleagues—one of whom called for impeachment—for his alleged role in appointments of three new justices.[69] In Nevada, the chief justice of the Supreme Court became embroiled in a battle with three of his colleagues, who strongly suggested in a confidential memo (which became public) that the chief justice retire.[70] In 1992 a long period of friction among

"The majority violates a fundamental tenet of appellate review by upholding a verdict on a theory that was never presented to the jury."

"My colleagues take a giant leap into a dangerous and heretofore uncharted no-man's land, ill-serving the causes of environmental hygiene, industrial safety and worker privacy."

"The majority also interprets Alaska law in a dangerous and unprecedented way, and wholly ignores serious public policy concerns."

"This strikes me as a result so preposterous it would be laughable if it were not so scary."

Alex Kozinski of the Ninth Circuit Court of Appeals, dissenting in *Sanders v. Parker Drilling Company*, 911 F.2d 191 (1991).

"The dissent claims that the result we reach today is 'so preposterous it would be laughable if it were not scary,' . . . a remarkable comment considering that the dissent not only flagrantly misconstrues an elementary legal principle . . . but does so in 'a dangerous and unprecedented way.' "

"If courts accepted the views of our dissenting colleague, the consequences would be staggering."

"Regretfully, I must add that in addition to its disregard for traditional tenets of job security, the dissent demonstrates an equally blatant disdain for the fundamental concept of guilt and innocence."

Stephen Reinhardt of the Ninth Circuit Court of Appeals, concurring in *Sanders*.

EXHIBIT 8.5 Two Federal Judges Disagree About a Decision

members of the Pennsylvania Supreme Court culminated in a vote to reprimand one justice for his involvement in a case at the trial level; that justice then charged that two colleagues had committed several misdeeds and that they had "enormous cravings and appetites for power and control."[71]

Among the courts that have experienced strong conflicts over a long period of time are the federal Court of Appeals for the District of Columbia and the Ohio Supreme Court; those conflicts are described in Exhibit 8.6. The two courts illustrate the differing sources of enmities among judges: the primary source in the District of Columbia court has been ideological differences, while political rivalries have been central to conflicts in the Ohio court. In these and other courts, personal enmities have also played a part in fostering bad feelings.

Interpersonal relations are likely to affect a court's functioning. Good relations facilitate consensus in cases and enhance a court's efficiency in handling its work, while bad relations may have just the opposite effect. Even efforts to prevent conflict may have an effect. The Rhode Island Supreme Court of the early 1970s, for instance, seemed to avoid major policy issues in order to maintain harmony among justices with diverse views.[72] This example suggests both that active involvement in difficult issues may be a source of

---

The Ohio Supreme Court

The Ohio court has had a good deal of internal conflict over the years, in part because of partisan rivalries. In the first half of the 1980s, Democratic Chief Justice Frank Celebrezze and a party colleague had a public conflict with some Republican justices—a conflict featuring some vitriolic language in opinions. The conflict was especially heated in 1985 and 1986. "On just one day," according to a reporter, "two jurists exchanged accusations of case-fixing, payoffs, lying, electronic surveillance and political orchestration. And then things really got nasty."

After a period of relative quiet, new conflicts arose between Republican Andy Douglas, relatively liberal in his positions, and some other court Republicans. In 1991 Douglas and a colleague had a physical scuffle, reportedly resulting from a leak of information to one of the state's newspapers. The next year Douglas and Republican Chief Justice Thomas Moyer accused each other of taking actions to hurt their chances for re-election.

The Federal Court of Appeals for the District of Columbia

The federal courts in the District of Columbia hear an unusually large number of cases that involve significant political and policy issues. Partly for this reason, there have been serious frictions between liberal and conservative judges on the court of appeals. During the 1960s the two ideological factions ate separately in the judges' dining room, and one moderate judge ate elsewhere because it was "more comfortable over here, away from the feuding."

During the 1980s and early 1990s strong conflicts within the court surfaced. The language in some opinions was bitter, and in one incident a judge told a colleague that "if you were ten years younger I would be tempted to punch you in the nose." The leak of a draft opinion in 1991 created difficulties for Clarence Thomas, a member of the court, during the battle over his confirmation to the Supreme Court. The next year the court's liberals and conservatives feuded publicly—in part through press releases—over investigation of the leak.

Sources: Reports in newspapers and other periodicals. The quotations are from, respectively, Lee Leonard, "Slugging It Out at the Ohio Supreme Court," *Columbus Monthly,* November 1985, p. 147; Joseph C. Goulden, *The Benchwarmers: The Private World of the Powerful Federal Judges* (New York: Weybright and Talley, 1974), p. 253; and Ann Pelham, "Silberman, Dogged by Story, Provides Details of Outburst," *Legal Times,* March 11, 1991, p. 7.

EXHIBIT 8.6 Conflicts in Two Appellate Courts

conflict and that willingness to face conflict may allow a court to address such issues.

The Court's Environment

Ultimately, everything that courts do can be traced to external forces. Judges' policy preferences, for instance, are the products of social influences on them.

But courts are also subject to more specific and direct influences from their environment. As suggested earlier, appellate courts enjoy a certain degree of insulation. Yet this insulation is not total, and some external forces are sufficiently strong to have a major impact on appellate court policies.

The Legal Environment   Appellate courts are part of a legal community that includes lawyers and other courts. This community exerts an impact on court decisions that goes beyond the general pressure to follow legal rules.

In making their decisions, judges pay attention to the positions of other courts— and not just the higher ones to which they owe obedience. The opinions of state and federal appellate courts constitute a body of doctrine from which judges on any court can draw ideas. Judges, like legislators and administrators, look to their counterparts elsewhere for solutions to policy problems. Thus, when the Illinois Supreme Court faces a domestic relations issue that is new to it, its members will be interested in how other state supreme courts and the Illinois Appellate Court have dealt with the same issue. Furthermore, if several courts have addressed an issue and the weight of judicial opinion lies primarily on one side, that weight may sway another court that faces the issue.

These kinds of influences can help produce broader doctrinal trends. In the period from the 1950s through the 1970s, state supreme courts adopted several new legal doctrines favorable to plaintiffs in personal injury cases. In doing so, they spurred each other on: as more and more courts adopted a particular doctrine, the impetus for others to jump on the bandwagon grew. Thus, when it eliminated one long-standing rule in 1973, the New Mexico Supreme Court pointed out that "in so doing, we join the growing number of States which have judicially abolished it," and the court attached an appendix to its opinion showing the numerical support for its position in other states.[73]

The opinions of lawyers can also influence a court. Of course, the lawyers who argue cases can influence specific decisions. Supreme Court Justice David Souter reported that, when he was on the New Hampshire Supreme Court, he kept track of his tentative positions in cases before and after oral argument; there were enough shifts "to indicate to me that oral argument was a matter of substantial importance to me in deciding cases."[74]

Lawyers' advocacy can have broader effects as well. In the late nineteenth and early twentieth centuries, for instance, some of the most skilled attorneys in the country represented businesses that sought to have government regulations of business practices declared unconstitutional, and their efforts influenced the views of federal judges on such regulation.[75] The lawyers representing civil rights and civil liberties groups in the past half century have played a similar role.

Another influence on judges is the general pattern of opinion within the bar on social and political issues. Not only do law school and legal practice shape the attitudes of people who later become judges, but these judges continue to interact with lawyers and to read what lawyers are saying about legal issues. As a result, judges are drawn toward prevailing opinions within the bar. Traditionally, the predominant viewpoint of the legal profession was conservative, but in recent years that viewpoint has become more liberal; one sign of this change is a striking shift in the positions taken by the American Bar Association on political issues. The more liberal legal profession may be one force helping to sustain judicial liberalism.

The Political Environment   As already noted, interest groups can have an impact on court decisions through their involvement in litigation. This is only one of several ways that courts can be affected by their political environment. Public opinion, like legal opinion, subtly influences appellate courts. Although judges do not always follow the majority view on issues that attract public interest, inevitably they are swayed by strong currents of opinion. For instance, current concern about illegal drugs has made some federal judges reluctant to overturn criminal convictions in drug cases. One lawyer, pointing to the impact of public opinion, said of the Court of Appeals for the Eleventh Circuit in Atlanta: "down here we have the 'drug exception to the rule of law' that says, in effect, that it's almost impossible to defend drug cases."[76]

A more direct source of potential influence for public opinion is the desire of judges to maintain their positions; most state judges must face the voters in regular or retention elections. We might assume that the prospect of elections would have little impact on judges' behavior since few appellate decisions attract much public interest and most sitting judges win re-election with little difficulty. But legislators from safe seats tend to exaggerate the threat of defeat and work hard to reduce that threat; to a lesser extent, judges can be expected to act in the same way.

Furthermore, the electoral accountability of appellate judges—especially on state supreme courts—has grown in recent years. It has become increasingly common for judges' decisions, particularly on criminal justice issues, to become an election issue. For instance, supreme court justices in several states have faced strong opposition based on their votes to overturn death sentences. According to Otto Kaus, a former member of the California Supreme Court, in this new climate, "there's no way a judge is going to be able to ignore the political consequences of certain decisions, especially if he or she has to make them near election time. That would be like ignoring a crocodile in your bathtub."[77]

Even more relevant to judges than voters are the other branches of government. Legislatures and chief executives affect appellate courts in several ways: they determine court budgets, they adopt legislation that has an impact on judges' working conditions, they can act to overturn or limit court decisions, and they can help determine whether decisions are enforced.

These powers sometimes come into play when courts adopt unpopular policies. In the last few decades, for example, the federal courts' prohibitions of school prayer and support for the rights of criminal defendants have aroused considerable congressional opposition, and members of Congress have threatened retaliation against the courts.

Judges are aware of the potential for negative reactions from the other branches. As Justice Christine Durham of the Utah Supreme Court said, "we live down the hall from the house and the senate and up the stairs from the governor's office. The things we do that have an impact on the law and on the other branches of government have immediate repercussions for us."[78]

The desire to avoid such negative reactions has at least a subtle effect on some judicial decisions. Judges generally seek to minimize confrontations with the other branches. This goal is one reason for the common practice by which courts avoid declaring laws unconstitutional when other alternatives exist. It is noteworthy that the Supreme Court has struck down nearly ten times as many state and local laws as federal laws;[79] in part, this ratio reflects the Court's dependence on Congress and its independence from state legislatures and city councils.

Occasionally, courts minimize conflict with the other branches in a more visible way. In this century, for example, the Supreme Court has twice retreated under fire. In 1937 it escaped the threat of President Roosevelt's proposal to "pack" the Court with additional members: two justices shifted position on the constitutionality of New Deal legislation, so that the Court ceased to be a roadblock to Roosevelt's program, and support for the proposal waned. Similarly, in the late 1950s the Court defused a congressional drive to attack its liberal policies on civil liberties issues by taking a more conservative tack. While such incidents are relatively rare, they do underline the impact of the legislature and the executive branch on the courts.

The Limits of Environmental Influence   Having considered the ways in which external forces can influence appellate courts, I should emphasize once again the general autonomy of these courts. For the most part, judges are free to choose their own policy directions. Pressure from the environment is seldom so strong that it forces judges into a particular position. If they wish, judges ordinarily can resist that pressure rather than bow to it.

There is abundant evidence of this freedom. For instance, state appellate judges often adhere to positions that may arouse the wrath of voters. Several state supreme courts have used their state constitutions to expand the rights of criminal defendants; some justices have voted to overturn large numbers of death sentences despite overwhelming public approval of capital punishment. Similarly, the Supreme Court has adopted some policies that were highly unpopular both in Congress and in the nation as a whole, such as its prohibition of laws that punish flag burning.

The strongest external forces on the courts are likely to be the most subtle and the least visible. Most important, currents of opinion in the legal and political communities often create constraints that rule out some possible policies and influence judges' choices among other policies. In this sense, the environments of courts are similar to the state of the law these courts apply; both direct appellate judges toward some decisions rather than others, while leaving room for judges to put their own stamp on the decisions that they reach.

CONCLUSIONS

This chapter examines several characteristics of appellate courts, including their use by litigants and interest groups as a vehicle to shape government policy and the broad freedom of appellate judges to chart their own course in choosing among alternative policies. Chapter 9 explores the policies that result from these and other characteristics of state and federal appellate courts.

One concern of this chapter merits further emphasis: to a degree, caseload pressures are undermining two traditional features of appellate courts, the central role of judges and the focus on individual cases. These pressures have created distinctions between types of cases. While some appellate cases continue to receive close attention from judges, others are handled in more routine ways, with judges' law clerks and central staff attorneys doing much of the work. In second-level courts, many petitions for hearings are denied with little consideration by judges, and in first-level courts many appeals are decided primarily by staff attorneys and reviewed only briefly by panels of judges.

The differentiation among cases has allowed judges to concentrate on the cases that seem to deserve the greatest attention rather than give all cases limited consideration. Thus judges can continue carrying out their traditional functions of correcting lower-court errors and enunciating legal principles in the face of growing caseloads. Yet the differentiation also may have produced some unintended and undesirable effects, such as weakening the right to appeal. One thing is clear, however: as appellate courts increasingly adopt new procedures to cope with greater workloads, they are subtly altering their own characteristics as institutions.

FOR FURTHER READING

Davis, Sue. *Justice Rehnquist and the Constitution*. Princeton, N.J.: Princeton University Press, 1989.

Epstein, Lee, and Joseph F. Kobylka. *The Supreme Court and Legal Change: Abortion and the Death Penalty*. Chapel Hill: University of North Carolina Press, 1992.

Grodin, Joseph R. *In Pursuit of Justice: Reflections of a State Supreme Court Justice*. Berkeley: University of California Press, 1989.

Lamb, Charles M., and Stephen C. Halpern, eds. *The Burger Court: Political and Judicial Profiles*. Urbana: University of Illinois Press, 1991.

Lawrence, Susan E. *The Poor in Court: The Legal Services Program and Supreme Court Decision Making*. Princeton, N.J.: Princeton University Press, 1990.

Perry, H. W., Jr. *Deciding to Decide: Agenda Setting in the United States Supreme Court*. Cambridge, Mass.: Harvard University Press, 1991.

Salokar, Rebecca Mae. *The Solicitor General: The Politics of Law*. Philadelphia: Temple University Press, 1992.

Tushnet, Mark. *The NAACP's Legal Strategy Against Segregated Education, 1925–1950*. Chapel Hill: University of North Carolina Press, 1987.

Walker, Samuel. *In Defense of American Liberties: A History of the ACLU*. New York: Oxford University Press, 1990.

NOTES

1. This discussion draws from Daniel J. Meador, *Appellate Courts: Staff and Process in the Crisis of Volume* (Saint Paul: West Publishing, 1974), pp. 1–3; and Robert S. Thompson and John B. Oakley, "From Information to Opinion in Appellate Courts: How Funny Things Happen on the Way Through the Forum," *Arizona State Law Journal* (1986), 10–13.
2. Joy A. Chapper and Roger A. Hanson, *Intermediate Appellate Courts: Improving Case Processing* (Williamsburg, Va.: National Center for State Courts, 1990), pp. 6–7.
3. This discussion draws from John Bilyeu Oakley and Robert S. Thompson, *Law Clerks and the Judicial Process* (Berkeley: University of California Press, 1980).
4. Harry Jupiter, " 'You're Sort of a Ghost Writer,' " *San Francisco Examiner*, October 13, 1991, p. E3.
5. Susan E. Grogan, "Judicial Apprentices? Law Clerks in the United States" (Paper presented at the 1991 meeting of the American Political Science Association, Washington, D.C.).
6. *Report to the Federal Courts Study Committee of the Subcommittee on the Role of the Federal Courts and Their Relation to the States* (Washington, D.C.: duplicated, 1990), pp. 72–73.
7. David Margolick, "At the Bar," *New York Times*, March 17, 1989, p. B4.
8. Patricia M. Wald, "Selecting Law Clerks," *Michigan Law Review*, 89 (October 1990), 153.
9. Frank J. Sorauf, *The Wall of Separation: The Constitutional Politics of Church and State* (Princeton, N.J.: Princeton University Press, 1976), p. 136.
10. Chapper and Hanson, *Intermediate Appellate Courts*, pp. 10–11.
11. Joseph R. Grodin, *In Pursuit of Justice: Reflections of a State Supreme Court Justice* (Berkeley: University of California Press, 1989), p. 19.
12. Ibid., p. 65.
13. *R.A.V. v. City of St. Paul*, 120 L. Ed. 2d 305 (1992).
14. Chapper and Hanson, *Intermediate Appellate Courts*, p. 16.
15. *Annual Report of the Director of the Administrative Office of the United States Courts, 1991* (Washington, D.C.: Government Printing Office, 1992), p. 163.
16. Chapper and Hanson, *Intermediate Appellate Courts*, p. 87.
17. Thomas Y. Davies, "Affirmed: A Study of Criminal Appeals and Decision-Making Norms in a California Court of Appeal," *American Bar Foundation Research Journal* (Summer 1982), p. 566.
18. Gregory J. Rathjen, "Lawyers and the Appellate Choice: An Analysis of Factors Affecting the Decision to Appeal," *American Politics Quarterly*, 6 (October 1978), 387–405.
19. See Rebecca Mae Salokar, *The Solicitor General: The Politics of Law* (Philadelphia: Temple University Press, 1992); Paul D. Carrington, "United States Appeals in Civil Cases: A Field and Statistical Study," *Houston Law Review*, 11 (July 1974), 1101–1123; and Lincoln Caplan, *The Tenth Justice: The Solicitor General and the Rule of Law* (New York: Alfred A. Knopf, 1987).
20. Salokar, *The Solicitor General*, p. 31; see Marc Galanter, "Why the 'Haves' Come Out Ahead: Speculations on the Limits of Legal Change," *Law and Society Review*, 9 (Fall 1974), 97–125.

21. *Bowsher v. Synar*, 478 U.S. 714 (1986); *Immigration and Naturalization Service v. Chadha*, 462 U.S. 919 (1983). See Linda Greenhouse, "Keeping Government's 3 Arms Minding Their Own Business," *New York Times*, December 26, 1988, p. A14.

22. H. Jane Lehman, "Owners Aren't Giving Ground in Property Battles," *Chicago Tribune*, February 9, 1992, sec. 16, pp. 1–2.

23. Bill Stanton, *Klanwatch: Bringing the Ku Klux Klan to Justice* (New York: Grove Weidenfeld, 1991).

24. Katherine Bishop, "Suit Seeks Ban on Shrimp From Nations Not Protecting Sea Turtles," *New York Times*, February 25, 1992, p. A6.

25. See Kim Lane Scheppele and Jack L. Walker, Jr., "The Litigation Strategies of Interest Groups," in Jack L. Walker, Jr., *Mobilizing Interest Groups in America* (Ann Arbor: University of Michigan Press, 1991), pp. 157–183.

26. Karen O'Connor and Lee Epstein, "The Rise of Conservative Interest Group Litigation," *Journal of Politics*, 45 (May 1983), 479–489; Lee Epstein, *Conservatives in Court* (Knoxville: University of Tennessee Press, 1985).

27. Lee Epstein, "Interest Groups in Judicial Systems: A Comparative Analysis of the Evolution, Rules, and Usage of Amicus Curiae Briefs in the U.S. Supreme Court and in State Courts of Last Resort" (Paper presented at the 1988 conference of the Southern Political Science Association), Table 2.

28. Susan M. Olson, "Interest-Group Litigation in Federal District Court: Beyond the Political Disadvantage Theory," *Journal of Politics*, 52 (August 1990), 869–870.

29. Lee Epstein and C. K. Rowland, "Debunking the Myth of Interest Group Invincibility in the Courts," *American Political Science Review*, 85 (March 1991), 205–217.

30. Jerry Goldman, "Federal District Courts and the Appellate Crisis," *Judicature*, 57 (December 1973), 212.

31. Thomas B. Marvell, "Appellate Court Caseloads: Historical Trends," *Appellate Court Administration Review*, 4 (1982–1983), 9. The main decision was *Douglas v. California*, 372 U.S. 353 (1963).

32. Myron Moskovitz, "Take My Case—Please," *California Lawyer*, 4 (December 1984), p. 49. Reprinted by permission.

33. See H. W. Perry, Jr., *Deciding to Decide: Agenda Setting in the United States Supreme Court* (Cambridge, Mass.: Harvard University Press, 1991), pp. 41–91.

34. Grodin, *In Pursuit of Justice*, pp. 59–60.

35. Maurice Kelman, "Case Selection by the Michigan Supreme Court: The Numerology of Choice," *Detroit College of Law Review* (Spring 1992), 1–2.

36. See Perry, *Deciding to Decide;* Gregory A. Caldeira and John R. Wright, "Organized Interests and Agenda Setting in the U.S. Supreme Court," *American Political Science Review*, 82 (December 1988), 1109–1127; and Grodin, *In Pursuit of Justice*, pp. 60–61.

37. Perry, *Deciding to Decide*, pp. 198–207.

38. Victor E. Flango, "Case Selection in the Georgia and Illinois Supreme Courts," *Justice System Journal*, 12 (Winter 1987), 398–401.

39. Lawrence Baum, *The Supreme Court*, 4th ed. (Washington, D.C.: CQ Press, 1992), p. 106.

40. Chapper and Hanson, *Intermediate Appellate Courts*, pp. 15–22; Donna Stienstra and Joe S. Cecil, *The Role of Staff Attorneys and Face-to-Face Conferencing in Non-Argument Decisionmaking* (Washington, D.C.: Federal Judicial Center, 1989), pp. 1–3.

41. Meador, *Appellate Courts*, pp. 104–105.

42. Thomas Y. Davies, "Gresham's Law Revisited: Expedited Processing Techniques and the Allocation of Appellate Resources," *Justice System Journal*, 6 (Fall 1981), 397–398.

43. Thompson and Oakley, "From Information to Opinion," p. 41.

44. Mary Lou Stow and Harold J. Spaeth, "Centralized Research Staff: Is There a Monster in the Judicial Closet?" *Judicature,* 75 (December–January 1992), 220.

45. David J. Brown, "Facing the Monster in the Judicial Closet: Rebutting a Presumption of Sloth," *Judicature,* 75 (April–May 1992), 291.

46. Charles R. Haworth, "Screening and Summary Procedures in the United States Courts of Appeals," *Washington University Law Quarterly* (Spring 1973), 309–319.

47. Jerry Goldman, "Appellate Justice Economized: Screening and Its Effect on Outcomes and Legitimacy," in *Restructuring Justice: The Innovations of the Ninth Circuit and the Future of the Federal Courts,* ed. Arthur D. Hellman (Ithaca, N.Y.: Cornell University Press, 1990), pp. 136–162.

48. Benjamin N. Cardozo, *The Growth of the Law* (New Haven, Conn.: Yale University Press, 1924), p. 60; see also Ruggero J. Aldisert, "Philosophy, Jurisprudence, and Jurisprudential Temperament of Federal Judges," *Indiana Law Review,* 20 (Spring 1987), 462, 466.

49. Douglas O. Linder, "How Judges Judge: A Study of Disagreement on the United States Court of Appeals for the Eighth Circuit," *Arkansas Law Review,* 38 (Summer 1985), 498 n. 72.

50. John T. Wold, "Going Through the Motions: The Monotony of Appellate Court Decisionmaking," *Judicature,* 62 (August 1978), 61–62.

51. Henry R. Glick and George W. Pruet, Jr., "Dissent in State Supreme Courts: Patterns and Correlates of Conflict," in *Judicial Conflict and Consensus,* ed. Sheldon Goldman and Charles M. Lamb (Lexington: University Press of Kentucky, 1986), pp. 202–203.

52. Jeffrey A. Segal and Albert D. Cover, "Ideological Values and the Votes of U.S. Supreme Court Justices," *American Political Science Review,* 83 (June 1989), 557–565.

53. See *Almanac of the Federal Judiciary* (Englewood Cliffs, N.J.: Prentice-Hall Law & Business, 1992), II [7th Circuit], 17–21.

54. Lisa Leff, "You Can't Accuse Md. High Court of Playing Politics," *Washington Post,* February 15, 1990, p. E1.

55. William E. Kovacic, "Reagan's Judicial Appointees and Antitrust in the 1990s," *Fordham Law Review,* 60 (October 1991), 49–124; William F. Kovacic, "The Reagan Judiciary and Environmental Policy: The Impact of Appointments to the Federal Courts of Appeals," *Boston College Environmental Affairs Law Review,* 18 (Summer 1991), 669–713.

56. Craig F. Emmert and Carol Ann Traut, "Integrating Streams of Judicial Research: The California Supreme Court and the Death Penalty" (Paper presented at the 1992 meeting of the Midwest Political Science Association, Chicago), p. 2.

57. *Planned Parenthood v. Casey,* 120 L. Ed. 2d 674 (1992).

58. Ruth Bader Ginsburg, "Styles of Collegial Judging: One Judge's Perspective," *Federal Bar News and Journal,* 39 (March–April 1992), 199–201.

59. Stephen L. Wasby, "Communication Within the Ninth Circuit Court of Appeals: The View from the Bench," *Golden Gate University Law Review,* 8 (Fall 1977), 125.

60. Daniel Egler, "Hallowed Chambers," *Chicago Tribune,* March 12, 1984, sec. 2, p. 8.

61. Judith S. Kaye, "My 'Freshman Years' on the Court of Appeals," *Judicature,* 70 (October–November 1986), 166.

62. Robert S. Thompson, "One Judge and No Judge Appellate Decisions," *California State Bar Journal,* 50 (November–December 1975), 476–480, 513–519.

63. Wold, "Going through the Motions," p. 64.

64. Linder, "How Judges Judge," pp. 484–486.

65. See Note, "Plurality Decisions and Judicial Decisionmaking," *Harvard Law Review,* 94 (March 1981), 1127–47.

66. Sanford S. McConkie, "Decision-Making in State Supreme Courts," *Judicature,* 59 (February 1976), 337–343.
67. David Margolick, "A Judicial Maverick Is Worn Down in Arkansas," *New York Times,* March 16, 1990, p. B11.
68. Scott Winokur, "Justice and Balance," *San Francisco Examiner,* March 3, 1991, p. E5.
69. Greg Casey, "Public Perceptions of Judicial Scandal: The Missouri Supreme Court 1982–88," *Justice System Journal,* 13 (Winter 1988), 288–290.
70. Michael W. Bowers, "Personality and Judicial Politics in Nevada," *State Constitutional Commentaries and Notes,* 2 (Summer 1991), 7–10.
71. Michael deCourcy Hinds, "Special Prosecutors Named in Pennsylvania Judicial Feud," *New York Times,* December 12, 1992, p. 1.
72. Edward Beiser, "The Rhode Island Supreme Court: A Well-Integrated Political System," *Law and Society Review,* 8 (Winter 1973), 167–186.
73. *Hicks* v. *State,* 544 P.2d 1153 (N.M. 1975). The quoted passage is from pp. 1155–56 of the opinion.
74. "Decision Process 'Helps to Discipline the Mind,' " *Legal Times,* September 24, 1990, p. 17.
75. Benjamin Twiss, *Lawyers and the Constitution* (Princeton, N.J.: Princeton University Press, 1942).
76. *Almanac of the Federal Judiciary,* II [11th Circuit], 1.
77. Paul Reidinger, "The Politics of Judging," *American Bar Association Journal,* 73 (April 1, 1987), 58.
78. Lawrence Baum and David Frohnmayer, eds., *The Courts: Sharing and Separating Powers* (New Brunswick, N.J.: Eagleton Institute of Politics, Rutgers University, 1989), pp. 21–22.
79. Baum, *The Supreme Court,* pp. 188, 190.

9

Appellate Courts as
Policy Makers

A
s policy makers, appellate courts differ from trial courts. The primary
task of trial courts is to apply existing legal rules to specific cases. In
contrast, appellate courts have more opportunities to establish new
rules—to make decisions whose implications extend far beyond individual
cases. This chapter examines what appellate courts do with these opportunities—what roles they play in the making of government policy.

One concern of this chapter is the significance of appellate courts as
policy makers. Appellate judges frequently address major issues, ranging
from abortion to compensation for personal injuries. Yet they do not always
take the opportunity to rule on such issues. And when courts do intervene
in the making of public policy, the impact of their decisions is frequently
narrowed by the reactions of other government institutions and of people
outside government.

Another concern is the content of the policies made by appellate courts—
particularly their ideological direction. At any given time, the decisions of
appellate courts are mixed, ranging from some that can be characterized as
quite liberal to others that appear to be quite conservative. But during a
particular era, there may be a dominant tendency, and these tendencies have
shifted over time.

This chapter examines the characteristics of appellate courts as policy
makers in two stages. The first section of the chapter looks at appellate court
decisions as government policies. The second discusses the actual impact of
the policies made by appellate courts.

APPELLATE COURT DECISIONS AS
POLICIES

We can think of appellate court decisions as having two components, which
correspond to the functions of these courts that are discussed in Chapter 8.
The first is a review of the way that the lower court treated the parties to the
case. The second is a judgment about the principles of law that are applicable
to the case—a judgment expressed in the opinion accompanying the decision.

I consider the policy outputs of appellate courts in terms of these two components of the decision, giving primary attention to the second.

Appellate Review of Lower-Court Decisions

In each case that an appellate court hears, its most specific task is to review the treatment of the parties by the court below it. The two levels of appellate courts take somewhat different approaches to this task.

Review by First-Level Courts   First-level appellate courts—which are intermediate courts in the federal system and in most states—review trial court decisions. Because of the general right to appeal adverse trial decisions and the growing tendency to exercise this right, they review a fairly high percentage of decisions by major state trial courts and federal district courts.

Most often they ratify trial decisions by affirming them. It appears that every first-level court approves well over half the decisions it reviews. In 1991 the federal courts of appeals affirmed lower courts in 80 percent of their decisions and dismissed appeals in another 6 percent.[1]

Furthermore, many decisions that are not affirmances (which I call disturbances of trial decisions) modify decisions in limited ways rather than overturning them altogether. A study of criminal appeals in five state courts found a 21 percent disturbance rate, but a majority of those disturbances were "little" wins for defendants—most often, a corrected sentence or a new sentencing hearing. Only 8.5 percent of the defendants who appealed had their convictions overturned, and three-quarters of those successful defendants faced the possibility of a new trial rather than having their cases dismissed.[2]

High affirmance rates can be explained in three ways.[3] The first is in terms of generally accepted legal doctrines. One of these doctrines is that a trial court's interpretation of the facts in a case will not be questioned if there is any *substantial evidence* for that interpretation. On the basis of this rule, appellate courts generally do not take a fresh look at the evidence as a whole in order to weigh it independently; rather, they seek out a basis in the evidence for upholding the trial court's ruling. This rule helps to explain one federal judge's argument that a decision should not be overturned when it is "just maybe or probably wrong" but only when it is "wrong with the force of a five-week-old, unrefrigerated dead fish."[4] Another important doctrine is the *harmless error* rule, which holds that even if a trial judge has erred in applying legal rules, an appellate court can still affirm the decision if it concludes the error was harmless, that it probably did not affect the trial court judgment.

High affirmance rates can also be explained by the institutional interests of appellate courts. Frequent reversals of trial court decisions would increase conflict between the two levels of courts, because many trial judges resent reversals as negative reviews of their work. More important, to proceed with full and thorough reviews of trial decisions, with no preconceptions, would consume the time and energy of appellate judges at an unacceptable rate.

And high reversal rates might encourage more litigants to appeal, increasing the burdens of appellate judges even more.

Finally, the past experience of appellate judges helps to account for their tendency to affirm. Because most appeals in the past have seemed suitable for affirmance, judges expect that this will continue to be true. Speaking of certain legal claims commonly made in appeals, two commentators note that "staff attorneys and judges, conditioned by case after case in which these claims have been rejected, come to associate them with meritless appeals. . . . Expectation can influence misperception of lack of merit, and . . . has done so in some of these cases."[5]

Affirmance rates are especially high in criminal cases. In 1991 federal courts of appeals reversed district court decisions 7.4 percent of the time; the reversal rate in civil cases was 12.7 percent.[6] One reason for this difference lies in patterns of appeals. Civil appeals carry significant monetary costs for most litigants, and civil litigants are ordinarily advised by attorneys. As a result, most appellants probably have fairly strong grounds on which to challenge trial decisions. In contrast, criminal defendants have considerable incentive to appeal when they have received substantial prison sentences, a high proportion of defendants do appeal, and a good many such appeals have little legal basis.

Nevertheless, as Thomas Y. Davies has argued, it misses the point simply to assume that most criminal appeals are frivolous, for frivolousness is a subjective concept. Indeed, Davies found that one California court of appeal cited trial court errors in about one-quarter of the decisions in which it affirmed convictions.[7] Hence the concept of the frivolous criminal appeal may be as much a justification for affirmance—and for limited judicial scrutiny of trials—as it is an explanation of high affirmance rates.

The inclination to affirm is linked with the growing use of abbreviated procedures in first-level appellate courts. The establishment of such procedures has been encouraged by the belief that a high proportion of appeals are easy affirmances that staff attorneys can identify and handle. And when certain cases are labeled as requiring only abbreviated consideration, court personnel may be encouraged to treat them as easy affirmances. Thus the use of abbreviated procedures can raise an affirmance rate that already is high.

Review by Second-Level Courts   Unlike first-level appellate courts, those at the second level disturb lower court decisions in a high proportion of the cases they decide. In its 1991–1992 term, for instance, the U.S. Supreme Court affirmed the lower court in only 31 percent of the decisions for which it provided full opinions.[8]

Such a high disturbance rate suggests that second-level appellate courts are quite willing to substitute their own judgments for those of the courts below them. But in this respect the disturbance rate is quite deceptive. As we have seen, judges on second-level courts are inclined to accept cases for hearings when they think that the lower court has erred in its decision. This means that they approach many of the cases they have accepted with a presumption of reversal rather than the presumption of affirmance that prevails in first-level courts; therefore, a high reversal rate is virtually guaranteed.

Yet if we take into account all the cases that are brought to the second-level courts, and not just those that are accepted for review, the disturbance of lower-court decisions is in fact quite limited. For example, the Supreme Court disturbs decisions in less than 5 percent of the cases it receives.[9] Thus appellate courts at both levels allow most decisions that they review to remain standing.

Overview   Because appellate courts uphold most decisions that are brought to them and because some decisions are not appealed, the great majority of decisions by trial courts and intermediate appellate courts become final. In this respect, then, appellate courts intervene rather little into the work of the courts below them.

Of course, this is only one aspect of the relationship between higher and lower courts. Even though appellate courts overturn relatively few decisions, the opinions they write influence what the courts below them do in a much larger number of cases. For example, one state supreme court decision on liability rules in auto accident cases can shape hundreds of trial court decisions. Thus, to gain a fuller sense of the roles of appellate courts within the judicial branch, we need to examine their agendas and the responses of lower courts to their decisions.

Appellate Court Agendas

The potential impact of courts on the rest of government and society is determined, first of all, by the types of issues they address. Consequently, we can begin to sketch out the roles of appellate courts in policy making by examining the sets of cases that appellate courts hear and decide with opinions—what I call their agendas. The more a court concentrates on cases in a particular field, the greater is its potential to shape public policy in that field. As suggested in Chapter 8, the agendas of appellate courts are the products of rules of jurisdiction, patterns of litigation and appeals, and the judges' choices of cases in which to write opinions. The 1991 agendas of three appellate courts at different levels are summarized in Exhibit 9.1.

The agendas of state supreme courts reflect the work of state courts generally.[10] Because state court litigation is quite diverse, so too is state supreme court business. In recent years, several areas have been frequent subjects of supreme court opinions: torts, particularly cases arising from accidents; criminal law and procedure; contract disputes, most often between debtors and creditors; government economic regulation; and family and estate issues, primarily concerning divorce and inheritance. As a result, state supreme courts make legal rulings in a broad range of policy areas.

The agendas of federal courts of appeals show both similarities and differences with those of state supreme courts.[11] Their opinions are primarily on issues of federal law, but they also deal with a good many state law issues in cases brought under the diversity jurisdiction. The two policy areas that stand

Category of Cases[a]	Pennsylvania Supreme Court	Federal Court of Appeals, Sixth Circuit[b]	U.S. Supreme Court[c]
Debt and contract	12.2	8.6	0.0
Real property	5.3	0.9	1.8
Business organization	0.0	2.6	7.9
Torts	13.0	9.0	5.3
Family and estates	7.6	0.4	0.9
Public law			
Criminal	38.9	24.9	24.6
Government regulation of economic activity	3.8	21.5	21.1
Other	19.1	32.2	38.6

[a]Many cases could have fit into multiple categories; different coding rules would have produced substantially different results. For this reason, the percentages should be viewed as illustrations of differences in the agendas of the three courts rather than as exact depictions of each court's agenda.
[b]The time period from which cases were drawn was January–June 1991.
[c]The time period from which cases were drawn was the 1991–1992 term of the Court.

EXHIBIT 9.1 Subject Matter of Cases Decided with Published Opinions in 1991, Selected Appellate Courts, in Percentages

out on their agendas are government economic regulation and criminal law and procedure, with regulation cases considerably more numerous than they are in state appellate courts. Also common are torts, tax cases, and contract cases.

The agenda of the U.S. Supreme Court is distinctive.[12] Broadly speaking, the Court devotes itself overwhelmingly to public law issues; as Exhibit 9.1 shows, all other cases account for only a small minority of its opinions. Within this category, the Court is primarily a civil liberties specialist; indeed, in recent years about half its opinions have involved civil liberties issues. The largest number of these cases concern criminal procedure, but the Court also writes a great many opinions on the right to equal treatment under the law and other individual liberties, such as freedom of expression and freedom of religion. Another significant part of the Court's agenda concerns economic regulation by federal and state governments. A third major area, which overlaps the first two, is federalism—that is, the constitutional relationship between national and state governments.

Even this brief discussion suggests two conclusions about the potential roles of appellate courts as policy makers. The first relates to the agendas of appellate courts taken as a whole. While the various state and federal courts cover a broad range of issues, there are some important areas of public policy in which appellate courts are largely inactive. The outstanding example is foreign policy, which state courts barely touch and in which federal courts make relatively few decisions. Even in fields where they are active, the courts may not deal with the most fundamental issues. In economic regulation, for instance, courts focus primarily on the details of regulatory policy rather than on the general form and scope of regulation.

The second conclusion concerns differences among courts. Some issue areas, such as criminal procedure, are important to appellate courts at all levels. Others are concentrated in certain courts. Property disputes and divorce are primarily the domain of state courts, while the Supreme Court gives civil liberties much greater emphasis than does any set of lower appellate courts. Thus different appellate courts have different domains in which to make policy.

Ideological Patterns in Appellate Court Policy

The agendas of appellate courts indicate the areas to which they devote the most attention. To get a sense of what they do in these areas, we need to examine the ideological direction and activism of appellate policies.

Ideologically, the policies of appellate courts at any given time are certain to be quite diverse. But diversity is not the same as randomness. For most of American history, appellate courts as a whole were fairly conservative in their policies, by the current definition of that term. In the past half century, while strong elements of that conservatism have remained, there have also been major liberal themes in the doctrinal positions of state and federal courts.

The traditional conservatism of appellate courts was best reflected in economic policies. Federal and state courts addressed a wide range of legal issues involving the interests of economically powerful groups, and the dominant theme in their decisions was support for those interests.

The U.S. Supreme Court did much to protect property rights and the freedom of business enterprises from restrictions by state and federal governments. As legislation to regulate and restrict business practices grew early in this century, the Court frequently struck laws down as unconstitutional; ultimately, the Court overturned much of President Franklin Roosevelt's New Deal economic program in the 1930s.

The economic policies of state courts, though quite mixed, also had a conservative emphasis.[13] As the industrial economy developed, state courts did much to protect the business sector from threats to its economic well-being. For instance, they adopted a set of rules for personal injury law that favored businesses over injured individuals.

This conservative emphasis in appellate court policy is not difficult to understand. Judges came primarily from economically advantaged segments of society and were imbued with the values of the elite. Trained in a legal profession in which conservative values predominated, they often embarked on legal careers that involved service to business enterprises. Furthermore, the most skilled advocates who came before their courts generally represented businesses and other institutions with conservative goals. Because of all these forces, perhaps it was almost inevitable that the dominant element in judicial policy was conservative.

Yet in the past half century judicial conservatism has been replaced by an ideologically mixed pattern of policy, in which the liberal element has often been more prominent. Across a range of issues, the courts have given significant support to the interests of relatively weak groups in society, groups that possess far fewer social and economic resources and far less conventional political power than the business interests that courts tended to favor in the past.

The most visible change has been in the Supreme Court. From 1937 on, the Court quickly abandoned its earlier support for business interests that sought protection from government regulation. It also began to provide support for the civil liberties of relatively powerless groups in American society, support that peaked in the 1960s. It applied the constitutional rights of criminal defendants to state proceedings and established new controls on police investigations and trial procedures. It required the desegregation of southern public schools and protected the rights of racial minority groups in other areas of life. It strengthened freedom of expression both for the mass media and for people who express their views through vehicles such as pamphlets and marches.

Since the 1970s the Supreme Court has supported civil liberties with less consistency. It narrowed the rights of criminal defendants, and it became more reluctant to establish new rights in any area. But even in the early 1990s, when the Court had its most conservative membership in decades, it maintained a surprising degree of support for individual liberties. And, despite some hints of a new direction, the Court continued to accept active government regulation of the economy.

In the past few decades the federal courts of appeals have differed a good deal in their ideological positions, but in general they have taken a path similar to that of the Supreme Court. The court of appeals for the District of Columbia stood out for its strong liberalism from the 1960s through the mid-1980s, as evidenced in its support for the rights of criminal defendants and the mentally ill, for the interests of consumers, and for protection of the environment. Standing out in another way was the Fifth Circuit Court of Appeals in the Deep South, which gave strong support to African American civil rights on school desegregation and other issues in the 1950s and 1960s despite the anti–civil rights pressures in that region. In the last decade the courts of appeals gradually have become more conservative in their policies. But, like the Supreme Court, they remain relatively liberal by historical standards.

Early in this century state supreme courts began to reduce their long-standing support for business in tort law, expanding the ability of people who suffer injuries to recover compensation.[14] This trend gradually gained momentum, as courts increasingly eliminated old rules that had favored defendants. Most dramatically, supreme courts in the 1960s and 1970s largely eliminated the requirement that those who are injured by defective products must prove that the manufacturer was negligent. Some other examples of changes in tort law since the 1950s are shown in Exhibit 9.2. In the past decade the movement to expand the rights of injured people has slowed considerably, and to some degree state courts have become more favorable to the interests of tort defendants,[15] but for the most part the revolution in personal injury law remains intact.

State courts have taken decidedly mixed positions in civil liberties. In the 1950s and 1960s some supreme courts openly resisted the Supreme Court's expansions of individual liberties, interpreting the Court's decisions narrowly. Since the 1970s, as the Supreme Court itself has narrowed some liberties, some state courts have accepted this direction enthusiastically.[16] But others, particularly in the West and Northeast, have undertaken their own expansions of liberties by finding independent sources of protections in their state constitutions.[17] The largest part of this activity has concerned criminal justice, but it has extended to other areas, such as freedom of expression and sex discrimination.

The relative liberalism of appellate courts in recent years is more difficult to explain than was their traditional conservatism. Undoubtedly, the recent liberalism is at least partially rooted in a changing pattern of social values. In this century support by the general public and political leaders for protection of business enterprises from government regulation has declined. Meanwhile, some civil liberties—especially those related to equality—have gained more support. This change in values is reflected in judges' own attitudes, as well as in the kinds of litigation and arguments that come to the appellate courts. Justice Christine Durham of the Utah Supreme Court has pointed to the effects of this change on civil liberties policy.

EXHIBIT 9.2 A Sampling of Widely Adopted Changes in Tort Law Doctrine Favoring Injured Parties

Doctrinal Change	Innovating State
Abolishing the immunity of charitable institutions from lawsuits	Minnesota, 1920
Abolishing the general immunity of local governments from lawsuits	Florida, 1957
Allowing parents and children to sue each other for torts	Wisconsin, 1963
Holding that builders or sellers of homes gave an implied warranty against negligent construction to buyers	Colorado, 1964
Allowing a person to sue for emotional distress without any physical injury	Hawaii, 1970

Note: The identity of the state that first adopted a legal doctrine is ambiguous for some doctrines.

Most of us who sit on state supreme courts, and most of the lawyers who appear before us, were educated during a generation of expansivist, creative, and enormously "generative" thinking on the subject of the federal constitution and in the context of civil liberties. We saw in the Warren Court era an enormous and impressive reshaping of our attitudes and our assumptions about what the constitution meant for individual liberties in the U.S.[18]

Another source of this ideological change is the kinds of people who become judges. Like judges in the past, most current judges come from families with high status. But there are more exceptions today; as a result, the attitudes of judges on economic and social issues are less likely to be conservative. Furthermore, at the federal level, liberal Democratic presidents have sought out appellate judges who shared their liberalism. Franklin Roosevelt's appointments turned the Supreme Court away from its traditional conservatism. Similarly, Roosevelt, Johnson, and Carter all used their appointments to move the lower federal courts in a liberal direction. At the state level, growing Democratic strength in the North from the 1930s on brought more liberal governors into office; in turn, these governors influenced the direction of state appellate courts with their own appointments.

To some extent, this shift to greater liberalism has been self-reinforcing. The courts' support for civil liberties encouraged interest groups to bring new cases, seeking further expansions of liberties. When the Supreme Court in the 1960s played a strong role in expanding civil liberties, many lawyers gained an appreciation for that role, and those who reached the bench themselves sought to follow it. As I suggested for torts in the state courts, a trend in judicial policy tends to gain a certain momentum of its own.

The partial reversal of this liberal trend in the past decade reflects events outside the courts. The success of Republican presidential candidates from 1968 through 1988 brought more conservatives into the federal courts, with an inevitable impact on their policies. In part because of activity by interest groups, fears about negative effects of expanded rights for injured people became widespread, and these fears undoubtedly affected state court decisions in tort law. Of course, further developments in the environments of appellate courts will shape their future directions; if Bill Clinton were to serve two full terms as president, for instance, his appointments would move the federal courts toward more liberal policy positions. The policy shifts that already have occurred in this century should remind us that the ideological stance of the courts is always subject to change.

Judicial Activism

Observers of the courts sometimes debate whether judges should "make policy." It should be clear by now that such debates have little value, for in deciding cases and writing opinions judges inevitably and unavoidably make public policy.

But if judges cannot avoid making policy, they do have some control over the *extent* of their involvement in policy making. In the cases that come

before any court, some decisions would increase the court's significance as a policy maker, while others would limit its importance. For instance, a court might decide a tort case on the basis of a narrow rule, or it might announce a broad rule that affects a whole class of tort cases. When facing an old issue, a court may follow the legal rules it laid down earlier or overturn precedent and establish new rules. Most important, where a policy of the legislature or executive branch is challenged, a court can uphold it and allow it to continue, or it can overturn the policy and make it inoperative.

These kinds of choices often are discussed in terms of a dichotomy between *judicial activism* and *judicial restraint*. Restraint involves an effort to minimize a court's role in policy making, whereas activism involves a willingness—even, perhaps, an eagerness—to go beyond that minimal role. These terms are problematic because of their ambiguity; activism can refer to several different characteristics of court decisions, which need not coincide.[19] Still, activism is a useful term with which to summarize the extent of judicial participation in the making of public policy.

One critical element and sign of judicial activism is the use of *judicial review*, the power to strike down policies of the other branches on the ground that they violate constitutional provisions. The striking down of a law as unconstitutional is the most dramatic and decisive way in which a court can involve itself in the governing process. It is also a good indicator of activism; a court that declares legislative and executive acts unconstitutional with some frequency is likely to be engaged in a good deal of activism in other forms.

Judicial Activism Today   American courts have always engaged in activism. In the nineteenth century, for instance, the Supreme Court laid down sweeping rules on issues of federalism and government power over the economy. In 1857 the Court sought to impose a legal resolution of the controversy over slavery, striking down a federal law of fundamental importance in doing so.[20] In the first four decades of the twentieth century both the Supreme Court and many lower courts were active in overturning federal and state laws that regulated economic activity.

If activism is far from new, however, the level of activism has been unusually high in the past few decades, perhaps higher than in any earlier period. The Supreme Court's recent record of activism has justifiably received wide attention. Its use of the judicial review power has been extraordinary: between 1960 and 1990, by one count, the Court struck down 54 federal statutes and 506 state and local laws.[21] Both figures constitute well over one-third of the total for the Court's entire history. In the period from 1961 through 1988 the Court overturned its own precedents in 94 cases, a number almost equal to the total from 1791 through 1960.[22]

These figures reflect the Court's involvement in a wide range of important policy questions. In the 1950s and 1960s it reshaped public policy on civil liberties questions ranging from school segregation to libel and obscenity. The more conservative Court since the 1970s has taken a more limited role in civil liberties, but it too has made some significant interventions in this field. The most dramatic example was its 1973 decisions striking down state

prohibitions of abortion, followed by two decades of decisions defining state power to regulate abortion.[23]

The Court of the 1980s was also willing to resolve disputes over the balance of power between Congress and the executive branch. In the process, the Court declared unconstitutional the legislative veto, perhaps the most important mechanism with which Congress has tried to control policy implementation in the executive branch.[24]

Federal courts of appeals have engaged in their own activism, often following the lead of the Supreme Court. One set of decisions has overturned regulatory policies of the executive branch on the ground that they did not follow relevant provisions of federal statutes. Several of these decisions concerned Reagan and Bush administration policies that allegedly failed to protect health and environmental interests to the degree required by Congress.

State supreme courts have also engaged in an impressive level of activism. The revolution in tort law is symbolized by the long list of precedents that were overturned. For instance, when the South Carolina Supreme Court abolished the immunity of state and local governments from lawsuits in 1985, it overruled at least 118 of its past decisions, handed down over 160 years.[25] The increased use of state constitutions by some supreme courts as independent protections for civil liberties is a significant expansion in their roles.

Particularly in the federal courts, this wave of activism has extended to the trial level. With some encouragement from appellate courts, federal district judges frequently intervene in the governance of public institutions such as schools, prisons, and mental institutions, holding existing conditions to be unconstitutional and then supervising closely the task of reforming them. Frank Johnson of Alabama was a leader in this development.[26] Many other trial judges have intervened quite significantly in these and other areas of public policy; Exhibit 9.3 provides some recent examples of such interventions.

The state of Texas illustrates the extent of judicial activism over the past two decades.[27] Federal district judge William Wayne Justice has handed down a series of rulings requiring important changes in state policies involving prisons and schools. As a result, he "has been called the most hated man in Texas, the most powerful man in Texas and the real governor of Texas."[28] Other federal judges have struck down state policies on mental health and election rules. In the early 1980s the Texas Supreme Court overturned a number of tort rules that had limited liability for personal injuries, and it has handed down a series of rulings requiring reform of the state's property tax-based system for school funding. Responding to all this activism, one newspaper headline asked, "So who's running Texas—the courts or the Legislature?"[29]

Some sources of this surge of activism lie within the courts themselves. To a degree, the heightened activism simply reflects the policy goals of the judges who have been responsible for activist decisions, particularly those whose commitment to civil liberties is expressed in their rulings. Undoubtedly, the Supreme Court has helped to foster activism in the lower courts through its own example, and the lower courts set examples for each other. It is easier

Judge	Court	Year	Decisions
Charles Grabau	State: Massachusetts	1987	Ordered Massachusetts to increase welfare benefits by nearly 30 percent
Marvin Katz	Federal: Pennsylvania	1988	Ordered public transportation systems throughout the country to provide service to the disabled without regard to cost
Terrence Evans	Federal: Wisconsin	1990	Suspended part of state program that reduced welfare benefits for families whose children had too many unexcused school absences
Alfred Wolin	Federal: New Jersey	1992	Struck down New Jersey system to provide funds for health care for the poor

Sources: "Judge Orders Welfare Rise in Massachusetts," *New York Times,* January 6, 1987, p. A14; Mary Thornton, "Judge Widens Transit Service for Disabled," *Washington Post,* January 6, 1988, p. A3; Rogers Worthington, "Judge Halts Program in Milwaukee That Links Aid Cuts to Teen Truancies," *Chicago Tribune,* July 11, 1990, sec. 1, p. 3; Joseph F. Sullivan, "Judge Stays Ruling on Hospital Billing in New Jersey," *New York Times,* June 5, 1992, p. A13.

EXHIBIT 9.3 Some Examples of Activist Decisions by Trial Judges

for a federal judge to order major prison reforms when a dozen judges in other districts have already done so. Discussion with Frank Johnson helped lead William Wayne Justice to establish a right to treatment for juveniles in reform schools.[30]

The high level of activism in recent years also reflects forces outside the courts. Perhaps its most fundamental source is the growth in government action at all levels. Because government policies now touch people more often and more deeply than in past eras, it is inevitable that more questions about the legal validity of government action will arise. Today the Supreme Court strikes down more laws than it did in the past, but there are more laws on the books than in the past. The 1940 edition of the *United States Code,* the compilation of federal statutes, was forty-five hundred pages long; in contrast, the 1988 edition contains more than twenty-five thousand pages.

The growth in government action has been paralleled by a growth in interest group litigation to challenge that action. Interest groups cannot force activism on a reluctant court, but they can facilitate activism by providing opportunities and by constructing arguments for it. Groups such as the American Civil Liberties Union have played a critical role in bringing civil liberties cases to court, just as groups such as the Sierra Club have done on environmental issues. Of course, as suggested earlier, courts have encouraged interest groups and others to challenge government action through decisions responding positively to such challenges. Judicial activism, like so many other phenomena in the courts, results from an interaction between judges and the larger society in which they work.

Debates over Judicial Activism   Judicial activism is a controversial matter. The recent surge of activism has led to a great deal of criticism in forums that range from newspaper editorials to political party platforms and presidential statements.

Much of this commentary is misleading in an important sense. People who profess to support or oppose judicial activism on principle are actually reacting, for the most part, to the ideological content of activist decisions. Today, when most activism supports liberal values, liberals generally defend activist courts and conservatives attack them. But early in this century, when conservative activism predominated, it was conservatives who supported the courts' policy interventions. Should a new wave of conservative activism arise, liberals and conservatives once again would switch their views on activism.

Yet judicial activism raises a serious set of issues that transcend the substance of activist policies at any given time.[31] Supporters of judicial restraint argue that activist policy making is undesirable on several grounds. They perceive activism as illegitimate because the courts are relatively free from popular control and accountability particularly the federal courts, whose judges are appointed for life. They also see activism as risky because it puts the courts into confrontations with more powerful policy makers and thus threatens their autonomy. And some commentators have attacked activism on a more practical level, arguing that the courts are not well equipped to make good policy choices on complex social issues.

Defenders of activism counter these arguments in several ways. Some minimize the alleged weaknesses of the courts—arguing, for instance, that their capacity to make good policy is greater than the critics have suggested. They view the courts' freedom from popular control as a virtue rather than a weakness because that freedom allows the courts to protect important but often unpopular values such as civil liberties.

This debate is impossible to resolve definitively because the issues involved are so complex and because some of them involve disagreements about values. In light of this difficulty, perhaps it is inevitable that most people react to activism on an ideological basis.

In any case, it is uncertain that the debate over judicial activism has much effect on the actual behavior of courts. The current surge of activism has developed and continued despite strong criticisms in government and in the legal community. And although the extent of activism can vary a good deal over time, some considerable degree of activism is a permanent feature of American courts. What is less permanent, as we have seen, is its ideological direction.

THE IMPACT OF APPELLATE COURT POLICIES

The activism of appellate courts gives them great potential influence over the rest of government and over American society as a whole. Court decisions on major public issues can have a massive impact on government and society. But the actual effects of such decisions depend on how people respond to them. To take one example, the Supreme Court has made several major decisions interpreting the scope of federal laws against employment discrimination. The ultimate impact of those rulings depends on a wide range of actions in government and the private sector: whether Congress allows the rulings to stand, how civil rights enforcement agencies interpret them, decisions by individuals whether to file lawsuits for discrimination, and decisions by employers whether to change their practices. As this example suggests, we cannot determine the effects of appellate court decisions from a reading of the decisions themselves; we have to investigate further.

Implementation by Lower Courts and Administrators

When an appellate court disturbs the decision of a lower court, it usually remands the case to that court for reconsideration. The lower court is then responsible for implementing the appellate decision, that is, for putting it into effect. It often retains a good deal of discretion in its treatment of the case, and the party that won in the Supreme Court may ultimately lose again in the lower court.

The decisions of appellate courts are also subject to a second, much broader implementation process. When a court rules on a legal issue, the courts and administrative bodies below it are responsible for applying that ruling, where it is relevant, to other cases and other situations. (Such administrative bodies include all the agencies in the executive branch of government, ranging from federal regulatory commissions to police departments and school systems.) I focus on this broader implementation process in the discussion that follows because it is chiefly through application to other cases that appellate court decisions gain their impact.

The Implementation Record   In responding to decisions by appellate courts, lower-court judges and administrators have choices to make. Most fundamentally, they must decide how fully they will put those decisions into effect. Responses to appellate court decisions differ a great deal. Noncompliance with the legal rules laid down in decisions is hardly rare, but the extent of such noncompliance varies considerably among decisions and among different policy makers responding to the same decision. These generalizations can be illustrated by examining some major areas of appellate court policy.

The first is school desegregation.[32] In *Brown v. Board of Education* (1954), the Supreme Court required that school districts with separate schools for black and white students desegregate their systems. In the Deep South, the federal Fifth Circuit Court of Appeals followed the *Brown* decision faithfully. But federal district judges, who had ultimate responsibility for applying the decision to specific cases, generally allowed successive delays in desegregation. Meanwhile, many southern school administrators and other public officials flatly refused to follow the Supreme Court's ruling. As a result, schools in the Deep South remained almost as segregated in 1964 as they had been ten years earlier. Only after Congress and the federal executive branch intervened, primarily by providing financial incentives, did significant desegregation begin in the Deep South.

Desegregation followed a different path in the rest of the country. The border states, such as Maryland and Missouri, also were subject to the *Brown* decision. Their school districts gradually desegregated while the Deep South maintained its resistance. In the 1970s and 1980s the Supreme Court required elimination of the more complex segregation found in many northern school districts. On the whole, northern federal judges followed the Court's rules, and school districts generally followed court desegregation orders.

The second area is police procedure.[33] In the 1960s the Supreme Court established major new restrictions on searches and seizures of physical evidence by police officers. It also laid down rules for police interrogation of suspects; its key decision in this regard was *Miranda v. Arizona* (1966), which required that certain warnings be read prior to questioning. Since then several state supreme courts have gone even further than the Supreme Court in restricting these types of police practices. Some lower courts, particularly at the trial level, have applied these rulings reluctantly and narrowly. In addition, police officers have engaged in a good deal of partial and full noncompliance with court-imposed restrictions. On the whole, they seem to have followed the rules for questioning of suspects reasonably well, but the record for searches and seizures is considerably more mixed.

The final area is school religious activities.[34] Over the past half century, federal courts have limited religious observances in public schools. Especially important were the decisions by the Supreme Court in 1962 and 1963 that prohibited schools from engaging in organized prayer or Bible reading exercises, a position that the Court reiterated and extended in 1985 and 1992. A great many schools eliminated observances that the courts struck down, but others maintained them despite their illegality. Thus, after the federal court of appeals in Atlanta prohibited public prayers before high school football games in 1989, some school systems immediately stopped using them, while others continued them.

How can we account for the imperfections of the implementation process that these areas illustrate? What causes variation in the responses of policy makers to appellate court rulings? We can address both questions by looking at several relevant factors.

Attitudes Toward Policy   Every appellate court decision embodies a position on a policy issue, whether it be school desegregation, liability for personal injuries, or government regulation of air pollution. The judges and administrators who deal with these issues do not respond to decisions of higher courts as neutrals. Indeed, their personal attitudes are perhaps the most powerful forces in determining their responses to the policies they are asked to implement. More specifically, two kinds of attitudes are important, *policy preferences* and *self-interest*.

The policy preferences of judges and administrators have an obvious relevance to their implementation of decisions. If asked to carry out an appellate court decision with which they agree, they can be expected to do so with alacrity. But, by the same token, if they are asked to implement a decision with which they disagree, it is unlikely that they will do so enthusiastically. When faced with an appellate court order that violated her "moral and ethical conscience," for instance, one federal district judge withdrew from the case rather than carry it out.[35]

This point helps to explain how decisions have been implemented in the three policy areas just discussed. The Supreme Court's decisions in each of these areas have been viewed as very bad policy by many of those responsible for carrying them out, and understandably people with such a view have often balked at following the Court's lead. This has been true, for instance, of teachers and school administrators who think that prayers are an essential part of school activities. This factor also helps to explain differences in responses to the same decision: the border states desegregated their schools more quickly than the Deep South largely because their school officials were not as strongly opposed to the idea of desegregation.

It follows that the implementation of appellate court decisions has an ideological dimension. As we have seen, the major thrust of activist judicial policies in recent years has been liberal; not surprisingly, conservative officials are the most likely to resist these policies. Similarly, the Supreme Court's conservative policies on some issues in the 1980s and early 1990s aroused resistance from liberal judges on the federal Ninth Circuit Court of Appeals on the Pacific Coast.[36]

Self-interest is also relevant to the implementation process. Appellate court rulings can affect the self-interest of judges and administrators in several ways. These rulings may, for instance, threaten or reinforce practices that officials find advantageous, such as the rapid processing of cases in trial courts. Or they may ask elected officials to take positions that are highly popular or unpopular with their constituents. Interest groups can also be important; a public utilities commission, for instance, might resist state supreme court decisions that run counter to the interests of a powerful utility company.[37]

The early failure to achieve school desegregation in the Deep South resulted in large part from constituency pressures. School officials typically faced overwhelmingly white electorates because of restrictions on voting by black citizens, and southern whites were strongly opposed to desegregation. Federal district judges held lifetime positions, but they faced ostracism and even possible violence if they demanded speedy desegregation.

Similarly, resistance by law enforcement officials to court decisions that limit investigative practices can be understood chiefly in terms of self-interest. Police officers have the inherently difficult job of solving crimes by identifying suspects and obtaining physical evidence. Court rulings that limit searches and seizures of evidence or the questioning of suspects complicate this job and threaten to make it even more difficult. Thus most officers initially take a negative view of these rulings. Ultimately, their compliance with such decisions depends on how much harm the decisions seem to cause. Police have found that court-imposed rules for searches and seizures often prevent them from obtaining the evidence they want, and so their compliance with these rules has been quite imperfect. In contrast, although there was considerable unhappiness with the *Miranda* decision when it was issued, officers gradually learned that minimal compliance with the decision did not make their job more difficult. If they read suspects their rights without giving any encouragement to make use of them, people seldom refused to answer questions. As a result, the *Miranda* rights generally have become a part of police routines.

Any court decision that requires major changes in policy is likely to conflict with the policy preferences or self-interest of many judges and administrators. One reason is that people and institutions left on their own will choose the policies that accord with their preferences and self-interest; hence, when an appellate court intervenes to demand a change, it is usually demanding that officials do what they find less desirable. Perhaps just as important, officials generally dislike any change that is imposed on their work because it is easier to continue doing things the same way than to adopt new routines.

Judicial Authority   If officials' self-interest and policy preferences may work against the full implementation of court decisions, other factors generally work in favor of effective implementation. One is acceptance of the *authority* of appellate courts: the right of those courts to bind legal subordinates with their rulings.

It appears that most people accept an obligation to follow the legal rules laid down by courts above them as part of the general obligation to obey the law. Lawyers are directly imbued with this duty through their training. Because most judges are lawyers and because they themselves benefit from judicial authority, judges tend to accept higher-court authority even more than do administrators.

The significance of court authority can be seen in the response to some unpopular decisions. A great many teachers and school administrators, for instance, have eliminated religious observances that they personally favored. This willingness to follow the courts' lead despite disagreement with their decisions stems chiefly from acceptance of the obligation to do what the Court asked.[38]

The impact of authority is sometimes quite explicit, as when judges proclaim their willingness to apply a higher-court precedent despite their disapproval of the policy expressed in that precedent. In one typical instance, a federal district judge in Louisiana wrote in a 1990 opinion that he was "respectfully disagreeing" with a ruling by the court of appeals above him but that this ruling was "binding and controlling in this cause," so that he had to follow it.[39]

Despite the authority of appellate courts, judges and administrators sometimes refuse to carry out an applicable decision. One reason is that some officials take a narrow view of the authority of appellate courts. Federal agencies such as the Social Security Administration and the Internal Revenue Service have engaged in selective "nonacquiescence" with rulings of lower federal courts that they disagree with, arguing that they need not change their policies across the country or adopt different policies in different parts of the country unless the Supreme Court rules definitively against them.[40] In 1983, in an incident noted in Chapter 5, a federal district judge in Alabama simply rejected the Supreme Court's interpretation of the First and Fourteenth Amendments concerning school prayer and substituted his own, implicitly taking the position that he was not bound by the Court's decisions.[41]

More important, officials can often reconcile their acceptance of a court's authority with evasion of its ruling. They may, for instance, seize upon the ambiguity in an appellate court opinion to avoid following its spirit. This was the response of many federal district judges to *Brown v. Board of Education,* in which the Supreme Court required that schools be desegregated "with all deliberate speed."[42] Judges who opposed desegregation interpreted this language as allowing them to delay the initiation of desegregation for many years, so long as any practical difficulties could be shown.

Similarly, officials may evade the spirit of a decision by engaging in narrow compliance with it. To take one example, a 1988 decision of the Ohio Supreme Court required that meetings of public bodies be open to the public when public business is discussed and a majority of members are present. In response, some agencies held private "educational" meetings, and a mayor asked to continue his private meetings with the city council—but with only three of seven council members in attendance.[43] One trial judge described informally his narrow compliance with appellate court decisions protecting the rights of criminal defendants:

> I've got to find some way to get around some rule that some court has pronounced about something, and I don't think we should have to admittedly—okay. I'm not great on defendants' rights. . . . So, you can argue until you're blue in the face. I'll agree with you that it is a close call, but I don't choose on close calls to read it in favor of the defendant. I just don't see that we have to do that.[44]

Another way to reconcile a court's authority with a failure to follow its ruling is to engage in selective misperception of the ruling. Some school personnel, for example, believe that they are in compliance with the Supreme Court's school prayer decisions when they allow students to absent themselves from prayer recitations. Such misperception is fostered by the poor communication of decisions to many administrators, who may learn of relevant decisions from imperfect reports by the mass media or by superiors. When communication is poor, people easily can interpret decisions as they see fit.

Sanctions   If the authority of appellate courts does not overcome resistance to their rulings, we might expect them to employ *sanctions*, penalties designed to force compliance. Appellate courts do possess some meaningful sanctions that they can threaten or actually employ against disobedient judges and administrators. However, these sanctions are fairly weak in comparison with those that exist in most other organizations. A federal court of appeals, for instance, cannot fire a district judge who refuses to follow its decisions.

For lower-court judges, the most significant sanction is the reversal of decisions that fail to follow an applicable ruling. Judges do not like to have their decisions reversed because this suggests that they have erred, and a judge who is frequently reversed may be perceived as incompetent. (Indeed, evidence of a high reversal rate contributed to the Senate vote against G. Harrold Carswell's nomination to the Supreme Court in 1970.) Hence judges have an incentive to apply appellate court rulings properly to the cases they decide. Yet reversal has limited practical consequences—usually only the requirement that a judge rehear a case. For this reason, judges who strongly oppose an appellate policy may be willing to accept reversals as a consequence of following their inclinations. As a federal district judge in Oregon liked to say, "We try to rule on the side of God. If the 9th Circuit wants to reverse, we'll know whose side it's on."[45] And reversals do not always follow disobedient decisions, in part because such decisions may not be appealed and reviewed.

For many administrative bodies, the most significant sanctions involve being taken to court and becoming subject to a court order that requires a change in policies. If, for example, a school continues to hold prayer exercises despite the Supreme Court's decisions, an unhappy parent can file suit and secure an order against such practices. The monetary costs of going to court and the embarrassment of an adverse court order can deter a certain amount of noncompliance. But, like reversal, this is not a very powerful set of sanctions. One reason is that someone with legal standing must go to court to seek an order requiring compliance with a decision, and frequently no one does so. Thus, for example, many school districts can continue religious observances because no lawsuit has ever been filed against them.

For administrative bodies that are more directly dependent on the courts, judges have a stronger sanction: the refusal to give needed support to agency policies. This sanction applies to some regulatory agencies, such as the National Labor Relations Board, which require court enforcement of their rulings. Less directly, police departments are dependent on courts to convict the defendants they arrest. Thus noncompliant behavior that jeopardizes enforcement of agency rulings or conviction of defendants carries real costs. Police officers, for instance, want to follow court requirements for obtaining evidence so that it will not be ruled inadmissible in court. But achieving a conviction is not always of great importance to individual police officers, who are judged chiefly on their ability to make "good arrests" rather than on the convictions of people they arrest. For this reason, they may be willing to jeopardize a conviction by violating judicial rules.

When judges or administrators violate a direct court order, those officials or their governments may be cited for contempt of court, usually with a monetary penalty. Though judges are reluctant to use such a strong sanction, fines for contempt against governments are not rare. As Exhibit 9.4 illustrates, federal judges have issued and enforced contempt citations against the District of Columbia government over several matters in recent years. And in 1988 a federal district judge temporarily overcame the resistance of Yonkers, New York, to housing desegregation by fining the city $100 and then doubling the fine each day. But this action, like some of the contempt citations against the District of Columbia, failed to bring about full compliance by the city.

Taken together, the sanctions that appellate courts can employ are significant but relatively weak. This weakness underlines the potential for inadequate implementation of their policies. Lower-court judges and administrators often hold attitudes that incline them against faithfully carrying out these policies. Although the authority of appellate courts and their sanctions do overcome some resistance, they are not strong enough to produce perfect compliance. As a result, the policies of appellate courts—like other government policies—are subject to implementation problems.

Responses by the Legislative and Executive Branches

Legislatures and the executive branch hold important powers over the courts, powers that make judges attentive to these other branches of government. This section examines how the legislative and executive branches actually use these powers in response to appellate court decisions.

EXHIBIT 9.4 Use of the Contempt Power Against the District of Columbia: Some Examples

Year	Court	Basis for Contempt Citation
1987	Federal District	Violation of a limit on the number of inmates at a local prison
1989	D.C. Superior	Failure to adhere to an agreement in court to improve shelters for the homeless
1990	Federal District	"Continuing obdurate resistance" to the obligation to provide adequate care at a home for the mentally retarded
1991	D.C. Superior	Violation of an order to transfer juvenile defendants and convicted criminals to shelters and foster care when incarceration in juvenile detention centers would be overly restrictive
1991	D.C. Superior	Failure to comply with legislation and a court order to increase nursing services in public schools

Sources: Articles in *Washington Post;* Aaron Freiwald and Daniel Klaidman, "The Nation's Capital: A City in Contempt," *Legal Times,* June 12, 1989, pp. 1, 16–17.

Responding to Statutory Interpretations   Most appellate court decisions interpret statutes, the laws that legislatures enact. Such decisions give additional form to the policies that are laid down in the legislation itself. In this way, state courts help shape legislative policy on such matters as divorce and occupational licensing, just as federal courts affect congressional policy on employment discrimination and taxation.

Most court interpretations of statutes attract little attention in the other branches of government because they are uncontroversial. But some statutory decisions arouse opposition from legislators or officials in the executive branch, who conclude that the court has misinterpreted their intent. These opponents can use a straightforward remedy: adoption of new legislation that clarifies the intent of the other branches and supersedes—in effect, overturns—the offending court decision.

Bills to undertake such corrective action are introduced quite often in Congress. Like other legislation, most of these bills fall by the wayside at some point, but many are enacted. One study found that between 1967 and 1990 Congress overturned 121 statutory decisions of the Supreme Court and 220 decisions of lower courts.[46] Exhibit 9.5 describes some recent overturnings of statutory decisions by Congress.

State legislatures also respond to statutory decisions with some frequency. In 1990, for instance, the New York legislature overturned a decision by the

Legislation	Decisions Overturned
Antitrust Amendments Act of 1990	1981 decision by Ninth Circuit Court of Appeals giving a broad interpretation to prohibitions on holding directorships in competing companies
Immigration Act of 1990	1983 Fifth Circuit decision allowing exclusion of homosexuals from immigration to the United States
Civil Rights Act of 1991	Nine Supreme Court decisions, 1985–1989, giving narrow interpretations to civil rights statutes
Copyright: Fair Use of Unpublished Works (1992)	Two Second Circuit decisions giving broad copyright protection to unpublished works

Sources: Based in part on compilation in William N. Eskridge, Jr., "Overriding Supreme Court Statutory Interpretation Decisions," *Yale Law Journal,* 101 (1991), 424–425. Reprinted by permission of the Yale Law Journal Company and Fred B. Rothman & Company from the *Yale Law Journal,* Vol. 101, pp. 331–445.

EXHIBIT 9.5 Some Recent Congressional Legislation Overturning Statutory Decisions by Federal Courts

state Court of Appeals that had interpreted narrowly the law allowing news organizations to withhold information from the courts.[47] Even more than members of Congress, state legislators are willing to work against decisions that they dislike.[48]

State legislatures can also supersede court decisions in areas such as property and torts, where the law has developed through court-made rules independent of statutes. Legislatures have been especially active in the tort field in recent years.[49] After state supreme courts adopted new doctrines expanding the legal rights of injured parties, legislatures often passed legislation to negate or limit these doctrines. Several legislatures, for instance, overturned decisions making social hosts liable for injuries caused by their serving of liquor to guests. This action has come at the behest of groups that must defend against lawsuits, particularly the insurance companies that usually pay the damages awarded against defendants; as discussed in Chapter 7, these groups have also obtained other legislation designed to improve their positions in court. In some instances, however, state supreme courts held that these new laws were unconstitutional. Courts in nine states, for instance, have overturned limits on the amounts that can be awarded to plaintiffs for certain kinds of damages.[50]

The discussion so far may suggest that legislation in response to judicial interpretation of a statute always involves direct conflict between the two branches, but this is not the case. The legislation that follows a statutory decision may ratify that decision, at least in part, rather than overturn it. And a court sometimes invites the legislature to overturn its decision if legislators see fit. In 1990, for instance, a California court of appeal ruled that the law did not allow some stockholders access to certain corporate records, but it recommended that the legislature change the legal provision in question.[51]

In most statutory fields, legislation in response to court decisions is only a small part of the process through which the law develops. In fields such as criminal law and environmental protection, each branch helps to shape and reshape public policy through a series of actions and decisions. Only occasionally in this process do the other branches react directly to court interpretations of statutes; more often the initiatives of each branch create a new status quo on which the other branches build.

Responding to Constitutional Interpretations   Ordinarily, a court decision that overturns a statute on constitutional grounds can itself be overturned only by a constitutional amendment. The federal and state constitutions have intentionally been made difficult to amend. The United States Constitution, for instance, is ordinarily amended by the agreement of two-thirds of each house of Congress and three-quarters of the state legislatures. Since the adoption of the Bill of Rights in 1791, only seventeen amendments have survived this process. State constitutions are usually amended through another two-stage process, which involves a proposal by the legislature and its ratification by the voters. This process is less cumbersome than its federal counterpart, but amendments to state constitutions are still considerably more difficult to achieve than simple legislation.

At both the state and federal levels, some constitutional amendments have overturned court decisions. Four amendments to the federal Constitution clearly were aimed at overturning Supreme Court decisions, and five others can also be put in that category. The most recent such amendment was the Twenty-sixth, which overturned a 1970 decision limiting congressional power to reduce the legal voting age.[52] In the states, several constitutional amendments have been adopted in recent years to overturn court decisions—most often on the death penalty and other criminal justice issues.

But these instances are exceptional. Because the amendment process is so difficult, even highly unpopular constitutional decisions generally are not overturned. The rarity of such action is especially striking at the federal level. In response to the liberal activism of the Supreme Court since the 1950s, members of Congress have introduced dozens of amendments designed to overturn particular decisions, yet none of these resolutions has received the necessary two-thirds majority in even one house of Congress. The Court's decisions opposing school prayer and supporting school busing do not enjoy anything like majority support in Congress or the nation at large, yet both sets of decisions remain standing.

Under some circumstances, a legislature can negate or limit the effect of a constitutional decision through statutory action. For example, when the Supreme Court struck down state death penalty laws in *Furman v. Georgia* (1972), its ambiguous decision seemed to indicate that redrafted versions would be constitutionally acceptable if they established clearer standards for imposing the death penalty. In response, most states did redraft their statutes, and the Court upheld some of the new statutes in 1976.[53] After *Roe v. Wade* (1973), the Supreme Court decision that struck down state prohibitions of abortion, Congress and many state legislatures adopted provisions that limited government funding of abortion; these provisions were also found acceptable under the U.S. Constitution.[54] (Some state supreme courts have held, however, that their own constitutions require state funding of abortion.)

Other statutory responses have been in more direct conflict with the court decisions in question. After *Brown v. Board of Education*, for example, southern states adopted a variety of laws to prevent desegregation, most of which were clearly unconstitutional and which were struck down by federal courts. Legislatures have also enacted statutes that directly contravened Supreme Court decisions on school prayer and abortion. An unusually concerted conflict occurred in California for several years after 1981, when the state supreme court ruled that the state must fund abortions for low-income women. The legislature continued to prohibit most such funding each year, even though these prohibitions all were struck down by the state courts.[55]

These kinds of actions may seem futile, but they can serve several purposes. First, legislators may express their own opposition to court decisions and appeal to constituents who are themselves opposed. Second, under some circumstances, such actions can delay the implementation of the decisions; this was the case with the web of segregation laws adopted by some southern states. Finally, legislators may perceive that a court's view on an issue has changed and enact a new law in order to seek a reversal of its position. This has been true of some recent statutes reinstating school prayer and regulating abortion.

Influencing the Implementation Process   There are several ways in which legislatures and chief executives can help determine how court decisions are put into practice.

First, they may influence the behavior of implementers by taking positions on controversial decisions. For example, the strong and active opposition of some southern governors to school desegregation contributed to the failure of the Deep South to initiate desegregation after 1954. President Kennedy's statement of support for the Supreme Court's 1962 school prayer decision may have helped induce compliance, while President Reagan's expressions of opposition to the Court's school prayer decisions may have had the opposite effect.

Second, the legislature and executive can provide—or fail to provide—tangible help in achieving effective implementation. After a decade of inaction in the Deep South, for example, Congress in 1964 gave the executive branch the power to withhold federal funds from school districts that refused to desegregate. The Johnson administration used this power with some vigor, and the result was that real desegregation finally began in that region. Ironically, Congress took several actions to try to impede desegregation of northern schools in the 1970s and 1980s, although these actions seemed to have little impact. In a different kind of action, Presidents Eisenhower and Kennedy each used federal troops in one instance to enforce school desegregation in the South.

Finally, some court decisions require compliance by legislatures or chief executives themselves. Perhaps the most famous example was the Supreme Court decision in *United States v. Nixon* (1974), which required that President Nixon turn over tape recordings of his conversations to a federal court. After some hesitation, Nixon complied, even though material in the recordings forced his resignation. His compliance, like that of some predecessors, suggests that the president's legitimacy might be seriously damaged by a failure to obey court rulings.

In recent years state legislatures have frequently been faced with court rulings that required them to make major changes in public institutions. For example, in many states, federal judges have ordered improvements in prisons and mental hospitals, and several state supreme courts have ordered changes in state systems for the financing of public schools. Legislators have good reasons to try to carry out these orders; most important, if they fail to do so, courts may take more drastic action, such as requiring that a prison be closed. But budgetary constraints may make effective implementation of a sweeping decision very difficult, and legislators often resent court rulings demanding institutional change.

As a result, the record of legislative action in response to these decisions is mixed. For instance, in 1973 the New Jersey Supreme Court issued a decision requiring a new school funding system. However, the state legislature adopted a tax measure needed to put the decision into effect only after the court had ordered the state's schools closed because of legislative inaction on its rulings. And in 1991, after a second major decision requiring a change in the funding system, low-income districts complained that the state still had not done enough to equalize funding.[56] In contrast, the Kentucky legislature responded enthusiastically to a 1989 state supreme court decision requiring a new system for school funding.[57]

Attacking the Courts as Institutions   Legislatures and chief executives typically control court jurisdiction, budgets, and staffing. If they are unhappy with court policies they can use these powers to attack the courts, either to limit what the courts can do as policy makers or simply to exact a measure of revenge.

At the federal level, the president and Congress frequently threaten to use their powers against the courts, but such an attack is seldom carried out. In 1937, for example, President Franklin Roosevelt proposed legislation that would allow him to "pack" the Supreme Court with six new members, thereby changing the Court's policy direction. The proposal died in Congress, partly because the Court retreated under this threat. Only once, in 1869, has Congress narrowed the Supreme Court's jurisdiction to keep the Court out of a controversial area—in that instance, Reconstruction of the South after the Civil War. Indeed, in the past thirty years a multitude of bills have been introduced to remove the jurisdiction of the Court or of all federal courts in such areas as abortion and school busing, but none was adopted.

In a number of instances, state legislatures have actually used their institutional powers to attack courts. In 1991 the California Supreme Court upheld an initiative measure that cut the state legislative budget by 38 percent; its opinion seemed to endorse the view that the legislature needed reform. In response, the legislature cut the supreme court's budget by the same 38 percent. One person who discussed that cut with legislators "discovered they had memorized the 'offensive' passages in the high court opinion, and quoted them back to her in the hallways of the Legislature."[58]

Another instance of financial retaliation was reported by a lawyer who argued a case before the Nevada Supreme Court during a rainstorm and found that rain was pouring into the courtroom itself. The chief justice explained that the court had asked the legislature for money to fix the problem, but the legislature refused because of its unhappiness with some of the court's decisions.[59]

Significant though these attacks are, some nineteenth-century legislatures took stronger action. Early in that century one legislature reportedly expressed its displeasure with a decision of the state supreme court by reducing the justices' annual salaries to twenty-five cents.[60] And the Kentucky legislature went even further in the 1820s:

> When the state supreme court adopted some unpopular doctrines relating to disputed land claims, the legislature abolished the court and appointed a new one. The first court refused to go out of existence, however, and for several years Kentucky had two supreme courts, reminiscent of the medieval episode when the Catholic church had two popes.[61]

The Courts and the Other Branches: The General Relationship   Even in the states, and certainly at the federal level, the other branches of government take action against courts and court decisions less frequently than we might expect. Congress and the president have vast powers to undo court decisions, both through legislation and through the proposal of constitutional amendments, and equally vast powers to attack the courts as institutions. Why have they not used these powers more extensively?

One reason is the sheer difficulty of such action. On controversial matters—and action against a court is almost always controversial—it is usually difficult to get past the many potential roadblocks in the legislative process. Senator Russell Long perhaps expressed this best: "It is absolutely beyond the power of any human mind to assess the various ways that something which appears destined to become law can fail to become law, but it happens all the time."[62] Because constitutional amendments require more than simple legislative majorities, they are even more difficult to adopt.

Another reason is the tinge of illegitimacy that is attached to many forms of anticourt action, particularly attacks on the courts as institutions. Even the adoption of constitutional amendments may seem illegitimate if the provisions to be amended are themselves regarded as sacrosanct. Most amendments to overturn Supreme Court decisions expanding civil liberties can be seen as cutting into the Bill of Rights, and such a step would bother members of Congress a good deal. For example, a 1985 proposal to remove federal court jurisdiction over school prayer was defeated in the Senate because liberal Democrats were joined in opposition by a good many moderate and conservative senators.

Thus the relationship between the courts and the other branches is somewhat different in practice from what formal legal powers would suggest. Legislatures and chief executives, which would seem to be in a dominant position over the courts, do not in fact employ their powers very fully. And this restraint increases the role of the courts in making public policy.

We also need to take into account the courts' own restraint, discussed in Chapter 8. Judges often avoid conflict with the other branches of government by limiting their intervention on policy questions. Courts adopt fewer innovative interpretations of statutes and declare fewer laws unconstitutional than we might expect, in part because of a desire to keep the peace with the legislature and the executive branch. In addition, courts sometimes retreat from their past policies in order to ease conflicts with the other branches.

Finally, we should keep in mind the narrow area of policy interventions that appellate courts make. The willingness of other policy makers to live with judicial initiatives in some fields may result in part from the courts' inactivity in others.

The Impact of the Courts on Society

The most important impact courts can have is on society as a whole—on people's behavior as individuals and on such social institutions as the family and the economy. We know relatively little about how much effect courts actually have in general or in particular situations, but we can explore this question on the basis of what we do know.

Types of Impact   Various observers have ascribed a wide range of effects to appellate courts. They include the following:

- Many people see the Supreme Court's 1973 decision in *Roe v. Wade* as the source of a massive growth in the rate of legal abortions.[63]
- Some commentators argue that state court decisions expanding the right to sue for personal injuries have resulted in a long list of bad effects, including economic costs as high as $300 billion a year.[64]
- According to some critics, court decisions limiting the legal regulation of obscenity produced a major increase in the volume of sexually oriented materials available to consumers.[65]
- A number of commentators assert that court decisions expanding the legal rights of public school students, mandating compensatory treatment for disadvantaged students, and prohibiting school prayer have damaged the educational process and had adverse effects on students.[66]
- Supreme Court decisions in support of racial equality are widely seen as an important spur to the civil rights revolution in the 1950s and 1960s and improvement in the status of African American citizens since that time.[67]
- More broadly, one legal scholar concluded that the Supreme Court's decisions "upholding personal rights secured by the Constitution" have "enhanced the liberties of many individuals and produced substantial consequences."[68]

The wide range of effects suggested by these examples can be divided into two categories. The more direct effects involve changing the incentives for people to engage in some kinds of behavior. For example, the Supreme Court may have encouraged the proliferation of sexually oriented books and magazines by reducing the likelihood that their publishers and retailers would be prosecuted and convicted under the obscenity laws. On the other hand, state courts may have increased the financial risk of making products that are subject to lawsuits as the causes of injuries, thereby leading manufacturers to stop making these products.

The less direct form of impact occurs when the courts trigger broader social change by influencing people's thinking and the structures in which they operate. For instance, the Supreme Court may have helped to spur the civil rights revolution by providing an important symbol (*Brown v. Board of Education*) and by giving legal protection to the incipient civil rights movement. By expanding the legal rights of students, the courts may have changed the attitudes of students toward authority, both within the schools and in the larger society. Of course, this second form of impact is linked to the first, in that changes in specific behavior may lead to broader social changes. For example, if school boards are required to integrate the schools, then that integration might well lead to changes in racial attitudes among students.

Limits on the Impact of Courts   There is reason to be skeptical about some claims regarding the impact of the courts because three conditions tend to limit the actual effects of judicial policies on social behavior and social institutions.

First, the policies that the courts adopt on any particular issue are seldom perfectly consistent in their direction. Thus, for example, the Supreme Court's decisions expanding some of the rights of criminal defendants coexist with other Court decisions that have narrowed the same rights; in addition, lower courts have differed a good deal in their own support of those rights. For some time the dominant trend in state supreme courts was one of expansion of liability for defective products, but some courts resisted this trend, and the trend itself has now been reversed. To a degree, these conflicting decisions cancel out each other's potential effects.

Second, policy makers in the other branches also act on issues that courts address, and these policy makers can reduce the impact of courts. Most directly, court decisions often have to be implemented by administrative policy makers, and we have seen the problems that can arise in this process. For instance, police departments and regulatory boards sometimes fail to follow court guidelines for regulation of obscenity, thereby reducing their impact. Similarly, legislatures can narrow the scope of a decision or overturn it altogether. Congress, for example, has limited the effects of the Supreme Court's legalization of abortion by its refusal to fund abortions.

More broadly, the policies made by the courts in any field coexist with the policies of the other branches of government, whose actions may amplify or blunt the courts' potential impact. Thus the great increase in legal abortion rates during the 1970s resulted in considerable part from action by state legislatures before the landmark Supreme Court decisions of 1973.[69] Similarly, a tremendous array of government policies might influence the education and behavior of young people, and it is the other branches rather than the courts that operate the schools.

Finally, and perhaps most significantly, government policies are only one of many forces that shape society as a whole. Indeed, for both politicians and scholars, one important lesson of the past quarter century is that the capacity of government to do either good or ill is constrained by more fundamental influences on people's behavior and on the social structure. Racial discrimination, for example, has proved at least moderately resistant to government action, in part because it is deeply rooted in some people's perceptions and attitudes. Courts are limited by these conditions just as the other branches are.

We can probe the limitations on the impact of courts by looking at two examples of potential impact, the incidence of crime and the status of women.

The Incidence of Crime   Beginning in the 1950s and then more concertedly in the 1960s, the Supreme Court expanded the procedural rights of criminal defendants in several areas. The most important of these expansions were its requirements that indigent defendants in any serious case be provided with attorneys, that suspects be warned of their rights prior to police questioning, and that evidence seized illegally be excluded from use in court. These decisions received a mixed response from lower appellate courts; however, some had taken similar steps even before the Supreme Court acted. And in the last two decades, as the Court has reduced its support for defendants' rights, several state supreme courts have adopted new doctrines expanding these rights.

The judicial expansion of defendants' rights—particularly restrictions on police practices—has aroused a good deal of criticism. In 1986 President Ronald Reagan said that "the proliferation of drugs has been part of a crime epidemic that can be traced to, among other things, liberal judges who are unwilling to get tough with the criminal element in this society."[70] The 1992 Republican party platform argued that widespread violent crime was, in part, "the legacy of a liberalism that elevates criminals' rights above victims' rights."[71]

How might this have happened? As critics see it, appellate court decisions make it more difficult to obtain and use needed evidence against criminals, thus reducing the likelihood that they will be convicted. As people who are contemplating criminal acts become aware that their chances of being convicted and punished have decreased, they in turn are more willing to commit such offenses.

On the basis of the available evidence, a partial evaluation of this analysis is possible. First of all, the effect of expanded defendants' rights on conviction rates is uncertain. Some studies of restrictions on police practices suggest that they have only a limited impact on the effectiveness of law enforcement. It does not appear that reading rights to suspects substantially reduces the numbers who are willing to answer questions; although restrictions on searches and seizures apparently lessen the number of arrests and convictions, these reductions do not seem to be substantial.[72] These findings do not mean that we can dismiss the possibility of a strong relationship between appellate court decisions and conviction rates. It may be that such a relationship exists, at least under certain circumstances.[73] But we should not simply assume that it exists.

It is likely that policy makers who participate more directly in the criminal justice system actually affect conviction rates a good deal more than do appellate courts. Police officers, prosecutors, and trial judges have more direct control over what happens in specific cases, and they also put appellate court policies into effect, reshaping and sometimes weakening these policies in the process. Legislatures exert considerable impact through their funding decisions. As a committee of the American Bar Association concluded in 1988,

> Constitutional restrictions, such as the exclusionary rule and Miranda, do not significantly handicap police and prosecutors in their efforts to arrest, prosecute, and obtain convictions of criminal defendants for most serious crimes. Rather, the major problem for the criminal justice system . . . is lack of sufficient resources.[74]

In addition, it is unclear just how much a moderate decline in the chances of conviction—if, indeed, one has resulted from court decisions—would affect the incidence of criminal behavior. Rational calculations appear to play only a small part in some decisions to commit crimes with a large emotional content, so conviction rates may not be very relevant in these cases. In contrast, such calculations seem to be more important for crimes with economic motives, such as burglary. (Indeed, one New Jersey kidnapper had done substantial research to determine the average sentence for the crime and then calculated how much ransom he would need to justify the risk of incarceration.[75]) Yet even a burglar's commitment to criminal behavior may be sufficiently deep that nothing less than a massive change in the likelihood of conviction—presuming, of course, that this change was evident to the burglar—could alter that behavior.

There are, then, some reasons to question the claims that appellate court decisions have encouraged crime. Historian Leonard Levy has expressed a particularly skeptical view, arguing that "decisions of appellate courts have approximately the same effect upon the causes of crime as gamma rays."[76] Levy may have exaggerated the limits of appellate court impact, but his statement underlines the uncertain relationship between appellate courts and crime.

The Status of Women   Until the 1960s courts generally ratified and accentuated the inequalities between women and men that were established by other institutions in society. The Supreme Court, for instance, upheld state laws that excluded women from the legal profession and restricted other employment opportunities and that prevented women from voting.

In the last three decades, however, courts have responded to society's changing attitudes toward women's status and roles. Through interpretations of the equal protection clause of the Fourteenth Amendment and provisions of state constitutions, courts have struck down a variety of legal rules that distinguished between women and men. The Supreme Court has been the most visible participant in this process; although the Court's record is mixed, it is clear that the majority of justices will hold unconstitutional any law that discriminates directly against women. Some state supreme courts have taken even stronger positions. The Pennsylvania Supreme Court, for example, has given expansive interpretations to the equal rights amendment in its state constitution.

This new wave of appellate court decisions has overthrown a large number of laws and legal rules that put women at a disadvantage, including provisions that limited the rights of women in marriage and laws that treated female criminal defendants in special ways. Indirectly, these decisions have also speeded the elimination of other laws that discriminate by sex and made unenforceable many laws that remain on the books. During the same period the status of women in American society has changed substantially; one example is the growing representation of women in such professions as law and medicine.

To what extent are appellate courts responsible for these changes? On the whole, it appears that they have played only a minor part.[77] One reason is that judges have not been entirely fervent or even consistent in attacking sex discrimination. But even a more concerted effort would have had only a limited effect when compared with other forces. Recent changes in the status and roles of women reflect a general social revolution in American society, a revolution that has been spurred chiefly by changes in such matters as women's educational attainments rather than by government action. To the extent that government has encouraged this revolution, legislatures and chief executives have done more than appellate courts, mainly because they are better situated to take actions with a major impact in this area. For example, state legislatures have initiated equal rights amendments, and protection for women in employment has come primarily through legislation.

Employment provides a good illustration of these general points.[78] The concentration of women in certain occupations and the relatively low wages of the average female worker result from a wide range of conditions, including the education of girls, the conflict between caring for children and professional careers, and discrimination by employers. Recent improvements in the employment status of women also derive from several sources. Government policies, especially prohibitions of employment discrimination, probably have played a part in these improvements. But these policies have come from the legislative and executive branches, not from the judiciary. Courts have made some important interpretations of antidiscrimination laws, yet the effects of their decisions appear to be quite limited in comparison with action by the other branches of government and with nongovernmental forces. In this area, and more generally, courts have played only a small part in changing the roles of women.

Areas of Significant Impact   I have given considerable attention to policy areas in which the courts seem to have relatively limited effects. This emphasis has been deliberate, in order to counter the prevailing tendency to exaggerate the impact of appellate courts. Yet the impression that the examples of crime and women's status may give—that courts actually make little difference— needs to be modified in two respects.

First, even in these two areas and in others like them, courts have significant effects. For example, although appellate courts may not have much of an influence on the patterns of crime, their decisions have changed the treatment of suspects and defendants by the criminal justice system. At least some people have escaped police searches, obtained more favorable terms in plea bargains, and avoided convictions because of the rights established in appellate court decisions. In the area of women's status, court decisions have helped determine when women can collect damages for employment discrimination and have brought about changes in insurance rates for women and men. These effects cannot be dismissed as trivial.

Second, there are other policy areas in which courts have played more central roles. One example, discussed in Chapter 3, is the marketing of lawyers' services. The development of low-cost legal clinics and widespread advertising over the past decade are changing the legal profession markedly. These changes could not have occurred without Supreme Court decisions that overturned prohibitions of advertising by lawyers. Pressures for change in the legal market already existed, but their effects would have been delayed and more limited without the Supreme Court's intervention.

Another example concerns abortion. The impact of the Supreme Court's 1973 decision in *Roe v. Wade* is often exaggerated because people do not take into account the changes in social attitudes and legislative policies that preceded *Roe*. Yet the Court greatly speeded up the process of legal change with its original decision and with later rulings that limited state regulation of abortion. Moreover, *Roe v. Wade* provided a focal point for the debate over abortion; among other things, the Court inadvertently helped to bring about a large-scale antiabortion movement. Thus the Court had a major effect on both the numbers of abortions that are performed and the political contention over abortion. Similarly, the Court's decisions since 1989, which have expanded the states' power to regulate and restrict abortion, caused both sides in the abortion debate to focus their attention on the state legislatures; in addition, the restrictions that the Court has allowed probably have reduced the numbers of abortions.

But perhaps the most important example of the courts' impact in recent years concerns the status and roles of African American citizens. It is important not to overstate this impact. Change in the situations of African American citizens has been limited in important respects. For instance, a good deal of racial segregation remains in schools and colleges, and the average income of blacks continues to be far below that of whites. And courts were not the primary source of the changes that have occurred. As with changes in women's rights, the most important sources of change were outside government. Moreover, much of the government policy supporting racial equality came from the legislature (such as prohibitions of employment discrimination) or was initiated by the courts but was largely ineffective until other branches of government acted (such as school desegregation and protection of the right to vote in the Deep South).

Yet courts played a major part in facilitating change. Although court decisions were insufficient to desegregate southern schools without congressional help, they did make desegregation possible. Perhaps more important, *Brown v. Board of Education* and other decisions were significant symbols; they declared that government support for discrimination was constitutionally unacceptable and encouraged other efforts to achieve racial equality. Once the civil rights movement became active, the Supreme Court took extraordinary steps to protect it, striking down convictions of people arrested in demonstrations and overturning state laws intended to cripple civil rights organizations. The Court's decisions were neither necessary to sustain the movement nor sufficient to protect it from harassment, but they strengthened it significantly.

Thus the courts, and especially the Supreme Court, have been important contributors to the process of social change in this area. Although court decisions would have had little impact in themselves, they served to bolster and stimulate other forces for change. Because the civil rights revolution has been so important, this example should dispel any doubt that the courts can make a difference in American society.

CONCLUSIONS

In this chapter, I have examined the roles of appellate courts as policy makers from several perspectives. As we have seen, those roles are complex and difficult to characterize, but a few conclusions are possible.

Perhaps the most important conclusion concerns limitations on the power of the courts as policy makers. The Supreme Court and other courts have a significant impact on the rest of government and society, but their impact is not nearly as great as it is sometimes depicted. For one thing, the courts focus on some kinds of policy issues rather than others; as a result, to take one example, they generally can have only a limited effect on foreign policy. Even in the areas where they are active, the courts often endorse rather than overturn policies of the other branches. Finally, where courts do act independently and decisively to create new policies, the impact of those policies may be limited severely by the actions of people in other government institutions.

Both this chapter and the book as a whole stress that the courts are closely linked with the rest of government and society, and those links largely determine the roles that courts play in the making of public policy. The opportunities that judges have to make policy decisions depend heavily on the jurisdiction that legislatures give them and on the actions of individuals and groups to bring cases to them. What judges do with those opportunities is shaped by their own socialization within the legal system and the larger society and by their perceptions of what their legal and political audiences will accept. As suggested earlier, the ultimate impact of a court decision depends on the ways that other policy makers and people outside of government react to it.

It should be clear by now that the roles of the courts are not static. Over the course of time, both the ideological pattern of appellate court policies and the extent of judicial activism have varied. The contribution of the courts to public policy today looks rather different from their contribution half a century ago. As relevant conditions continue to change, we can expect further changes in what the courts do—in some instances, changes that we cannot predict today.

FOR FURTHER READING

Chilton, Bradley Stewart. *Prisons Under the Gavel: The Federal Court Take-over of Georgia Prisons*. Columbus: Ohio State University Press, 1992.

Gates, John B. *The Supreme Court and Partisan Realignment: A Macro- and Microlevel Perspective*. Boulder, Colo.: Westview Press, 1992.

Johnson, Charles A., and Bradley C. Canon. *Judicial Policies: Implementation and Impact*. Washington, D.C.: CQ Press, 1984.

Keynes, Edward, with Randall K. Miller. *The Court vs. Congress: Prayer, Busing, and Abortion*. Durham, N.C.: Duke University Press, 1989.

Pacelle, Richard L., Jr. *The Transformation of the Supreme Court's Agenda From the New Deal to the Reagan Administration*. Boulder, Colo.: Westview Press, 1991.

Rosenberg, Gerald N. *The Hollow Hope: Can Courts Bring About Social Change?* Chicago: University of Chicago Press, 1991.

Yackle, Larry W. *Reform and Regret: The Story of Federal Judicial Involvement in the Alabama Prison System*. New York: Oxford University Press, 1989.

NOTES

1. *Annual Report of the Director of the Administrative Office of the United States Courts, 1991* (Washington, D.C.: Government Printing Office, 1992), p. 177.
2. Joy A. Chapper and Roger A. Hanson, *Understanding Reversible Error in Criminal Appeals* (Williamsburg, Va.: National Center for State Courts, 1989), pp. 34–35. See also Thomas Y. Davies, "Affirmed: A Study of Criminal Appeals and Decision-Making Norms in a California Court of Appeal," *American Bar Foundation Research Journal* (Summer 1982), 576.
3. See Davies, "Affirmed."
4. *Parts and Electric Motors v. Sterling Electric*, 866 F.2d 228, 233 (7th Cir. 1988).
5. John B. Oakley and Robert S. Thompson, "Screening, Delegation, and the Values of Appeal: An Appraisal of the Ninth Circuit's Screening Docket During the Browning Years," in *Restructuring Justice: The Innovations of the Ninth Circuit and the Future of the Federal Courts*, ed. Arthur D. Hellman (Ithaca, N.Y.: Cornell University Press, 1990), p. 130.
6. *Annual Report of the Administrative Office, 1991*, p. 177.
7. Davies, "Affirmed," pp. 582–583.
8. "The Supreme Court, 1991 Term," *Harvard Law Review*, 106 (November 1992), 382.
9. This figure is estimated from the Court's rates of acceptance of cases and of disturbances in the cases it accepts. See "Statistical Recap of Supreme Court's Workload during Last Three Terms," *United States Law Week*, 61 (August 11, 1992), 3098; and J. Woodford Howard, Jr., *Courts of Appeals in the Federal Judicial System: A Study of the Second, Fifth, and District of Columbia Circuits* (Princeton, N.J.: Princeton University Press, 1981), p. 59.
10. See Robert A. Kagan, Bliss Cartwright, Lawrence M. Friedman, and Stanton Wheeler, "The Business of State Supreme Courts, 1870–1970," *Stanford Law Review*, 30 (November 1977), 132–151; and Burton M. Atkins and Henry R. Glick, "Environmental and Structural Variables as Determinants of Issues in State Courts of Last Resort," *American Journal of Political Science*, 20 (February 1976), 98–101.
11. See Howard, *Courts of Appeals in the Federal Judicial System*, pp. 315–318; and Lawrence Baum, Sheldon Goldman, and Austin Sarat, "The Evolution of Litigation in the Federal Courts of Appeals, 1895–1975," *Law and Society Review*, 16 (1981–1982), 291–309.
12. See Richard L. Pacelle, Jr., *The Transformation of the Supreme Court's Agenda From the New Deal to the Reagan Administration* (Boulder, Colo.: Westview Press, 1991).
13. See Lawrence M. Friedman, *A History of American Law*, rev. ed. (New York: Simon & Schuster, 1985); Stanton Wheeler, Bliss Cartwright, Robert A. Kagan, and Lawrence M. Friedman, "Do the 'Haves' Come Out Ahead? Winning and Losing in State Supreme Courts, 1870–1970," *Law and Society Review*, 21 (1987), 403–445; Melvin I. Urofsky, "State Courts and Progressive Legislation during the Progressive

Era: A Reevaluation," *Journal of American History*, 72 (June 1985), 63–91; and Gary T. Schwartz, "Tort Law and the Economy in Nineteenth-Century America: A Reinterpretation," *Yale Law Journal*, 90 (July 1981), 1717–1775.

14. Lawrence Baum and Bradley C. Canon, "State Supreme Courts as Activists: New Doctrines in the Law of Torts," in *State Supreme Courts: Policymakers in the Federal System*, ed. Mary Cornelia Porter and G. Alan Tarr (Westport, Conn.: Greenwood Press, 1982), pp. 83–108.

15. James A. Henderson, Jr., and Theodore Eisenberg, "The Quiet Revolution in Products Liability: An Empirical Study of Legal Change," *UCLA Law Review*, 37 (February 1990), 479–553.

16. Barry Latzer, "The Hidden Conservatism of the State Court 'Revolution,' " *Judicature*, 74 (December–January 1991), 190–197.

17. See Ronald K. L. Collins, Peter J. Galie, and John Kincaid, "State High Courts, State Constitutions, and Individual Rights Litigation since 1980: A Judicial Survey," *Publius*, 16 (Summer 1986), 141–161; and Stanley H. Friedelbaum, ed., *Human Rights in the States: New Directions in Constitutional Policymaking* (New York: Greenwood Press, 1988).

18. Lawrence Baum and David Frohnmayer, eds., *The Courts: Sharing and Separating Powers* (New Brunswick, N.J.: Eagleton Institute of Politics, Rutgers University, 1989), p. 17.

19. Bradley C. Canon, "A Framework for the Analysis of Judicial Activism," in *Supreme Court Activism and Restraint* ed. Stephen C. Halpern and Charles M. Lamb (Lexington, Mass.: Lexington Books, 1982), pp. 385–419

20. The case was *Scott v. Sandford*, 19 Howard 393 (1857).

21. These figures were calculated from data in Congressional Research Service, *The Constitution of the United States of America: Analysis and Interpretation* (Washington, D.C.: Government Printing Office, 1987), pp. 1885–2113; *1988 Supplement* (Washington, D.C. Government Printing Office, 1989), pp. 187–206; and more recent decisions.

22. Congressional Research Service, *Constitution of the United States*, pp. 2117–2127; *1988 Supplement*, pp. 208–209.

23. The 1973 decisions were *Roe v. Wade*, 410 U.S. 113, and *Doe v. Bolton*, 410 U.S. 179. The most recent decision on state regulation was *Planned Parenthood v. Casey*, 120 L. Ed. 2d 674 (1992).

24. *Immigration and Naturalization Service v. Chadha*, 462 U.S. 919 (1983).

25. *McCall v. Batson*, 329 S.E.2d 741 (S.C. 1985).

26. Tinsley E. Yarbrough, *Judge Frank Johnson and Human Rights in Alabama* (University: University of Alabama Press, 1981); Larry W. Yackle, *Reform and Regret: The Story of Federal Judicial Involvement in the Alabama Prison System* (New York: Oxford University Press, 1989); Ronald Smothers, "Cursed and Praised, Retiring Judge Recalls Storm," *New York Times*, November 8, 1991, p. B9.

27. See Gary Taylor, "Mighty Lone Star Standoff," *National Law Journal*, January 14, 1991, pp. 1, 30–31.

28. David Maraniss, "Justice, Texas Style," *Washington Post*, February 28, 1987, p. G1. See Frank R. Kemerer, *William Wayne Justice: A Judicial Biography* (Austin: University of Texas Press, 1991).

29. Taylor, "Mighty Lone Star Standoff," p. 1.

30. Kemerer, *William Wayne Justice*, p. 163.

31. See Halpern and Lamb, eds., *Supreme Court Activism and Restraint*.

32. J. W. Peltason, *Fifty-Eight Lonely Men: Southern Federal Judges and School Desegregation*, 2d ed. (Urbana: University of Illinois Press, 1971); Charles S. Bullock III, "Equal Education Opportunity," in *Implementation of Civil Rights Policy*, ed. Charles S. Bullock III and Charles M. Lamb (Monterey, Calif.: Brooks/Cole, 1984), pp. 55–92.

33. Neal Milner, *The Courts and Local Law Enforcement: The Impact of Miranda* (Beverly Hills, Calif.: Sage Publications, 1971); Charles A. Johnson and Bradley

C. Canon, *Judicial Policies: Implementation and Impact* (Washington, D.C.: CQ Press, 1984), pp. 95–97; Stephen J. Schulhofer, "Reconsidering *Miranda*," *University of Chicago Law Review*, 54 (Spring 1987), 435–461.

34. H. Frank Way, Jr., "Survey Research on Judicial Decisions: The Prayer and Bible Reading Cases," *Western Political Quarterly*, 21 (June 1968), 191; Kenneth Paul Nuger, "Teacher Compliance with *Wallace v. Jaffree* in Mobile County Schools" (Paper presented at the annual conference of the Midwest Political Science Association in Chicago, April 1987); Gary Abramson and David Goldberg, "7 School Systems to Ignore Ruling on Prayer," *Atlanta Constitution*, August 29, 1989, pp. D1, D4.

35. Leslie Guevarra, "Judge Won't Absolve Late Drug King," *San Francisco Chronicle*, August 14, 1987, p. 4.

36. Katherine Bishop, "When an Appeals Court Becomes the Big Issue in Death Penalty Cases," *New York Times*, May 22, 1992, p. B9.

37. Rob Karwath, "ICC Acts as If It's in the Dark," *Chicago Tribune*, December 18, 1991, sec. 1, p. 7.

38. Richard M. Johnson, *The Dynamics of Compliance* (Evanston, Ill.: Northwestern University Press, 1967); William K. Muir, Jr., *Prayer in the Public Schools: Law and Attitude Change* (Chicago: University of Chicago Press, 1967).

39. *United States v. State of Louisiana*, 751 F. Supp. 606, 608 (E.D. La. 1990).

40. Susan Gluck Mezey, *No Longer Disabled: The Federal Courts and the Politics of Social Security Disability* (New York: Greenwood Press, 1988), pp. 121–139; Marianne Lavelle, "Sometimes the U.S. Just Says 'No,' " *National Law Journal*, July 24, 1989, pp. 1, 36–37.

41. *Jaffree v. Board of School Commissioners*, 554 F. Supp. 1104, 1128 (S.D. Ala. 1983).

42. *Brown v. Board of Education*, 349 U.S. 294, 301 (1955).

43. Alan Johnson, "Public Officials Find Ways to Pull Shades on Sunshine Law," *Columbus Dispatch*, September 11, 1988, p. 4C. The decision was *State, ex rel. Plain Dealer Publishing Co. v. Barnes*, 527 N.E.2d 807 (Ohio 1988).

44. Charles M. Sevilla, *Disorder in the Court: Great Fractured Moments in Courtroom History* (New York: W. W. Norton, 1992), pp. 108–109.

45. Stephen Gillers, "Gus J. Solomon: 'On the Side of God,' " *National Law Journal*, April 27, 1987, p. 13.

46. William N. Eskridge, Jr., "Overriding Supreme Court Statutory Intrepretation Decisions," *Yale Law Journal*, 101 (November 1991), 338.

47. Sam Howe Verhovek, "New York State Votes Stricter Law Protecting Reporters' Notes," *New York Times*, March 22, 1990, p. A16.

48. See Mark C. Miller, "Court-Legislative Relations: The Policy Role of the Courts in Three American Governmental Systems" (Paper presented at the annual conference of the Midwest Political Science Association in Chicago, April 1992).

49. See Linda Lipsen, "The Evolution of Products Liability as a Federal Policy Issue," in *Tort Law and the Public Interest: Competition, Innovation, and Consumer Welfare*, ed. Peter H. Schuck (New York: W. W. Norton, 1991), pp. 262–271.

50. "Record on 'Reform' Mixed in Courts," *National Law Journal*, November 9, 1992, p. 34.

51. *Feldman v. San Mateo Financial Corporation*, 276 Cal. Rptr. 285 (Cal. App. 1st Dist. 1990).

52. *Oregon v. Mitchell*, 400 U.S. 112 (1970).

53. *Gregg v. Georgia*, 428 U.S. 153 (1976).

54. *Harris v. McRae*, 448 U.S. 297 (1980).

55. See William Carlsen, "Court Again Refuses to Hear Abortion Case," *San Francisco Chronicle*, December 16, 1988, p. A9.

56. Richard Lehne, *The Quest for Justice: The Politics of School Finance Reform* (New York: Longman, 1978); Rorie Sherman, "Tackling Education Financing," *National Law Journal*, July 22, 1991, p. 22.

57. William Celis III, "Kentucky Begins Drive to Revitalize Its Schools," *New York Times,* September 26, 1990, p. B6.
58. Victoria Slind-Flor, "Calif. Bar Criticized by Judges," *National Law Journal,* October 19, 1992, p. 27. The decision was *Legislature v. Eu,* 54 Cal. 3d 492 (1991).
59. Baum and Frohnmayer, *The Courts,* p. 35.
60. Evan Haynes, *The Selection and Tenure of Judges* (Newark, N.J.: National Conference of Judicial Councils, 1944), p. 95.
61. Johnson and Canon, *Judicial Policies,* p. 156.
62. Peter Masley, "The Capitol," *Washington Post,* April 23, 1977, p. A3.
63. See Walter Isaacson, "The Battle Over Abortion," *Time,* April 6, 1981, pp. 20–28.
64. Peter W. Huber, *Liability: The Legal Revolution and Its Consequences* (New York: Basic Books, 1988), pp. 3–5.
65. Walter Berns, "Beyond the (Garbage) Pale, or Democracy, Censorship and the Arts," in *The Pornography Controversy,* ed. Ray C. Rist (New Brunswick, N.J.: Transaction Books, 1975), pp. 43–45.
66. Edward A. Wynne, "What Are the Courts Doing to Our Children?" *The Public Interest,* 64 (Summer 1981), 3–18; H. Wesley Smith, "Holding Court in the Schools," *Newsweek,* February 4, 1985, pp. 12–13; "Remarks to the 47th National Conference . . ." *Weekly Compilation of Presidential Documents,* 19 (July 1, 1983), 953–954.
67. Johnson and Canon, *Judicial Policies,* pp. 256–260.
68. Jesse H. Choper, "Consequences of Supreme Court Decisions Upholding Individual Constitutional Rights," *Michigan Law Review,* 83 (October 1984), 12.
69. Susan B. Hansen, "State Implementation of Supreme Court Decisions: Abortion Rates since *Roe v. Wade,*" *Journal of Politics* 42 (May 1980), 372–395; Gerald N. Rosenberg, *The Hollow Hope: Can Courts Bring About Social Change?* (Chicago: University of Chicago Press, 1991), pp. 178–180.
70. "Remarks at a Rally for Senator James T. Broyhill, October 8, 1986," *Weekly Compilation of Presidential Documents,* 22 (October 13, 1986), 1353.
71. "Party Stresses Family Values, Decentralized Authority," *Congressional Quarterly Weekly Report,* August 22, 1992, p. 2566.
72. Thomas Y. Davies, "A Hard Look at What We Know (and Still Need to Learn) About the 'Costs' of the Exclusionary Rule: The NIJ Study and Other Studies of 'Lost' Arrests," *American Bar Foundation Research Journal* (Summer 1983), 611–690; Peter F. Nardulli, "The Societal Costs of the Exclusionary Rule Revisited," *University of Illinois Law Review* (Spring 1987), 223–239.
73. Sheldon Goldman and Thomas P. Jahnige, *The Federal Courts as a Political System,* 3d ed. (New York: Harper & Row, 1985), pp. 101–103.
74. Special Committee on Criminal Justice in a Free Society, American Bar Association, *Criminal Justice in Crisis* (Washington, D.C.: American Bar Association, 1988), p. 5.
75. Chuck Shepherd, "News of the Weird," *The Reader* (Chicago), April 5, 1991, sec. 3, p. 33.
76. Leonard W. Levy, *Against the Law: The Nixon Court and Criminal Justice* (New York: Harper & Row, 1974), p. 3.
77. See Rosenberg, *The Hollow Hope,* pp. 202–246.
78. Elaine Sorensen, *Exploring the Reasons Behind the Narrowing Gender Gap in Earnings* (Washington, D.C.: Urban Institute Press, 1991); Paul Burstein, *Discrimination, Jobs, and Politics: The Struggle for Equal Employment Opportunity in the United States since the New Deal* (Chicago: University of Chicago Press, 1985), pp. 130–154.

Index of Cases

In citations of court decisions, the first number is the volume of the court reports in which the decision is found, the designation of the court reports (such as "U.S." for the United States Reports) follows that number, and the second number is the first page of the decision. The year of the decision is in parentheses; except for the Supreme Court or where the name of the reporter indicates which court decided the case, the designation of that court is indicated before the year. A state name (such as "Mass.") indicates a state supreme court; a state name preceded by a district (such as "N.D. Fla.") indicates a federal district court; a circuit number (such as "9th Cir.") indicates a federal court of appeals.

Abood v. Detroit Board of Education, 431 U.S. 209 (1977), 285
American Civil Liberties Union v. Florida Bar, 744 F. Supp. 1094 (N.D. Fla. 1990), 132
American National Red Cross v. S.G., 120 L. Ed. 2d 201 (1992), 20
Bates v. State Bar, 433 U.S. 350 (1975), 98
Bowsher v. Synar, 478 U.S. 714 (1986), 312
Brown v. Board of Education, 347 U.S. 483 (1954), 349 U.S. 294 (1955), 285, 328, 332, 337, 341, 346, 350
Chapman v. United States, 114 L. Ed. 2d 524 (1991), 222
Chisom v. Roemer, 115 L. Ed. 2d 348 (1991), 167
Commonwealth v. Gordon, 574 N.E.2d 974 (Mass. 1991), 217
DF Activities Corporation v. Brown, 851 F.2d 920 (7th Cir. 1988), 262
Doe v. Bolton, 410 U.S. 179 (1973), 349
Doggett v. United States, 120 L. Ed. 2d 520 (1992), 298
Feldman v. San Mateo Financial Corporation, 276 Cal. Rptr. 285 (1990), 350
Furman v. Georgia, 408 U.S. 238 (1972), 337
Gault, In re, 387 U.S. 1 (1967), 216
Gideon v. Wainwright, 372 U.S. 335 (1963), 78, 98
Goldfarb v. State Bar, 421 U.S. 773 (1975), 99
Gregg v. Georgia, 428 U.S. 153 (1976), 350
Harris v. McRae, 448 U.S. 297 (1980), 350
Hicks v. State, 544 P.2d 1153 (N.M. 1975), 314
Hudson v. McMillian, 117 L. Ed. 2d 156 (1992), 298

judges, 158
selection of judges, 118, 121
North Dakota lawyers, 62
North, Oliver, 147
Nowlin, James, 41
Nuger, Kenneth Paul, 350
Nunes, Don, 217

Oakley, John Bilyeu, 311, 313, 348
O'Brien, John, 169
Ocasal, Christopher, 96
O'Connor, Karen, 285, 312
O'Connor, Matt, 169
O'Connor, Sandra Day, 106, 144, 298, 300
Ohio
courts, 2, 53, 249, 257, 286, 301, 305, 306
judges, 25
lawyers, 62, 83, 142
selection of judges, 103, 116, 119, 120, 123, 301
Oklahoma
courts, 46, 47
judges, 27
Olson, Susan M., 312
Olson, Walter K., 99, 262
O'Neill, C. William, 142
Opinions, court, 276–278, 293, 301, 303
Oregon
courts, 184, 187
judges, 133, 158
Ostrom, Brian J., 98, 216

Pace, Nicholas M., 262, 267
Pacelle, Richard, 348
Packer, Herbert L., 18, 20
Padgett, John F., 188, 217
Page, Alan, 122, 123
Palay, Thomas, 94, 96, 97
Palermo, B. J., 57
Paltrow, Scot J., 220
Papadakos, Nicholas, 52
Parker, Jim, 56
Patterson, Philip C., 162
Pelham, Ann, 306
Pell, Eve, 241
Peltason, Jack W., 350
Penney, J.C., company, 245
Pennington, Nancy, 215
Pennsylvania
courts, 52, 194, 195, 245, 305, 319
judges, 15, 146, 159, 193, 212
laws, 1, 344
lawyers, 175
Penrod, Steven D., 215
Percival, Robert V., 265
Perkins, Craig, 216
Perpich, Rudy, 145

Perry, H. W., Jr., 311, 312
Personal injury cases
appellate court policies, 19, 119, 121, 225, 227, 300, 301, 307, 321–323, 325, 341
as area of court activity, 226, 318, 319
handling, 234, 235, 248–251
legislation, 244
litigation, 233–236, 240, 247
outcomes, 228, 255–257, 260, 261
Peters, Ellen Ash, 140, 141
Petersilia, Joan, 217, 220
Peterson, Mark A., 265, 266
Phelps, Timothy M., 131
Philadelphia
courts, 52, 194, 195
judges, 146, 212
lawyers, 70, 82
Phillippe, Donald R., 119
Phoenix courts, 255, 271
Pianin, Eric, 55
Pittsburgh
courts, 194, 245
judges, 159
Plea bargaining, 149, 151, 181, 186, 187
abolition and reform efforts, 196, 197
evaluations, 195–197
exceptions, 194, 195
explanations, 15, 191–193
forms, 187–189
prevalence, 191–193
process, 177, 189–191
Polaroid company, 242
Police
arrests, 182, 183
responses to court decisions, 10, 328–331, 333, 334
roles in court, 174–176, 184, 206, 229
Political parties
as influence on courts, 146, 147, 160
in selection of judges, 102, 103, 106, 107, 109–111, 113, 114, 120–123, 125, 128, 137–139
Porter, John F., 57
Porter, Mary Cornelia Aldis, 133
Portland courts, 184, 187
Posner, Richard, 299
Pound, Roscoe, 42, 56
Powell, Lewis, 106, 108, 141
Pozzo, Joanne F., 99
Prepaid legal services, 83, 84
Presidents. *See also individual presidents*
appointments of federal judges, 103–114, 299, 300, 323
responses to court decisions, 308, 309, 338–341
Press, Aric, 99, 132
Pressman, Steven, 218